Democracy Disrupted

Communication in the Volatile 2020 Presidential Election

Benjamin R. Warner, Dianne G. Bystrom,
Mitchell S. McKinney, and Mary C. Banwart, Editors

PRAEGER®

An Imprint of ABC-CLIO, LLC

Santa Barbara, California • Denver, Colorado

Library of Congress Cataloging-in-Publication Data

Names: Warner, Benjamin R., editor. | Bystrom, Dianne G., editor. |
McKinney, Mitchell S., editor. | Banwart, Mary C., 1968- editor.
Title: Democracy disrupted : communication in the volatile 2020
presidential election / Benjamin R. Warner, Dianne G. Bystrom, Mitchell
S. McKinney, and Mary C. Banwart, Editors.
Description: Santa Barbara : Praeger, [2022] | Includes bibliographical
references and index.
Identifiers: LCCN 2022015746 (print) | LCCN 2022015747 (ebook) |
ISBN 9781440879234 (cloth) | ISBN 9781440879241 (ebook)
Subjects: LCSH: Presidents—United States—Election—2020. | Political
campaigns—United States. | Communication in politics—United States. |
COVID-19 Pandemic, 2020—United States. | Social justice—United
States. | BISAC: POLITICAL SCIENCE / Political Process / Campaigns &
Elections | POLITICAL SCIENCE / Political Ideologies / Democracy
Classification: LCC JK526 2020 .D46 2022 (print) | LCC JK526 2020 (ebook) |
DDC 324.973—dc23/eng/20220225
LC record available at https://lccn.loc.gov/2022015746
LC ebook record available at https://lccn.loc.gov/2022015747

ISBN: 978-1-4408-7923-4 (print)
      978-1-4408-7924-1 (ebook)

26 25 24 23 22   1 2 3 4 5

This book is also available as an eBook.

Praeger
An Imprint of ABC-CLIO, LLC

ABC-CLIO, LLC
147 Castilian Drive
Santa Barbara, California 93117
www.abc-clio.com

This book is printed on acid-free paper ∞

Manufactured in the United States of America

Contents

Introduction

Exploring the Disruptive 2020 Campaign: Contextualizing the Role of the Push for Progress, the Pandemic, and the Insurrection at the Capitol

Benjamin R. Warner and Dianne G. Bystrom

On January 6, 2021, U.S. Senator Mitch McConnell (R-KY), then majority leader, had just delivered a speech on the Senate floor in which he warned that any effort to overturn the results of an election that was "not unusually close" would send our democracy into a "death spiral" (McConnell, 2021, para. 2). He was referring, of course, to Donald Trump's "clear and multifaceted effort to use any tool available to overturn the election" (Blake, 2021, para. 19). Less than an hour later, insurrectionists had stormed the U.S. Capitol, hoping to prevent the peaceful transfer of power for the first time since the establishment of the precedent of 1800 (Georgini, 2020).

The harrowing events of January 6, 2021, were the culmination of more than a year of disruptions to the 2020 presidential election. Disruptions interrupt the status quo by challenging the inertia of historical patterns and systems. In this book, we consider the co-occurrence of three historical disruptions: a 100-year pandemic coinciding with the presidential campaign, the diversification of the field of candidates for president preceding a reinvigorated civil rights movement in response to the murder of George Floyd, and the authoritarian lurch that emerged in reaction to Trump's norm-challenging presidency. Our contributors adopt diverse theories and methods to understand these events. Experiments, longitudinal surveys, case studies, and close textual analysis illuminate essential features of this once-in-a-generation campaign.

The first section of this book analyzes the role of diversity—especially regarding issues of race, gender, and sexuality as they affected the 2020 campaign. In one sense, 2020 signaled incredible (if astonishingly slow) progress. Throughout the 59 presidential elections held over the 224-year history of the U.S. presidency, all 46 people selected by the Electoral College have been men—45 of whom were White, cisgender, and straight presenting. Only once before has one of the major parties nominated a woman for the presidency (Democrat Hillary Clinton in 2016), and only one Black man (Democrat Barack Obama in 2008 and 2012) has ever been nominated.

Representation in the vice presidency has scarcely been better. As a result of the 2020 presidential election, former U.S. Senator Kamala Harris (D-CA) is the first woman, the first South Asian, and the first Black person to hold the office. Prior to Harris, an uninterrupted line of 48 White, cisgender, and straight-presenting men served as vice president. Indeed, of the more than 100 vice presidential candidates of the two major political parties, only three women (Democrat Geraldine Ferraro in 1984, Republican Sarah Palin in 2008, and Democrat Harris in 2020) have ever been nominated.

Suffice it to say, the executive office has historically looked nothing like the diverse country it seeks to represent. The 2020 election was disruptive of this status quo not only because of the election of Harris but also due to the diversity of the pool of candidates vying for the presidency. When Obama won the presidency in 2008, he did so after emerging from a field of largely traditional candidates—defeating five White men, one White woman, and one Latino man, all straight-presenting. The 2016 election was the next to feature a competitive Democratic primary and, had either candidate seeking the nomination won the presidency, they would have represented a historical first. Former Secretary of State Clinton would have been the first woman president, and Senator Bernie Sanders (I-VT) would have been the first Jewish president.

The 2020 Democratic primary presents a clear departure from even recent history. Of the 12 candidates that participated in at least three primary debates, four were women, four were candidates of color, and one was an out gay man (the first in U.S. history to seek the office). Two more women participated in at least two primary debates. In total, straight-presenting White men were still overrepresented, comprising 13 of the 23 candidates who participated in at least one debate. Nevertheless, this set of candidates presents a stark contrast to preceding election years. The diversity of the Democratic primary illustrates both progress and constraint. Chapters in this volume consider the historical significance of these candidates while also documenting the ways in which this progress was constrained by the intersecting systems of racism, sexism, and other discriminations imposed by the electorate and, in some cases, by the media.

Just as the diversity in the presidential candidates illustrates the push-pull of progress, so too do the events in the summer of 2020 that engaged—and in many ways overshadowed—the campaign. That summer saw a reinvigorated call for social and racial justice in the wake of high-profile police killings, notably the murder of George Floyd by Derek Chauvin in Minneapolis, Minnesota. These protests established the Black Lives Matter movement as the largest in the history of the United States. It is estimated that 15 to 26 million people (up to 10% of the U.S. population) participated in one of the nearly 5,000 protests that occurred in approximately 2,500 cities (Buchanan et al., 2020). Although Floyd's murder was the proximate cause of the protests, they were also reacting to a long list of police killings that preceded it, as well as the violent way police responded to protesters and the countless other ways Black lives have been denigrated both before and as a consequence of the COVID-19 pandemic (Bouie, 2020). More than a year after these protests, progress on the injustices that called so many to the streets has been stymied (Booker, 2021).

Just as protest and calls for progress disrupted the 2020 campaign, so too did the ongoing pandemic. In the spring of 2020, not long after the Iowa Caucuses, the United States entered a prolonged shutdown to minimize the spread of COVID-19. This shutdown overlapped with a period of time in which, during a traditional campaign, the candidates would be crisscrossing the country holding large in-person rallies, meeting potential voters in diners, and spending extensive time interacting with people in various states ahead of their primary elections.

Although each political campaign was forced to react and adjust to the pandemic, the 2020 presidential candidates adopted different approaches. Whereas Biden engaged in a largely virtual campaign strategy, avoided holding in-person events in times and places when infections were surging, and encouraged social distancing and mask-wearing when in-person events were held, the Trump campaign seemed to flaunt these guidelines, opting instead for numerous large rallies with little social distancing or mask-wearing (Blanco, 2020). One study of the effects of 18 Trump rallies estimated that these events resulted in 30,000 additional cases of COVID-19 and 700 additional deaths beyond what would be expected had Trump not held these rallies (Bernheim et al., 2020).

Perhaps the most infamous of Trump's pandemic-era rallies was the first in-person rally to be held after the pandemic halted regular campaign events. Trump returned to the campaign trail in Tulsa, Oklahoma, on June 20, 2020, against the wishes of local public health officials (Seddiq, 2021). These health officials later suggested that the rally was responsible for a subsequent surge in cases in the area (Jones, 2020). As part of the rally, Trump's team flew in former presidential candidate Herman Cain, who was photographed without a mask in close proximity to others. Eight Trump campaign staffers would later test positive for COVID-19, as would Cain, who was hospitalized and ultimately died as a result of his infection. Although it is unknown whether Cain contracted COVID-19 at the event, Trump staffers reportedly blame themselves for his death (Seddiq, 2021).

As the Trump campaign disregarded public health warnings—seemingly heedless of the death and disease left in their wake—it also focused on Biden's cautious approach as a point of contrast. The Trump campaign persistently criticized Biden's virtual campaign, arguing that he was hiding in his basement to obscure his propensity to make gaffes while speaking extemporaneously (Jansen, 2020). Trump also repeatedly mocked Biden for the size of his masks and his commitment to wearing a mask when campaigning (Yglesias, 2020).

The Trump campaign's dismissiveness toward public health precautions was in evidence at a Rose Garden ceremony hosted on September 26, 2020, to celebrate the appointment of Amy Coney Barrett to the U.S. Supreme Court. Dr. Anthony Fauci—the nation's leading infectious disease expert and a member of Trump's White House Coronavirus Task Force—would later confirm that this ceremony was a super spreader event (Clark, 2020). That day, Trump tested positive for COVID-19, though a subsequent test would return a negative result (Pengelly, 2021). In the days between initially testing positive and publicly announcing that he and his wife had contracted the virus, Trump would expose more than 500 people, including top aid Chris Christie, who helped him prepare for the first presidential debate and would later blame Trump for infecting him (Reimann, 2021). Christie spent seven days battling COVID-19 in an intensive care unit. Trump's infection was sufficiently severe that doctors feared he would need to be put on a ventilator—an indication that the disease had reached late stages and was potentially life-threatening (Singh, 2021).

Trump's infection necessitated the cancelation of the second presidential debate and limited his campaign activity in the month preceding the 2020 election. In addition to these disruptions, the party nominating conventions were held virtually for the first time since they became a staple of presidential campaigns. Chapters in this volume examine the various ways the pandemic disrupted the 2020 campaign and how those vying for the presidency and other elected offices adapted.

The third disruption to receive attention in this collection is the challenge to democratic norms posed by Trump's campaign, culminating in his attempts to reverse the outcome of the 2020 election. Trump engaged in early and frequent challenges to the legitimacy of the election that precipitated a violent insurrection on January 6, 2021, and resulted in his second impeachment. In the impeachment trial, prosecutors cited a persistent effort by

Trump to undermine faith in a fair election. After the election, Trump refused to accept the legitimacy of the outcome and repeatedly made statements that appeared to encourage the eventual insurrection. Research has documented a connection between distrust of democratic outcomes and acceptance of political violence that has been identified in Trump supporters since his first rallies as a candidate for the presidency in 2016 (Warner et al., 2019).

Seven months before the November 3, 2020, election, Trump began undermining faith in mail-in ballots, calling them "very dangerous," "cheaters," and "fraudulent" (Inskeep, 2021, para. 7). He later told *Fox News* host Chris Wallace that mail-in voting would "rig the election" (Inskeep, 2021, para. 12). In the same interview with Wallace, Trump refused to commit to accepting the results of the election. *The Washington Post* documented more than 150 instances in which Trump made similar claims about a fraudulent election (Kessler & Rizzo, 2020).

In the first presidential debate, Wallace (serving as moderator) again pressed Trump to accept the outcome of the election and again Trump refused, citing what he referred to as ballot manipulation. Wallace also asked Trump to denounce right-wing militants who had been exacerbating violence during the summer protests of police killings. When Trump asked for a name of an organization, Biden interjected, asking Trump to denounce the Proud Boys. Trump responded by saying the Proud Boys should "stand back and stand by," a statement that was celebrated by the organization online (Murphy, 2020). Members of the Proud Boys began including the phrase "stand back and stand by" in their online logos and sharing it with memes. Their leader, Enrique Tarro, said that he interpreted the message to mean that the Proud Boys should continue with their activity (Murphy, 2020).

Because the election was being held during the COVID-19 pandemic, people were increasingly encouraged to vote by mail rather than gather at in-person voting locations. Trump's focus on the legitimacy of mail-in votes strategically coincided, therefore, with an election in which many more votes would be cast by mail than in the past. The consequence of this uptick in mail-in balloting was that it took much longer to count the ballots and identify who had won crucial states. Thus, although the election occurred on November 3, media organizations did not name Biden the victor until November 7, 2020. Nevertheless, it was widely anticipated that Trump would declare victory on election night before most mail-in ballots had been counted—and indeed he did, saying "we did win this election" (Inskeep, 2020, para. 22).

In the time between Trump declaring victory and Biden being named the winner, Trump repeatedly advanced false allegations of voter fraud. For example, Trump often tweeted about mail-in ballots being fraudulently manufactured to change the outcome in key states (Kessler & Rizzo, 2020). In one tweet sent on November 5, Trump claimed (in all caps), "If you count the legal votes, I easily win the election! If you count the illegal and legal votes, they can steal the election from us" (Kessler & Rizzo, 2020, para. 58). In the weeks following the election, Trump, his family, and his legal team repeatedly encouraged his supporters to "rise up against the outcome of the national election" (Ballhaus et al., 2021, para. 2). When the Electoral College confirmed Biden's victory on December 14, Trump called for Republicans to "get moving," stating that "this fake election can no longer stand" (Ballhaus et al., 2021, para. 6). Trump then began targeting January 6, the day Congress was scheduled to certify the Electoral College count, as a day for his supporters to intervene to prevent the transfer of power to Biden. On December 19 he told his followers, "Big protest in D.C. on January 6. Be there, will be wild" (Ballhaus et al., 2021, para. 7).

Trump's efforts to overturn Biden's victory included scores of lawsuits, many litigated by vocal Trump supporter and ally L. Lin Wood, who repeatedly stoked the flames of political violence. Wood said the country was "on brink of civil war" (Ballhaus et al., 2021, para. 17); asked, "Do you think our country is on the verge of an attempted coup/revolution in the disguise of a civil war or is it just me?" (Ballhaus et al., 2021, para. 20); and publicly encouraged Trump to declare martial law (Ballhaus et al., 2021). At a "Stop the Steal" rally, Wood said, "We're going to slay Goliath, the communists, the liberals, the phonies, Joe Biden will never set foot in the Oval Office of this country" (Ballhaus et al., 2021, para. 25) and predicted there would be "violence in our streets soon" (Ballhaus et al., 2021, para. 26).

Sidney Powell, another legal ally of Trump, sent 116 tweets about election fraud in the time between the day of the election and the Electoral College certification, according to an analysis conducted by *The Wall Street Journal* (Ballhaus et al., 2021). Powell called the efforts of Trump and his supporters, "essentially a new American revolution," encouraging "anyone who wants this country to remain free needs to step up right now" (Ballhaus et al., 2021, para. 22). On Twitter, she encouraged supporters to "rise up" and "swarm the state capital, Congress" (Ballhaus et al., 2021, para. 27). In a rally in Georgia on January 5, Trump led his supporters in a "fight for Trump" chant and delivered a speech in which he said, "When you win in a landslide and they steal it and it's rigged, it's not acceptable. . . . They're not taking this White House. We're going to fight like hell" (Ballhaus et al., 2021, para. 35).

On January 6, the violent rhetoric reached a crescendo. Wood told supporters, "The time has come . . . time to fight for our freedom. Pledge your lives, your fortunes, your sacred honor . . . TODAY IS OUR DAY" (Ballhaus et al., 2021, para. 38). Trump's personal lawyer, Rudy Giuliani, told the January 6 crowd, "If we are right, a lot of them will go to jail. So let's have trial by combat" (Ballhaus et al., 2021, para. 40). In his speech, Trump told his supporters "We're going to have to fight much harder" (Rupar, 2021, para. 2). "You'll never take back our country with weakness. You have to show strength," he said (Rupar, 2021, para. 3).

In total, events leading up to and including January 6 included an extensive effort to pressure Vice President Mike Pence to refuse to certify the Electoral College result. The morning of January 6, just after 8 a.m., Trump tweeted: "States want to correct their votes, which they now know were based on irregularities and fraud, plus corrupt process never received legislative approval. All Mike Pence has to do is send them back to the States, AND WE WIN. Do it Mike, this is a time for extreme courage!" (Forgey, 2021, para. 2).

In his speech, Trump rallied supporters in front of the White House, where he urged them to "never give up . . . never concede" (Naylor, 2021, para. 12) and "fight like hell" (Naylor, 2021, para. 259). He then instructed his supporters: "We're going to the Capitol . . . to try and give [Republicans] the kind of pride and boldness that they need to take back our country" (Naylor, 2021, para. 262–263). At Trump's behest, many who attended Trump's speech stormed the U.S. Capitol, hoping to prevent the peaceful transfer of power (Rubin et al, 2021). The insurrectionists planted pipe bombs (Godfrey, 2022), assaulted 140 police officers (Davis et al., 2021), searched for prominent members of Congress with means and apparent intent to capture and detain them, chanted "hang Mike Pence," and erected gallows in front of the Capitol building. The insurrection resulted in five deaths (Davis et al., 2021).

Among those who stormed the Capitol were members of the far-right groups Trump had courted leading up to the election. The Proud Boys were heavily represented, heeding calls from their leadership to "turn out in record numbers" (Parloff, 2022, para. 2) for an "epic" day (Parloff, 2022, para. 4). Along with the far-right group the Oath Keepers, the Proud Boys comprise a majority of those charged with conspiracy for their involvement in the insurrection (Parloff, 2022). On January 13, 2022, 11 members of the Oath Keepers were charged with sedition by the U.S. Department of Justice. The Oath Keepers' membership includes a substantial number of people from law enforcement and the military. Their leadership had been calling for civil war in reaction to the election (Giglio, 2020).

The sedition charge is a formal allegation that the Oath Keepers were working to overthrow the government or prevent the execution of its laws. The indictment cites the transportation of firearms and ammunition to the Capitol; combat training in Washington, DC, prior to the attack; and plans to provide armed support for the insurrectionists (Ioanes, 2022). Stewart Rhodes, the leader of the Oath Keepers and one of the 11 members of the organization charged with sedition, "promised a 'bloody, massively bloody revolution'" (Ioanes, 2022, para. 7), indicating that the transfer of the presidency from Biden to Trump would not happen "without a civil war" (Ioanes, 2022, para. 7).

As this introduction makes clear, the 2020 presidential campaign saw significant disruptions to the U.S. democracy. Some of these disruptions represent signs of progress; 2020 saw some of the most robust challenges to the 200-year monopoly on power held by straight, White, cisgender men. However, we suspect that most readers, like us, will find the disruptions posed by the global pandemic and attempted autocoup to be the more memorable. In the following chapters, our contributors explore each in turn.

The book's first section—Disrupting the Status Quo—opens with three chapters that consider the greater diversity of presidential candidates during the Democratic primary campaign (including the eventual vice president). These chapters feature qualitative studies that examine the historical candidacies of an openly gay man—former South Bend, Indiana, Mayor Pete Buttigieg—and the six women seeking the Democratic Party nomination for president, including Harris, who went on to make history as the first woman, Black, and South Asian vice president of the United States.

In Chapter 1, "Looking In/Looking Out: Pete Buttigieg's Not-So-Queer Run for the Presidency," Bryan G. Pepper and Mitchell S. McKinney argue that the historic candidacy of the first openly gay man seeking a major political party's nomination to the U.S. presidency was driven by his desire to be accepted as a traditional (i.e., normal) public figure. By eschewing an identity or agenda that might be viewed as violating the values and expectations of normative politics, Buttigieg often framed his gayness in terms of his military service, his faith and religious practice, and his marriage. The authors assess Buttigieg's quest for the presidency, including his rise as an early front-runner for the 2020 presidential nomination in a crowded and diverse field of Democratic candidates; reactions to his campaign, particularly from gay activists; and its impact on the status of gay, trans, bisexual, and intersex individuals in the United States.

Chapter 2, "Mediating Race and Gender in Campaign 2020: The Cooking with Kamala Videos," examines how the Black, South Asian, female candidate for the Democratic nomination for president confronted racialized and gendered campaign discourses through a series of videos that showed her cooking with different celebrities and voters. In this chapter, Trevor Parry-Giles and eight doctoral students at the University of Maryland contend that Harris transcended the rhetorical double bind faced by all women and particularly women of color who seek high political office by relying on her multiracial consciousness to appeal to a broader American audience. Thus, they argue, Harris addressed and recaptured control over her political identity—which has been defined by discourses of race and gender from the earliest days of her political career to her ascendancy to the vice presidency— through a multiethnic rhetorical framing of cooking.

In Chapter 3, "Rhetoric of Optimism and Promise of Transformation: Concession Speeches by U.S. Presidential Women Candidates in 2020," Julia A. Spiker examines the rhetorical strategies used by each of the record six women who sought the Democratic nomination for president when they exited the primary campaign. Framing her analysis of their concession speeches via the gendered voice, Spiker argues that each of these women candidates broadened voters' perspectives of what a powerful woman political leader looks like in 2020 and beyond through their communication styles, messages, focus on issues important to their constituencies, and their unique worldviews. Her study also serves to extend the findings of previous research on the genre of concession speeches through its focus on gender and the presidential primary.

The final two chapters in this section explore the impact of the reinvigorated calls for social and racial justice in the wake of high-profile police killings in the summer of 2020 through quantitative analyses of survey data.

In Chapter 4, "Partisan Motivations for News Use: Implications for Threat Perceptions during the 2020 U.S. Election," Andrea Figueroa-Caballero and Julius Matthew Riles examine under what conditions the relationship between partisan and like-minded news consumption was exacerbated or diminished in the 2020 political campaign. Specifically, through an analysis of survey data using the differential susceptibility to media effects model, they focus on how certain social identities—Chinese people, Black people, and the police—were presented as threats in news coverage of the COVID-19 global pandemic and the 2020 summer demonstrations against police brutality and other forms of ongoing racial inequity following the high-profile killings of George Floyd, Breonna Taylor, Ahmaud Arbery, and others.

Chapter 5, "Navigating Difficult Conversations in the Family in the 2020 Election Environment," utilizes family communication patterns theory to better understand how families managed difficult conversations about race relations, the COVID-19 pandemic, and the 2020 election. Authors Xavier Scruggs and Colleen Warner Colaner analyze survey research data to examine family communication patterns along four dimensions of conformity orientation—ranging from pressure to adopt parental values to being allowed to question parental authority and beliefs—and the frequency of political talk between young adults and their families. Their study offers socially relevant insights into parent–child communication as family dyads navigate communication on such difficult topics as those presented during the 2020 election.

The book's second part—Disrupting the Campaign—includes five chapters that focus on how the COVID-19 pandemic affected political campaigns on the state and national level. Chapters in this section analyze how candidates, political parties, and celebrities organized and communicated amidst the constraints presented by the pandemic through content analyses, surveys, ethnography, and case studies.

This section opens with a content analysis by Daniel Montez and Kate Kenski of tweets posted by the Democratic and Republican national committees during the 2020 presidential campaign. In Chapter 6, "Political Party

Tweets during the 2020 Presidential Campaign," the authors first identify the issues that voters believed were important that year. Using a computerized, dictionary-driven content analysis, they then analyze the frequency and policy emphasis of tweets posted by the two major political parties. The authors also examine how Twitter users engaged with the issues put forth by the political parties through retweets. Their findings demonstrate how the two major political parties used the Twitter platform differently in 2020, as well as how issues identified as important by voters were reflected in their social media communication in what was a unique campaign year.

In Chapter 7, "Donald Trump and the COVID-19 Information Environment in Campaign 2020," authors Joshua M. Scacco, Jonathon Smith, and Kevin Coe analyze the content of the White House Coronavirus Task Force press briefings and the possibility that they may have influenced knowledge acquisition in the electorally important state of Florida. They first conduct a keyword analysis of the transcripts of 41 press briefings where Trump spoke about the virus's origins, "cures," and negative outcomes. Using survey research data, they then examine the influence of such briefings on the knowledge acquisition of Floridians as to the origins, treatments, and negative outcomes of the coronavirus. When considering the possibility of knowledge acquisition, they place Trump's potential contribution within the broader sociocultural environment in which COVID information—and misinformation—emerged and circulated.

Chapter 8, "Forced Online: The Promise and Challenge of Relational Organizing Technology in a 2020 State-Level Campaign," examines whether creative new digital technologies adopted in the midst of the COVID-19 pandemic were successful in building relationships with supporters and voters with whom the campaign could not interact in person. Authors Ashley Muddiman and Cameron W. Piercy were invited to join weekly meetings conducted as part of a state-level Senate race in a small midwestern state as the campaign transitioned to online canvassing. They analyze their data using a constant comparison approach, which incorporates the verbatim meeting transcripts and the researchers' ethnographic observations to generate intersubjective understanding of the context. In all, their findings reveal a tension in the campaign between building and controlling relationships.

In Chapter 9, "'The SPN Family Votes!': Celebrity Endorsements in Online Fan Communities," Ashley A. Hinck employs a case study approach to examine the tweets and YouTube videos of the creator and actors of the CW program, *Supernatural*, in their support for the Biden-Harris campaign. She argues that personalizing popular culture celebrities transforms them from a cultural elite to a friend and fellow citizen, while the personalization of political surrogates transforms them from a political elite to a fellow fan. Ultimately, Hinck shows that the personalization of politicians and popular culture celebrities makes fandom a significant location for political campaigning. Further, she demonstrates that celebrity endorsements don't have to be empty proclamations, devoid of civic value, but can—and do—function as sites of civic practices and audience engagement.

Chapter 10, "Hope and Fear in a Pandemic: Videostyle in 2020 Presidential Advertising," analyzes the content of candidate-sponsored television ads to better understand the messaging of the Biden and Trump campaigns and provide insights into the outcome of the election. Author Kelly L. Winfrey provides a thorough examination of the previous research findings on the effects of political advertising, as well as the content of TV ads through the theoretical lens of videostyle. She then reports the findings of a content analysis on the verbal, nonverbal, and production elements of 218 television ads sponsored by presidential candidates Biden and Trump. Her analysis reveals that the candidates employed fundamentally different strategies in their TV ads—some of which may have been informed by the successes and mistakes of the 2016 campaign and some of which were related to the unique context of the 2020 election.

The book's third part—Disrupting Democratic Norms—includes five chapters that consider the early and frequent challenges to the legitimacy of the 2020 election that culminated in the violent insurrection on January 6, 2021, at the U.S. Capitol and the second impeachment of former President Trump. Chapters in this section examine Trump's disruptive rhetoric—in his acceptance speech, the presidential debates, and on social media—as well as Republicans who "crossed over" to endorse Biden. The effects of the campaign on voters—including racism, sexism, and polarization—are also explored in this section.

Chapter 11, "Donald Trump, Emotional Activation, and Authoritarianism," offers a rhetorical analysis by Robert C. Rowland of Trump's acceptance speech at the Republican National Convention, debate performance, and use of social media on Twitter. He argues that the power (and weakness) of Trump's rhetoric and its hold over core supporters did not relate to ideology, but rather to emotion. Lacking a coherent ideological perspective, Trump's rhetoric activated the emotions of his supporters through nationalist appeals related largely to racial identity, grievances against elites and the media, self-presentation as a charismatic outsider, and the use of a colloquial style. Unlike former presidents running for re-election—who often extend the themes of their first campaign, lay out an agenda for a second term, respond to current issues, and attack their opponent—this was the only message Trump had, no matter what the context.

In Chapter 12, "Reclaiming the Center: Constitutive Rhetoric and the 'Moderate Ethos' in Crossover Endorsements for Joe Biden," Ryan Neville-Shepard argues that the crossover discourse in 2020 marked a critical redefinition of what it means to be politically moderate. The historic number of crossover endorsements constituted a specific kind of moderate politics that is perceived as a last resort, focused on character and procedure over policy, while defining extremism in a way that might build winning coalitions, but ultimately can impair a party. Neville-Shepard suggests that this particular kind of moderate politics—which he terms "procedural centrism"—served not only as a direct backlash to Trumpism but also simultaneously undermined party-driven reforms that may have helped reverse the trends it allegedly condemned.

In Chapter 13, "Trump's Disruptive Debate: Analyzing the Candidate Branding Costs," authors Josh C. Bramlett, Benjamin R. Warner, and Mitchell S. McKinney examine voter evaluations of Trump and Biden after each of the two general election presidential debates in 2020 using post-debate surveys of 339 viewers from both political parties and independents. Specifically, they assess the candidate brand association effects of each debate performance, as well as the constraints of partisan-motivated reasoning. The researchers report the positive and negative brand associations for both Trump and Biden across time and party to test four hypotheses. Results from their study support prior research on debate candidate branding and candidate evaluations and illustrate the branding risks associated with outlier performances such as that delivered by Trump in the first presidential debate.

Chapter 14, "Social Dominance, Sexism, and the Lasting Effects on Political Communication from the 2020 Election" examines the relationship between social dominance orientation, sexism, and candidate image in 2020. Extending their work from the 2016 presidential election—where they found evidence of sexism and social dominance orientation influencing voter perceptions of Hillary Clinton and Donald Trump—authors Mary C. Banwart and Michael W. Kearney asked if these correlations would emerge in the 2020 race between Biden and Trump without a woman candidate activating any threat to masculinity. Their study provides not only some answers about the 2020 election but also raises questions about how dominant attitudes develop around the role of women in politics, the men who disparage them, and the men who promise to provide them with protection.

Finally, in Chapter 15, "Partisan Media and Polarization in the 2020 Campaign," Benjamin R. Warner, Jihye Park, Go-Eun Kim, and Alyssa N. Coffey report the results of their analysis of responses drawn from the *American National Election Study*, a nationally representative survey of 6,291 U.S. citizens. Specifically, the researchers investigate the association of partisan media use and the polarization that defined and disrupted the 2020 campaign. They assess whether the association between partisan media use and polarization is stronger among those with more partisan strength, political interest, and attention to the election. They also consider the type of media consumed—pro-partisan versus cross-partisan—on the political polarization of voters. The researchers report their results about the direct and conditional effects of partisan media use on polarization with a series of linear regression models. Ultimately, they find some good news for democracy.

In summary, this book responds to the unique circumstances that combined to disrupt the 2020 campaign and election—as well as its aftermath—through 15 studies authored by leading and emerging scholars of political communication. In total, these contributions represent an important archive of one of the most historically significant campaigns in the history of the United States. They also advance crucial conversations in the field of political communication about the nature of campaign media effects, presidential rhetoric, the content of campaign communication, and how all of these important fields of scholarship hold up (or are altered by) the striking circumstances of the 2020 election.

References

Ballhaus, R., Palazzolo, J., & Restuccia, A. (2021, January 8). Trump and his allies set the stage for riot well before January 6. *The Wall Street Journal.* https://www.wsj.com/articles/trump-and-his-allies-set-the-stage-for-riot -well-before-january-6-11610156283

Bernheim, B. D., Buchmann, N., Freitas-Groff, Z., & Otero, S. (2020). The effects of large group meetings on the spread of COVID-19: The case of Trump rallies. *SSRN.* https://papers.ssrn.com/sol3/papers.cfm?abstract_id=3722299

Blake, A. (2021, October 7). 3 takeaways from the Senate report on Trump's brazen efforts to overturn the 2020 election. *The Washington Post.* https:// www.washingtonpost.com/politics/2021/10/07/3-takeaways-senate -report-trumps-brazen-efforts-overturn-2020-election/

Blanco, A. (2020, November 2). Amid the pandemic, Trump and Biden traveled most often to Pennsylvania and Florida. *The Washington Post.* https:// www.washingtonpost.com/elections/2020/11/02/campaign-rallies -covid/

Booker, B. (2021, May 25). George Floyd and the new civil rights era. *Politico.* https://www.politico.com/newsletters/the-recast/2021/05/25 /george-floyd-death-anniversary-civil-rights-492986

Bouie, J. (2020, June 12). To overturn Trump, we need to overturn white supremacy. *The New York Times.* https://www.nytimes.com/2020/06/12/opinion /sunday/floyd-protests-white-supremacy.html

Buchanan, L., Bui, Q., & Patel, J. K. (2020, July 3). Black Lives Matter may be the largest movement in U.S. history. *The New York Times.* https://www .nytimes.com/interactive/2020/07/03/us/george-floyd-protests-crowd -size.html

Clark, D. (2020, October 9). Fauci calls Amy Coney Barrett ceremony in Rose Garden "superspreader event." *NBC News.* https://www.nbcnews.com /politics/white-house/fauci-calls-amy-coney-barrett-ceremony-rose -garden-superspreader-event-n1242781

Davis, A. C., Rucker, P., Gardner, A., & Helderman, R. S. (2021, October 31). The attack: The Jan. 6 siege of the U.S. Capitol was neither a spontaneous act nor an isolated event. *The Washington Post*. https://www.washingtonpost .com/politics/interactive/2021/jan-6-insurrection-capitol/?itid=lk_inline _manual_4

Forgey, Q. (2021, January 6). "Do it Mike": Trump leans on Pence to reject Biden's Electoral College certification. *Politico*. https://www.politico.com/news /2021/01/06/do-it-mike-trump-leans-on-pence-to-reject-bidens-electoral -college-certification-455319

Georgini, S. (2020, December 7). How John Adams managed a peaceful transition of presidential power. *Smithsonian Magazine*. https://www .smithsonianmag.com/history/how-john-adams-managed-peaceful -transition-presidential-power-180976451/

Giglio, M. (2020, November). A pro-Trump militant group has recruited thousands of police, soldiers, and veterans. *The Atlantic*. https://www .theatlantic.com/magazine/archive/2020/11/right-wing-militias-civil -war/616473/

Godfrey, E. (2022, January 6). The strangest ongoing mystery of January 7: Who planted the Capitol Hill pipe bombs? *The Atlantic*. https://www.theatlantic .com/politics/archive/2022/01/january-6-capitol-hill-pipe-bomb/621178/

Ioanes, E. (2022, January 16). How seditious conspiracy charges change the January 6 narrative. *Vox*. https://www.vox.com/2022/1/16/22886516 /stewart-rhodes-seditious-conspiracy-january-6-oath-keepers

Inskeep, S. (2021, February 8). Timeline: What Trump told supporters for months before they attacked. *NPR*. https://www.npr.org/2021/02/08 /965342252/timeline-what-trump-told-supporters-for-months-before -they-attacked

Jansen, B. (2020, August 10). 'There is no playbook': How Trump and Biden are trying to run virtual campaigns during the coronavirus. *USA Today*. https://www.usatoday.com/story/news/politics/2020/08/10/donald -trump-joe-biden-running-virtual-campaigns-amid-coronavirus /3288147001/

Jones, C. (2020, July 9). 'Connect the dots': Tulsa County COVID-19 cases soaring weeks after Trump rally, related large-scale events. *Tulsa World*. https://tulsaworld.com/news/local/connect-the-dots-tulsa-county-covid-19 -cases-soaring-weeks-after-trump-rally-related-large/article_7c6dfef3 -230a-5314-94bc-bab491189960.html

Kessler, G. & Rizzo, S. (2020, November 5). President Trump's false claims of vote fraud: A chronology. *The Washington Post*. https://www.washingtonpost .com/politics/2020/11/05/president-trumps-false-claims-vote-fraud -chronology/

McConnell, M. (2021, January 6). *Mitch McConnell Senate speech on election confirmation* [Speech transcript]. *Rev.com*. https://www.rev.com/blog/transcripts /mitch-mcconnell-senate-speech-on-election-confirmation-transcript -january-6

Murphy, P. (2020, October 1). Trump's debate callout bolsters far-right Proud Boys. *CNN.* https://www.cnn.com/2020/09/30/politics/proud-boys-trump -debate-trnd/index.html

Naylor, B. (2021, February 10). Read Trump's Jan. 6 speech, a key part of impeachment trial. *NPR.* https://www.npr.org/2021/02/10/966396848 /read-trumps-jan-6-speech-a-key-part-of-impeachment-trial

Parloff, R. (2022, January 6). The conspirators: The Proud Boys and Oath Keepers on Jan. 6. *Lawfare.* https://www.lawfareblog.com/conspirators-proud -boys-and-oath-keepers-jan-6

Pengelly, M. (2021, December 1). Trump tested positive for COVID few days before Biden debate, chief of staff says in new book. *The Guardian.* https:// www.theguardian.com/us-news/2021/dec/01/trump-tested-positive -covid-before-biden-debate-chief-staff-mark-meadows-book

Reimann, N. (2021, December 9). Christie says it's 'undeniable' Trump gave him COVID. *Forbes.* https://www.forbes.com/sites/nicholasreimann /2021/12/09/christie-says-its-undeniable-trump-gave-him-covid/?sh =12fbd82c54e7

Rubin, O., Mallin, A., & Hosenball, A. (2021, February 9). 'Because President Trump said to': Over a dozen Capitol rioters say they were following Trump's guidance. *ABC News.* https://abcnews.go.com/US/president -trump-dozen-capitol-rioters-trumps-guidance/story?id=75757601

Rupar, A. (2021, January 8). How Trump's speech led to the Capitol riot. *Vox.* https://www.vox.com/22220746/trump-speech-incite-capitol-riot

Seddiq, O. (2021, November 11). 'We killed Herman Cain': Trump staffers say they blame themselves for Cain's COVID-19 death after he attended Tulsa rally. *Business Insider.* https://www.businessinsider.com/trump-staffers -blame-themselves-for-herman-cains-covid-19-death-book-2021-11

Singh, M. (2021, February 11). Trump's case of coronavirus was far worse than he admitted, report says. *The Guardian.* https://www.theguardian.com /us-news/2021/feb/11/trump-coronavirus-ventilator-covid-illness

Warner, B. R., Galarza, R., Coker, C. R., Tschirhart, P., Hoeun, S., Jennings, F. J., & McKinney, M. S. (2019). Comic agonism in the 2016 campaign: A study of Iowa Caucus rallies. *American Behavioral Scientist, 63*(7), 836–855. https://doi.org/10.1177%2F0002764217704868

Yglesias, M. (2020, October 2). Trump has consistently mocked adherence to public health guidelines. *Vox.* https://www.vox.com/2020/10/2/21498574 /trump-covid-biden-basement

PART 1

Disrupting the Status Quo

CHAPTER ONE

Looking In/Looking Out: Pete Buttigieg's Not-So-Queer Run for the Presidency

Bryan G. Pepper and Mitchell S. McKinney

Central to understanding the significance of Pete Buttigieg's quest for the U.S. presidency is considering the distinction between the proverbial outsider and insider of normative politics. By normative politics we mean those social institutions—such as faith, marriage, and family—grounded in so-called traditional values and behaviors that are seen as the accepted (read normal) ways in which one seeks political power and how our systems of governing and social rule function. Of course, the traditional insider to this process and political club has been the predominately Christian and White cisgender male, though this representation in our electoral politics has been slowly changing with greater numbers of women and racial and ethnic minority candidates and elected officials. The normative face of American politics continues to evolve to reflect the voices and concerns of a now emerging minority majority U.S. electorate.

Still, as we argue in this chapter and reflective in the presidential campaign of Buttigieg, the most frequent road to political power, and certainly when seeking the U.S. presidency, is navigated by presenting oneself as nothing but normal. The process of normativization, however, is pursued chiefly through the homogenization of differences, and the rules that guide this type of political engagement exact an assuming price in which certain concerns are marginalized, representation quieted, time and struggle yielded. The central thesis we develop in this chapter is that the historic candidacy of the first openly gay man seeking nomination to the U.S. presidency by a major political party was driven by his desire to be accepted as a traditional—read normal—public figure. Essentially eschewing any sense of a gay identity or agenda that might be viewed as violating the values and expectations of normative politics, Buttigieg most frequently framed his gayness in terms of his military service, his faith and religious practice, and his marriage. Certainly, to seek public office with appeals grounded in faith, family, and freedom is far from a radical candidacy—again, which Buttigieg avoided at all costs—and not at all a particularly progressive path for a trailblazing would-be first openly gay president.

The crux of our argument is that the status and struggle of gay men and women and of bisexual, trans, and intersex citizens was largely underrepresented—even misrepresented—by the candidacy of the gay community's first out, yet not always apparently and completely proud, presidential aspirant. These individuals and their agenda remained marginal to Buttigieg's normativization of gay identity and politics, much as a queer politics remains on the fringe of our nation's social and political fabric. This chapter begins the story of Buttigieg's quest for the presidency by tracing his rather unplausible and rapid rise as an early frontrunner for the 2020 presidential nomination in a crowded field of Democratic candidates. We next focus on reactions to Buttigieg's campaign, particularly the challenges from gay activists, and finally consider some troubling consequences of his attempts to normativize gay politics for our fellow citizens who remain at the margins of political power and recognition.

(Gay) Mayor Pete Wants to Go to Washington

We begin our account of Buttigieg's quixotic, if not entirely queer, quest for the presidency with his politically spurred coming-out story. At the age of 29, and by garnering just under 11,000 of the nearly 15,000 votes cast, Buttigieg was elected mayor of the somewhat small town of South Bend, Indiana, with a population of approximately 100,000, in November 2011. As he was nearing the end of his first term as mayor, and just before he would announce his bid for re-election, Mayor Pete penned an essay in the *South Bend Tribune* on June 10, 2015, titled "Why Coming Out Matters" (Buttigieg, 2015). He began by confessing, "I was well into adulthood before I was prepared to acknowledge the simple fact that I am gay . . . putting something this personal on the pages of a newspaper does not come easy. We Midwesterners are instinctively private to begin with, and I'm not used to viewing this as anyone else's business" (paras. 5–6). Until this point, and now 33 years old, Buttigieg had not publicly acknowledged he was a gay man, including during his first mayoral campaign. He described his life removed from gay admission and LGBTQ exposure when he recounted, "My high school in South Bend had nearly a thousand students. Statistically, that means that several dozen were gay or lesbian. Yet, when I graduated in 2000, I had yet to encounter a single openly LGBT student" (para. 4). He concluded his coming-out confessional by proclaiming:

> Like most people, I would like to get married one day and eventually raise a family. I hope that when my children are old enough to understand politics, they will be puzzled that someone like me revealing he is gay was ever considered to be newsworthy. By then, all the relevant laws and court decisions will be seen as steps along the path to equality. But the true compass that will have guided us there will be the basic regard and concern that we have for one another as fellow human beings—based not on categories of politics, orientation, background, status or creed, but on our shared knowledge that the greatest thing any of us has to offer is love. (Buttigieg, 2015, para. 12)

Here we see for Buttigieg that his gayness is something almost inconsequential, a rather insignificant and not at all newsworthy part of who he is. Rather than something to be celebrated or championed in a quest for greater inclusion and representation, in Mayor Pete's vision, the steps to full LGBTQ legal and social equality will simply happen along the way so that one day the Buttigieg family will live happily ever after in a time of full inclusion and acceptance. Certainly until this point for the just-out Buttigieg, there has been no real struggle, no restraint or rejection encountered based on his identity as a gay man—hidden as it had been. Not only has there been no struggle for Buttigieg, but there is also absolutely no evidence proffered of any sort of advocacy or defense of the LGBTQ effort to achieve acceptance and equality.

What is also quite clear in the Buttigieg coming-out narrative is his instinct to normativize his gayness, translating his being as a gay man into what he views as the normal desires to be "like most people," with the ultimate prize of acceptance and inclusion that of marriage and children. Perhaps not coincidentally, just 10 days after Buttigieg came out—and as one who yearned for the normality of marriage and a family—the U.S. Supreme Court ruled on June 26, 2015, in its landmark *Obergefell v. Hodges* decision that same-sex couples had a constitutionally protected right to marry (Liptak, 2015). With such timing, we can glean what appears to be the rather calculated approach by Buttigieg to "managing" his gayness and, particularly, his approach in handling the public/private duality created by his status and aspirations as a gay public official.

The Buttigieg biography clearly demonstrates an eagerness for increasing public and professional success. When he launched his bid for the U.S. presidency at 37, Buttigieg barely cleared the constitutionally prescribed age requirement of 35 years old to serve as our nation's chief executive. Had he been successful in his quest for the presidency, Buttigieg, at 39 years of age, would have been the youngest president ever elected (Teddy Roosevelt currently holds that record, as he assumed the presidency when he was 42). Buttigieg was first elected mayor at age 29, and at that time was the youngest serving mayor of a U.S. city with at least 100,000 residents (Pak et al., 2020). Yet until he was ready to seek his second term as mayor, the position that he would shortly attempt to parlay into the U.S. presidency, his identity as a gay man was not something he would openly acknowledge or attempt to reconcile with his public life. Indeed, from his journey as a Harvard University graduate and Rhodes scholar to his time as a U.S. Navy reserve officer with service in Afghanistan, Buttigieg had more important matters to attend to. He explained, "Yeah, I'd been dragging my feet on coming out, because my two careers were military and elected office in Indiana, neither of which is super gay-friendly" (DeCosta-Klipa, 2019, para. 6). It was actually his military service in Afghanistan that ultimately led him to openly acknowledge his homosexuality. As he noted, the possibility of his life ending in battle prompted him to examine who he truly was and how he wished to live his life:

> Then the thing that really put me over the top was the military deployment, where I took a leave from serving as mayor to go serve overseas. And it just . . . something about that really clarified my awareness of the extent to which you only get to live one life and be one person. . . . Well, part of it was just the exposure to danger, even the fact of writing the letter that I wrote to my family before I left, just in case. . . . Well, a lot of it was about why I felt that my life, how I felt my life fit together, and why I didn't want them to think that I'd been cheated if I didn't come back, because I had such a full life up till then, I was thirty-two, thirty-three. But, at the same time, I realized that there was something really important that was missing, and I began to feel a little bit humiliated about the idea that I could, my life could come to an end, and I could be a visible public official and a grown man and a homeowner and have no idea what it was like to be in love. (*The New Yorker*, 2019, paras. 50, 52, & 54)

Yet now with his political career firmly established, it was time for Buttigieg to get on with pursing love and a life "like most people want[ed]"—that of marriage and children.

Once Buttigieg checked off public acknowledgment of his homosexuality from his list of things to do, the now openly gay mayor of South Bend would pursue his quest for a normal life—and the presidency—with deliberate dispatch. After coming out in June 2015, it was finally time to get out and about in pursuit of Mr. Right, and, in fact, like much of Buttigieg's life of acceler-ated success, it only took a matter of weeks to make the match. In Septem-ber 2015, Buttigieg would meet Chasten Glezman on the dating app Hinge, and they would have their first date (Schwedel, 2019). From this point, the calendar of dating, marriage, and seeking the presidency becomes a rather amazing marathon run. In June 2018, Buttigieg and Glezman were married, complete with an obsequious pictorial spread of their nuptials in the vows section of *The New York Times* (Trebay, 2018). The same-sex marriage of great political interest was described this way:

> Dressed in three-piece Ted Baker suits from Nordstrom of differing but complementary shades of blue and matching socks—Mr. Glezman and Mr. Buttigieg were married by the Rev. Brian G. Grantz at the Episcopal Cathedral of St. James before 200 guests from their newly blended fami-lies and divergent worlds. In a nod to the significance of the event, the 30-minute ceremony, which was livestreamed on YouTube, featured a reading from Justice Anthony Kennedy's majority opinion in *Obergefell v. Hodges*, the landmark 2015 case that granted marriage equality to same-sex couples in the United States. . . . After the ceremony, the newlyweds were driven in the back of a cherry red 1961 Studebaker Lark VIII to stop briefly at a South Bend Gay Pride Week block party, where the beam-ing couple donned rainbow-colored beads, greeted the crowd and took photos with joyful attendees. . . . They then joined 200 more friends for a reception at LangLab, an arts- and co-working space in a former furniture factory that is a prime example of the revitalized city Mr. Buttigieg helped transform. Under soft indigo lights on the concrete floor, Mr. Buttigieg and Mr. Glezman danced for the first time as a couple while the band David Wax Museum played a slow-tempo, soulful cover of the 1988 song "When You Say Nothing At All." (paras. 22–24)

Mixed with the *New York Time's* description of gay pomp and pageantry was also the political, with speculation of what might come next for Mayor Pete and his new husband. One of the political VIPs attending the wedding was President Barack Obama's senior adviser and chief strategist David Axel-rod, who predicted, "Pete's going to be a force in the Democratic Party . . . the question is just whether that's as a candidate for president, or something else" (Trebay, 2018, para. 8). Well, it didn't take long at all for this question to be answered. Just nine months after Buttigieg and Glezman wed, Mayor Pete announced his candidacy for the Democratic Party's presidential nomination (Burns, 2019b).

Less than a year following the launch of his presidential campaign, Butti-gieg would emerge as one of the front-runners in the large Democratic field of candidates, actually winning the first-in-the-nation Iowa caucuses, narrowly edging out Bernie Sanders (Becker & Martina, 2020). With his Iowa victory,

Buttigieg became the first openly gay person to ever win a state's presidential primary election. Following his win in Iowa, Buttigieg delivered a second-place showing in New Hampshire (this time with Sanders narrowly besting him). In the third state to vote in the Democratic presidential primary in 2020, Buttigieg dropped to third place in the Nevada caucuses. He continued his slide in vote-taking with a fourth-place finish in the South Carolina Democratic presidential primary (Epstein & Gabriel, 2020).

With his defeat in the South Carolina primary, a contest that was won overwhelmingly by Joe Biden, Buttigieg withdrew from the race. Along with several other Democratic presidential candidates, including U.S. Senator Amy Klobuchar of Minnesota and former U.S. Representative Beto O'Rourke of Texas, Buttigieg endorsed Biden before Super Tuesday voting (Epstein & Gabriel, 2020). Following Biden's victory in the November 2020 presidential election, Buttigieg was nominated to serve as secretary of transportation in the new administration. The 39-year-old mayor from South Bend continued to make history as he became the youngest member to ever serve in a presidential cabinet. Buttigieg also became the first openly gay cabinet member confirmed by the U.S. Senate (Shepardson, 2021).

Without question, Buttigieg mounted the most successful run for the U.S. presidency by any openly gay person in our nation's history. That his bid for the White House fell short should in no way be viewed as a damning failure of his political acumen or a defeat to be attributed principally to his status as a gay man. As a novice on the national political scene with limited experience as an elected official, and especially for one so young, Buttigieg was haunted throughout his campaign by the suggestion that he was too inexperienced and not ready to assume the awesome responsibilities of the most powerful leader in the world. For many, acceptance of Buttigieg as a gay man did not seem to be an issue at all. His victory in Iowa, a largely rural and mostly White electorate, illustrates the appeal the millennial mayor from South Bend had among some voters. In fact, Buttigieg's strong showing in both Iowa and New Hampshire demonstrated that he performed much better with older, White, rural, and even religious voters—the very types of voters that one might expect would be resistant to a trailblazing gay politician. Of course, Buttigieg was far from any sort of radical or revolutionary gay activist who wished to reside at 1600 Pennsylvania Avenue.

The Buttigieg campaign message was infused with themes of family, faith, and military service framed in middle- and working-class values and centrist appeals to unite political partisans and country. Buttigieg, it bears pointing out, was never a champion for the LGBTQ cause or struggle. In fact, during the campaign, his critics, and particularly gay activists, argued that Buttigieg was "not gay enough" (Gessen, 2020, para. 1). And more to the point, gay activists argued that Buttigieg engaged in a type of "pinkwashing" when it came to his identity as a gay man. When convenient or if it served his political purposes, he invoked solidarity with the LGBTQ community and agenda, yet in the main he actually downplayed his gay identity or commitments, often ignoring gay and other marginalized citizens' struggle for acceptance and social justice (Santus, 2019). Rather than a message that acknowledged and championed the mosaic of diversity within our society, Mayor Pete's campaign appeals, grounded in normativization, expressed a desire for sameness—to pursue a life like "most people want[ed]" (Buttigieg, 2015, para. 15). Describing Buttigieg's propensity for "pinkwashing," one critic noted:

> He chose to wait a long time: until after he graduated from college, after he had served in the military, after he had been elected mayor. He has made it clear that he feared that, if he had come out sooner, his political career might have suffered. But he didn't just wait until he was established in his political career. He also waited until after attitudes toward homosexuality had changed and same-sex marriage had become legal in more than half the states and was recognized by the federal government—all thanks to the courage and work of people who came out before Buttigieg did. Then, in 2015, he had the chutzpah to write an op-ed titled "Why Coming Out Matters," in which he praised himself for "putting something this personal on the pages of a newspaper." (Gessen, 2020, paras. 3–4)

Other instantiations of Mayor Pete's pinkwashing might be found, for example, in his campaign announcement speech in which the nation's first openly gay candidate seeking the presidency never once utters the word "gay" (nor any references at all to LGBTQ, sexuality, identity, or same-sex). *New York Times* reporter Alexander Burns (2019b) notes the "gay" omission and points out Buttigieg acknowledges the historic nature of his candidacy only indirectly in four references throughout the speech to his "husband" Chasten and their "marriage," with Buttigieg describing his partner as "my love." Again, for Buttigieg, he is now "like most people" with husband in tow and ready for the campaign trail that will hopefully take him and Chasten Glezman to the White House. Rejecting Buttigieg's normativization, *New Yorker* columnist Masha Gessen (2020) argues, "But the politics of being 'just like you' leaves out the people who cannot or do not want to be just like conventional straight people, whether in appearance or in the way we construct our lives and families" (para. 6).

In yet another example demonstrating Buttigieg and his husband's desire to appear like a normal married couple, Gessen goes on to discuss Greta LaFleur's analysis of a *Times* magazine cover that became a rather iconic image during the 2020 Democratic primary campaign. We quote from Gessen's description of LaFleur's critique of this image at length:

> In a beautiful essay published in the *Los Angeles Review of Books*, Greta LaFleur, a professor of American studies at Yale, analyzed a photograph

of Buttigieg and his husband, Chasten, that appeared on the cover of *Time* magazine in May of last year [2019]. "This photo is about a lot of things," LaFleur wrote. "But one of its defining features is its heterosexuality. It's offering us the promise that our first gay first family might actually be a straight one." Time had captioned the photo "First Family." How can a family that consists of two men be heterosexual? LaFleur's use of the term is a bit tongue-in-cheek, but she explains that the "unmistakable heraldry of 'FIRST FAMILY,' alongside the rest of the photograph—the tulips; the Chinos; the notably charming but insistently generic porch; the awkwardly minimal touching that invokes the most uncomfortable, unfamiliar, culturally-heterosexual embrace any of us have ever received—offers a vision of heterosexuality without straight people." And without women. (2020, para. 7)

The Buttigieg campaign's striving for gay normativization, in our view, was little more than a plea for sameness at the sacrifice or erasure of gay identity and full inclusion. As Gessen (2019, para. 6) concludes, Mayor Pete's "message to straight people is 'We are just like you, and all we want is the right to have what you have: marriage, children, a house with a picket fence, and the right to serve in the military.'" This experiment in the mainstreaming of gay politics can be most troubling for those outside the White and elite world that Buttigieg inhabits. Thinking more critically about the Buttigieg presidential campaign places us at the center of questions about intersectionality, marginalization, and the possibilities—and limits—of LGBTQ inclusion, social justice, and liberation.

To this end, we next turn to an exploration of the views of those critics within the LGBTQ community who were altogether impatient with the Buttigieg campaign's approach to gay politics. We place these voices in conversation with the decidedly more friendly stances of gay opinion leaders and writers sympathetic to Buttigieg's positioning and message. Finally, we consider the implications of Buttigieg's "traditional values" approach to gay identity and its impact on the future and advancement of LGBTQ politics. Our central contention is that we believe Buttigieg's candidacy furthers the ascendency of privileged gay White males to an uncritical inclusion that leaves larger progressive issues of race, class, and gender unexamined. Such inclusion prioritizes a seat at the table over the priorities of liberation and transformation.

Mayor Pete, We Hardly Knew Ye

We begin our critique of Buttigieg's gay politics from within the LGBTQ community with a focus on Dale Peck's controversial July 12, 2019, editorial, "My Mayor Pete Problem," published online by *The New Republic* (Lederman,

2019). Peck is known for inviting controversy with his political commentary and satire, including his 2011 *Daily Beast* column titled, "If I Have to Read Another Book about the Holocaust, I'll Kill a Jew Myself" (Franklin, 2011). Both Peck essays noted here were removed from online posting shortly after their publication. In both instances, Peck decried what he viewed as censorship and his misunderstood "jokes." In the case of his *New Republic* piece on Buttigieg, Peck seemed less interested in informed, ethical journalism than in creating the type of sensational and dramatic political punditry that typifies so much of today's social media maelstrom. What garnered the greatest reaction to Peck's essay was his homophobic speculation regarding Buttigieg's sex life. He wrote, "The only thing that distinguishes [Buttigieg] . . . is what he does with his dick . . . I get a definite top-by-default vibe . . . I bet he's too uptight to [bottom]" (Roberts, 2019, para. 3). Within just a few hours following the posting of the essay, and with immediate condemnation by multiple gay rights groups, *The New Republic* replaced the article with a brief apology in an editor's note that stated, "Dale Peck's post 'My Mayor Pete Problem' was removed from the site in response to criticism of the piece's inappropriate and invasive content. We regret its publication" ("Editor's note," 2019).

While we in no way endorse Peck's homophobic slurs, we would like to explore his critique of Buttigieg on the much more significant issues of LGBTQ inclusion and normativization and also the mayor's policy proposals. Peck's central beef with Buttigieg centers on two issues. The first is the idea of passing in a world of heteronormative class biases. Peck delivers the following screed:

> I actually want to tell Mayor Pete to take a good look at this world, at his experiences and his view of the public good as somehow synonymous with his own success and I want him to reject it all . . . because I made a similar journey, or at least started out from a familiar place and I was lucky enough to realize . . . that the only place that leads to is a gay parody of heteronormative bourgeois domesticity. (Juzwiak, 2019b, para. 16)

Peck goes on to offer up a laundry list of the parody he has in mind that describes Mayor Pete and his husband's manufactured normativity: the "historic home" in which they live, their "specialty kitchen appliances," their "book club," and "summer and winter vacations" (Juzwiak, 2019b, para. 16). To this vision of happy domesticity, Peck retorts:

> Sorry boys, that's not a life. It's something you buy from a catalog. It's a strange set you build so you can convince everybody (or maybe just yourself) that you're as normal as they are. Call me a hick from the sticks, but I don't want someone who fills out his life like he fills out an AP exam serving as the country's moral compass. (Juzwiak, 2019b, para. 16)

Despite Peck's self-serving attitude throughout his piece, he manages a useful critique of Buttigieg and his gay supporters' self-image and emerging self-righteousness born of an allegiance to heteronormative dreams of comfort and inclusion, a critique that is largely lost in the controversy that surrounds the essay.

The second issue Peck articulates centers on Buttigieg's neoliberal positions throughout his campaign. He pays particular attention to health insurance:

> It's right there in his "Medicare for all . . . who want it" song and dance. To Mayor Pete this is simple egalitarianism and freedom of choice. If you want Medicare, you should be able to have it. And if you want private insurance you should be able to pay three or four or ten times more for health care than you have to. . . . Embedded in this oblivion are both the liberal delusion that people are naturally good and the neoliberal sophistry that the market, like the tide, will raise everyone. (Juzwiak, 2019b, para. 11)

We quote at length here to what amounts to be one of the more trenchant critiques of Buttigieg's policies throughout the campaign. In fact, critics often decried Buttigieg's campaign as lacking in policy details, opting instead for a politics by aphorisms (Burns, 2019a).

Unfortunately, Peck's discussion of race and class and neoliberal deficits were lost in the charges of homophobia, jealousy, and self-serving asides. As one critic wrote, "With Peck, *TNR* exposed the wider culture to a facet of gay culture with particularly rough edges and when people found it unsightly, they did their best to make it unseen" (Juzwiak, 2019a, para. 18). Much of the effort to unsee involved a weaponizing of charges of homophobia aimed at Peck, who credits ACT-UP and the power of creative and disruptive LGBTQ activism for his brand of politics. Homophobia is typically an outsider-insider charge, one hurled from outside the community. Peck's airing of well-established arguments within the community, which if he had delivered in more polite or constructive terms, would perhaps have diminished the long history of shade and reading as essential to the gay public sphere and would have been itself a pinkwashing of the radical politics that brought LGBTQ activists—indeed all of us—into the 21st century. It is along these lines that Peck's arguments can be seen as brave given the media's excessive flattery over Buttigieg's clean-cut, boy-next-door appeal and the heteronormative pull of gay politics post ACT-UP.

For the purpose of our argument, Peck is a stand-in for radical politics, even with all its messiness and self-promotion. Reactions to the piece were almost entirely negative as opposition formed around the predictable insults and charges of homophobia. And there was a great deal of pearl clutching among mainstream media outlets, including *The New Republic*. Most notably heard were the Buttigieg partisans whose central aim was to defend Mayor Pete and his husband's honor and respectability, but not much else.

Too easily ignored by mainstream media until Peck's article in *The New Republic* calling out Buttigieg for not being queer enough was the disquieting gap for many in the LGBTQ community separating the moral force of activism and the staid, satisfied nature of Mayor Pete's campaign and bio. In Buttigieg, LGBTQ activists found a caricature of an upper-middle-class son of a privileged background with an Ivy League education. A closet case lacking the guts of his inner desire is what his more biting critics alleged; an opportunist with no connections to the gay grassroots except for a few speeches to Hillary Rodham Clinton donors was how many activists felt about Buttigieg's rise.

For its part, the mainstream media pitted a wild-eyed LGBTQ activism at odds with the quiet decency of the Buttigieg campaign and whose appearances on the stump would always end with a simple—and staged—kiss between Pete and Chasten, a peck, not a lingering; an honest, relatable jest that only faintly bears the imprint of the radical kiss-ins of the ACT-UP era, an act that was both clarifying and controversial. A kiss, ACT-UP demonstrated, is not just a kiss. Long after it leaves the lips, a same-sex kiss stirs a range of views—opening a politics that at once is dangerous and defiant.

Frank Bruni, writing for *The New York Times*, describes the contrast between activists and the Buttigieg campaign in this manner:

> While some critics on the left conducted an offensive discussion about whether he was gay enough, he performed an important balancing act, integrating his gayness into his campaign without letting his candidacy be defined by it, seizing teachable moments without ever becoming tendentious or tedious, showing the world that being gay or lesbian or bisexual or transgender or queer is an essential part of who we L.G.B.T.Q. people are but not all of who we are. (2020, para. 12)

Undergirding Bruni's argument is the image of an unrealistic, single-minded, and impatient LGBTQ protester over-determined by a "tendentious and tedious" identity politics. This contrasts with the overt grace and charm he affords Buttigieg, whose politics he no doubt shares.

Writing for *The Atlantic*, whose politics remain largely centrist, Spencer Kornhaber (2020) notes:

> Conflating gayness with any particular moral, political, or aesthetic value the observer has deemed *good*, though, is an act of hijacking . . . one weirdly similar to the rhetorical move homophobes use when they say gay people are immoral . . . the chatter painting Buttigieg as virtually straight points to something that's harder to talk about: the ways in which the Democratic front-runner is, in fact, unmissably gay, and how the backlash to him is itself tinged with its own strain of queer shame. (paras. 4–5)

Here, again, we find a caricature of a queer left more concerned exclusively with identity politics than with the centrist brand of political normativity moderates prefer. While there is nothing new here, it is striking that both Bruni and Kornhaber aggressively campaign against what is essentially a minority within a minority. The LGBTQ community's reaction to Buttigieg produced—thanks to the media we've examined so far—more fire than light. Nowhere by *The New York Times* or *The Atlantic*'s pro-Buttigieg columnists was there any attempt to clarify the notably complex contentions emerging out of the queer community. One such attempt in *The New Yorker*—again, an elite liberal publication—stands out: "One kind of queer politics is rooted in the ideas of liberation, revolutionary change, and solidarity" (Gessen, 2020, para. 5). A second form of gay politics, by contrast, rests on largely white assimilationist versions of marriage and white picket fences. It is assumed in the discourses presented here that the latter is of a greater moral weight, and certainly more suitable to the Democratic Party and its primary voters. What Gessen (2020) terms a "passable life" is rife with ethical, political, and class pitfalls made clear by the emancipatory trajectory of the first approach.

Several thousand activists working under the tutelage of "#QueersAgainstPete" published an open letter, arguing in part:

> We are clear that LGBTQ2IA people are directly and disproportionately impacted by police violence, incarceration, unaffordable healthcare, homelessness, deportation and economic inequality among other things. (Gessen, 2020, para. 5)

Here we find a coalition of issues with the potential to unite political outsiders poised against Buttigieg, who is considered an insider to the political world of White male liberalism uncomfortable with issues of class and race, of casualty and history. The group further charges:

> As LGBTQ2IA our lives are layered and must have an intersectional framework . . . during this critical election it's important (we) demand more from our leaders and from a candidate claiming to be in community with us. (#QueersAgainstPete, n.d., para.16)

As a candidate, Buttigieg found himself caught between a passable, safe life awash in privilege and the demands of a political force pressing in from the outside against those privileges. He is both an insider to an elite world few imagine and an outsider to the queer critiques of that world. In the aftermath of his campaign announcement, Buttigieg was awash in requests from media outlets and magazine covers. One such cover from *New York* magazine featured Buttigieg dressed in his requisite white dress shirt and chinos staring up into some imagined promised land (White, 2019). The lighting and the fix of his eyes suggest an almost angelic, anointed figure awash in optimism and faith in a country that served up a Harvard degree and a fawning wedding spread in *The New York Times*. Just what this promised land looks like for Americans of unequal birth, societal ridicule, and repudiation is lost on a cover boy flooded in the warm glow of bright white lights. Buttigieg is at once a symbol of hope and a shiny token for a hungry media reading too much into his appeal to a narrow band of largely White and elite liberals. South Carolina, for example, exposed the Buttigieg appeal to the scrutiny of Black voters. Sixty percent of South Carolina's Democratic voters are African American, and Buttigieg managed a rousing 2% of these primary voters (Epstein & Gabriel, 2020).

Indeed, the Buttigieg flattery presented in mainstream media accounts built up his image as the normal, steady-as-she-goes, wonder boy who lives a life far removed from any sort of radical gay trailblazing. These media depictions would often stress his safe and comfortable demeanor and basic attire, as Nathan Heller (2019) wrote for *Vogue* magazine:

> In person, Buttigieg's style is amiable and controlled. He speaks, like a newscaster, in lucid paragraphs, with a solid baritone and boxed-in decorum. He seems to live in white shirts and pressed slacks—it's his dress even now, around the house—and wears his hair in the same tame coif as Mike Pence, who was elected Indiana's governor the year he was sworn in as mayor. Showing me into a living room where books on display range from Thomas Piketty's *Capital in the Twenty-First Century* to *Peanuts: A Golden Celebration*, he takes a seat in front of a huge resource-and-mineral map of Afghanistan. A burl-wood chessboard sits beside a folded-over copy of *The New Yorker*; most other surfaces, including the dining-room table in the other room, are piled with work papers and the castoffs of a busy life. The home is one of the nicest in the city and serves as a reminder of South Bend's distance from the coasts: The mortgage payment, according to Buttigieg, is about $450 a month. (para. 2)

Here, the description of a studied approach to a careful life is clear. All the markers of a comfortable life with a worn copy of the iconic *The New Yorker* magazine on display reinforce a cultural elitism along with the obligatory copy of Picketty's *Capital*. Lest we miss the hint of acceptable humor on display throughout most of his campaign, Buttigieg's drawing room is tempered by the Midwestern values of the Peanuts cartoons. Yes, Charles Shultz was a lifelong Republican. To readers of *Vogue*—mostly White and affluent—this sort of style piece is familiar terrain. Consider also this from Heller's 2019 article:

> He defaults toward a wonky interiority (he's at his most animated talking about policy reform) and lives with a longtime wunderkind's self-minimizing streak: a habit of demurely absorbing admiration as a matter of course. His air is one of quiet, recessive confidence. (para. 3)

Here Heller (2019) locates in Buttigieg an affect aligned with an upper middle-class upbringing, hailing from a dual PhD household where things like intellect and conversation mattered more than TV and schoolchild crushes. That's how privilege works; you gain the access, the habits of mind and confidence needed to soar above the messy issues involved in the life experiences of those outside your world. You assume your dreams are the center of a moral universe of meritocracy and hard work. Privilege assumes we all dream to the sounds of a single lullaby. Further, privilege accrues in a knowing and a studied and steady approach to, well, everything. It is an inbred demeanor and becomes a "habit of demurely absorbing admiration as a matter of course" (para. 3). It is the resources, leisure, and self-confidence to master seven languages in a country where most Americans perform at an eighth-grade reading level. For too many, the ability—or inability—to dream and live in the main is determined largely by your proximity to power and privilege.

Our critique is not meant to be a blanket criticism of intellect, of poise, or of discernment. Instead, we are most interested in how these constructs play out in our political discourse and the false assumptions that they accrue particularly, and somewhat naturally, to those who are defined as in the main and as pursuing the normal course to power, in this case Pete Buttigieg. The analysis we offer acknowledges the voices and views of the presumed radical gay left who read in Buttigieg's normativized vision of the American Dream a rather blind and crushing inclusion for any number of people of color, working and queer folks, a vision that is narrowly revelatory in the spaces and representation of those who most often find themselves at the margins of our national politics and society.

Conclusion

Certainly, Pete Buttigieg's presidential candidacy was historic, occurring at a time when greater numbers of LGBTQ candidates are seeking and gaining elected office at all levels. Preceding Buttigieg's run for the presidency, the 2018 midterm elections were viewed as a "rainbow wave" with more than 150 LGBTQ candidates taking office (Caron, 2018). Notable victories included Jared Polis of Colorado, the first openly gay man to be elected governor of a state, and Sharice Davids who was elected to a U.S. House seat as the first lesbian congresswoman from Kansas. At that time, Kansas was one of only seven states who had never elected an openly LGBTQ official at the state or federal level.

Notable LGBTQ incumbents re-elected in 2018 included Governor Kate Brown in Oregon, a bisexual, and U.S. Senator Tammy Baldwin of Wisconsin, who was the first openly LGBTQ person elected to the U.S. Senate.

While LGBTQ candidates have found increasing success at the ballot box, the campaign trail is fraught with peril for these candidates, who are frequently subjected to discrimination and even threats from voters as well as their opponents. Annise Parker, president of the LGBTQ Victory Fund, noted: "As we in the LGBTQ community achieve more visibility and acceptance, those who are deeply opposed to the community are alarmed and they strike out . . . sometimes the attacks take the form of overt anti-gay messages or they are dog whistles or sideways references based on stereotypes" (Stack, 2018, para. 8). Employing a more overt gay slur, for example, a state Republican official in Kansas described U.S. House candidate Sharice Davids, a Native American and lesbian, as a "radical socialist kickboxing lesbian Indian" who should be "sent back packing to the reservation" (Caron, 2018, para. 19). Other LGBTQ candidates have been attacked with a barrage of anti-gay discrimination, including these instances:

> Rick Neal, a White gay House candidate in Ohio, found white supremacist material outside the home he shares with his husband and black children. In New Hampshire, a primary opponent accused congressional candidate Chris Pappas of being a weakling—a common trope used against gay men—and in Maryland, State Senator Richard Madaleno, who ran unsuccessfully in the Democratic primary for governor, was mocked by an opponent as someone who "prances around Annapolis." In Vermont, Christine Hallquist, the first transgender person nominated for governor by a major party, stopped publicizing her campaign schedule and started traveling everywhere with an aide after she received a dozen or more death threats. (Stack, 2018, paras. 11–13)

Clearly, the path to acceptance for LGBTQ candidates has not been an easy road, and perhaps because of this struggle, the candidacy of Buttigieg as the first openly gay candidate for the U.S. presidency was seen as potentially emancipatory, especially for those within the LGBTQ community, and possibly the dawn of something if not radicalizing at least liberating in our current political order.

Mayor Pete, however, stepped into the presidential arena and sought above all else to be seen as normal—"like most people"—with a campaign driven by normative appeals grounded in the traditional and wholesome values of faith, family, and freedom. The Buttigieg centrist Democratic campaign playbook contained very little of the historic discrimination that gay men and women have sustained and continue to endure, with hardly any nod to the struggles of those who remain outside the main of American politics. This struggle, as we have described, was never part of Buttigieg's lived experience. The central thesis developed in this essay is that the status of gay men and women and of trans, bisexual, and intersex individuals remains marginal to the normative strain of politics peddled by Buttigieg. In a normativized political discourse, the plight and pleas of the outsider are abated by the promise of inclusion—that one can achieve insider status if only they mask their identity and dreams in the beliefs and values of the majority.

As we suggest, such inclusion brings with it a set of expectations and norms that favor gradualism and elides questions of social justice and the potential for systemic change. As an insider to privilege, Buttigieg's norma- tivization of gay life sacrificed the gay struggle and agenda for the assurance and comfort of broader acceptance. Our intent is not to burden Buttigieg with the weight of gay liberation or acceptance in our social and political order. Rather, we subject him, and his supporters, to a scrutiny only fitting their privilege and access to power and influence. With respect to Buttigieg, and to quote scripture as he would so often do, to whom much is given, much is expected. This is essential.

References

Becker, A. & Martina, M. (2020, February 6). Buttigieg wins Iowa caucuses: State party rules. *Reuters.* https://www.reuters.com/article/us-usa-elections /buttigieg-narrowly-wins-iowa-caucuses-state-party-results-idUSKBN2002JS

Bruni, F. (2020, March 1). Mayor Pete flew sky high. *The New York Times.* https:// www.nytimes.com/2020/03/01/opinion/Pete-Buttigieg-speech.html

Burns, A. (2019a, April 14). Pete Buttigieg's focus: Storytelling first. Policy details later. *The New York Times.* https://www.nytimes.com/2019/04/14/us/politics /pete-buttigieg-2020-writing-message.html

Burns, A. (2019b, April 15). Pete Buttigieg's campaign kickoff: Full speech, annotated. *The New York Times.* https://www.nytimes.com/2019/04/15/us /politics/pete-buttigieg-speech.html

Buttigieg, P. (2015, June 16). South Bend mayor: Why coming out matters. *South Bend Tribune.* https://www.southbendtribune.com/story/news/local /2015/06/16/south-bend-mayor-why-coming-out-matters/45761773/

Caron, C. (2018, November 7). In 'rainbow wave,' L.G.B.T. candidates are elected in record numbers. *The New York Times.* https://www.nytimes .com/2018/11/07/us/politics/lgbt-election-winners-midterms.html

DeCosta-Klipa, N. (2019, April 3). Pete Buttigieg explains why he didn't come out until nearly his second term as South Bend mayor. *The Boston Globe.* https://www.boston.com/news/politics/2019/04/03/pete-buttigieg -gay-coming-out/

Editor's note. (2019, July 12). *The New Republic.* https://newrepublic.com /article/154457/editors-note

Epstein, R. J. & Gabriel, T. (2020, February 29). For Buttigieg, a search for black support that never came. *The New York Times.* https://www.nytimes .com/2020/02/29/us/politics/buttigieg-black-voters-south-carolina.html

Franklin, R. (2011, May 19). "[I]f I have to read another book about the holocaust, I'll kill a Jew myself." *The New Republic.* https://newrepublic.com/article/88712/holocaust-jokes-dale-peck-daily-beast-lars-von-trier

Gessen, M. (2020, February 12). The queer opposition to Pete Buttigieg, explained. *The New Yorker.* https://www.newyorker.com/news/our-columnists/the-queer-opposition-to-pete-buttigieg-explained

Heller, N. (2019, April 29). Pete! Pete! Pete! Inside the underdog campaign shaking up the 2020 race. *Vogue.* https://www.vogue.com/article/pete-buttigieg-interview

Juzwiak, R. (2019a, July 15). Define 'homophobic.' *Jezebel.* https://jezebel.com/define-homophobic-1836367531

Juzwiak, R. (2019b, July 16). The article on Buttigieg that the New Republic published and then unpublished. *Louis Proyect: The Unrepentant Marxist.* https://louisproyect.org/2019/07/16/the-article-on-buttigieg-that-the-new-republic-published-and-then-unpublished/

Kornhaber, S. (2020, February 29). The shame of Pete Buttigieg. *The Atlantic.* https://www.theatlantic.com/culture/archive/2020/02/why-policing-pete-buttigiegs-gayness-essentialist/607129/

Lederman, J. (2019, July 13). New Republic magazine pulls down homophobic op-ed about Pete Buttigieg by an openly gay literary critic. *NBC News.* https://www.nbcnews.com/politics/2020-election/new-republic-removes-homophobic-op-ed-attacking-buttigieg-n1029546

Liptak, A. (2015, June 26). Supreme Court ruling makes same-sex marriage a right nationwide. *The New York Times.* https://www.nytimes.com/2015/06/27/us/supreme-court-same-sex-marriage.html

The New Yorker. (2019, April 2). Interview: Pete Buttigieg on how he plans to win the Democratic nomination and defeat Trump. https://www.newyorker.com/news/the-new-yorker-interview/pete-buttigieg-plans-win-democratic-presidential-nomination-defeat-trump

Pak, N., Scanlan, Q., & Thomas, E. (2020, March 2). Pete Buttigieg: Everything you need to know about the 2020 presidential candidates. *ABC News.* https://abcnews.go.com/Politics/peter-buttigieg/story?id=60731298

#QueersAgainstPete. (n.d.). Open letter. https://www.queersagainstpete.com/letter

Roberts, Q. (2019, August 1). The Dale Peck is over party: Mayor Pete, Dale Peck, and the limits of queer rhetorical flourishes. [Blog post]. *Los Angeles Review of Books.* https://blog.lareviewofbooks.org/essays/dale-peck-party-mayor-pete-dale-peck-limits-queer-rhetorical-flourishes/

Santus, R. (2019, April 15). Cutting through the Mayor Pete hype. *Vice News.* https://www.vice.com/en/article/neawkw/cutting-through-the-mayor-pete-hype

Schwedel, H. (2019, April 17). Hinge in the White House: Pete and Chasten Buttigieg's other potential first. *Slate.* https://slate.com/human-interest/2019/04/pete-chasten-buttigieg-hinge-marriage-dating-app-president.html

Shepardson, D. (2021, February 2). Pete Buttigieg becomes first openly gay cabinet secretary confirmed by U.S. Senate. *Reuters*. https://www.reuters.com/article/us-usa-biden-transportation/pete-buttigieg-becomes-first-openly-gay-cabinet-secretary-confirmed-by-u-s-senate-idUSKBN2A22IQ

Stack, L. (2018, November 5). Facing threats and bias, L.G.B.T. candidates are running in record numbers. *The New York Times*. https://www.nytimes.com/2018/11/05/us/politics/lgbt-candidates.html

Trebay, G. (2018, June 18). Pete Buttigieg might be president someday. He's already got his first man. *The New York Times*. https://www.nytimes.com/2018/06/18/fashion/weddings/mayor-peter-buttigieg-wedding-democratic-party.html

White, A. (2019, April 14). On the cover: Wonder boy Pete Buttigieg. *New York*. https://nymag.com/press/2019/04/on-the-cover-wonder-boy-pete-buttigieg.html

CHAPTER TWO

Mediating Race and Gender in Campaign 2020: The Cooking with Kamala Videos

*Trevor Parry-Giles, Divine Narkotey Aboagye,
Jin R. Choi, Taylor Hourigan, Meg Itoh,
Carolyn Robbins, Matthew Salzano,
Kalin Schultz, and Shelby Sturm*

It was a typically cool spring Thursday in the San Francisco Bay area when the president of the United States, Barack Obama, chose to introduce and recognize, somewhat awkwardly, a unique and compelling California political leader on April 4, 2013. In his introductory remarks to a crowd of supporters gathered in Atherton to raise funds for the California Democratic Party, Obama said, "You have to be careful to, first of all, say she is brilliant and she is dedicated and she is tough, and she is exactly what you'd want in anybody who is administering the law, and making sure that everybody is getting a fair shake. She also happens to be by far the best-looking attorney general in the country; Kamala Harris is here. It's true. Come on. [Laughter] And she is a great friend and has just been a great supporter for many, many years" (2013, p. 276).

There is much to parse in Obama's off-hand introductory comments. Of course, Obama was being genial, even jovial, in this setting—it was a festive occasion with an audience of supporters and just the sort of context where a usually careful president lets his guard down. In so doing, Obama betrays a lot—a defensiveness about his sexism most of all. Note the construction at the outset of the comments: "You have to be careful to, first of all, say she is brilliant . . . ." The construct "you have to be careful" signals that Obama knew what was coming next might be offensive or read the wrong way. To cover his tracks, Obama takes care, is "careful," to praise Harris's brilliance, dedication, and toughness so as to create a permission to go down the sexist road of labelling Harris "by far the best-looking attorney general in the country" (Obama, 2013, p. 276).

The reaction must have been immediate—Obama says, defensively, "It's true. Come on," while the transcript of the remarks reports laughter from the gathered audience. Presumably, the audience's laughter was, in part, derisive. The national reaction over the next few days was similarly immediate and sometimes also derisive. By Saturday, April 6, 2013, *CNN* featured an interview with Sam Bennett, the president and CEO of the She Should Run foundation, who said of Obama's comments, "It's sexist. That simple comment drops her like a stone electorally and makes voters much more likely to see her—much less likely to see her as qualified or worthy of their vote" (*CNN*, 2013). In *New York Magazine*, columnist Jonathan Chait (2013) opined that while Obama sought to overcome his own sexism by praising Harris's brilliance, "Discussing their appearance in the context of evaluating their job performance makes it worse" (para. 2). Chait (2013) concluded that "the example [Obama's] setting here is disgraceful" (para. 3). And in the White House briefing room, Press Secretary Jay Carney was asked specifically about Obama's comments about Harris on April 5, 2013. Carney replied, somewhat opaquely, that the president "called her [Harris] to apologize for the distraction created by his comments" (para. 152, 2013).

This incident from 2013 was, in important and material ways, Harris's political introduction to a national audience. Having risen quickly from a municipal to a statewide official, she was known in California but not well-known nationally except, perhaps, in rarified political circles. More telling is the fact that Harris's national introduction was wrapped in controversy and couched in specifically sexist (and to a lesser extent, racialized) terms, putting forward those sexist and racialized grammars as a framework for understanding this political figure. Like many public, political women, Harris's foray into the national spotlight was shaped and framed by overtly gendered dynamics, which have and will affect the rest of Harris's political career. Add to that a clearly racialized dimension occasioned by the remarks of America's first Black president about a Black, Asian American state attorney general resulting in comments that were not only overtly sexist but also implicitly racialized.

Six years after Obama's fundraiser comments about Harris, the then U.S. senator from California stood at the podium in Oakland in front of more than 20,000 supporters on January 27, 2019, to announce that she was running for president of the United States. Within a few months of that announcement, Harris was out of the presidential race on December 3, 2019, before any actual votes were cast. She emerged quickly as a leading contender for the Democratic vice presidential nomination once Joe Biden secured the presidential nomination. And on August 11, 2020, Biden named Harris as his running mate. With Biden's victory in November 2020 and inauguration in January 2021, Harris became the first woman and the first Black/South Asian vice president of the United States.

Harris's remarkable, history-making journey to the second-highest office in the United States was defined and framed by the same sex- and race-based political grammars that defined her introduction to the national political audience in 2013. Such sex-based grammars are endemic to American politics; they have organized political communication in a campaign context since at least 1872 when the first woman (Victoria Woodhull) ran for president. Race-based appeals and logics are also endemic to political campaign rhetorics and have been for the entirety of the nation's history. It is therefore hardly surprising that when Harris sought, in turn, the presidency and the vice presidency, her political efforts and communications were and are shaped by the long-lingering racism and sexism so common in American politics.

Of more significant interest than the simple identification of the exclusionary, discriminatory nature of presidential politics is the recognition and assessment of how women candidates and candidates of color navigate those politics. Contemporary politics is driven by the complex interaction between broad, large public audiences; candidates and their messages; and the media outlets that convey those messages and offer their own reads and interpretations. Deep into that complexity are the intervening forces of race and sex/gender. In important ways, the dynamics of race and sex/gender inflect all dimensions of contemporary political communication, with all parties involved addressing those dynamics in rich and varied ways. Here, we consider specifically one approach employed by Senator Harris to confront the racialized and gendered discourses that were occasioned by her candidacy for president.

Starting in late 2019, prior to withdrawing from the presidential contest, Harris was featured in a series of videos that appeared on YouTube and other social media outlets showing her cooking with different celebrities and voters. Harris had long proclaimed her fondness for cooking, and cooking had become a central part of her political identity, especially as reinforced by these videos. Our examination of these unique political rhetorics highlights the stereotypical mediation and representation of women of color in political communication and notes how these videos work to shift and occlude these stereotypes in unique and compelling ways. By rhetorically reconfiguring her identity as a Black/South Asian woman via these videos, we contend that Harris transcended the double-bind rhetorical scenarios faced by all women and women of color who seek high office; she did so by relying on her multiracial consciousness to appeal to a broader American audience.

While operating within spheres that are distinctly coded as feminine (e.g., cooking, domesticity), Harris reclaims the feminine coding of cooking as an act of gendered resistance, largely via a multiethnic framing of cooking. Another double bind is implicated here, as Harris uses some of the videos to cater to a nonimmigrant gaze while simultaneously creating image rhetorics carefully engineered to be digestible by nonimmigrant American voters. Harris has thus reclaimed her heritage through food, un-containing herself by cooking, to ultimately shift gridded, gendered power structures in the service of her political identity and carefully constructed political image.

Kamala Harris: For the People

A common truth about presidential campaigns is that they begin in earnest with the publication of books by would-be candidates; these books are useful for candidates as they seek to establish their political image and articulate their presidential identity in advance of the first caucuses and primaries. Such was the case in 2020, with a series of books published by noted Democrats in the years preceding 2020, including books by Joe Biden (*Promise Me, Dad*), Bernie Sanders (*Where Do We Go From Here*), and Elizabeth Warren (*This Fight Is Our Fight: The Battle to Save America's Middle Class*). Into this collection came Harris's book, *The Truths We Hold: An American Journey*, in early 2019. Like so many of these campaign books, Harris's is part autobiography, part policy manifesto, part confessional, and part promises for the future. And as she had done throughout her political career, Harris infuses her political identity with healthy doses of family life, narratives about her mother, and cooking.

The Truths We Hold, and so many of the profiles and comments from Harris in 2019 and 2020, speak powerfully to the challenges women and women of color face as they pursue high office. These candidates are forced to simultaneously appear competent, but humble; powerful, but demure; ambitious, but modest. The failure or inability to navigate these dynamics of contemporary political communication may portend the collapse of a campaign and the end of political advancement. Beginning with *The Truths We Hold* (Harris, 2019a) and continuing throughout her different candidacies for president and vice president, Harris negotiated the uncertain terrain of political identity construction in a context decidedly unfavorable for women and especially women of color.

To American women in the political sphere, questions of qualifications and charges of overambition are not new. Qualities that are seen in political men as markers of good leadership, such as confidence and assertiveness, are often entirely recontextualized when identified in political women. Confidence becomes "bossiness"; assertiveness translates into being a "bitch" (Anderson, 1999). Rhetorics of political identity, then, may function to contain these political women, shutting down space for them to act within the political sphere and allowing for a dismissal of their voices.

This containment is a manifestation of the particular form of "otherizing" that established power structures of political communication may often employ when challenged by female candidates and women of color. According to Homi Bhabha, the concept of the Other is constructed within "the overlap and displacement of domains of difference" (2004, p. 2). This notion of difference as a marker of the Other is evident throughout cultural analyses and anthropological inquiry; it is a "part of this strategy of containment where the Other text is forever the exegetical horizon of difference" (Bhabha, 2004, p. 2). To contain is thus to enclose the Other behind a door of vast difference; to contain is to entertain the voyeuristic, fetishizing, colonial gaze that writes inherent difference and Otherness onto a certain cultural space, becoming a sort of fantasy, ultimately never giving the Other the chance to be the "active agent of articulation" (Bhabha, 2004, p. 2).

In contemporary political communication, containment via otherizing is a common strategy as candidates vie for public office. American political history is replete with examples of such otherizing, from Jesse Helms's use of White hands in 1990 to argue against affirmative action (and his Black opponent, Harvey Gantt), to the infamous Willie Horton TV ads of 1988, to the Republican attempts to otherize John Kerry in 2004. Otherizing is frequently used to attack and dismiss another's candidacy, to suggest that a political opponent just is not "one of us." As such, we are particularly concerned with political containment as a process of identifying difference between Self and Other and as a strategy of maintaining dominant power. Moreover, germane to Harris, this containment is especially potent for the subjects that lie in the in-between, a space that Harris occupies as a multiracial woman on the stage of traditional (and White, male) American politics (Bhabha, 2004; see also Poirot, 2009; Smith, 2010; Vats & Nishime, 2013).

Consideration of Harris's race is thus vital to understanding her political identity formation. As Anne Norton contends, "Culture is political" because politics exists "as an aspect of culture, and culture as the field in which politics is conceived and enacted" (2004, pp. 9–12). Harris's multicultural identity indicates a new "field" in which American politics will be enacted—a political change which, in turn, has the potential to change American culture and that may have a significant influence on the American people because "representation alters the represented . . . representatives [refine] the opinions of the people," which "alter[s] the public world" (Norton, 2004, pp. 93–95). Furthermore, the interchange between the larger political culture and Harris (and her campaign) illustrates the important cultural and rhetorical negotiations that all female candidates and women of color candidates face and enact.

Yet another dimension of Harris's political identity and image is her frequently mentioned status as a "first." The rhetoric of "firsts"—often taking the form of adjectives like "historic," "ground-breaking," and "momentous"—rings of a "pioneer frame" through which politicians are painted in the spirit of Western "rugged individualism" as "facing hardship as they pursue a new goal," "making it easier for those who follow" (Sheeler & Anderson, 2013 p. 17). While the pioneer frame arguably carries some positive connotations for the male candidates to which it is applied, Sheeler and Anderson contend that it "undermines the credibility of women candidates, under-scoring the transgressive and oxymoronic quality of all woman presidential candidates" (2013, p. 17). Consistently painting female (and women of color) candidates as the "first" works to "situate women as perpetual novices" while simultaneously ignoring and obfuscating the "ideological, cultural and political forces" that constrain female agency as political actors (Sheeler & Anderson, 2013, p. 17).

By the time the Cooking with Kamala videos began to circulate, Harris was already confronting the power-laden, exclusionary dynamics of presidential politics and contemporary political communication. While her announcement was heralded generally as a success, an op-ed had appeared in *The New York Times* a few days earlier that had the potential to stymie any Harris momentum (Bazelon, 2019). The op-ed maintained that Harris was not the "progressive prosecutor" that she purported to be and that many of her policies as San Francisco district attorney and as California attorney general were far from "progressive" (para. 1). The op-ed's criticism of Harris was particularly potent for the progressive left; this leftist *topos* was prominent in discourse regarding her presidential campaign, especially when journalistic coverage addressed Harris's racial identity.

For example, in November 2019, *The New York Times* ran a story titled "Black voters to Black candidates: representation is not enough." The article begins by featuring a 20-year-old Black woman, Chyna Hester, sharing that "Ms. Harris was not her preferred choice . . . supporting Ms. Harris was a particularly uncool thing to do" (Herndon, 2019, para. 3). "Kamala Harris is a cop" memes circulated widely. Multiple news articles mention how the meme spread in various ways—photoshopped Harris clad in police gear, jokes about how she (as a cop) would treat citizens, and just simple reminders that Harris is a cop (Reese, 2019; Squires, 2019; Starr, 2019). In all, the public discussion about "Kamala is a cop" and her record as a progressive prosecutor was deeply implicated with powerful questions of race and gender; indeed, by the time Harris was the Democratic vice presidential nominee, the discussion surrounding her prosecutorial record abated somewhat when its highly racialized and gendered foundation was emphasized.

Cooking with Kamala

The entirety of Harris's political identity, from the earliest days of her career to her ascendancy to the vice presidency, has been defined by discourses of race and gender. If contemporary political communication is understood as a conversation between different agents (political candidates, voters and citizens, news media and social media) and all of those agents are discussing the same thing (e.g., a candidate's race, a candidate's gender), those messages then rise to the top and become a dominant image for the candidate—everything comes to be defined by those rhetorics. Such was the case with Harris, and our focus shifts to how she and her campaign sought to address and recapture control over her political identity, at least via one small set of rhetorics about cooking.

The Cooking with Kamala videos are certainly a unique addition to the annals of political identity definition and political communication. As a response to the ways in which Harris is othered as an unsuitable presidential candidate via her race and gender, the campaign created a set of videos (seven in total) that offers food as a vessel that embodies this differentiation. Cooking and food have an inherent rhetoricity and are activities and materialities that are imbued with power. As such, we also recognize that the Cooking with Kamala videos are alternative containment rhetorics, coming from the candidate (and/or the campaign) that attempt to (re)contain her political image; in particular, we observe how some of these videos work, in part, to contain Harris as "ethnic" through her heritage that associates her with "ethnic food." At the same time, Harris uses this same ethnic food as a method of resisting dominant power, to un-contain herself. Specifically, Harris cooks "ethnic food" for her audience, reclaiming these dishes as heritage food, and thus invites them to participate in a form of what Lucy Long calls "culinary tourism" and to change their understanding of Harris in the process (2013, p. 20).

Bacon-Fried Apples

Two of the Cooking with Kamala videos were specifically aimed at Iowa caucus-goers and were released in late 2019; by the time they were broadcast, *Politico* had released reports that the Harris campaign was dramatically restructuring and placing heavy focus on Iowa ahead of the first primaries (Cadelago & Bland, 2019). During this time, Harris's official YouTube channel released a playlist of videos titled Cooking with Kamala. Harris traveled to Iowa campaign chair Deidre DeJear's home in Des Moines to make bacon-fried apples. The recipe comes from Harris's mother, who is pictured onscreen in an archival photograph that also features Harris and her sister. Deidre (she's referred to by first name only throughout the video) remarks that "your mama was a wise woman putting bacon in this!" and Harris retorts: "Look, bacon is a spice as far as I'm concerned" (Harris, 2019b).

The "Kamala Harris Cooks Bacon-Fried Apples" video uses cooking to connect Harris's Black ancestry with the state of Iowa. The video works to enhance and expand on her identity in ways that are designed to work specifically for an Iowa audience. It also functions to address Harris's broader political identity as a Black woman candidate. The video speaks to these themes in two major ways.

First, making and enjoying the recipe with Deidre connects their experiences as Black Americans and thus recaptures this dimension of Harris's political identity. After the line about Harris's wise mama, the two women cook with a cast iron skillet in Deidre's kitchen and share stories about Harris's mother. Harris complains that there were never exact measurements in the recipes; then they share a joyous laugh when Harris continues to measure by eye. Harris and Deidre finish the bacon-fried apples and put them on a stack of pancakes. Deidre takes the first bite while Harris watches. After a closeup of her forkful, the camera cuts to a medium shot where Harris watches Deidre close her eyes and sigh. Next is a close-up shot of Deidre's face: "Life, liberty, and the pursuit of happiness is right here."

The line goes unanswered—it is punctuated by more close-up shots of the bacon-fried apples on forks, and then they start a new conversation about Harris's experience in Iowa. But the line is a poignant moment in the video's narrative, as it completes the arc that opened with Harris's mother, rose in action with the assembling of the dish, and concluded with the first bite from Deidre—who ends it with a reference to the Declaration of Independence. Significantly, the video frames this patriotic allusion as the resolution to the stories about generations of women of color making food in the kitchen.

On the one hand, this reference is a powerful refutation of the original document that excluded people of color and women from its citizenry. But it also manages to suggest that participation in life, liberty, and the pursuit of happiness from these women of color is manifested in the kitchen. Joshua Meyrowitz (1985) suggests that politicians revealing "behind the scenes" is necessary for achieving some political success because it shows the audience the "true character" of the candidate (see also Parry-Giles & Parry-Giles, 1996). Here, Harris's authenticity is generated by relying on White, patriarchal visions of Black women's patriotism being connected to their role in the kitchen.

Second, in the "Kamala Harris Cooks Bacon-Fried Apples" video, the candidate shares stories about Black Iowans, stories that are deeply connected to food. Deidre asks Harris about her first time in Iowa in 2007, when she campaigned for Obama right before the new year. Harris describes one of the most memorable moments for her was visiting an African American senior home. "Invariably, folks would answer the door, and I remember at least a couple of them saying: 'Oh, baby, come on in, Can I give you a cup of coffee? Oh, you look a little skinny, you want something to eat?'" The two women laugh, as the video switches between close-up shots between them throughout Harris's story, and Deidre says, "They always want to feed you."

Just after eating the bacon-fried apples together—food as campaigning—they return to food during campaigning. The experience that connected Harris to her mother also connects her to the Black community in Iowa. She starts to tell a story about a specific occupant, a "petite lady, must have been well into her 80s, perfectly coiffed wig, perfect makeup, elegantly dressed." The rest of the story is so profound we will quote it at length:

> *Kamala*: And so she answers the door with the chain on, and I was really excited, and I said, "Hi, I'm Kamala Harris, and I'm here for the caucuses. And they're tomorrow, and I'm supporting Barack Obama. And are you gonna come and join us at the caucuses?" And I was all excited, and she looked at me with a straight face and said, "They're not gonna let him win." And I looked at her, and I realized what I was looking at. Which is, this lady, in probably the 85 years of her life. . . . All the indignity she has faced, all the injustice she has witnessed, and she is holding onto her dignity. And she wasn't about to suffer another disappointment at this stage of her life. And, at that moment, I just decided I am not leaving here. And I put my purse down, and I just kept talking with her, and she opened the door a little bit more. . . . She never took that chain off the door.
>
> *Deidre*: She didn't offer you anything to eat.
>
> *Kamala*: . . . And Deidre, the next night at the caucuses, guess who was there?
>
> *Deidre*: I hope she was.
>
> *Kamala*: In the corner all by herself, with her perfect kinda like fox stole. And she was there, and Barack won.

This story is then a jumping point for Harris's own barrier-breaking career. She has not claimed a racial identity or spoken directly about her gender in this video so far—instead, the audience is left to pick this up on their own. As Harris shares about her career, she explicitly claims particular identities for the first time: "When I ran for district attorney of San Francisco, there had never been a woman, there had never been a person of color. People said 'Oh, nobody like you has done it before.'" Deidre wonders: "What did you tell yourself to keep going, just to bypass all that?" Harris responds, quickly, with remarkable wit—"I eat no for breakfast," using another food reference to make a claim about her tenacious political character. The food connects Harris and Deidre, then it connects Harris and Black Iowans, and then Harris with barrier-breaking generally.

Navigating these multiple identities is an important constraint for Harris, who, as a multiracial woman, cannot parse her identities as if they were separate. The two stories told in this video reveal how food is marshalled to connect racial, gender, and political identities. Harking to Harris's mother and life, liberty, and the pursuit of happiness in the kitchen is an example of how racial identity is never separate from gender identity—they are mutually constituted (Crenshaw, 1989; Nash, 2011). And the story of the elegant 85-year-old shows how the experience of "they always want to feed you" can connect Harris to Black identities in Iowa and resistance to oppression generally.

Masala Dosas with Mindy Kaling

Just a month later, Harris's YouTube channel released another cooking video, this time featuring prominent Indian American actress Mindy Kaling as they teamed up to cook masala dosas (Harris, 2019c). During this video, they share similar stories of their Indian heritage as the daughters of immigrant Indian women who earned advanced degrees and pursued careers in medicine (Kaling's mother) and as a biomedical scientist (Harris's mother). The video is set at Kaling's home kitchen, where Harris enters through the kitchen door. They share a moment of shared heritage right away, as Harris notices that Kaling's dad has stored her spices in Taster's Choice jars, just like Harris's mother did. "That's so funny," Harris remarks. "Did they tell each other about it?" The two then proceed to introduce the purpose of the video. Similar to the video with Deidre, their Indian American identity is made possible by being Indian American women as they cook food together and share stories about how their mothers always had home-cooked meals ready. With this context in mind, we want to highlight two moments throughout this video as revealing about how it meets the exigence of making appeals to authenticity.

First, Harris never directly claims an Indian American identity in the video. In the "Bacon-Fried Apples" video, Harris associates with her Black identity by telling stories about and with Black Iowans and only briefly claims her racial identity as she refers to being a person of color. In the video with Kaling, Harris only accepts Indian American identity as it is ascribed by Kaling. There are multiple exchanges where Kaling claims Indian American identity for Harris. The video begins with an exchange where Kaling asks if she should refer to her as "Senator Harris," and Harris insists on a first-name basis. "Just don't call me auntie," Harris says, laughing about a traditional way of referring to an elder in Indian American communities. The conversation continues:

> *Kaling*: Okay. (laughing) I won't call you auntie. They'll be like, how could you call her by her first name? She's worked so hard. Okay, so what we're gonna cook today . . . is an Indian recipe.
>
> *Harris*: Yes.
>
> *Kaling*: Because you are Indian.
>
> *Harris*: Yes, yes, yes.
>
> *Kaling*: Okay and I don't know that everybody knows that. But I find that wherever I go and I see Indian people at the supermarket, on the street, everyone's like, "you know Kamala Harris is Indian, right?" It's like our thing we're so excited about to have you running for president.
>
> *Harris*: Yeah.
>
> *Kaling*: So we're both Indian.
>
> *Harris*: Yes.
>
> *Kaling*: But actually, we're both South Indian.
>
> *Harris*: Yes, you look like the entire one half of my family.
>
> *Kaling*: Okay, thank you.

"I don't know that everybody knows that," Kaling says, getting right to the point about Harris's multiracial identity. Kaling references the casual racial identity invalidation that biracial and multiracial people experience (Campion, 2019; Franco et al., 2016). Harris is not "seen" as Indian because of her perceived racial ambiguity. In the identity politics landscape that she faced in 2020, Harris needs to establish her various racial identities in order to fully inculcate her political identity. By allowing Kaling to ascribe that Indian identity to her, she avoids the micro-aggressive question, "Are you really _____?" that questions her racial authenticity, and, in turn, her political authenticity. Kaling instead proudly claims—for herself and for Harris— "You are Indian."

Second, one moment in the video stands out where the desire to project authentic Indian American identity is inflected by her status as a political and class elite. The dynamic of Harris being an elite is already thrown into play with Kaling's concern about calling her Senator Harris vs. Kamala, and it returns as Harris chops an onion. As Kaling chops up ginger, Harris is working on chopping an onion. They are also talking about mischievous antics they and their cousins engaged in while avoiding elderly family members' religious diets. While this is happening, Harris is using a sophisticated method for chopping an onion advocated by food magazines like *Cook's Illustrated*. The camera jumps between a medium-wide shot where the viewer sees both Harris and Kaling and close ups watching Harris and Kaling work on their onion and ginger. Harris gets to the chopping portion as Kaling starts telling her a story about lamb burgers. Kaling glances down a few times, and then stops and says:

> *Kaling:* That's a fine chop.
>
> *Harris:* Right.
>
> *Kaling:* Okay, Senator Harris, I say this with respect, you're kind of a show-off. (laughing) It's like, meanwhile it's taking me 20 minutes to do this much ginger. Okay, what can't she do? You got my vote.

It's an endearing moment where both women laugh and behave like they are friends, teasing each other as they work together in the kitchen. And yet, at the same time, Kaling awkwardly reveals—and quickly redirects from— the issues that constitute the exigence for these Cooking with Kamala videos. Is Harris an authentic person, a home cook who can make jokes with her friends, or is she an elite who professionally chops onions?

Harris is known as a foodie, but despite this aspect of her identity, some might suggest displaying her cooking expertise is a visual manifestation of how she cuts into power, unabashedly claiming her status as a second-generation immigrant and woman, whose precise cuts in the kitchen echo her incisive political mind (Heil, 2020). And surely, it is possible to celebrate how Harris navigates a double bind placed on all political women via these videos. At the same time, the Cooking with Kamala videos are campaign videos created for political purposes and that her appeals to identity function strategically to activate voters and cultivate Harris's political image. And that image is complicated—the videos navigate multiple avenues of Harris's political identity, at once speaking to her Blackness, her South Asian heritage, the fact that she's a female, her relatively privileged class position, and her identity as a "foodie." With the onion discussion, Kaling's comments bring up, lightheartedly, these contradictions in Harris's persona. Despite changing subjects from the initial encounter quickly, the matter comes back up, as Harris describes her mother's cooking.

> *Harris:* So all of that stuff, everything was from scratch. And this is why maybe I've become, hopefully, not a snob about food—

Kaling: Someone who could cut up onions like that, like we're on a cooking show.

Immediately following, Harris critiques Kaling's approach to dosas:

Kaling: Yeah. Listen, this is controversial, I put peas and cashews in mine. Yay or nay?

Harris: I noticed that. That, you know, I mean—

Kaling: Okay, all right.

Harris: It's fine. You could do it—

Kaling: Your silence was very damning . . .

Harris: Okay, put a couple in. Just put a couple in. Can I just tell you something?

Kaling: Yeah.

Harris: I've never made dosas.

Kaling: Okay, but you're really good about critiquing them. Great. (laughing) This is gonna be great for me.

The "cooking show" reference, paired with the confession that Harris has never made dosas, a traditional Indian dish, reveals the contradictions and oppositions within Harris's political identity. Such a rhetorical strategy is not without risk—as she lets Kaling ascribe her identities, Harris risks being ascribed the elitism these videos were meant to avoid. Moreover, by recounting the experiences of living in an Indian immigrant household, Harris openly claims the culinary practices of her "ethnic" mother and the "ethnic" food that she cooked. Furthermore, Harris acknowledges her mother's influence as something that continues to shape her own culinary practices, thus reclaiming her heritage by emphasizing the ways in which it is the backbone of her political identity.

Conclusion

On November 24, 2020—just a year after she posted the video with Kaling—Vice President-elect Harris posted a cornbread recipe on social media. She captioned the tweet as follows: "During difficult times I have always turned to cooking. This year, I wanted to share one of my family's favorite Thanksgiving recipes with you. I hope whenever you're able to make it in life, it brings you as much warmth as it has brought me—even when separated from those I love" (Harris, 2020). Also, another video of Harris offering recommendations on how people could "brine their Turkeys" went viral. *HuffPost* journalist Kristen Aiken (2020) reported that "if anyone knows how to roast a turkey, it's the Senator who just helped Joe Biden defeat Donald Trump in the 2020 presidential election" (para. 1). A food reporter for *The Washington Post*, Becky Krystal (2020), also praised Harris's recipe. She wrote, "Normally, there's not a whole lot of breaking news involved. But when Vice President-elect Kamala Harris—a person known for her kitchen prowess—drops a dressing recipe on Twitter less than two days before Thanksgiving, well, that's the food writer's equivalent of the Friday afternoon political news dump" (para. 1). These testimonials about Harris's cooking "powers" reinforce the idea of an authentic political candidate who is adept at whatever she does. It also communicates the mediating role of social media and how this has enhanced Harris's candidacy, making her a culinary celebrity-politician in American politics.

These videos, by contextualizing Harris's political identity in food and cooking, contribute to the building of "culinary citizenship" (Lindenfeld, 2001). For Sylvie Durmelat (2015), culinary citizenship denotes "how one's perceived or proclaimed foodways, as well as the degrees and styles of participation in consumer culture that they entail, define one's place in the imagined culinary pantheon and repertoire of specific nations" (p. 108). As a political candidate, Harris pursues her cooking hobby or interacts with the public. In the video with Kaling, Harris underscores this notion of food as it is linked to identity and political image. The "culinary citizenship" emerges from these videos as nuanced and multifaceted—as personified by Harris, the culinary citizen is female and a person of color, someone who proudly and humorously embraces a nonwhite, immigrant ethnic identity.

The 2020 elections were historical in several ways, one of which was Harris's election into the seat of the vice presidency both as a woman and multiracial child of immigrants. The scope of American politics remains exclusionary along lines of race and gender, creating grids of power that contain politicians such as Harris. Recognizing the American presidency as a symbolic and historical place of what it means to be American, Harris's identity as vice president is contained within the lines of race and gender.

With her YouTube cooking videos, Harris cooks herself out of containment in a reformative, although not revolutionary, way. Still operating within the bounds of the "exotic" and the feminine, Harris takes the topic of her heritage to reinvent her Otherness into a curious yet safe experience of culinary tourism and culinary citizenship for her largely nonimmigrant audience. Her differences are just interesting, curious, and fresh enough to be enjoyable, not threatening; her similarities are familiar enough to avoid being banal; and just familiar enough for her audience to feel safe. She identifies herself as the ethnically diverse, immigrant-mother character that is exotic enough to be interesting, familiar enough to be safe, strong enough to be capable, and nurturing enough to be comforting. Furthermore, Harris utilizes cooking and food as modes of resistance, insisting on performing her heritage and centering her own subjectivity. As such, Harris's videos serve as a case study on how politically othered subjects may reclaim their subjectivity, embracing the othering gaze that is placed upon them to meet with a gaze of their own.

References

Aiken, K. (2020, November 24). Kamala Harris shares her Thanksgiving turkey recipe, and it's a good one. *HuffPost*. https://www.huffpost.com/entry/kamala-harris-turkey-recipe_l_5fbd4e17c5b68ca87f7f35a2

Anderson, K. V. (1999). "Rhymes with rich": "Bitch" as a tool of containment in contemporary American politics. *Rhetoric & Public Affairs*, 2(4), 599–623. doi:10.1353/rap.2010.0082

Bazelon, L. (2019, January 17). Kamala Harris was not a "progressive prosecutor." *The New York Times*. https://www.nytimes.com/2019/01/17/opinion/kamala-harris-criminal-justice.html

Bhabha, H. (2004). *The location of culture*. New York, NY: Routledge.

Cadelago, C. & Bland, S. (2019, October 30). Kamala Harris to slash staff, restructure campaign as she hemorrhages cash. *Politico*. https://www.politico.com/news/2019/10/30/kamala-harris-campaign-layoffs-061112.

Campion, K. (2019). "You think you're Black?" Exploring Black mixed-race experiences of Black rejection. *Ethnic and Racial Studies*, 42(16), 196–213. doi:10.1080/01419870.2019.1642503

Carney, J. (2013, April 5). Press briefing by press secretary Jay Carney. https://obamawhitehouse.archives.gov/the-press-office/2013/04/05/press-briefing-press-secretary-jay-carney-452013

Chait, J. (2013). Obama in need of gender-sensitivity training. *New York Magazine*. https://nymag.com/intelligencer/2013/04/obama-in-need-of-gender-sensitivity-training.html

CNN. (2013, April 6). *CNN Saturday morning news* [Television broadcast transcript]. http://www.cnn.com/TRANSCRIPTS/1304/06/smn.05.html

Crenshaw, K. (1989). Demarginalizing the intersection of race and sex: A Black feminist critique of antidiscrimination doctrine, feminist theory and antiracist politics. *University of Chicago Legal Forum*, 1989(1), 139–167. https://chicagounbound.uchicago.edu/uclf/vol1989/iss1/8

Durmelat, S. (2015). Tasting displacement: Couscous and culinary citizenship in Maghrebi-French diasporic cinema. *Food and Foodways*, 23(1–2), 104–126. doi:10.1080/07409710.2015.1012007

Franco, M. G., Katz, R., & O'Brien, K. M. (2016). Forbidden identities: A qualitative examination of racial identity invalidation for Black/White biracial individuals. *International Journal of Intercultural Relations*, 50, 96–109. doi:10.1016/j.ijintrel.2015.12.004

Harris, K. (2019a). *The truths we hold: An American journey*. New York, NY: Penguin.

Harris, K. (2019b, October 22). *Kamala Harris cooks bacon-fried apples* [Video]. *YouTube*. https://youtu.be/ql7YHR4Dwg0

Harris, K. (2019c, November 25). *Kamala Harris & Mindy Kaling cook masala dosa* [Video]. *YouTube*. https://youtu.be/xz7rNOAFkgE

Harris, K. [@KamalaHarris]. (2020, November 24). *During difficult times I have always turned to cooking. This year, I wanted to share one of my family's favorite Thanksgiving recipes with you* [Tweet]. Twitter. https://twitter.com/KamalaHarris/status/1331425347112493056

Heil, E. (2020, August 26). For female politicians, talking about cooking can be fraught. Kamala Harris is breaking that mold, too. *The Washington Post*. https://www.washingtonpost.com/news/voraciously/wp/2020/08/26/for-female-politicians-talking-about-cooking-can-be-fraught-kamala-harris-is-breaking-that-mold-too/

Herndon, A. W. (2019, November 25). Black voters to Black candidates: Representation is not enough. *The New York Times*. https://www.nytimes.com/2019/11/25/us/politics/2020-election-black-voters.html.

Krystal, B. (2020, November 25). I made Kamala Harris's cornbread dressing—and filled in all the details so you can make it, too. *The Washington Post*. https://www.washingtonpost.com/food/2020/11/25/kamala-harris-cornbread-dressing-recipe/

Lindenfeld, L. A. (2001). Feasts for our eyes: Viewing films on food through new lenses. In J. M. Cramer, C. P. Greene, & L. M. Walters (Eds.), *Food as communication, communication as food* (pp. 3–22). New York, NY: Peter Lang

Long, L. M. (2013). Culinary tourism. In P. B. Thompson & D. M. Kaplan (Eds.), *Encyclopedia of food and agricultural ethics*. New York, NY: Springer. https://doi.org/10.1007/978-94-007-6167-4_416-1

Meyrowitz, J. (1985). *No sense of place: The impact of electronic media on social behavior*. Oxford, UK: Oxford University Press.

Nash, J. C. (2011). "Home truths" on intersectionality. *Yale Journal of Law and Feminism, 23*(2), 445–470. https://digitalcommons.law.yale.edu/yjlf/vol23/iss2/5

Norton, A. (2004). *95 theses on politics, culture, and method*. New Haven, CT: Yale University Press.

Obama, B. H. (2013, April 4). Remarks at a Democratic National Committee fundraiser in Atherton, CA. *Public papers of the presidents of the United States: Barack Obama, 276–279*. https://www.govinfo.gov/content/pkg/PPP-2013-book1/pdf/PPP-2013-book1-doc-pg276.pdf.

Parry-Giles, T. & Parry-Giles, S. J. (1996). Political scopophilia, presidential campaigning and the intimacy of American politics. *Communication Studies, 47*(3), 191–205. doi:10.1080/10510979609368475

Poirot, K. (2009). Domesticating the liberated woman: Containment rhetorics of second wave radical/lesbian feminism. *Women's Studies in Communication, 32*(3), 263–292. doi:10.1080/07491409.2009.10162391

Reese, A. (2019, December 3). Did the "Kamala is a cop" meme help tank Harris's campaign? *Jezebel*. https://theslot.jezebel.com/did-the-kamala-is-a-cop -meme-help-tank-harriss-campaign-1840056843

Sheeler, K. H. & Anderson, K. V. (2013). *Woman president: Confronting postfeminist political culture*. College Station, TX: Texas A&M University Press.

Smith, M. (2010). Containment rhetoric and the public sphere: Imagining Amana, inscribing America. *Rhetoric Society Quarterly, 40*(2), 128–145. doi:10.1080/02773940903413423

Squires, C. (2019, December 9). Kamala was a cop. Black people knew it first. *Mother Jones*. https://www.motherjones.com/politics/2019/12/kamala-was-a-cop -black-people-knew-it-first/

Starr, T. J. (2019, December 6). Kamala Harris wasn't allowed to fail up like a White boy. *The Root*. https://www.theroot.com/kamala-harris-wasnt -allowed-to-fail-up-like-a-white-boy-1840273699

Vats, A. & Nishime, L. (2013). Containment as neocolonial visual rhetoric: Fashion, yellowface, and Karl Lagerfeld's "Idea of China." *Quarterly Journal of Speech, 99*(4): 423–447. doi:10.1080/00335630.2013.833668

Rhetoric of Optimism and Promise of Transformation: Concession Speeches by U.S. Presidential Women Candidates in 2020[1]

Julia A. Spiker

Women candidates running for the U.S. presidency share a common goal of breaking the ultimate glass ceiling in politics even as their communication messages and styles vary during a race. Hillary Rodham Clinton was a serious contender in 2008 but lost the Democratic Party nomination to Barack Obama. In her concession speech, Clinton (2008) described her impact with the metaphor of making "18 million cracks" in the glass ceiling. Joining the race again in 2016, Clinton became the first woman to secure a major U.S. party nomination for the office of president of the United States. Clinton's political progress paved the way for more women to run for president as

---

[1] An earlier version of this chapter was presented at the 2021 Midwest Political Science Association conference.

more voters shifted their perspectives to seriously consider the electability of a woman candidate.

In the subsequent 2020 presidential election, a record number of six Democratic women joined the large number of primary contenders vying for their party's nomination, representing a transformative and significant departure from previous election cycles. However, one by one, each woman candidate left the race without gaining the coveted party nomination. Exploring how a woman political candidate rhetorically ends her campaign offers insight into her campaign's impact on the political race, her political legacy, and her future plans. This research examines the campaign exit rhetoric of the Democratic women candidates guided by the question, "How do women presidential candidates rhetorically frame their primary concession speeches?"

Political Concession Speeches

Conceding defeat in politics is a necessary component in the pageantry of elections. Signaling that one's campaign has run its course is a ritual expected by both the remaining candidates and the citizenry. Ritter and Howell (2001) argue that concession speeches are necessary to "promote national unity and legitimize election results" (p. 2329). This was especially true in the 2020 and 2000 presidential elections. In the 2020 presidential election, after months of turmoil, legal fights, the January 6 attack on the U.S. Capitol, and the certification of the election by the U.S. Congress, Trump finally conceded on January 7, 2021 (Williams, 2021). In the 2000 presidential election between George W. Bush and Al Gore, concession speeches were important due to the legal recounts that took place (Ritter & Howell, 2001).

The concession speech has been examined through the message of defeat. As Corcoran (1994) states, the concession speech is "a quintessential narrative of democratic action: a supremely painful personal resignation, symbolic of the public moral drama, and a disarming revelation of the commitments and costs of seeking the nation's highest office" (p. 128). The influence of the context and the speaker on concession speeches has been examined. Willyard and Ritter (2005) viewed concession speeches as a "theatrical performance" in which the "context, the character, personality, and speaking habits" of candidates may lead to a "departure from some generic expectations" (p. 507). The influence of the personal characteristics of the candidates has also been studied. The 2008 presidential race between Barack Obama and John McCain with his vice presidential nominee Sarah Palin highlighted the important issues of race, gender, and age, which influenced their political rhetoric in victory and defeat (Howell, 2011).

Previous research has examined the genre of U.S. presidential concession speeches in the general election in order to decipher key characteristics, message, and rhetorical style. The genre of presidential concession speeches is framed through six key characteristics, including formal declaration of defeat or victory, call for national unity, tribute to American democracy, affirming the candidate's campaign, transformed roles for candidates, and thanking supporters (Corcoran, 1994; Howell, 2011; Ritter & Howell, 2001; Willyard & Ritter, 2005). Concession speeches by third-party candidates have been examined to add to our understanding of additional factors that may influence the rhetorical message (Neville-Shepard, 2014). How a candidate signals the end of their campaign via Twitter has been examined to help understand how a new channel can influence the rhetorical message (Mirer & Bode, 2015). According to Mirer and Bode (2015), substantive themes in Twitter concession speeches include "declares result formally; affirmation of campaign; acknowledgement of role transformation; and thanking supporters" (p. 464).

This research examines the presidential primary concession speeches of major political party candidates. Focusing on primary concession speeches contributes to our understanding of this rhetorical genre. In particular, this research frames the analysis of primary concession speeches via the gendered voice, more specifically six Democratic women candidates who tried to win the White House as president. The focus on women political leaders' rhetoric offers an opportunity to reveal their voices in the 2020 election, pointing to political shifts in 2020 and future presidential elections. According to Kunin (2008), many women politicians may lead differently from men, but not all women politicians behave differently from their male counterparts. Women political leaders may follow the traditional pattern for giving a concession speech, or their concession rhetoric may vary. The findings from this analysis expand the study of the genre of concession speeches to address political primaries, the manner and style in which women candidates concede defeat, and the context and method by which they deliver their messages.

Candidate Concession Speech Analysis

Six women candidates ran in the Democratic primary for the U.S. presidency in 2020. The concession speeches of Democratic candidates Kirsten Gillibrand, Kamala Harris, Marianne Williamson, Amy Klobuchar, Elizabeth Warren, and Tulsi Gabbard are analyzed in the order they ended their campaigns. A rhetorical analysis is used to examine each candidate's style and message. The communication channel used by each candidate and the context of the message are also considered. A thematic analysis is used to study their speech transcripts and media coverage of their remarks to identify key issues and topics in their messages.

Kirsten Gillibrand: August 28, 2019

Senator Kirsten Gillibrand (D-NY) was the first candidate to officially end her bid for the White House on August 28, 2019. First, she informed her campaign staff via telephone. Gillibrand then announced her decision to the world in a written speech on Twitter. In her brief concession speech, Gillibrand states:

> Today, I am ending my campaign for president. I am so proud of this team and all we've accomplished. But I think it's important to know how you can best serve. To our supporters: Thank you, from the bottom of my heart. Now let's go beat Donald Trump and win back the Senate (Merica, 2019, para. 2).

Gillibrand is direct about the purpose of her message. She first announces the end of her campaign before addressing her pride in her campaign team. She acknowledges the contributions of her campaign staff and connects their efforts to the campaign's accomplishments. Gillibrand offers the transformation of her political career as an explanation of why she is leaving the race. She indicates that her 2020 campaign experience helped her to discern that she will be able to contribute more politically at this time and in a different capacity, just not as a presidential candidate. Gillibrand thanks her supporters with an emotional statement. She ends her brief concession speech with the charge to fight the Republican candidate. The end offers a statement of party unity for the purpose of fighting the common opponent. Overall, her speech addresses key characteristics of admitting defeat with a brief explanation on political transformation, thanking her campaign staff and supporters, and challenging her constituency to stay united and continue the fight for victory over a common opponent.

Gillibrand's speech is concise, organized, and offers a clear message and path forward for her supporters. This type of speech and message supports a political party's election efforts and demonstrates that the defeated candidate is a team player. Gillibrand ran her campaign on issues of women's equality (Burns, 2019), but her concession speech did not include key issues from her campaign platform. By focusing on generic statements of unity and support for the Democratic political party election goals, Gillibrand's concession speech message was devoid of her unique perspectives in the political race. Perhaps because her own campaign failed to "catch wind" or because she was the first woman candidate to drop out of the race or due to other factors, Gillibrand cut her losses with this simple but clear speech. She returned to the U.S. Senate to continue her fight for the issues she highlighted in her presidential campaign—women's equality, reproductive rights, and paid family leave (Merica, 2019).

Kamala Harris: December 3, 2019

Then Senator Kamala Harris (D-CA) suspended her campaign on December 3, 2019, due to a lack of financial resources to fund her efforts. She informed her staff via a phone call. In an email to her supporters, Harris said that she "lacked money needed to fully finance a competitive campaign" (Herndon, 2019, para. 2). She used *Medium*, an online publishing platform for blogs, to publish her concession speech in its entirety. Harris opened her concession speech by citing herself when she first launched her campaign in order to describe how she would act as a leader, in particular that she would tell the truth. Within this context of the importance of truth, Harris outlines her inability to raise enough campaign money to continue in the race. She uses these facts to reinforce her ethos of truth-telling with her supporters.

Harris announces that even though she is suspending her campaign, she will continue to fight for her campaign agenda. She builds a rhetorical pattern into her speech by highlighting a key issue from her campaign platform followed by the phrase, "We will keep up that fight" (Harris, 2019, paras. 11, 13, 15, 17, 19). Harris's key fight message focuses on "justice for the people" (para. 9). She fights for "people whose voices that have not been heard or too often ignored," teacher pay, protecting children from gun violence, "unconstitutional state abortion laws," "speaking to the experience of Black women and people of color," and creating opportunity for all children because her "campaign showed every child in America—regardless of their color or gender—that there are no limits to who can lead and hold positions of power in our country" (2019, paras. 10, 16, 18, 20).

By detailing the importance of each of these issues, Harris stresses that her campaign focused on something bigger than herself. Also, before concluding her speech, Harris thanks her staff for their sacrifices on behalf of her campaign. She thanks her husband Doug, her family, and friends for their support. She thanks the volunteers and contributors "who put their faith and trust in me" (Harris, 2019, para. 24). Before ending her speech, Harris declares that she will continue working to defeat Trump and to fight "for an America we believe in, an America free of injustice" (2019, para. 27).

Harris's speech portrays a candidate who still wants to fight for the issues in which she believes. She uses this opportunity to draw attention to key issues that she hopes to keep in the policy and political spotlight. She builds her public ethos with her supporters by stressing her value on transparency and truth for herself and her campaign, thus laying the foundation for a continued relationship with her stakeholders. She acknowledges and thanks her supporters in order to demonstrate appreciation for their support. After these important concepts are established, Harris ends her speech by demonstrating that she is a team player who will help the Democratic Party retake the White House.

Besides the lack of funds, Harris's campaign faced challenges due to strategic miscalculations about which primaries to focus on and her difficulties framing her stance on healthcare issues. However, Harris frames her speech as a suspension of the presidential campaign efforts, but not an end to her political future. She subsequently became Joe Biden's vice presidential running mate on the Democratic Party ticket to the White House. Harris made history as the first woman, first Black, and first South Asian vice president of the United States when the Biden–Harris ticket was elected in November 2020.

Marianne Williamson: January 10, 2020

Author and self-help guru Marianne Williamson suspended her presidential campaign on January 10, 2020, in an email to her supporters (Breuninger & Block, 2020). Williamson "built her campaign around an eclectic mix of progressive policies and lofty pronouncements" (Astor, 2020, para. 4). During her campaign she claimed that "President Trump's election was a symptom of a spiritually diseased society . . . and only love, not plans, could defeat him" (Astor, 2020, para. 4). In her final campaign speech, Williamson states:

> I ran for president to help forge another direction for our country. I wanted to discuss things I felt needed to be discussed that otherwise were not. I feel that we have done that. I stayed in the race to take advantage of every possible opportunity to share our message. With caucuses and primaries now about to begin, however, we will not be able to garner enough votes in the election to elevate our conversation any more than it is now. (2020, paras. 1–2)

With this opening statement, Williamson offers her reason for running for president. By staying in the race until January, she makes her case that she was successful in her goal of drawing public attention to issues which she believed were important. Williamson also demonstrates her support for the other progressive candidates during the upcoming primaries as she states, "I don't want to get in the way of a progressive candidate winning any of them [primaries]" (2020, para. 2). Williamson frames her key issues within the metaphor of a growing season using images of a growing "season" and a "seed" as she states, "I hope they'll [her key issues] find seed in other ways and in other campaigns" (2020, para. 4). Her key issues include "rescuing underserved at risk and traumatized children," "waging an agenda for peace," integrative health models, "reparations to achieve deeper reconciliation between races," "repudiating corporate aristocracy," "the creation of a more mindful politics," "changing from an economic to a humanitarian bottom line," and "initiating a season of moral repair" (2020, para. 4).

Williamson broadens her perspective to address America's foundation as she explains how her run for president helped her to learn more about the United States. Williamson states she is "more convinced than ever that we're a good and decent people, that democracy matters, and that what our country has always stood for is worth struggling for. I will continue in that struggle and I know that you will too" (2020, para. 5). Williamson thanks her volunteers, contributors, and campaign staff for their hard work. She sends well wishes to the remaining political candidates. She states, "Whichever one of you wins the nomination, I will be there with all my energy and in full support" (2020, para. 7). Ending her speech with a vision of hope for the country, she states:

These are not times to despair; they are simply times to rise up. Things are changing swiftly and dramatically in this country, and I have faith that something is awakening among us. A politics of conscience is still yet possible. And yes . . . love *will* prevail (para. 8)

Williamson's concession speech did not blame anyone or anything for having to end her campaign. She made no attacks on any candidate from either party. She focused the message on her campaign platform. Williamson emphasized her key issues in the hope that they would be incorporated into the agenda of other candidates. She focused her message on her worldview of the power of love and how it would save America. Her speech used a soft tone that reflected her personal style as a self-help author.

Amy Klobuchar: March 2, 2020

Senator Amy Klobuchar (D-MN) ended her presidential campaign on March 2, 2020, at a rally for Joe Biden and endorsed him. In one sentence, Klobuchar states, "Today I am ending my campaign and endorsing Joe Biden for president" (Corasaniti & Burns, 2020, para. 2). She demonstrated her commitment to the Democratic Party and to Biden by leading her supporters to join Biden. She states:

He can bring our country together and build that coalition of our fired-up Democratic base as well as independents and moderate Republicans. We do not in our party want to just eke by a victory. We want to win big. (Corasaniti & Burns, 2020, para. 2)

Klobuchar's abrupt departure from the campaign on March 2 took her staff members by surprise, as they were still planning campaign events for later in the week (Corasaniti & Burns, 2020). She made a decision and adapted for the next phase of her political career by aligning her support for Biden. A moderate candidate with a career of a bipartisan voting record, Klobuchar had difficulty gaining support from minority communities. According to Corasaniti and Burns (2020), she ran her campaign "with a calm but prosecutorial demeanor mixed with a dry sense of humor" (para. 17). They added:

> Ms. Klobuchar slowly built momentum through consecutive debate performances, seeing immediate spikes in cash and volunteers. But she never experienced a true "viral moment"—something she lamented in the closing days of her campaign while speaking in Nashville—forcing her to run a threadbare operation in every state outside of Iowa. (para. 17)

During the primaries, Klobuchar won "a third-place finish in New Hampshire [but] lagged her moderate rivals in every other state" (Corasaniti & Burns, 2020, para. 10). Even an increase of funds ($12 million) after New Hampshire was not enough to help Klobuchar's campaign continue to compete.

Elizabeth Warren: March 5, 2020

Senator Elizabeth Warren (D-MA) held a press conference in front of her home on March 5, 2020, during which she formally suspended her presidential campaign (Hagen, 2020). She made a brief statement and then took questions from the media. Earlier the same day, Warren first announced her decision to her campaign staff in a phone call (Hagen, 2020). Later the same day, Warren and her husband walked out of their home to face the waiting media. She states:

> So, I announced this morning that I am suspending my campaign for president. I say this with a deep sense of gratitude for every single person who got in this fight, every single person who tried on a new idea. Every single person who just moved a little in their notion of what a president of the United States should look like. I will not be running for president in 2020, but I guarantee I will stay in the fight for the hardworking folks across this country who've gotten the short end of the stick over and over. That's been the fight of my life and it will continue to be so. So, anyone have a question? (2020, paras. 1–2)

Warren's announcement extends the message beyond the expected elements of why she is leaving the race to address how the public holds two different perspectives toward women and men running for the White House. She thanks not only her supporters for accepting her identity as a woman leader but also those who may not have supported her but who did change their worldview somewhat to seriously consider that a president could be a woman.

What a president "looks like" is an important issue in politics, as well as a foundational element in Warren's campaign. Her message stays true to her campaign platform. Warren frames the presidential election as a fight for "hardworking folks" who have not been treated fairly in society. However, she also directs attention to the divide in U.S. culture of how women political leaders are perceived and evaluated. She emphasizes the key issue of "hardworking folks" to continue to draw public attention to this foundational message of her career as she ends by saying that she will continue the fight because "That's been the fight of my life" (Warren, 2020, para. 2). To further highlight her intention to keep fighting, Warren goes beyond the standard announcement to engage in a Q and A with media during the press conference.

The press conference afforded Warren the opportunity to direct public attention to her key issues. Warren fielded questions about who she would endorse, how women and girls would be affected by her decision, whether she had regrets about running, why she lost her home state of Massachusetts, and the role gender played in the political race. When asked who she would endorse, Warren states, "Well, let's take a deep breath and spend a little time on that. We don't have to decide that this minute" (2020, para. 4). Warren chose not to endorse another candidate; instead, she remained focused on her campaign and her issues. When asked how her decision to leave the race affects women and girls, she states, "I know one of the hardest parts of this is all those pinky promises and all those little girls who are going to have to wait four more years. That's going to be hard" (2020, para. 6).

When asked if she had regrets about running, Warren states, "I have no regrets at all. This has been the honor of a lifetime. Ten years ago, [I've talked] about what was broken in America, and ideas for how to fix it . . . nobody wanted to hear it" (2020, para. 12). She lists the issues and ideas that people continue to talk about, including a 2 cent wealth tax, universal childcare, canceling student debt, and raising Social Security payments (Warren, 2020).

Immediately prior to Warren's announcement to suspend her campaign, she suffered defeat by losing Massachusetts, the state she represents in the U.S. Senate, and Oklahoma, the state where she was born and raised. When asked about why she lost Massachusetts in the Democratic primary, Warren said that when she entered the race, she was told that there were two lanes— Bernie Sanders's progressive lane and Joe Biden's moderate lane—and there was "no room for anyone else" (2020, para. 16). She continues, "I thought there was more room and more room to run another kind of campaign. But evidently that wasn't the case" (2020, para. 18). When asked about the role of gender in the race, Warren said:

> Gender in this race, you know, that is the trap question for every woman. If you say "Yeah, there was sexism in this race," everyone says, "Whiner!" And if you say, "No, there was no sexism," about a bazillion women think, "What planet do you live on?" (2020, para. 24)

Warren ended the press conference by reaffirming her intention to keep fighting for her key issues by framing her decision to leave the presidential race as based on "what is the best place for me to go to keep fighting those fights" because she wants "to keep fighting and to fight this smartly and effectively as I can" (2020, para. 32). She acknowledges defeat through the transformation of her political role moving forward.

Warren frames her concession message as a fighter who changes course to remain in the battle. To Warren, her issues are what drives her political career. In her rhetorical message, she remains true to her campaign platform to offer a sense of authenticity as she builds her ethos with other individuals who believe in and who support the fight for these issues. She portrays an image of progress and hope for more societal change to occur. Warren's method of face-to-face engagement and interaction with media in front of her home offers a very personal context. The setting of her home suggests a retreat from the broader national public eye while still demonstrating a willingness to directly confront important issues and engage in dialogue.

Tulsi Gabbard: March 19, 2020

U.S. Representative Tulsi Gabbard (D-HI) suspended her presidential campaign in a video posted to social media on March 19, 2020. She was the last woman presidential candidate to leave the Democratic primary. Gabbard "broke barriers as the first Hindu and the first American Samoan elected to Congress" (Lerer & Astor, 2020, para. 15). She had already announced that she was not seeking re-election to Congress. Her campaign stirred controversy due to support from her mixed group of stakeholders. According to Lerer and Astor (2020):

> Her unorthodox platform, a mix of noninterventionist foreign policy, liberal social policy and libertarian leanings on issues like drug decriminalization attracted support from an unusual array of public backers. Alt-right internet stars, white nationalists, libertarian activists and some of the biggest boosters of Mr. Trump heaped praise on Gabbard. (para. 11)

As Gabbard's profile visibility increased, she raised needed campaign funds when she engaged in a public fight with Hillary Clinton over Clinton's charge that Russia backed Gabbard's campaign. She gained support from different stakeholders but lost support from the Democratic Party's traditional base.

In her concession speech, Gabbard framed her message within the context of the COVID-19 crisis. She states:

> Our nation is facing an unprecedented global crisis that highlights the inextricable bonds of humanity, and how foreign policy and domestic policy are inseparable. We are all in this together and we must all rise to meet this moment—in service to our country and our fellow man. (2020, para. 1)

This opening of Gabbard's speech demonstrates concern for the nation during a crisis. Gabbard calls for national unity as she states, "This is not the first time we have faced adversity together. And it will not be the last" (2020, para. 1). Within this crisis context, Gabbard outlines her transformed role in politics and society as she states:

> Throughout my life, and this campaign, my motivation has been to serve God, our country, and the American people as best I can. I feel that the best way that I can be of service at this time is to continue to work for the health and wellbeing of the people of Hawaii and our country in Congress, and to stand ready to serve in uniform should the Hawaii National Guard be activated. (2020, para. 2)

Although Gabbard lays the foundation for explaining why she will suspend her campaign, she first offers reasons why she is endorsing Joe Biden—including his support among Democratic voters in the primaries; her friendship with Biden, his wife, and his late son, Beau; and because of his character. She states:

> I know that he has a good heart and is motivated by his love of our country and the American people. I'm confident that he will lead our country guided by the spirit of aloha—respect and compassion—and thus help heal the divisiveness that has been tearing our country apart. (2020, paras. 2–3)

Gabbard blends her sense of optimism and Hawaiian cultural values into her endorsement of Biden. It is at this point that she officially suspends her presidential campaign and once again offers her full support to Biden "in his quest to bring our country together" (2020, para. 3). Gabbard declares that she will be an advocate for the key issues of her campaign, namely a

"21st century foreign policy," "tackle climate change," "combat terrorism," "end the new Cold War," and "end regime change wars," so as to invest resources into the "needs of the American people—health care, rebuilding our infrastructure, education" (2020, paras. 3–4). She extends well wishes to a few individuals by name, including Sanders, because she appreciates his "love for our country and the American people" (2020, para. 4). She ends her speech by thanking the people who supported her and who worked "tirelessly to get our message out" (2020, para. 4). Gabbard indicates that she will continue "to work together [with her supporters] for our common course" (2020, para. 4).

Gabbard's speech is characterized by expressions of hope, optimism, and unity. She uses a more feminine rhetorical style by portraying her worldview as an advocate rather than the traditional male perspective as a fighter. She presents her political role as one who serves the American people as a politician using a servant leadership style. While her message identifies key issues, they are framed within a "care perspective" incorporating the Hawaiian cultural values of respect and compassion in the "spirit of aloha."

Transformation, Disruption, or New Status Quo?

Kendall (1994) asserts that "conceding is a settled convention in the campaign drama" (p. 107). There is still more to learn about how a political candidate concedes an election. In 2020, Gillibrand, Harris, Williamson, Klobuchar, Warren, and Gabbard challenged the societal norm for who could be president. Their concession speeches offered voters a unique perspective into how each candidate framed her 2020 political exit. In addition, their speeches expand our understanding of the nuances of presidential primary exit rhetoric.

In the 2020 election, multiple factors influenced the six women candidates' decision to run for the presidency, and there were multiple reasons why each left the race. How they communicated their exit offers insight into the genre of concession speeches, more specifically, how presidential primary concession speeches are framed by women candidates. Based on the analysis of the primary concession speeches, this research offers a modification of the six characteristics used to frame the genre of concession speeches, namely the call for national unity to reflect the call for party unity that is more unique to the primary concession speech. Gillibrand and Klobuchar made very clear that they were loyal members of the Democratic Party with their statements by asking their supporters to unite with the party to win back the White House and to join the call to beat Donald Trump and, in the case of Klobuchar, declaring her endorsement of Joe Biden.

Another contribution of this research to the genre of concession speeches is an additional characteristic. The hope of influencing and/or joining the presidential ticket is a seventh characteristic unique to the primary concession speech. In their concession speeches, many of the candidates identified key issues that they fought for during their campaign. Continuing to draw attention to their political issues indicates their hope that they could influence the platform of the party nominee and possibly be considered for the vice presidential candidate on the ticket. A major component of the concession speeches by Harris and Warren included fight rhetoric for their key political issues. This rhetorical strategy keeps their ideas and their names associated with the ethos of a strong leader. Biden later chose Harris as his running mate on the Democratic presidential ticket.

The six candidates offered different reasons for leaving the presidential race. Gillibrand's message indicated that she learned how she "could best serve" the country, and it was not as a presidential candidate. Harris did not have enough campaign funds to continue, but she really wanted to keep fighting. Williamson believed that she was successful in raising awareness of her key issues, so it was okay to leave the race. Klobuchar did not give a reason in her concession speech. Warren indicated that she entered the race because she thought there was room in the presidential race for her approach to politics, but she found out there was no room for her—only a path for Biden's approach and another for Sanders's approach. Gabbard left the race because she believed she could better serve the country by being ready to be called up for active duty in the Hawaiian National Guard during the pandemic.

The communication styles in the concession speeches of the six women candidates were displayed through their different means of communicating their message, different reasons for leaving the race, and different political issues in their campaign. The six women political leaders seeking the presidency chose different means of communicating their message. Each candidate communicated with their various stakeholders—campaign staff and volunteers, supporters, and family—through a variety of channels, including face-to-face conversations, phone calls, and emails. However, each candidate chose a different channel to make her official announcement to either end or suspend their campaign. Gillibrand used Twitter to end her campaign. Harris posted her announcement to suspend her campaign via an online blog platform. Williamson suspended her campaign in an email. Klobuchar ended her campaign at a rally for Biden. Warren suspended her campaign at a press conference held in front of her home, during which she made her announcement and then answered questions. Gabbard posted a video of her speech on social media in which she announced that she was suspending her campaign.

Most of the candidates chose a no-contact communication channel that fulfilled their responsibility to inform the electorate that they were leaving the race. Klobuchar chose a public rally to visually communicate that she had thrown her support behind Biden. Warren chose to engage with the media directly and personally when she spoke face-to-face with them while standing on the sidewalk in front of her house. She made direct eye contact and engaged in a Q and A on her decision and key dimensions of her presidential race, including gender.

The concession speeches by the 2020 women presidential candidates are characterized by the rhetoric of fight, hope, and promise of the future. Both Gillibrand and Gabbard use their 2020 presidential election experience to find a new avenue for their skill sets. Gillibrand modifies the concept of defeat with rhetoric of fighting for the Democratic Party to defeat Trump. Gabbard states she wants to be an advocate and to serve the country through a different path, namely the National Guard. Klobuchar changes her rhetoric of defeat into rhetoric of support for Biden and fighting for his success. Williamson does not acknowledge defeat, but rather stresses the success of bringing attention to her key issues and expresses optimism and hope for the spiritual healing of a divided nation. Both Harris and Warren transform their defeat and the end of their campaigns into the ongoing fight rhetoric directed toward their key issues and their future presidential ambitions.

The women political candidates vying for the U.S. presidency in 2020 offer inspiration and hope for the future. Their presence in the fight for the White House pushed the door open even wider. And they may have even permanently propped the door open for women and girls to enter future elections. Empowering women to step through the door is important. Krawcheck (2017) expresses hope for women being themselves in society because "by owning our diversity, we women can do better for our families, our economy, and our society, and we can make the world where our daughters and daughter's daughters can succeed not in spite of being female, but because of it" (pp. 26–27). Empowering young girls to consider a career in politics is important. Warren's "pinky promises" with young girls on the campaign trail demonstrate her belief in empowering girls. Warren states, "It matters a lot to me that little girls see themselves as future presidents of the United States" (Norvell, 2019, para. 14).

Prior women presidential candidates helped to pave the way for the six women running for the Democratic nomination in 2020. Gutgold (2006) contends that these earlier women presidential candidates "had the optimism to try and the courage to dare to move women a little further on the path to political equality" (p. 17). The six women Democratic candidates in 2020 made an impact on the political process. Kunin (2008) claims that women political leaders "bring their experiences, values, and priorities into the political process" (p. 83). The six women candidates influenced 2020 election conversations through their communication styles, their messages, their focus on issues important to their constituencies, and their unique worldview as women. The six women running for the U.S. president in 2020 offered voters the opportunity to see leadership in a new light, changing the image of what a president could look like.

In 2020, voters had the opportunity to consider changing the image of a U.S. president to that of a powerful woman political leader, a transformative and potentially significant shift for the future. It is important to consider the image of a powerful woman political leader, because according to Beard (2017), "we have no template for what a powerful woman looks like, except that she looks rather like a man" (p. 54). In their run for the White House, each of these six Democratic women presidential candidates broadened U.S. voters' perspectives of what a powerful woman political leader looks like in 2020 and beyond.

References

Astor, M. (2020, January 10). Marianne Williamson drops out of 2020 race. *The New York Times*. https://www.nytimes.com/2020/01/10/us/politics/marianne-williamson-drops-out.html

Beard, M. (2017). *Women & power: A manifesto*. New York, NY: Liveright Publishing Corporation.

Breuninger, K. & Block, V. (2020, January 10). Author and self-help guru Marianne Williamson is out of the 2020 presidential race. *CNBC*. https://www.cnbc.com/2020/01/10/marianne-williamson-out-of-2020-presidential-race.html

Burns, A. (2019, August 30). Gillibrand drops out of 2020 Democratic presidential race. *The New York Times*. https://www.nytimes.com/2019/08/28/us/politics/kirsten-gillibrand-2020-drop-out.html

Clinton, H. R. (2008, June 7). *Hillary Clinton endorses Barack Obama* [Speech transcript]. *The New York Times*. https://www.nytimes.com/2008/06/07/us/politics/07text-clinton.html

Corasaniti, N. & Burns, A. (2020, March 3). Amy Klobuchar drops out of presidential race and endorses Biden. *The New York Times*. https://www.nytimes.com/2020/03/02/us/politics/amy-klobuchar-drops-out.html

Corcoran, P. E. (1994). Presidential concession speeches: The Rhetoric of defeat. *Political Communication, 11,* 109–131. doi: 10.1080/10584609.1994.9963019

Gabbard, T. (2020, March 19). *Transcript: Tulsi Gabbard drops out of race, endorses Biden* [Speech transcript]. *Rev.* https://www.rev.com/blog/transcripts/transcript-tulsi-gabbard-drops-out-of-race-endorses-biden

Gutgold, N. D. (2006). *Paving the way for madam president*. Lanham, MD: Lexington Books.

Hagen, L. (2020, March 5). Elizabeth Warren ends presidential campaign. *U.S. News & World Report.* https://www.usnews.com/news/elections/articles/2020-03-05/elizabeth-warren-to-end-presidential-campaign-report

Harris, K. (2019, December 3). *I am suspending my campaign today.* [Online forum post]. *Medium.* https://kamalaharris.medium.com/i-am-suspending-my-campaign-today-6dca8cefb252

Herndon, A. (2019, December 6). Kamala Harris says she's still 'in this fight,' but out of the 2020 race. *The New York Times.* https://www.nytimes.com/2019/12/03/us/politics/kamala-harris-campaign-drops-out.html

Howell, B. W. (2011). Change and continuity in concession and victory speeches: Race, gender, and age in the closing statements of the 2008 presidential campaign. *American Behavioral Scientist, 55*(6), 765–783. doi: 10.1177/000276-4211406082

Kendall, K. E. (1994). Strategic communication problems in presidential campaigns. *Political Communication, 11,* 107–108.

Krawcheck, S. (2017). *Own it: The power of women at work.* New York, NY: Crown Business.

Kunin, M. M. (2008). *Pearls, politics, & power: How women can win and lead.* White River Junction, VT: Chelsea Green Publishing Company.

Lerer, L. & Astor, M. (2020, March 19). Tulsi Gabbard drops out of presidential race. *The New York Times.* https://www.nytimes.com/2020/03/19/us/politics/tulsi-gabbard-drops-out.html

Merica, D. (2019, August 28). Kirsten Gillibrand drops out of 2020 presidential race. *CNN.* https://www.cnn.com/2019/08/28/politics/gillibrand-drops-out-of-race/index.html

Mirer, M. L. & Bode, L. (2015). Tweeting in defeat: How candidates concede and claim victory in 140 characters. *New Media & Society, 17*(3), 453–469. doi:10.1177/1461444813505364

Neville-Shepard, R. (2014). Triumph in defeat: The genre of third party presidential concessions. *Communication Quarterly, 62*(2), 214–232. doi: 10.1080/01463373.2014.890119

Norvell, K. (2019, May 19). "That's what girls do": Elizabeth Warren tells young Iowa girls why she's running for president, with a pinky promise. *Des Moines Register.* https://www.desmoinesregister.com/story/news/elections/presidential/caucus/2019/05/09/elizabeth-warren-election-2020-girls-female-candidates-pinky-promise-iowa-caucus-women/1122078001/

Ritter, K. & Howell, B. (2001). Ending the 2000 presidential election: Gore's concession speech and Bush's victory speech. *American Behavioral Scientist, 44*(12), 2314–2330. doi:10.1177/00027640121958348

Warren, E. (2020, March 5). *Transcript: Elizabeth Warren speaks after suspending campaign* [Speech transcript]. *WBUR News.* https://www.wbur.org/news/2020/03/05/elizabeth-warren-speech-suspends-campaign-drops-out

Williams, A. (2021, January 8). Trump concedes election and condemns attack on Capitol for first time. *Financial Times*. https://www.ft.com/content/5875dfa8-689f-43bd-8cd6-d0cbb152fb66

Williamson, M. (2020, January 10). With love and gratitude . . . *Marianne 2020*. https://marianne2020.com/posts/with-love-and-gratitude

Willyard, J. & Ritter, K. (2005). Election 2004 concession and victory speeches. *American Behavioral Scientist, 49*(3), 488–509. doi: 10.1177/0002764205279439

Partisan Motivations for News Use: Implications for Threat Perceptions during the 2020 U.S. Election

Andrea Figueroa-Caballero and Julius Matthew Riles

Evidence suggests that most Americans do not perceive others in society as trustworthy (General Social Survey, 2021). One notable influence on the trust individuals perceive toward specific others is the media to which they are exposed. Specifically, when certain social identities are presented as a threat to audiences—for example, in the news—this exposure can influence the degree to which audiences hold positive evaluations of those social identities (Riles et al., 2020). In the run-up to the 2020 U.S. presidential election, the focus of news on two societal issues—COVID-19 and police brutality— has been described as producing threat perception influences regarding particular social identities. Indeed, the events leading to the 2020 summer protests and the global pandemic created a social climate that arguably functions to facilitate social animus toward a number of social identities (Anand & Hsu, 2020).

During the months leading up to the election, the United States, along with the rest of the world, experienced a pandemic that took or disrupted the lives of millions of individuals and had far-reaching economic impacts. News coverage of COVID-19 was omnipresent during 2020 (Zafri et al., 2021), and, unfortunately, this coverage routinely described the pandemic and its effects using terms that often attributed the cause to ethnically Chinese individuals. Consequently, this misattribution has had the unwarranted outcome of placing blame for the health consequences of the pandemic broadly on this particular social group (Jia & Lu, 2021). Additionally, following the high-profile 2020 killings of George Floyd, Breonna Taylor, Ahmaud Arbery, and others, demonstrations and protests were mobilized throughout the United States that sought to confront police brutality and other forms of ongoing racial inequity (Coleburn, 2020). News coverage and discussion of these events saw discourses about the threat that both police and (often Black) protestors posed to members of society (Anand & Hsu, 2020). In all, 2020 was associated with different news outlets variously promoting threat associations with Chinese and Black individuals in addition to police officers.

This chapter explores intertwining precursors to threat perceptions of these groups as related to palpable election themes during 2020 in the hopes of contributing to the conceptual and practical understanding of politically oriented identity threat. More specifically, based on the theoretical reasoning of the differential susceptibility to media effects model (DSMM; Valkenburg & Peter, 2013), the aim of the current study is to provide a more nuanced understanding of how mediated and political communication researchers understand people who differ in identity put similarly partisaned media to use for divergent reasons, potentially resulting in disparate threat outcomes.

Differential Susceptibility to Media Effects Model

Within the landscape of the 2020 U.S. presidential election, there is value to be obtained via examining how ideologically opposed media users may form different threat perceptions as a function of potentially distinct motivations for consuming news. Indeed, prevailing theory in mediated communication suggests that different people use media for different reasons and that these divergent reasons can produce divergent outcomes (Valkenburg & Peter, 2013). This line of reasoning has been relatively comprehensively addressed by the DSMM, which has been employed, in part, to explore the antecedents to media use that could inform various mediated outcomes (e.g., Houston et al., 2018). Within this model, different personal conditions (i.e., susceptibilities) are assessed for how they may directly predict patterns of media use. Routinely, these susceptibilities are investigated in terms of their direct effects on media use. However, in the current investigation, key susceptibilities (e.g., ideology, media use motivations) will be examined in terms of their interactive effects on political news use, as well as the indirect effect of these dispositional conditions on threat perceptions toward Chinese and Black individuals and police officers.

Building off prior conceptual frameworks suggesting that different traits could influence the use and experience of media in divergent and transactional ways (e.g., uses and gratifications theory, elaboration likelihood model, reinforcing spiral model), Valkenburg and Peter (2013) sought to develop a comprehensive and robust means of conceptualizing the multifaceted influences of, and influences upon, media use. Their DSMM was developed to suggest that what happens before and after media use is critical in understanding the nature, causes, and influences of ultimate outcomes.

In terms of antecedents to media use, it is suggested that various susceptibilities (i.e., reactivities; Piotrowski & Valkenburg, 2015) determine the selection and experience of media offerings. These conditions may be dispositional (e.g., social demographics, ideology, motivations), developmental (e.g., childhood and adolescent experiences), or social (e.g., interpersonal, institutional, and societal experiences) in nature. Furthermore, each susceptibility can contribute to if, and how, a media offering is used (Valkenburg & Peter, 2013).

In terms of aftermath of media use, the DSMM suggests that usage directly influences various response states (although this association can also be moderated by the aforementioned susceptibilities) which, themselves, are responsible for any number of ultimate outcomes (e.g., threat perceptions). These ultimate outcomes are then predicted to transactionally influence this process in a reflexive fashion. The DSMM has been notably integrated into research examining the exposure to, and influence of, media violence on various threat perceptions and behavioral outcomes (e.g., Piotrowski & Valkenburg, 2015), though it has also been incorporated into other areas, including examinations of risk and crisis communication events (Houston et al., 2018).

Ideology, Political Segmentation, and Polarization of Threat Perceptions

The notion that the modern era of digital media is associated with an increasingly fragmented populace has been promoted and discussed since its inception (e.g., Tewksbury, 2005). Indeed, evidence of growing polarization of news use has been observed going back to the dawn of the millennium (Hollander, 2008) with option-rich media—both cable (Chalif, 2011) and online news (Tewksbury & Rittenberg, 2012)—observed to be associated with a tendency to selectively expose oneself to media content that is familiar and comforting. Although in practical terms, fragmented selectivity is not without its limits (Riles et al., 2018), extant research of political news use has consistently revealed polarized selection of news content such that conservatives tend to congregate around news with conservative-leaning viewpoints, while liberals tend to congregate around news with relatively more liberal-leaning viewpoints (e.g., Chalif, 2011; Hollander 2008). Typically, ideological selectivity is more often characterized by news consumers seeking out the familiar, rather than engaging in deliberate avoidant behaviors (Weeks et al., 2016). However, the outcome is a systemically similar worldview among those who are politically similar (Tewksbury & Riles, 2015) and the attribution of malevolent motivations to dissimilar others (Warner et al., 2019; Warner et al., 2020). Thus, we offer the following hypothesis:

H1: Ideology will predict news use such that (a) those who are conservatively oriented will consume more conservative-leaning news and (b) those who are liberally oriented will consume more liberal-leaning news.

Political ideology, and its associated news use patterns, have routinely been demonstrated to predict disparate societal concerns and fear regarding potentially threatening circumstances. For example, in one examination of more than a decade of news coverage and public concern regarding climate change, Carmichael and colleagues (2017) observed substantial evidence that ideologically oriented media exposure was an important determinant of concerns about this global environmental phenomenon (with liberal news consumers viewing it as more of a threat and conservative news consumers viewing it as less of a threat). Indeed, evidence was observed that when exposed to news that was viewed as ideologically opposing, individuals became increasingly entrenched in their perceptions about the level of threat posed by climate change. In terms of COVID-19, it has been observed that conservative identification was associated with perceptions of COVID-19 as a conspiratorial threat on the American public (Calvillo et al., 2020). Such an association may be a function of researchers' observations that ideologically divergent news outlets have covered the pandemic in different ways, with particularly conservative outlets playing down the threat of COVID-19 while also playing up the threat posed by Chinese individuals for their regional association with coronavirus origins and the spread of the virus (Calvillo, et al., 2020; Jia & Lu, 2021). In sum, this research indicates that increased exposure to ideologically consistent news coverage that depicts particular social groups (e.g., Chinese individuals) as threatening can result in increased threat perceptions of that group.

Exposure to coverage of racial justice protests like Black Lives Matter (BLM) events, much like exposure to ideologically oriented news about COVID-19, has been associated with disparate outcomes, depending on the news outlet. For example, Kilgo and Mourão (2019) observed that the more respondents were exposed to news from conservative-leaning outlets like Fox News and Breitbart News, the more negative their attitudes were toward protest groups like BLM. In addition, a later study observed a negative relationship between positive attitudes toward police and support for protestors in general (Kilgo & Mourão, 2021). Taken together, this evidence suggests that ideologically oriented news use may facilitate opposing evaluative judgments about police and Black people as a function of who is relatively more associated with threat and in what capacity.

Like the patterns observed for news exposure about COVID-19 and Chinese individuals, this evidence suggests that conservative-leaning news outlet exposure may be associated with enhanced threat perceptions for Black people, whereas a similar magnitude of perceived threat about police may be more apparent from liberal-leaning news exposure. As such, we offer the following hypotheses:

H2: Exposure to liberal-leaning news outlets will be negatively associated with threat perceptions for (a) Chinese and (b) Black people and positively associated with threat perceptions regarding (c) police officers.

H3: Exposure to conservative-leaning news outlets will be positively associated with threat perceptions for (a) Chinese and (b) Black people and negatively associated with threat perceptions regarding (c) police officers.

Role of Disparate Media Motivations

In addition to assessing the role of political ideology as a dispositional susceptibility, media use motivations have a rich history of predicting divergent patterns of media use as they relate to divergent outcomes. The uses and gratifications approach has been used as a framework for conceptualizing the role of media motivations for several decades (Katz et al., 1974). This approach "takes the broad perspective that, by understanding why we choose the media we do and how we use it, researchers can gain a better understanding of the entire media use process from selective exposure to media outcomes and effects" (Krcmar, 2017, p. 1997). Much of the prior research in this tradition has largely sought to articulate the various motivations that exist for engagement in media use. Although many and more motivations have been enumerated over time, scholars have more recently tended to emphasize several notable motivational domains, including information seeking, entertainment, social engagement, self-presentation, and personal identity exploration (Krcmar, 2017; Rubin, 2009).

Information seeking pertains to the impetus of using media to learn about people, places, events, and other phenomena. It is a surveillance motivation to understand what is occurring in one's environment. *Entertainment* is a motivation that encompasses the seeking of arousal or the avoidance of boredom. A desire to experience stimulation or relieve stress would each be relevant to this motivation. *Social engagement* pertains to using media for its interpersonal functions. Using media as a social activity with others or because it will be a context for future interpersonal interaction relates to social engagement. The motivation of *self-presentation* relates to using media as a means of promoting some aspect of oneself in a social setting. This motivation is more often associated with digital and social media venues than nondigital media given the networked characteristics of these platforms. Finally, *personal identity exploration* can be characterized as the use of media to better understand those that one sees as like oneself—in terms of current situation or future aspirations—to better understand oneself and one's own perspective. This may often be accomplished via social comparison processes.

Far less understood in the domain of uses and gratifications, the overarching DSMM framework, or within the current understanding of polarization, is how specific identities may align with particular motivations to produce identity-oriented news exposure. Moreover, current research has yet to reveal how such ideology-motivation constellations could indirectly, via ideologically consistent news exposure, influence the degree to which various others are viewed as a threat. It is possible that political partisans view the role and utility of partisan news in unique ways that have specific ramifications for the influences of news exposure on social orientations.

The DSMM framework suggests that dispositions, such as ideology and motivations, serve as differential susceptibilities that may explain media engagement (Valkenburg & Peter, 2013). Although not employing all elements of the DSMM, the current investigation examines key components of it in answering the call of Valkenburg and Peter (2013) for "future researchers [to] elaborate on [their] insights even if they utilize only parts of the DSMM as their theoretical basis" (p. 236). Specifically, dispositional susceptibilities—in the form of political ideology and media use motivations—are analyzed in terms of their influence on the use of partisan news outlets. Although articulations of the DSMM have generally described direct main effects of susceptibilities on media use, the current investigation seeks to extend the explanatory power of this model by examining the conditional and interactive influences of dispositional susceptibilities as they moderate one another. Although response states will not be examined in the current investigation, the influence of partisan news use will be examined in terms of influences on threat perceptions related to the aforementioned three social identities (i.e., Chinese and Black individuals, police officers) routinely discussed in news coverage throughout the 2020 presidential election cycle. Based on these theoretical goals, we articulate the following research questions:

RQ1: Which motivations (i.e., information seeking, entertainment, social engagement, self-presentation, and personal identity exploration) predict (a) liberal and (b) conservative news use?

RQ2: Which motivations moderate the influence of ideology on news use?

RQ3: Which political ideology-by-motivation interactions indirectly, via politically aligned news use, influence threat perceptions regarding (a) Chinese and (b) Black people and (c) police officers?

Method

Participants and Procedures

Participants (N = 451) were recruited from an introductory communication course at a large midwestern university in fall 2020. They took part on a voluntary and anonymous basis. Due to the nature of the study, non-White participants were excluded from our analysis (N = 115). Subsequently, participants who failed to complete 100% of the survey (n = 33) were excluded from the final analysis, leaving a final sample of N = 303.

The mean sample age was 19.68 (SD = 2.39). Among the 303 participants included in the final analysis, 45.5% (n = 138) identified as male, 54.1% (n = 164) identified as female, and 0.3% (n = 1) identified as nonbinary. Approximately 49.6% (n = 69) identified as a Democrat, 26.6% (n = 37) as Independent, 16.5% (n = 23) as Republican, and 7.2% (n = 10) as other.

Measures

Media Motivations

To assess distinct media motivations, we incorporated items from prior studies on media use motivations (Khang et al., 2013; Rhee et al., 2006; Sheldon & Bryant, 2016) and provided the following instructions, "We are also curious about what motivates you to get the news. The following questions assess a lot of different reasons people have for following news and current events." All media motivations items were scored on a 7-point scale from (1) Strongly disagree to (7) Strongly agree, with higher scores indicating stronger levels of motivation.

Information seeking (α = 0.72, M = 5.19, SD = 1.10). A composite measure of three items was used to measure information seeking. Items include "When I consume news, it is usually because, on some level, I'm motivated to . . . get new ideas/learn new things/know what is going on in the world."

Social relationships (α = 0.80, M = 4.26, SD = 1.41). A composite measure of three items was used to measure social relationships. Items include "When I consume news, it is usually because, on some level, I'm motivated to . . . better socialize with others/read about other people's lives/have more to talk about in conversation on in the world."

Entertainment (α = 0.87, M = 3.85, SD = 1.49). A composite measure of four items was used to measure entertainment motivations. Items include "When I consume news, it is usually because, on some level, I'm motivated to . . . kill time/amuse myself/have fun/avoid boredom."

Self-presence (α = 0.84, M = 3.49, SD = 1.45). A composite measure of three items was used to measure self-presence motivations. Items include "When I consume news, it is usually because, on some level, I'm motivated to . . . gain significant identification of myself from others/make a good impression on others/appear to others as if I am knowledgeable."

Personal identity (α = 0.86, M = 4.41, SD = 1.36). A composite measure of three items was used to measure personal identity motivations. Items include "When I consume news, it is usually because, on some level, I'm motivated to . . . learn something about people with whom I identify/see how my values are playing out in the world/better understand how people like me are living."

Partisan Media

Participants were asked, "How many days in the past week did you read national news on a [liberal-leaning (M = 1.55, SD = 1.37)/conservative-leaning website (M = 1.49, SD = 1.31).]?"

Threat Perceptions

A four-item composite measure (adapted from Cottrell & Neuburg, 2005 and Cottrell et al., 2010) was created to assess threat perceptions for the social groups of interest (i.e., Black people, Chinese people, the police). The same four items were asked regarding each group: "To what extent to you feel that [Black people (α = 0.90, M = 2.66, SD = 1.27)/Chinese people or Chinese immigrants (α = 0.92, M = 2.59, SD = 1.27)/the police (α = 0.88, M = 3.20, SD = 1.43)] . . . advocate values that are morally inferior to the values of people like me/endanger the physical safety of people like me/do not want to contribute as much to people like me/choose to take more from people like me than they give back." All items were scored on a 7-point scale from (1) Strongly disagree to (7) Strongly agree, with higher scores indicating higher levels of perceived threat.

Political Ideology

Participants were asked, "To what extent do you consider yourself liberal or conservative" on a 7-point scale from (1) Extremely liberal to (7) Extremely conservative, with higher scores indicating greater belief in conservative ideology (M = 4.15, SD = 1.65).

Data Analysis Procedure

Several path analyses were conducted using PROCESS model 7 to test the proposed hypotheses. The significance of indirect effect was tested using 10,000 bootstrap resamples and a 95% bias-corrected confidence interval. Given the nature of the hypotheses, the single-item continuous variable for political ideology was treated as the exogenous variable (X); exposure to liberal-leaning (M_1) and conservative-leaning websites (M_2) were specified as the mediator variables.

Due to the limitations of PROCESS, only one dependent variable (Y) can be specified per model; as such, threat perceptions for each group were tested in separate models. Moreover, in order to look at each media motivation independently as the specified moderator (W) of the path between X and M_1 and X and M_2, these were also tested separately. In all, 15 different path analyses were conducted. These results are detailed in Tables 4.1 through 4.5.

Results

As posited in H1, we expected that political ideology would predict similarly aligned partisan media consumption. To examine this relationship without the presence of a moderator (i.e., media motivations), the Pearson correlation between the two variables was examined. These results support our hypothesis—consumption of liberal-leaning media was negatively correlated with ideology ($r = -0.35$, $p < 0.001$), whereas exposure to conservative-leaning media was significantly positively correlated with ideology ($r = 0.27$, $p < 0.001$).

To examine the role of media motivations in the relationship between ideology and partisan media consumption (RQ1 and RQ2), the direct and conditional effects of each media motivation was examined separately (see Tables 4.1–4.5). These data indicate that information seeking ($b = 0.84$), social relationships ($b = 0.34$), self-presence ($b = 0.28$), and personal identity ($b = 0.40$) motivations all directly positively predicted liberal-leaning media consumption. Moreover, conditional effects of media motivations and ideology on liberal-leaning media consumption were found for information seeking ($b = -0.14$) and social relationships ($b = -0.07$) motivations.

The data regarding conservative-leaning media consumption indicate that only the personal relationships motivation directly predicted this type of

Table 4.1   Results of Moderated Mediation Model with Information Seeking as the Moderator

	M_1	M_2	Black T.P. (Y_1)	Chinese T.P. (Y_2)	Police T.P. (Y_3)
Ideology (X)	0.51*	−0.28	0.31***	0.26***	−0.40***
Info. seeking (W)	0.84***	−0.21			
X*W	−0.14**	0.10*			
Liberal News (M_1)			−0.15**	−0.15**	−0.07
Conservative News (M_2)			0.08	−0.003	−0.05
	$R^2 = 0.19$	$R^2 = 0.11$	$R^2 = 0.23$	$R^2 = 0.18$	$R^2 = 0.21$

Note: $*p < 0.05$. $**p < 0.01$. $***p < 0.001$.

Table 4.2   Results of Moderated Mediation Model with Social
Relationships as the Moderator

	M_1	M_2	Black T.P. (Y_1)	Chinese T.P. (Y_2)	Police T.P. (Y_3)
Ideology (X)	0.03	−0.14	0.31***	0.26***	−0.41***
Social Relations (W)	0.34***	−0.25			
X*W	−0.07*	0.09*			
Liberal News (M_1)			−0.16**	−0.15**	−0.07
Conservative News (M_2)			0.08	−0.001	−0.05
	$R^2 = 0.14$	$R^2 = 0.11$	$R^2 = 0.25$	$R^2 = 0.23$	$R^2 = 0.22$

Note: *$p < 0.05$. **$p < 0.01$. ***$p < 0.001$.

Table 4.3   Results of Moderated Mediation Model with Entertainment
as the Moderator

	M_1	M_2	Black T.P. (Y_1)	Chinese T.P. (Y_2)	Police T.P. (Y_3)
Ideology (X)	−0.27*	−0.05	0.33***	0.25***	−0.39***
Entertainment (W)	0.08	−0.17			
X*W	−0.01	0.07*			
Liberal News (M_1)			−0.15**	−0.16**	−0.04
Conservative News (M_2)			0.07	0.01	−0.05
	$R^2 = 0.13$	$R^2 = 0.11$	$R^2 = 0.23$	$R^2 = 0.18$	$R^2 = 0.21$

Note: *$p < 0.05$. **$p < 0.01$. ***$p < 0.001$.

media exposure ($b = -0.34$). However, conditional effects of media motivations and ideology on conservative-leaning media consumption were found for information seeking ($b = 0.10$), social relationships ($b = 0.09$), entertainment ($b = 0.07$), and personal identity ($b = 0.11$).

Hypotheses 2 and 3 predicted that liberal- and conservative-leaning media exposure would have opposite effects on threat perceptions of distinct social groups. Specifically, it was posited that liberal-leaning news outlets would be negatively associated with threat perceptions for (a) Chinese and (b) Black people and positively associated with threat perceptions regarding (c) police officers. The data indicate support for this hypothesis across all models for threat perceptions of Chinese and Black people in the expected direction (see Tables 4.1–4.5 for direct effects) but not for threat perceptions of police officers. Conservative-leaning news exposure failed to directly predict threat perceptions for any of these groups.

Given these results, only the conditional indirect effects of ideology by media motivation on threat perceptions via liberal-leaning media exposure were also examined (RQ3). These data (see Table 4.6) indicate a consistent

Table 4.4 Results of Moderated Mediation Model with Self-Presence as the Moderator

	M_1	M_2	Black T.P. (Y_1)	Chinese T.P. (Y_2)	Police T.P. (Y_3)
Ideology (X)	−0.09	−0.04	0.31***	0.26***	−0.41***
Self-Presence (W)	0.28*	−0.10			
X*W	−0.05	0.05			
Liberal News (M_1)			−0.15**	−0.15**	−0.06
Conservative News (M_2)			0.07	0.003	−0.04
	$R^2 = 0.13$	$R^2 = 0.09$	$R^2 = 0.23$	$R^2 = 0.18$	$R^2 = 0.21$

*Note: *p < 0.05. **p < 0.01. ***p < 0.001.*

Table 4.5 Results of Moderated Mediation Model with Personal Identity as the Moderator

	M_1	M_2	Black T.P. (Y_1)	Chinese T.P. (Y_2)	Police T.P. (Y_3)
Ideology (X)	−0.02	−0.31	0.31***	0.26***	−0.41***
Personal Identity (W)	0.40*	−0.34*			
X*W	−0.06	0.11*			
Liberal News (M_1)			−0.16**	−0.16**	−0.06
Conservative News (M_2)			0.08	0.003	−0.04
	$R^2 = 0.15$	$R^2 = 0.13$	$R^2 = 0.23$	$R^2 = 0.18$	$R^2 = 0.21$

*Note: *p < 0.05. **p < 0.01. ***p < 0.001.*

Table 4.6 Conditional Indirect Effects of Ideology and Liberal Media on Threat Perceptions at Different Values of Moderator[†]

	Black Threat Perceptions				Chinese Threat Perceptions				Police Threat Perceptions			
	b	SE	LLCI	ULCI	b	SE	LLCI	ULCI	b	SE	LLCI	ULCI
Info. seeking (low)	0.01	0.01	-0.01	0.04	0.01	0.01	-0.01	0.03	0.01	0.01	-0.01	0.02
Info. seeking (mean)	0.04	0.01	0.02	0.06	0.04	0.01	0.01	0.06	0.02	0.02	-0.02	0.06
Info. seeking (high)	0.06	0.02	0.03	0.10	0.06	0.02	0.02	0.10	0.03	0.03	-0.04	0.09
Social Rela. (low)	0.03	0.02	0.001	0.06	0.02	0.01	0.001	0.06	0.01	0.02	-0.02	0.05
Social Rela. (mean)	0.04	0.01	0.02	0.07	0.04	0.01	0.02	0.07	0.02	0.02	-0.02	0.06
Social Rela. (high)	0.06	0.02	0.03	0.10	0.06	0.02	0.02	0.10	0.03	0.03	-0.03	0.09
Entertain. (low)	0.04	0.02	0.01	0.09	0.05	0.02	0.02	0.08	0.01	0.02	-0.04	0.05
Entertain. (mean)	0.05	0.01	0.02	0.07	0.05	0.01	0.02	0.08	0.01	0.02	-0.04	0.06
Entertain. (high)	0.05	0.02	0.02	0.08	0.05	0.02	0.02	0.09	0.01	0.03	-0.03	0.07

	b	SE	LLCI	ULCI	b	SE	LLCI	ULCI	b	SE	LLCI	ULCI
Self-Pres. (low)	**0.03**	**0.02**	**0.01**	**0.07**	**0.03**	**0.01**	**0.01**	**0.06**	0.01	0.02	−0.02	0.05
Self-Pres. (mean)	**0.05**	**0.01**	**0.02**	**0.07**	**0.04**	**0.01**	**0.02**	**0.07**	0.02	0.02	−0.03	0.06
Self-Pres. (high)	**0.06**	**0.02**	**0.03**	**0.09**	**0.06**	**0.02**	**0.02**	**0.09**	0.02	0.03	−0.04	0.08
Personal Id. (low)	**0.03**	**0.02**	**0.01**	**0.06**	**0.03**	**0.02**	**0.01**	**0.06**	0.01	0.01	−0.02	0.04
Personal Id. (mean)	**0.04**	**0.01**	**0.02**	**0.07**	**0.04**	**0.01**	**0.02**	**0.07**	0.01	0.02	−0.03	0.06
Personal Id. (high)	**0.06**	**0.02**	**0.02**	**0.09**	**0.05**	**0.02**	**0.02**	**0.09**	0.02	0.03	−0.04	0.08

Note: †Bolded estimates indicate significance at 95% CI.

pattern across the different levels (1 SD above, below, and at the mean) of the distinct media motivations regarding their effects on threat perceptions of Chinese and Black individuals. Of note, however, an examination of the pairwise contrast effects reveals that only for information seeking (for both groups) and social relationships (only for Chinese threat perceptions) motivations can a true significant difference between the levels be established. In other words, though a conditional indirect effect can be detected for the remaining motivations, the specified cutoff points failed to capture where true differences might be occurring.

Conclusion

Recent research by Peterson, Goel, and Iyengar (2021) reveals three notable trends in online news consumption among partisans. The first is that partisan isolation (i.e., partisans gravitating toward congenial news media sources) has increased significantly over the past two decades. Relatedly, this isolation exists even though most of the news sources visited by partisans vary relatively little in terms of content. The authors note, "We suspect that the segregation of the online news audience is more the result of beliefs about outlets' partisan leanings rather than changes in the content of campaign news" (pg. 257). In other words, partisans choose their news sources based on the source's perceived partisan preferences, regardless of the content it provides. With that in mind, the study presented in this chapter examined under what conditions the relationship between partisan and like-minded news source consumption was exacerbated or diminished.

This chapter reveals several ways in which partisans appear to differ in their view of the role of partisaned news use, as well as their motivations for using it. These distinctions were observed to be constituent elements of a process predicting a number of disparate perceptions about perceived social peril related to events leading up to the 2020 presidential election. Employing the DSMM in our investigation, the data suggest that various susceptibilities for media use do condition one another in a manner that predicts media use patterns that favor ideology. Ideological news use was observed to have a one-sided influence on threat perceptions, although observed patterns operated as predicted. Later, we articulate implications of the various ideology-partisaned news use motivation constellations observed and tease out possible explanations for the influences of notably liberal news use on threat perceptions.

The data presented here suggest that different types of media motivations drive news use for partisans in similar and dissimilar ways. For example, our findings indicated that the information-seeking motivation moderated both liberal and conservative news consumption—indicating that partisans on both sides are eager to learn from like-minded media outlets. Similarly, at least in the current sample, the social relationships motivation moderated the use of both types of news outlets as a means of connecting and interacting with others. This is somewhat contrary with recent studies that suggest that liberals are more active social media users and are more likely to use social media for political purposes (Anderson & Jiang, 2018; Vogels et al., 2021). Thus, this suggests that liberals might seek out like-minded news sources as a way of staying caught up with the current discourse within their group. However, conservatives may be motivated to consume conservative news or less traditional news outlets and meet offline to meet social needs.

Personal identity motivations solely moderated conservative partisaned news use, suggesting that conservatives were more likely to use this type of news to bolster the self. Recall that this motivation focuses on using media to learn about one's own group, their values, and their standing in society. Research by Haidt and Graham (2007) on moral foundations theory and Hoewe, Peacock, Kim, and Barnidge (2020) might shed light on this finding. Haidt and Graham (2007) suggest that the Democratic and Republican parties stress distinct moral foundations—or moral concerns—that can be largely categorized into two groups: binding and individualizing foundations. Republicans tend to emphasize the importance of binding foundations: loyalty, authority, and sanctity. Of relevance to the current study is loyalty, which can be characterized as unconditional devotion to one's group. Consequently, Hoewe et al. (2021) posit that when news sources emphasize certain foundations over others, they become increasingly salient and shape how audiences understand the content they are consuming. Indeed, their content analytic findings of *Foxnews.com*, *CNN.com*, and *MSNBC* coverage of refugees and immigrants indicates that *Foxnews.com* used language that emphasized binding foundations more so than the other, more liberal sources. Thus, it is not surprising that our findings regarding personal identity are specific to conservative media consumption. It is likely that conservative and conservative-leaning individuals turn to conservative media to reinforce their group identity, as this content tends to be laden with group-binding messages.

This research also elucidates our findings regarding the failure of conservative news consumption to predict threat perceptions. As stated previously (Carmichael et al., 2017; Peterson et al., 2021), the electorate—particularly the conservative electorate—is heavily entrenched in their political beliefs and attitudes. Thus, any effect that conservative media use might have is simply subsumed by ideological beliefs more broadly. In other words, if conservative media functions to merely reinforce, but not shape, existing beliefs regarding the threat posed by Black and Chinese individuals, then the lack of mediation is explicable.

In the same vein, this also helps understand why indirect and conditional indirect effects were found for liberal media consumption. Specifically, as liberals tend to emphasize individualizing foundations over binding foundations, there is less of a group-centric undercurrent in liberal media (Hoewe et al., 2021). Thus, it might be the case that liberal or liberal-leaning individuals are more malleable or more susceptible in their beliefs and their perceptions of threats to the content they consume—regardless of their motivation. Finally, our lack of findings regarding perceptions of police officer threat could have several explanations. For example, it might simply reflect a deeply ingrained trust in police officers among our sample. Relatedly, due to the nature of the study, we limited our analysis to only White participants— which is not a group typically associated with a hostile history with the police, and the questions asked might not have been able to capture the kind of threat police posed to this (or any) group. Ultimately, more research, ideally with more inclusive sampling approaches, is needed to identify how perceptions of this group are formed and communicated.

References

Anand, D. & Hsu, L. (2020). COVID-19 and Black Lives Matter: Examining anti-Asian racism and anti-Blackness in US education. *International Journal of Multidisciplinary Perspectives in Higher Education, 5,* 190–199. doi:10.32674/jimphe.v5i1.2656

Anderson, M. & Jiang, J. (2018, November 5). Liberal Democrats more likely to be politically active on social media than other groups. *Pew Research Center.* https://www.pewresearch.org/fact-tank/2018/11/05/liberal-democrats-more-likely-than-other-groups-to-be-politically-active-on-social-media/

Calvillo, D. P., Ross, B. J., Garcia, R. J., Smelter, T. J., & Rutchick, A. M. (2020). Political ideology predicts perceptions of the threat of COVID-19 (and susceptibility to fake news about it). *Social Psychological and Personality Science, 11,* 1119–1128. doi:10.1177/1948550620940539

Carmichael, J. T., Brulle, R. J., & Huxster, J. K. (2017). The great divide: Understanding the role of media and other drivers of the partisan divide in public concern over climate change in the USA, 2001–2014. *Climatic Change, 141,* 599–612. doi:10.1007/s10584-017-1908-1

Chalif, R. S. (2011). *Selective politics: The fragmentation and polarization of news on cable TV* (Master's Thesis). *Georgetown University Repository Digital Library.* https://repository.library.georgetown.edu/b]itstream/handle/10822/552906/chalifRebecca.pdf?sequence=1&isAllowed=y.

Coleburn, C. (2020). The ostrich rears its head: America's 2020 racial reckoning is a victory and opportunity. *Harvard Civil Rights—Civil Liberties Law Review.* https://harvardcrcl.org/the-ostrich-rears-its-head-americas -2020-racial-reckoning-is-a-victory-and-opportunity/

Cottrell, C. A. & Neuberg, S. L. (2005). Different emotional reactions to different groups: A sociofunctional threat-based approach to "prejudice." *Journal of Personality and Social Psychology, 88,* 770. doi:10.1037/0022-3514.88.5.770

Cottrell, C. A., Richards, D. A., & Nichols, A. L. (2010). Predicting policy attitudes from general prejudice versus specific intergroup emotions. *Journal of Experimental Social Psychology, 46,* 247–254. doi:10.1016/j .jesp.2009.10.008

General Social Survey (2021). *GSS data explorer: Can people be trusted.* https:// gssdataexplorer.norc.org/variables/441/vshow

Haidt, J. & Graham, J. (2007). When morality opposes justice: Conservatives have moral intuitions that liberals may not recognize. *Social Justice Research, 20,* 98–116. doi:10.1007/s11211-007-0034-z

Hoewe, J., Peacock, C., Kim, B., & Barnidge, M. (2020). The relationship between Fox News use and Americans' policy preferences regarding refugees and immigrants. *International Journal of Communication, 14,* 21. https://ijoc .org/index.php/ijoc/article/view/12402

Hollander, B. A. (2008). Tuning out or tuning elsewhere? Partisanship, polarization, and media migration from 1998 to 2006. *Journalism & Mass Communication Quarterly, 85,* 23–40. doi:10.1177/107769900808500103

Houston, J. B., Spialek, M. L., & First, J. (2018). Disaster media effects: A systematic review and synthesis based on the differential susceptibility to media effects model. *Journal of Communication, 68,* 734–757. doi:10.1093 /joc/jqy023

Jia, W. & Lu, F. (2021). US media's coverage of China's handling of COVID-19: Playing the role of the fourth branch of government or the fourth estate? *Global Media and China, 6,* 8–23. doi:10.1177/2059436421994003

Katz, E., Blumler, J. G., & Gurevitch, M. (1974). Uses and gratifications research. *The Public Opinion Quarterly, 37,* 509–523. doi:10.1086/268109

Khang, H., Kim, J. K., & Kim, Y. (2013). Self-traits and motivations as antecedents of digital media flow and addiction: The Internet, mobile phones, and video games. *Computers in Human Behavior, 29,* 2416–2424. doi:10.1016/j .chb.2013.05.027

Kilgo, D. K. & Mourão, R. R. (2021). Protest coverage matters: How media framing and visual communication affects support for Black civil rights protests. *Mass Communication and Society,* 1–21. doi:10.1080/15205436.2021 .1884724

Kilgo, D., & Mourão, R. R. (2019). Media effects and marginalized ideas: Relationships among media consumption and support for Black Lives Matter. *International Journal of Communication, 13,* 4287–4305. https://ijoc.org /index.php/ijoc/article/view/10518

Krcmar, M. (2017) Uses and gratifications: Basic concepts theory. In Rossler, P. (Ed.) *The International Encyclopedia of Media Effects*. https://onlinelibrary .wiley.com/doi/10.1002/9781118783764.wbieme0045

Piotrowski, J. T. & Valkenburg, P. M. (2015). Finding orchids in a field of dandelions: Understanding children's differential susceptibility to media effects. *American Behavioral Scientist, 59*, 1776–1789. doi:10.1177 /0002764215596552

Peterson, E., Goel, S., & Iyengar, S. (2021). Partisan selective exposure in online news consumption: Evidence from the 2016 presidential campaign. *Political Science Research and Methods, 9*, 242–258. doi:10.1017/psrm.2019.55

Rhee, J. W., Kim, E. M., & Shim, M. S. (2006). Exploring dispositional media use motives: an extension of the "uses and gratification" theory in the multimedia environment. *Korean Journal of Journalism and Communication Studies, 5*, 252–284. doi:10.1080/10510974.2016.1156006

Riles, J. M., Behm-Morawitz, E., Shin, H., & Funk, M. (2020). The effect of news peril-type on social inclinations: A social group comparison. *Journalism & Mass Communication Quarterly, 97*, 721–742. doi:10.1177 /1077699019855633

Riles, J. M., Pilny, A., & Tewksbury, D. (2018). Media fragmentation in the context of bounded social networks: How far can it go? *New Media & Society, 20*, 1415–1432. doi: 10.1177/1461444817696242

Rubin, A. M. (2009). Uses and gratifications. In R. L. Nabi & M. B. Oliver (Eds), *The SAGE handbook of media processes and effects* (pp. 147–159). Thousand Oaks, CA: SAGE Publications Inc.

Sheldon, P. & Bryant, K. (2016). Instagram: Motives for its use and relationship to narcissism and contextual age. *Computers in Human Behavior, 58*, 89–97. doi:10.1016/j.chb.2015.12.059

Tewksbury, D. (2005). The seeds of audience fragmentation: Specialization in the use of online news sites. *Journal of Broadcasting & Electronic Media, 49*, 332–348. doi:10.1207/s15506878jobem4903_5

Tewksbury, D. & Riles, J. M. (2015). Polarization as a function of citizen predispositions and exposure to news on the Internet. *Journal of Broadcasting & Electronic Media, 59*, 381–398. doi:10.1080/08838151.2015.1054996

Tewksbury, D. & Rittenberg, J. (2012). *News on the Internet: Information and citizenship in the 21st century.* Oxford, UK: Oxford University Press.

Valkenburg, P. M. & Peter, J. (2013). The differential susceptibility to media effects model. *Journal of Communication, 63*, 221–243. doi:10.1111/jcom .12024

Vogels, E. A., Auxier, B., & Anderson, M. (2021, April 7). Partisan differences in social media use show up for some platforms, but not Facebook. *Pew Research Center*. https://www.pewresearch.org/fact-tank/2021/04/07 /partisan-differences-in-social-media-use-show-up-for-some-platforms -but-not-facebook/

Warner, B. R., Galarza, R., Coker, C. R., Tschirhart, P., Hoeun, S., Jennings, F. J., & McKinney, M. S. (2019). Comic agonism in the 2016 campaign: A study of Iowa Caucus rallies. *American Behavioral Scientist, 63,* 836–855. doi:10.1177/0002764217704868

Warner, B. R., Horstman, H. K., & Kearney, C. C. (2020). Reducing political polarization through narrative writing. *Journal of Applied Communication Research, 48,* 459–477. doi:10.1080/00909882.2020.1789195

Weeks, B. E., Ksiazek, T. B., & Holbert, R. L. (2016). Partisan enclaves or shared media experiences? A network approach to understanding citizens' political news environments. *Journal of Broadcasting & Electronic Media, 60,* 248–268. doi:10.1080/08838151.2016.1164170

Zafri, N. M., Afroj, S., Nafi, I. M., & Hasan, M. M. U. (2021). A content analysis of newspaper coverage of COVID-19 pandemic for developing a pandemic management framework. *Heliyon, 7*(3). https://doi.org/10.1016/j.heliyon.2021.e06544

Navigating Difficult Conversations in the Family in the 2020 Election Environment

Xavier Scruggs and Colleen Warner Colaner

Families range in their willingness to engage in communication across a wide range of topics. Whereas some families participate in free-flowing conversations on even controversial topics, other families tend to restrict interactions and suppress exchanges in areas where there might be disagreement (Horstman et al., 2018). The current sociopolitical environment has brought controversial issues to the forefront of social interactions, including interactions in our closest personal relationships (Rittenour, 2020). Specifically, the 2016 and 2020 presidential elections introduced the most divisive political climate in recent memory, with lasting effects on civil discourse. Family relationships have also experienced an impact wherein opposing political stances and voting behaviors have stifled conversation, limited family interactions, and caused strife between parent–child and spousal dyads (Afifi et al., 2020; Warner et al., 2021).

Additionally, the COVID-19 global pandemic created strife in social agreements about best practices for preventing and managing the novel coronavirus; these disagreements have also affected family relationships, causing disagreements, relationship distance, and frustration in family units (Hernandez & Colaner, 2021). Concurrently, the murder of George Floyd and subsequent Black Lives Matter protests across the United States have elevated long-standing race-based discrimination, prejudice, and violence to public consciousness. Intergenerational differences and experiences with race relations pose a challenge to families as they navigate institutionalized racism, white supremacy, and equality efforts (Watson et al., 2020).

Families in the modern era must navigate these ever-present social issues while maintaining relational solidarity, even in the face of disagreement over closely held beliefs about politics, public health, and racial equality (Colaner & Soliz, 2020). Thus, it is important to better understand the kind of family environment that is the best for talking about these difficult topics. To better understand how families are managing difficult conversations about these three key events in 2020, the current chapter utilizes family communication patterns theory (FCPT).

Family Communication Patterns Theory

FCPT posits that parents socialize their children through two dimensions: conversation and conformity orientations (Koerner & Schrodt, 2014). These communicative dimensions give insight into the degree to which family communication in encouraged and/or restricted. FCPT sheds light on the communication behaviors that give structure to family interactions. FCPT is oriented around two dimensions. First, *conversation orientation* is the degree to which families create an environment that encourages unrestricted dialogue on a variety of topics and encourages every family member (regardless of age) to express their opinion (Koerner et al., 2018). Families that are high in this dimension view communication as a means to exchange ideas (Koerner & Schrodt, 2014). Families that are low in this dimension communicate less frequently on a variety of topics, including personal thoughts, feelings, and activities.

Conversation-oriented families have conversations on a wide variety topics, even on topics that are potentially sensitive or divisive (e.g., race or politics). Because of this, conversation-oriented families typically are more willing to communicate to their children about race, privilege, and other systemic issues that affect racial minorities. Even on other issues like health (e.g., COVID-19) and politics, these families will likely engage frequently and exchange opinions on these topics. Thus, we pose the following hypothesis:

H1: Conversation orientation will positively predict young adults' reports of family talk about (a) race relations, (b) COVID-19, and (c) the 2020 election.

The second dimension, *conformity orientation*, is the degree to which families stress a climate of homogenous beliefs, values, and attitudes (Koerner et al., 2018). Families that are high in this dimension stress uniformity of ideas and obedience to parental authority (Koerner et al., 2018). Parents in this dimension also believe that they know what is best for their children, so they typically do not include them in the decision-making process. Families low on this dimension value every family member's opinion, even if it is different from their own.

Conformity-oriented families tend to stress uniformity of beliefs and attitudes, likely will not discuss topics such as race, and talk about politics infrequently. Horstman and colleagues (2018) operationalized conformity orientation to consist of four dimensions: respect for parental authority, experiencing parental control, adopting parents' values/beliefs, and questioning parents' beliefs/authority. Most recently, scholars have examined how each dimension of conformity orientation has been associated with varying outcomes (Scruggs & Schrodt, 2020). Because these families view communication as a means to stress uniformity of ideas, conversations about sensitive topics, even health-related ones (i.e., COVID-19), will likely be discussed infrequently. Because of this, we posit the following hypothesis:

H2: Conformity orientation will negatively predict young adults' reports of family talk about (a) race relations, (b) COVID-19, and (c) the 2020 election.

Conversation and conformity orientation do not occur in a vacuum. Rather, the interaction between conversation and conformity provides nuanced information concerning how these constructs work together to create a family's global communication environment (Koerner & Schrodt, 2014). Past research reveals that conformity moderates the relationship between conversation orientation and individual and relational outcomes (Koerner et al., 2018). Thus, it is important to consider how conformity orientation may attenuate the role of conversation orientation in promoting family dialogue. Four family types emerge from the orthogonal relationship between conversation and conformity orientation. *Consensual* families have high levels of conversation and conformity orientation, whereas *laissez faire* families are low in both orientations. *Protective* families are those that are high in conformity yet low in conversation, and *pluralistic* families are high in conversation and low in conformity. With regard to the present study, a family's insistence that all individuals agree and adhere to parental values and beliefs (i.e., those families who are high in conformity orientation) is likely to suppress the degree to which parents and children discuss difficult topics. Thus, we offer the final hypothesis:

H3: Conformity orientation will weaken the association between conversation orientation and young adults' reports of family talk about (a) race relations, (b) COVID-19, and (c) the 2020 election.

Method

Participants

Participants (*n* = 466) were recruited from the basic public speaking course at a midwestern university. The average age of the participant was 18.77 (SD = 4.55). Participants included 260 males (56%) and 203 females (44%), and most identified as White (74%, *n* = 346), although some identified as African American/Black (8%, *n* = 40) and Hispanic/Latinx (4%, *n* = 22).

Procedures

After obtaining institutional review board approval, undergraduate students were asked to complete the survey. Qualtrics software was used to conduct the survey. Participant responses were all confidential, yet some information was gathered so that students could receive credit from instructors. All participation took place outside of regular class time.

Measures

Family Communication Patterns

Participants' family communication patterns (FCPs) were measured using the conversation orientation subscale of the Revised Family Communication Patterns (RFCP) instrument (Ritchie & Fitzpatrick, 1990) and Horstman et al.'s (2018) Expanded Conformity Orientation Scale (ECOS). The RFCP subscale consisted of 15 items asking respondents to evaluate the extent to which their FCPs reflect a conversation orientation (e.g., "My parents encourage me to challenge their beliefs and ideas," "I can tell my parents almost anything"). The ECOS consisted of 24 items that assess four dimensions of family conformity orientation: respect for parental authority (e.g., "My parents insist that I respect those who have been placed in positions of authority"); experiencing parental control (e.g., "My parents try to persuade me to view things the way they see them"); questioning parental authority and beliefs (e.g., "In our home, we are allowed to question my parents' authority"); and pressure to adopt parental values (e.g., "My parents encourage me to adopt their values"). Responses to both measures were solicited using a 7-point Likert scale that ranged from strongly disagree (1) to strongly agree (7). The validity and reliability of both FCP measures are well established (Horstman et al., 2018; Schrodt et al., 2008). In this study, the conversation orientation subscale produced an alpha coefficient of 0.93. The ECOS produced alpha coefficients ranging from 0.86 for questioning parental authority to 0.85 for parental control, 0.86 for pressure to adopt parental values, and 0.89 for respecting authority, with an overall alpha reliability of 0.84 for the 24-item measure.

Political Talk

We created three measures to assess the frequency with which young adults talk to their families on the following political topics: COVID-19, racial tensions, and the 2020 election. Participants were asked to indicate how frequently they discussed each topic with their family using a 5-point scale. Responses ranged from none at all (1) to a great deal (5).

Political talk about COVID-19 consisted of three items ("the COVID-19"; "social distancing, mask wearing, and other precautions related to COVID-19"; and "decisions about whether to 're-open', go out, and other returning to normal facets of life-related to COVID-19"). Political talk about COVID-19 produced an alpha reliability of 0.86. Political talk about the 2020 election consisted of three items ("Donald Trump," "Joe Biden," and "the 2020 presidential election"). Political talk about the 2020 election produced an alpha reliability of 0.84. Political talk about racial tensions consisted of three items: ("protests surrounding police shootings," "racial discrimination," and "Black Lives Matter movement"). Political talk about racial tensions produced an alpha reliability of 0.90.

Data Analysis

Analyses were conducted using structural equation modeling (SEM) with a robust maximum likelihood estimator using the lavaan package (Rosseel, 2012), an open-source package for latent variable modeling housed in the R environment. Because χ^2 can be affected by large sample sizes, we also examined the comparative fit index (CFI), the root mean square error of approximation (RMSEA), and the standardized root mean square residual (SRMR) to determine model fit.

The hypothesized model had five latent constructs (conversation orientation, conformity orientation, family talk about race relations, family talk about COVID-19, and family talk about the 2020 election), as well as an interaction term (conversation × conformity orientation). Latent variables were identified by creating three parcels, or indicators consisting of the average of two or more items (Little et al., 2013). Parcels for conformity orientation were created using domain-representative parceling wherein items from each of the four subconstructs (respect for parental authority, experiencing parental control, adopting parents' values/beliefs, and questioning parents' beliefs/authority) were dispersed among the three parcels. This distributes the unique elements of each facet across parcels to ensure each facet is represented in the latent construct.

Standardized coefficients were examined to assess significant relationships between latent variables. Significance of the interaction terms were evaluated using the χ^2 difference test, wherein each regression path is constrained to 0 and each nested, constrained model is compared to the baseline structural model (Kline, 2005). A significant worsening of the constrained model indicates a significant regression path.

Results

The parceled measurement model had 15 observations (three indicators each for five latent variables) and, using the formula $p(p + 1)/2$, we can establish that the model has 120 elements. We had 40 freely estimated parameters (15 loadings, 15 error terms, and 10 latent covariances). Thus, our measurement model had 80 degrees of freedom. The parceled measurement model had acceptable fit, $\chi^2 (80) = 160.33$, $p < 0.00$, $\chi^2/df = 1.98$, CFI = 0.98; RMSEA = 0.06; (*CI* [confidence interval] = 0.04–0.07), SRMR = 0.04. Following the recommendations of Goodboy and Kline (2016), the residual matrix and modification indices were examined to identify possible local model misfit. No evident misfit was identified by the residual matrix, nor did the modification indices suggest the need for model revision. All items loaded onto their respective factors ($\lambda > 0.7$), suggesting convergent and divergent validity of the measures.

Table 5.1 displays coefficients, standard errors, and *p* values. Conversation orientation was positively associated with all outcomes of family talk

Table 5.1   Regression Estimates from Structural Equation Model

	B	S.E.	β	p
Talk about race				
Conversation orientation	0.34	0.06	0.31	<0.001
Conformity orientation	−0.06	0.05	0.05	0.27
Conversation × Conformity	0.16	0.06	0.15	<0.01
Talk about COVID-19				
Conversation orientation	0.34	0.06	0.31	<0.001
Conformity orientation	0.09	0.05	0.08	0.07
Conversation × Conformity	0.22	0.10	0.20	<0.05
Talk about 2020 election				
Conversation orientation	0.27	0.06	0.26	<0.001
Conformity orientation	−0.08	0.05	−0.08	0.10
Conversation × Conformity	0.13	0.06	0.13	<0.05

($H1_a$, $H1_b$, and $H1_c$ supported). Conformity orientation was not significantly associated with any of the family talk outcomes ($H2_a$, $H2_b$, and $H2_c$ not supported). Conformity orientation approached statistical significance with talk about COVID-19. Conformity orientation was a significant moderator of the association between conversation orientation and all outcomes of family talk ($H3_a$, $H3_b$, and $H3_c$ supported), such that conformity increases the value of conversation with regard to difficult conversations about race relations, COVID-19, and the 2020 election.

Discussion

Families in the modern era are increasingly diverse in values and beliefs (Colaner & Soliz, 2020). Family identification often constitutes the ultimate ingroup identity, given that our families tend to provide a strong source of identity and belonging (Rittenour, 2020). At the same time, social identity differences increasingly appear within family units. Family members hold unique views on controversial social issues, such as race relations, COVID-19, and the 2020 election. These differences within a family unit have the potential to cause relationship strain unless managed through inclusive communication (Warner et al., 2020). The present study offers socially relevant insight into parent–child communication as these family dyads navigate communication on these difficult topics.

At the heart of FCP, parents are the primary agents in socializing their (young adult) children to achieve agreement on conversational topics (Koerner & Schrodt, 2014; Koerner et al., 2018; Scruggs & Schrodt, 2020). Certain family communication environments enhance or diminish children's willingness and ability to talk about certain topics with families. The primary purpose of this study was to understand how family communication environments shaped talk about three key events in 2020. Overall, the results showed modest support for our theoretical line of reasoning. The most consistent findings pertain to conversation orientation. As expected, families high in this dimension exhibited more talk on all three difficult conversations. Findings surrounding conformity were more nuanced. Conformity did not predict family talk on any of the family talk outcomes. However, conformity increased the positive effect of conversation on family talk on race, COVID-19, and the election, contrary to our predictions. These findings offer theoretical implications and directions for future research.

First, family conversation orientation likely equips young adult children to have challenging conversations such as those about race relations, political elections, and even politicized health topics such as COVID-19. Family communication environments that stress open and frequent communication across a variety of topics allow all family members to participate in decision making and encourage alternative viewpoints may allow children to gain the necessary communication skills needed to have these conversations. Such conversations within the family may also encourage young adults to feel efficacious to communicate about these topics outside the family. These conversations likely allow young adult children to gain information-processing skills (Keaten & Kelly, 2008; Koesten et al., 2009) and increase their communication competence (Schrodt et al., 2009). Findings in the present study continue to reiterate the beneficial role of conversation orientation for family communication and child development.

Second, conformity orientation seems to help facilitate conversation about difficult topics in parent–child relationships. Conformity orientation is a dense and long-misunderstood concept in family communication (Horstman et al., 2018). Previous conceptualizations of conformity tended to emphasize this orientation as one characterized by domination and control. Findings from RFCP instrument have upheld this notion. For example, families with high levels of conformity were unable to talk about a health condition, another difficult topic (Hays et al., 2017). Importantly, conformity measured via the RFCPI suppressed the role of conversation orientation on this topic, suggesting that families with high levels of conversation but also high levels of conformity were unable to freely discuss health issues. Such a finding suggests that conformity creates barriers to open communication, especially on difficult topics, even when the family environment is largely characterized by openness.

However, findings in the current study show the reverse, namely that conversation orientation is more valuable in families with more conformity orientation. This finding suggests that conversations about difficult topics such as a combative election, a politicized global pandemic, and strained race relations are aided by conversation orientation, but also that those conversations are even more likely when bolstered by high conformity orientation. An explanation for the difference in these findings likely stems from the use of the newly constructed, multifaceted ECOS measure of conformity orientation in the present study that has replaced the unidimensional RFCPI measure of conformity used in previous research.

ECOS was born out of family scholars' efforts to reconceptualize conformity as reflecting a family communication environment that fosters homogeneity of values and beliefs among all family members rather than one that is controlling or stifling (Horstman et al., 2018; Koerner & Schrodt, 2014). Parsing out unique features of conformity orientation seems to offer important nuance to this variable, providing more granularity to this construct. Whereas the ECOS subconstruct *experiencing parental control* certainly points to the potentially stifling experience of feeling pressured to conform to parental values, other subconstructs allow for families to come into alignment with one another on individual approaches to social issues.

For example, *respect for parental authority* and *adopting parents' values/beliefs* offer room for child agency in considering the value of parental insights and choosing to align those beliefs, values, and attitudes. *Questioning parents' beliefs/authority* seems to extend beyond the original conformity orientation construct. The respect and control dimensions are measured with items containing words such as "insist" and "persuade" with regard to parental values. Questioning, however, measures the ability of a child to push back on parental views. Such questioning likely has an important developmental function that facilitates parent–child conversation about difficult topics. Parents who are high in this questioning aspect are likely more able to create a safe space for their child to engage in controversial discussions to better understand and make sense of important social issues.

This line of reflection on conformity orientation implores family communication scholars to continue to carefully consider what conformity orientation really is, how it operates in the family, and how it supplements conversation orientation in productive ways. Conformity orientation has clear parallels to other parent–child theorizing. Authoritarian parenting, for example, is a parenting style that emphasizes parental control over the child (Trifan et al., 2014). Authoritarian parenting is contrasted with permissive parenting in which parents prioritize connection with and warmth for their child over control (Barton & Hirsch, 2016).

Research is clear that too much emphasis on either warmth or control relates to difficult outcomes for child development and relational solidarity. The balance of warmth and control—characterized as authoritative parenting—has the best outcomes for individuals and relationships. Parental influence is best manifested when parents are responsive to child needs, offer structure to keep the child safe and secure, provide explanations for limits, and negotiate boundaries with the child that allow for moderate amounts of autonomy and risk (Larzelere et al., 2013). Authoritarian parents tend to have children who are more open with them, more respectful of established boundaries, and more connected to the family unit.

Authoritarian parenting suggests that family communication environments which have both openness and homogeneity might be ideal for managing difficult topics. Consensual families, or those families who are high in conformity and conversation, align with authoritarian parenting in that both warmth and control are present in equal measure. Conversation orientation opens up dialogue on difficult topics, as seen in the current study, as well as previous literature (e.g., Hays et al., 2017; Schrodt et al., 2009). Importantly, however, conformity increases the value of conversation for family talk about race, the 2020 election, and COVID-19. The specific mechanisms of why this might be the case remain unclear. Assessing the association between the subconstructs of conformity and conversation in future research will likely provide important insight into the role of conformity.

The current study utilized a parsimonious model of FCPT by modeling conformity as a latent construct created through facet parceling of items across the four subdimensions. Thus, the current model does not speak to which of the subconstructs might moderate the positive relationship between conversation and family talk about difficult topics. This parsimonious model has many benefits for modeling. Modeling each of the four constructs is methodologically difficult and puts considerable burden on the statistical model. Yet it will be important for future research to find ways to maximize the potential of ECOS to produce a granular perspective of conformity orientation.

One possibility for future researchers to better assess ECOS is to simplify other aspects of their study. For example, assessing the role of conversation orientation alongside the conformity subconstructs of respect for parental authority, experiencing parental control, adopting parents' values/beliefs, and questioning parents' beliefs/authority might mean that researchers will need to focus on one dependent variable and limit the examination of meditators. Assessing conformity subconstructs also may mean that moderations between conversation and conformity are limited, given that measuring moderation would create four interaction terms between conversation and each conformity subconstruct. Researchers can manage this by building models in which moderations are only assessed for variables with significant direct effects on the dependent variable.

Finally, FCPT theorists might engage in incremental model building in which they include specific conformity constructs based on study goals. For example, measuring and analyzing the role of conversation and adopting parental beliefs in predicting voting behaviors will give a more nuanced approach to a pertinent aspect of parent–child political alignment. Alternatively, focusing on the role of questioning parental beliefs as it interacts with conversation orientation on coming-out conversations may illuminate how LGBTQ+ children express their sexual identity with their family.

In these such examples, homing in on one subconstruct leaves room for researchers to assess mediation, moderation, and associations to multiple outcome variables. Over time, theorists can aggregate findings about conformity subconstructs, conduct meta-analyses, and draw conclusions about the conformity construct that is mindful of the granularity of this dense orientation. These and other routes of researching conformity suggest that there is an increased opportunity to learn more using ECOS than the RFCPI.

The intersection of political and family communication is ripe for scholarly investigation, and FCPT is a useful lens to understand how families and politics interact. This study provides several avenues for future research with important implications for both managing difficult topics in parent–child communication and gaining a better understanding of the role of conversation and conformity orientation in creating global communication environments.

As families continue to diversify in structure, experiences, social identities, and values (Colaner & Soliz, 2020), there will be increased opportunity to discuss and potentially come to agreement on divisive social issues. Harnessing the role of conversation orientation alongside the multiple manifestations of the conformity orientation to best facilitate these interactions and support family solidarity can aid families as they navigate this rocky terrain.

References

Afifi, T. D., Zamanzadeh, N., Harrison, K., & Torrez, D. P. (2020). Explaining the impact of differences in voting patterns on resilience and relational load in romantic relationships during the transition to the Trump presidency. *Journal of Social and Personal Relationships, 37,* 3–26. https://doi.org/10.1177/0265407519846566

Barton, A. L. & Hirsch, J. K. (2016). Permissive parenting and mental health in college students: Mediating effects of academic entitlement. *Journal of American College Health, 64*(1), 1–8. https://doi.org/10.1080/07448481.2015.1060597

Colaner, C. W. & Soliz, J. (2020). Preface. In J. Soliz & C. W. Colaner (Eds.), *Navigating relationships in the modern family: Communication, identity, and difference.* New York, NY: Peter Lang.

Goodboy, A. K. & Kline, R. B. (2016). Statistical and practical concerns with published communication research featuring structural equation modeling. *Communication Research Reports, 34,* 68–77. doi: 10.1080/08824096.2016.1214121

Hays, A., Maliski, R., & Warner, B. (2017). Analyzing the effects of family communication patterns on the decision to disclose a health issue to a parent: The benefits of conversation and dangers of conformity. *Health Communication, 32*(7), 837–844. https://doi.org/10.1080/10410236.2016.1177898

Hernandez, R. A. & Colaner, C. (2021). "This is not the hill to die on. Even if we literally could die on this hill": Examining communication ecologies of uncertainty and family communication about COVID-19. *American Behavioral Scientist, 65*(7), 956–975. https://doi.org/10.1177/0002764221992840

Horstman, H. K., Schrodt, P., Warner, B., Koerner, A., Maliski, R., Hays, A., & Colaner, C. (2018). Expanding the conceptual and empirical boundaries of family communication patterns: The development and validation of an expanded conformity orientation scale. *Communication Monographs, 85*(2), 157–180. https://doi.org/10.1080/03637751.2018.1428354

Keaten, J. & Kelly, L. (2008). Emotional intelligence as a mediator of family communication patterns and reticence. *Communication Reports, 21*(2), 104–116. https://doi.org/10.1080/08934210802393008

Kline, R. B. (2005). *Principles and practice of structural equation modeling* (2nd ed). New York, NY: Guilford Press.

Koerner, A. F. & Schrodt, P. (2014). An introduction to the special issue on family communication patterns theory. *Journal of Family Communication*, *14*(1), 1–15. https://doi.org/10.1080/15267431.2013.857328

Koerner, A. F., Schrodt, P., & Fitzpatrick, M. A. (2018). Family communication patterns theory: A grand theory of family communication. In D. O. Braithwaite, E. A. Suter, & K. Floyd's (Eds.), *Engaging theories in family communication: Multiple perspectives* (2nd ed., pp. 142–153). New York, NY: Routledge.

Koesten, J., Schrodt, P., & Ford, D. (2009). Cognitive flexibility as a mediator of family communication environments and young adults' well-being. *Health Communication, 24*(1), 82–94. https://doi.org/10.1080/10410230802607024

Larzelere, R. E., Morris, A. S. E., & Harrist, A. W. (2013). *Authoritative parenting: Synthesizing nurturance and discipline for optimal child development*. Washington, DC: American Psychological Association.

Little, T. D., Rhemtulla, M., Gibson, K., & Schoemann, A. M. (2013). Why the items versus parcels controversy needn't be one. *Psychological Methods, 18*, 285–300. https://doi.org/10.1037/a0033266

Ritchie, L. D. & Fitzpatrick, M. A. (1990). Family communication patterns: Measuring intrapersonal perceptions of interpersonal relationships. *Communication Research, 17*(4), 523–544. https://doi.org/10.1177/009365090017004007

Rittenour, C. E. (2020). Family socialization of "otherness." In J. Soliz & C. W. Colaner (Eds.), *Navigating relationships in the modern family: Communication, identity, and difference*. New York, NY: Peter Lang.

Rosseel, Y. (2012). Lavaan: An R package for structural equation modeling. *Journal of Statistical Software, 48*, 1–36. www.jstatsoft.org/v48/i02/

Scruggs, X. & Schrodt, P. (2020). The frequency and comfort of political conversations with parents as mediators of family communication patterns and relational quality in parent-child relationships. *Journal of Family Communication, 21*(1), 17–33. https://doi.org/10.1080/15267431.2020.1860053

Schrodt, P., Ledbetter, A. M., Jernberg, K. A., Larson, L., Brown, N., & Glonek, K. (2009). Family communication patterns as mediators of communication competence in the parent-child relationship. *Journal of Social and Personal Relationships, 26*(6–7), 853–874. https://doi.org/10.1177/0265407509345649

Schrodt, P., Witt, P. L., & Messersmith, A. (2008). A meta-analytical review of family communication patterns and their associations with information processing, behavioral, and psychosocial outcomes. *Communication Monographs, 75*(3), 248–269. https://doi.org/10.1080/03637750802256318

Trifan, T. A., Stattin, H., & Tilton-Weaver, L. (2014). Have authoritarian parenting practices and roles changed in the last 50 years? *Journal of Marriage and Family, 76*(4), 744–761. https://doi.org/10.1111/jomf.12124

Warner, B. R., Colaner, C. W., & Park, J. (2021). Political difference and polarization in the family: The role of (non) accommodating communication for navigating identity differences. *Journal of Social and Personal Relationships, 38*(2). https://doi.org/10.1177/0265407520967438

Watson, M. F., Turner, W. L., & Hines, P. M. (2020). Black Lives Matter: We are in the same storm but we are not in the same boat. *Family Process, 59*(4), 1362–1373. https://doi.org/10.1111/famp.12613

PART 2

Disrupting the Campaign

CHAPTER SIX

Political Party Tweets during the 2020 Presidential Campaign

Daniel Montez and Kate Kenski

It has become a sine qua non for candidates, journalists, pundits, and citizens to consider the most recent or upcoming presidential campaign the most important campaign in their lifetime. Writing for *The New York Times*, Stuart Taylor, Jr. (1984), contended that "[t]he 1984 Presidential election could be the most important in a half-century" (sect. 1, p. 30). During the Republican National Convention in 2008, former New York mayor Rudy Giuliani said, "2008 is the most important election in our lifetime" (para. 2). In his acceptance speech for the Republican nomination in 2020, President Donald J. Trump said, "This is the most important election in the history of our country" (Bucktin, 2020, para. 6).

Despite almost every election having someone, if not many people, argue that it is the most important, author Christopher Clausen (2008) maintains, "Whether or not it suits candidates and the press to say so, most elections are fortunately a lot more like 1924 than 1932, let alone 1860" (para. 8), meaning that most elections are not necessarily transformative. Relative stability has dominated our system, not upheaval, even in tough times.

The ranking of importance of the 2020 election campaign against other election years may be debated, but few would question that 2020 was indeed important and undeniably unique owing to growing tensions between Republicans and Democrats, the novel coronavirus pandemic, and protests and riots that resulted from building racial injustice concerns. In the United States, levels of affective polarization are extremely high and have increased greatly over four decades, more so than in other countries, including Australia, Canada, Germany, New Zealand, Norway, Sweden, Switzerland, and the United Kingdom (Boxell et al., 2020). The spread of the novel coronavirus reached pandemic levels in March 2020 and dominated the last year of Trump's presidency and the presidential campaign. The murder of George Floyd by a police officer in Minneapolis was digitally recorded, disseminated on social media, and resulted in protests over racial issues. Either of these issues alone would have made the year exceptional, but the combination of these concerns made it especially complex. Concerns over electoral integrity, noted candidate messaging, and the lack of acceptance of the election outcome by the Trump administration foreshadowed the storming of the U.S. Capitol on January 6, 2021, as the Congress had assembled to count the electoral votes.

In light of these unique events, this chapter focuses on how these important issues of the day were presented by the Democratic National Committee and the Republican National Committee on their Twitter feeds. While candidates come and go, the major parties are more enduring and are thus worthy of examination. Social media communication is important because it both reflects and plays a role in shaping people's understanding of political events and attitudes. We, therefore, ask the question: In what ways did the major parties differ in their tweeting frequency and emphasis on key policy issues? And how did Twitter users engage with those issues put forth by the major parties?

According to Pew researchers Elisa Shearer and Amy Mitchell (2021), an August/September 2020 survey revealed that more than one-half of adults in the United States report getting news from social media either "often" or "sometimes." Twitter is among the top three social media sites that serves as a regular news source for Americans, with 15% of U.S. adults turning to it regularly. Candidates and parties use the platform to respond to issues raised by the news media and to shape news media in turn (Conway et al., 2015; Conway et al., 2018).

To understand how the Republican and Democratic parties handled issue messaging on Twitter, we first explain the process of identifying party tweets and discuss the top issues that voters and citizens believed were important during the year. Next, we examine differences in the frequency of their tweets, as well as their issue emphases. Then, we turn our attention to how the major parties handled the most important issues facing the nation in detail.

Tracking Political Parties and Issues on Twitter

It is not unusual for political organizations to have different Twitter accounts that serve different purposes for them. Candidates also have different accounts, some personal and others unique to their campaigns or elective offices. In this research, we focus on the primary accounts from the Republican National Committee (RNC) and Democratic National Committee (DNC) via their respective party Twitter accounts, @GOP and @TheDemocrats.

The data used in this chapter come from Zignal Discover, a historical archive of Twitter activity and conversations capable of pulling content from the very first tweet, powered by Zignal Labs. We focus on the time frame between January 1, 2020, and December 14, 2020, because of its relevance to the concurrent party primary elections, party national conventions, and general election. December 14 was chosen as the stopping point of data collection because of its correspondence with the Electoral College's final vote, thereby legally signaling a final vote count. Our study incorporated both original tweets and retweets from each party's account. In contrast to other forms of Twitter audience response (e.g., quote tweets, replies, mentions), only retweets were evaluated as engagement because they tend to connote endorsement (Borchers, 2017; Metaxas et al., 2015).

During the 2020 presidential campaign, many polling organizations (e.g., Statista, Gallup, YouGov, Pew Research) asked citizens what the most important issues facing the nation were. Among the top five common issues were healthcare, economy, pandemic, crime, and race relations. According to one Pew Research Center study conducted July 27 to August 2, 2020, 79% of registered voters said that the economy was "very important" to their vote in the presidential election, 68% said healthcare, 62% said the coronavirus outbreak, 59% said crime, and 52% said race relations (Pew Research Center, 2020).

Using these issues as a starting point, we produced keyword lists for each issue in order to perform a computerized, dictionary-driven content analysis.[1] From these baseline issues, other issues, such as voter fraud and party voting campaigns, emerged after observing trends in Twitter activity for each party's account. Final keyword lists were developed through multiple iterations of analyses and adjustment to be as exhaustive as possible. Exclusions were also built into the keyword lists to prevent irrelevant items from being coded. Once completed, the keyword lists comprised the five major issues (healthcare, economy, pandemic, crime, race relations), voter fraud, party voting campaigns, and various other issues (climate change, courts, education, impeachment, immigration, law enforcement). Voter fraud and voting campaign issue keywords were modified across party handles to avoid oversampling irrelevant discussions. For a list of the complete keyword lists for some of the major issues, see the appendix at the end of this chapter.

Additionally, keyword lists were created to search for mentions of party/ideology (Democrats/Liberals; Republicans/Conservatives) and presidential candidates (Biden/Harris; Trump/Pence). Keyword lists for each issue were then run for each party's handle in Zignal Discover to determine raw issue tweet counts for each Twitter account. When needed, keyword lists could be run jointly to determine more nuanced discussions. For example, keyword lists for economy and Democrats/Liberals could be searched together among tweets authored by the RNC to examine how the committee was targeting the opposition in their economic discussion.

It is important to note that individual tweets could include multiple issues. For example, a tweet from the @GOP on November 12, 2020, read, "While Democrats fight amongst themselves, Republicans are going to hold the line against the Democrat Party's radical agenda of defunding the police, middle class tax hikes, the Green New Deal, and a government takeover of health care" (GOP, 2020f). This tweet incorporated the issues of economy, taxes, healthcare, law enforcement, and climate change. Because individual tweets were inclusive of multiple issues, it is helpful to discuss issues in terms of the percentage makeup of total Twitter conversation in a given context (e.g., total from candidate, total from candidate mentioning opponent, total within another issue), as well as raw totals.

Frequency of Party Messaging and Issue Emphasis on Twitter

Between January 1, 2020, and December 14, 2020, the RNC and DNC generated substantially different volumes of tweets using their primary Twitter accounts. As shown in Table 6.1, the DNC posted 26,856 tweets, averaging 77 tweets per day. Important to note is that surrounding the voting registration deadlines for the general election and on the day of the presidential election, the DNC utilized a targeted voting campaign using their custom URL IWillVote.com, which was accompanied by personal

Table 6.1   Original Tweets vs. Retweets among Party Twitter Accounts

Issues	DNC	DNC (Omitting Personalized Tweets)	RNC
Original Tweets	26,117 (97.2%)	3,256 (81.5%)	5,286 (73.1%)
Retweets From	739 (2.8%)	739 (18.5%)	1,937 (26.9%)
Total Tweets	26,856 (100%)	3,995 (100%)	7,223 (100%)

Note: Among total tweets authored by @TheDemocrats, 85.1% were personalized voting campaign tweets that reminded specific constituents to vote in the presidential election.

reminder tweets to individual Twitter accounts. When excluding these personalized reminder tweets, the DNC generated a total of 3,995 tweets for the time range, including 1,484 general voting campaign tweets, and averaged 11.5 tweets per day. The DNC produced 3,256 original tweets (i.e., excluding retweets), averaging 9.3 tweets per day. When excluding the DNC's personalized voting tweets, the RNC posted almost twice as many tweets, totaling 7,223 tweets, and averaged 20.8 tweets per day. Regarding original content, the RNC posted 5,286 original tweets and averaged 15.2 original tweets per day.

Interestingly, not only did the RNC produce more total and original tweets, but it also received significantly higher engagement (i.e., retweets). The DNC received a total of 499,464 retweets, while the RNC received more than 2.3 million retweets, a difference of 367.2%. Additionally, each original tweet that was generated by the RNC had, on average, significantly more engagement than did individual original tweets from the DNC. While the DNC averaged 153.5 retweets per tweet and 1,431.8 retweets per day, the RNC averaged 441.4 retweets per tweet and 6,686.9 retweets per day, a difference of 367% compared to average daily retweets received by the DNC.

As seen in Table 6.2, both party Twitter accounts prioritized key issues at varying proportions of overall Twitter activity. For example, healthcare was given more attention by the DNC than it was by the RNC in relation to total tweets. On the other hand, while differing in raw totals, the issue of race relations was discussed at similar percentage levels for both parties. In our analysis, we will examine how each party discussed the pandemic along with other salient issues during most of 2020, which issues received pronounced audience engagement, and how each party framed itself and the opposing party within each issue.

Table 6.2 Main Issue Count and Percentage among Party Account Totals

Issue	DNC	RNC
Crime	62 (1.6%)	226 (3.1%)
COVID-19 Pandemic	878 (22.0%)	890 (12.3%)
Economy	490 (12.3%)	1,202 (16.6%)
Healthcare	350 (8.8%)	194 (2.7%)
Race Relations	166 (4.2%)	316 (4.4%)
Voting Campaign	1,484 (37.1%)	663 (9.2%)
Voter Fraud	211 (5.3%)	234 (3.2%)

Note: Issues are not mutually exclusive; issue counts include original tweets and retweets.

Party Response to the Pandemic

The pandemic was the second-most discussed topic among both parties' Twitter activity, with the RNC using pandemic-related terms in 12.3% of its total tweets and the DNC discussing the pandemic in 22% of its tweets (when excluding personalized voting campaign). Table 6.3 shows party pandemic-related tweets by month and year. Despite the substantial percentage point difference between the parties' pandemic tweet counts, raw tweet counts were similar, with the RNC producing 890 tweets and the DNC authoring 878 tweets.[2] During March and April 2020, when major government lockdowns and safety mandates were first initiated, the RNC authored the greatest percentage (48.4%; 431 total tweets) of its pandemic-related tweets for the year. On the other hand, the DNC had a significantly lower percentage for the same two-month period, with 26.4% (232 total tweets) of its pandemic-related discussion for the year. As RNC pandemic-related tweets decreased during the summer, the DNC steadily increased pandemic-related discussion from May through July 2020, which was consequently the highest-volume month (154 tweets).

We will next look at how the pandemic was interrelated with specific sub-issues of interest, as well as how each party discussed the opposition within pandemic-related discussion.

Table 6.3   Party Pandemic-Related Tweets by Month

Month	DNC	RNC
January	0 (0%)	1 (0.1%)
February	2 (0.2%)	8 (0.9%)
March	90 (10.3%)	229 (25.7%)
April	142 (16.2%)	202 (22.7%)
May	149 (17.0%)	105 (11.8%)
June	105 (12.0%)	35 (3.9%)
July	154 (17.5%)	56 (6.3%)
August	66 (7.5%)	66 (7.4%)
September	29 (3.3%)	58 (6.5%)
October	38 (4.3%)	49 (5.5%)
November	47 (5.4%)	51 (5.7%)
December	56 (6.4%)	30 (3.4%)
Total	878 (100%)	890 (100%)

Note: Time range was January 1 to December 14, 2020.

Framing of the Pandemic

Politicians and parties use language to draw attention to crises in order to shape public support for their positions. Murray Edelman (1988) states that a crisis "is a creation of the language used to depict it" (p. 31). We therefore examined the extent to which parties framed tweets to include words related to "crisis." In 2020, the DNC produced 180 pandemic-related tweets using "crisis," while the RNC produced 75 pandemic-related tweets using "crisis." During March and April 2020, both the RNC and DNC used the word "crisis" almost equally, with the DNC producing 55 total tweets and the RNC producing 53 total tweets. Tweets including the word "crisis" to describe the pandemic were mixed with messages of unity and division by both parties. Starting in May 2020, the RNC began to use the term "crisis" significantly less, posting 12 tweets during the month using "crisis" and only nine more "crisis" tweets for the rest of the year. The DNC, on the other hand, continued to refer to the pandemic as a "crisis" in 79 more tweets from May through July, before easing use of the term. Throughout the rest of our analysis, the pandemic will be a frequent theme among major key issues such as the economy, healthcare, and voting. For now, we will focus on specific health-promotion items within the pandemic discussion.

Face Masks. Face mask discussion was relatively low among both parties, but saw more concentration from the DNC, which mentioned face masks in 7.4% (61 total tweets) of pandemic-related tweets, while the RNC mentioned masks in 3.3% (26 total tweets) of its pandemic-related tweets. The DNC diligently urged its constituents to do their part, take the pandemic seriously, and wear a mask, producing the highest number of mask-related tweets during December 2020 (25 total tweets) as the state of the pandemic became exponentially dire. The DNC mentioned face masks more than vaccines, which only totaled 10 tweets throughout the year and only 3 tweets in November and December. The focus on face masks as the most practical defense against the virus more than vaccines is telling of the vaccine development. Perhaps Democrats felt less inclined to make promises on vaccines associated with Trump's administration.

To further demonstrate this assumption, the RNC generated 119 tweets mentioning the vaccine, with November being the highest-volume month (31 total tweets). The RNC heralded vaccine development as a major victory for Trump and his Operation Warp Speed. This sentiment is illustrated by the RNC's retweet of RNC chairwoman Ronna McDaniel on December 11, 2020. McDaniel quoted a list posted by Fox Business' Charles Payne honoring healthcare workers in place of Time's Person of the Year and commented, "Also adding @realDonaldTrump and Operation Warp Speed for getting a vaccine ready in less than a year. Unprecedented leadership and results."

Additionally, the RNC hailed Republican leadership for responsibly mobilizing companies to produce personal protection equipment, like masks and face shields. Surprisingly, few tweets criticized Democratic face mask mandates. Rather, the RNC avoided mask mandates almost completely. During November and December, as the pandemic worsened, the RNC produced no mask-related tweets, in complete contrast to its vaccine messaging.

Education. On the issue of education, the RNC was much more involved than was the DNC, particularly along the theme of reopening schools and the well-being of students and school children. For example, when analyzing keywords involving "schools," the RNC produced a total of 116 tweets, whereas the DNC produced 43 tweets. Similarly, when discussing "school children," the RNC generated 97 tweets and the DNC only generated 38 tweets. The RNC supported the reopening of schools, arguing that continued school closures would harm students' educational pursuits and mental and emotional well-being. Likewise, the RNC emphasized repeatedly the Centers for Disease Control and Prevention's (CDC's) recommendation that students' physical and emotional health would be better served in in-person environments than via online learning. The RNC even connected school closures back to school choice, contending that should schools remain closed, parents should receive funds to send their children to private and charter schools.

Neither party strongly associated the issue of education with teachers or instructors, with the RNC producing 30 total tweets and the DNC producing 21 total tweets. Among the few tweets that mentioned "teachers," the RNC attacked teachers' unions as an obstacle to reopening schools and targeted Joe Biden as being more concerned with the success of unions than the effects closures had on students. Democratic tweets promoted teachers' safety upon reopening schools and teachers' pay.

Pandemic Tweets Targeting Opposition

While the general pandemic-related trends assist our understanding of each party's overall concern, it is also helpful to analyze how each party framed the opposition within its pandemic discussion. The DNC and RNC routinely targeted the opposing party and presidential candidate when constructing pandemic-related tweets. This was done at a substantially higher rate by the DNC, which mentioned Trump, Mike Pence, or Republicans among 55.8% (490 total tweets) of its total pandemic discussion. The RNC targeted the opposition at a much lower level, with 21.2% (185 total tweets) of pandemic-related discussion including Biden, Kamala Harris, or Democrats. This finding demonstrates how Democrats composed pandemic discussion primarily in terms of the Trump administration's incompetence and unpreparedness to address a public health crisis. Again, looking at the first months of the pandemic outbreak will illustrate this point.

During March and April 2020, the DNC targeted Republicans among 43.1% of its pandemic-related tweets, totaling 32 and 68 tweets, respectively. By early March 2020, the DNC was already accusing the Trump administration of not taking the pandemic seriously and attacking Trump for incompetence and unpreparedness. Additionally, the DNC pushed back on their efforts to secure mail-in voting funding, describing Trump and Republicans' dismissal of the issue as voter suppression. DNC tweets focusing on Republican incompetence increased throughout the summer and highlighted Republican efforts to end the Affordable Care Act (ACA) and Trump's claims that virus tests were skewing case numbers. DNC attacks on Republicans within pandemic-related discussion spiked during the second week of July 2020. That week, the DNC leveled the Trump administration's concern for the economy over public safety and argued that the economy could not be strengthened until the pandemic was controlled. This move was most likely in response to the growing cases of COVID-19 throughout the country, which was at its highest peak at that point ("Coronavirus in the U.S.," n.d.). After July 2020, the DNC's pandemic-related tweets attacking Trump and Republicans decreased dramatically, dropping 62% from July to August (47 total tweets) and another 60% from August to September (19 total tweets). By the end of the time range, pandemic-related attacks were almost nonexistent, with only one tweet mentioning Trump in November 2020.

While the RNC's pandemic-related attacks against the opposition were much less frequent compared to the DNC's attacks on Republicans, the RNC reacted quickly to criticism from Democrats surrounding Trump's pandemic response. During March and April 2020, the RNC targeted Democrats among 17.4% of its pandemic-related tweets, totaling 32 and 43 tweets for each month, respectively. The RNC blasted Democrats for politicizing the pandemic and delaying economic relief to Americans. As early as March 27, 2020, the RNC also launched attacks on Biden's response to the 2009 H1N1 outbreak as vice president. By April, the RNC turned its criticism toward Democrats' calls for mail-in ballot funding as part of the pandemic relief stimulus. Interestingly, after May 2020, monthly pandemic-related attacks on Democrats decreased drastically, as the RNC only produced eight antagonistic tweets during June 2020. Each month for the rest of the year averaged 11.3 pandemic-related tweets targeting Democrats.

Pandemic Tweets Mentioning Trump. A majority (57.1%) of the RNC's pandemic-related tweets included references to Trump (508 total tweets). The RNC mentioned Trump in pandemic-related discussion even at a greater rate than the DNC (50.5%; 443 total tweets). This method of candidate promotion was not utilized by the DNC, who mentioned Biden in 12.8% of its pandemic-related tweets (112 total tweets). Although the DNC didn't begin to include Biden in pandemic-related tweets until May 2020, this percentage was still relatively low compared to the RNC's focus on

Trump in pandemic-related discussion from May through the end of the year (49.4%; 251 total tweets). In fact, half of the DNC's pandemic-related tweets mentioning Biden (56 total tweets) were posted after Biden won the general election. It seems that during the campaign period, the DNC was more invested in linking the pandemic to Trump's response (or lack thereof) than to how a future president Biden would respond.

The RNC emphasized the praise Trump received from governors of both parties and the development of several effective vaccinations toward the end of the year. On the other hand, the DNC attacked the lack of Trump's pandemic response, his knowing about the virus' deadly potential as early as February 2020, and the Trump administration's urgency to confirm a new conservative Supreme Court justice.

Other Salient Issues

Republican Focus on Economy

From a strategic communication offensive, the RNC rallying cry surrounding the importance of the economy, before and during the pandemic, made up 16.6% (1,202 total tweets) of the party's Twitter activity. While the economy was often discussed in terms of the threats that the Democratic agenda presented to economic freedom and the progress made by the Trump administration, the discussion was heavily influenced by the issues of the pandemic and healthcare. Early in the year, the RNC routinely discussed the economy to praise the Trump administration and disparage Democratic presidential candidates and the Democratic Party in general. After the initial pandemic outbreak, the RNC turned its attention to promoting the Trump administration's efforts to save small businesses, highlighting both the CARES act and the Paycheck Protection Program, while simultaneously attacking Democratic efforts to hinder economic relief.

May and June 2020, however, saw drastically lighter economy-related discussion from the RNC. From April to May, economic-related tweets decreased by 56.6%, reaching a monthly high in April with 189 tweets and dropping to 82 tweets in May. Perhaps the low level of economic-related tweets during May could be attributed to the reality of a vulnerable economy during statewide shutdowns. Additionally, in June, the RNC turned its attention to supporting law enforcement in light of the nationwide protests of police violence toward Black Americans. Nevertheless, the RNC still touted Trump's and Republicans' ability to lead in an economic recovery.

By mid-August, the economy had recovered to its previous performance in mid-February (S&P 500 Index, 2021). It was also during the weeks of the Democratic National Convention and Republican National Convention in mid-August 2020 that the RNC generated the most economic-related discussion. During the week of August 17, 2020, the RNC attacked Biden's former economic record, including his support of the North American Free Trade Agreement (NAFTA); his connection with the progressive wing of the Democratic Party (e.g., U.S. Representative Alexandria Ocasio-Cortez and U.S. Senators Elizabeth Warren and Bernie Sanders); and what it considered an "anemic" economic recovery following the Great Recession in 2009. The following week, the RNC switched gears in light of the Republican National Convention, emphasizing the "Great American Comeback" that Trump's administration had generated following the pandemic outbreak and the economic records of congressional Republicans up for re-election.

As the presidential debates and general election approached, the RNC doubled down on Biden's alleged promises to restrict fossil fuel production and fracking. For example, on October 31, 2020, several days before the general election, the RNC posted a quote from Trump during his rally in Butler, Pennsylvania, stating, "'A vote for Biden and Harris is a vote to Ban Fracking, Ban Mining, and Completely Destroy Pennsylvania.'—@realDonaldTrump" (GOP, 2020e). The tweet was accompanied by a video of the event and was able to generate a remarkable 3,776 retweets.

Biden/Harris and Democrat/Liberal Economic Mentions. The RNC's economy discussion also yielded the most references to Biden and Harris in comparison to the other issues. Biden and Harris were mentioned in 20% of the RNC's economic-related tweets (241 total tweets), even at a higher rate than Democrats/Liberals were mentioned (17.1%; 206 total tweets). Toward the beginning of the year, the RNC's opponent-targeted tweets primarily attacked Democrats/Liberals emanating from the Democratic primary elections and spiked during the week of April 13, 2020 (28 total tweets). During that week, the RNC took issue with Democrats' refusal to replenish the Paycheck Protection Program, framing Democratic actions as "obstruction" and "killing jobs."

By July 15, 2020, the last day of the tax filing period extension, the majority of RNC opponent-targeted attacks shifted against Biden, contrasting the potential effects Biden's economic proposals would place on taxes to the tax cuts imposed by Trump's administration. This increased effort makes sense, as the month of July also saw the DNC's promotion of Biden's Build Back Better initiative, which we will discuss further. The RNC was potentially counteracting the DNC's economic proposals. Other time periods of increased economic-related discussion surrounding Biden (and his running mate Harris) occurred during the weeks of the Democratic National Convention and the first and final general election debates.

Republican Focus on Voter Fraud

While not a top issue among opinion polls throughout the year, we believe an examination of how the RNC discussed voting fraud is merited, considering Trump's vigorous claims following the general election. Throughout 2020, the RNC posted 234 tweets related to voter fraud. Although the bulk of voter fraud discussion occurred later in the year, concerns surfaced shortly after the pandemic outbreak as a result of Democratic efforts to include funding for mail-in ballots in the first stimulus relief bill. For example, on March 24, 2020, @GOP tweeted a quotation from an article written by Harmeet K. Dillion of the Republican National Lawyers Association, "In these times of emergency we need to hew to existing safeguards to ensure that only citizens are voting . . . only once & voting safely . . . Speaker Pelosi sees an opportunity & won't let patriotism or duty get in the way of partisan rent-seeking" (GOP, 2020a). Two weeks later, on April 6, 2020, @GOP quoted an op-ed from RNC Chairwoman McDaniel, "Speaker Nancy Pelosi, D-Calif., & former VP Joe Biden say we must throw election integrity to the wayside in favor of an all-mail election. . . . The overhaul would vastly expand opportunities for fraud & weaken confidence in our elections" (GOP, 2020b).

The majority of tweets about voter fraud was generated in November, following the general election. During the two-week period from October 26 through November 8, 2020, the RNC's election fraud mentions saw a 300% increase and were marked by repeated calls for protecting election integrity. Starting November 4, 2020, the RNC routinely shared hyperlinks to secure. winred.com, the party's fundraising page accepting donations to combat voter fraud. Although voter fraud discussion only made up 3.1% of the RNC's original tweets—experiencing intermittent spikes in May, August, and November 2020—audience engagement (i.e., retweets) per tweet was substantially higher than that for other key issues. For example, voter fraud tweets generated almost 496 retweets per tweet, whereas the pandemic and economy generated 368 and 425 retweets per tweet, respectively. Voter fraud was therefore a much more resonating issue among Twitter audiences than were issues the RNC was actively trying to promote throughout the time range.

Despite the large volume of voter fraud tweets at the end of the year, only 52.5% were original tweets (123 tweets), the lowest original tweet to total tweet ratio among all issues discussed by the RNC in this analysis. For context, issues like economy and crime saw original tweet to total tweet ratios of 80.8% and 79.2%, respectively. This finding suggests the RNC's potential hesitation to author directly and disseminate claims of widescale voter fraud leading up to and following the 2020 general election. Voter fraud and election integrity have long been issues that conservatives have championed. The RNC, though, may have viewed Trump's personal efforts as overbearing, especially considering the lack of consistent evidence. In other words, election integrity, while hyper-salient to constituents, was not a priority for the party at large, at least not on Twitter.

Republican Focus on Crime and Law Enforcement

Significant issues for the RNC were its condemnation of riots associated with the Black Lives Matter protests and its unequivocal support of law enforcement in contrast to progressive calls to "defund the police." Crime-related discussion totaled 229 tweets, whereas law enforcement discussion yielded 261 total tweets. What made discussion surrounding these issues so unique was that 80.5% of crime-related tweets and 96.5% of law enforcement–related tweets were posted after June 1, 2020. Several days following the tragic murder of George Floyd, he was mentioned in a total of 15 original tweets by the RNC, most of which acknowledged the wrongdoing of the Minneapolis police and the need for police reform to protect Black Americans from injustice. Nevertheless, the RNC quickly reframed its acknowledgement of injustice as insufficient to motivate acts of civil unrest and focused most of its attention on restoring law and order and supporting law enforcement. This shift occurred approximately one week after Floyd's death, when on June 2, 2020, the RNC recognized a retired African American police captain who was killed during the St. Louis riots while protecting his friend's pawn shop. In its opposition to the Defund the Police movement, Democrats and liberals, including Biden, became a major target within the discussion, with 39.2% of law enforcement tweets and 44.5% of crime-related tweets mentioning Democrats/Liberals or Biden/Harris.

Engagement with Crime and Law Enforcement Tweets. Although the RNC issue that generated the most total retweets was the economy (367,548 retweets), it appears that Republican constituents resonated much more with other issues at an individual tweet level. As discussed, voter fraud tweets averaged a significant retweet rate (476 retweets per tweet), but even more engaging was the issue of crime, which yielded 518.9 retweets per tweet. The related issue of law enforcement had the second highest retweet rate, yielding 515.2 retweets per tweet. Both of these trends demonstrate the priority that Republican constituents placed on law and order. In other words, individual tweets for these issues carried much more weight than volume-heavy issues like the pandemic or healthcare.

Republican Race Relations

With a pandemic raging nationally and globally, 2020 was also marked by growing racial tensions and the need for racial harmony in the United States. Surprisingly, the RNC discussed race relations, which totaled 316 tweets, at much higher level than the DNC, which produced 166 race-related tweets.

Throughout the year, the RNC appeared to make a conscientious effort to highlight minority groups supporting Trump and all minority Republican candidates. The RNC also accused Biden of harming the Black community via problematic legislation and racial insensitivity. The RNC took issue with Biden's comments to an undecided Black voter as evidence in its tweet on June 2, 2020:

> Joe Biden's record does not bring healing to our country: Less than two weeks ago, Biden insinuated that black people couldn't think for themselves when he said, "If you have a problem figuring out whether you're for me or Trump, then you ain't black" (GOP, 2020d).

Other tweets like this demonstrated the RNC's deliberate attempts to portray itself as more inclusive than Democrats, while also providing minorities more opportunities to prosper.

Democratic Voting Campaign

When analyzing salient issues among tweets produced by the DNC, we identified a significant Twitter blitz leading up to the general election. The "I Will Vote" campaign consisted of both personalized tweets that encouraged, thanked, and followed up with individual Twitter accounts in their individual voting efforts and general voting promotion to motivate Democratic constituents. The campaign made up 90.7% of the DNC's total tweets during the year alone (24,345 tweets). Tweets usually featured a link to IWillVote. com, the DNC's landing page to help voters register. The URL appears to have been launched on July 1, 2019, and was used minimally before August 2020. Starting October 1, 2020, use of the URL increased dramatically, with the highest spike occurring on October 21 (6,360 total tweets), the last day to register for the general election in states like California, Michigan, and Pennsylvania. The template for each reply by @TheDemocrats to individual Twitter addresses included the following:

> [Twitter Address] Thanks for the ♥! We'll send you reminders to help with your plan to vote. It's going to take all of us to take back the White House. Don't forget to make your voting plan if you haven't already. Reply with #stop to opt out any time (e.g., see The Democrats, 2020).

The DNC launched a final blitz on November 3, 2020, which saw a total of 7,381 tweets. The DNC shifted its tweet content by addressing Twitter users who registered to vote using the web page, reminding them of polling hours and informing voters that should they be in line when polls close, they could still cast their vote. The majority of tweets during the day were posted in the morning before 11 a.m. Pacific Standard Time.

Both personalized tweets and general voting tweets were nearly exclusively dedicated to encouraging constituents to vote and did not refer to other issues to motivate voters. For example, general voting tweets included few references to Trump/Pence (9.0%) or Republicans (7.2%). It appears that the DNC did not believe that its urgency to remove Trump from office should be a motive to encourage voters to the ballot box. Additionally, this strategy was able to avoid negativity, which could possibly lead to political cynicism.

I Will Vote Campaign Engagement

Despite the anomaly of the voting campaign tweets toward the end of the election period, encouragement to vote generated a much higher level of engagement (i.e., retweets) when compared to the other key issues. Throughout the total period, the voting campaign produced 184,506 retweets, with the greatest concentration generated from mid-August through Election Day on November 3, 2020. Other issues that generated significantly lower engagement included the pandemic (94,591 retweets), economy (66,465), and healthcare (43,462). More impressively, 99.3% (183,243 total retweets) of engagement were with tweets that generally encouraged constituents to vote (1,346 original tweets), as opposed to the personalized tweets the DNC sent to individual registrants (22,861 original tweets). The campaign was ultimately successful in terms of audience engagement.

When excluding personalized voting campaign tweets, the voting campaign saw smaller retweet rates (136 retweets per tweet) compared to the economy (176 retweets per tweet) or crime (209 retweets per tweet). The biggest takeaway here was that the sheer level of personalized and general tweets was able to achieve a relatively moderate engagement level without Twitter users tiring of the message.

Democratic Focus on Economy

The second-most mentioned topic by the DNC was the economy (490 total tweets). The DNC framed the economy in a series of interrelated issues affected by the pandemic, such as the need for caregiving workers and addressing racial disparity (i.e., minority-owned small businesses). The highest-volume month was July 2020 (114 total tweets), when Biden released his Build Back Better economic proposal. Toward the beginning of July, the DNC established Trump's problematic top-down economic policies, which they claimed left millions unemployed amidst the pandemic. By mid-July, tweets accentuated Biden's agenda for infrastructure and clean energy job creation to address climate change. The DNC also blasted Trump's "Find Something New" campaign, which it claimed did not invest enough in job opportunities and acted as an empty statement of motivation.

By month's end, as extended unemployment benefits were set to expire, the DNC blamed Senate Republicans for failing to act and bickering with the White House. The DNC also recognized the caregiving crisis, which would prevent parents from assimilating back into full-time work as the economy recovered.

After July 2020, economy-themed Twitter discussion tapered dramatically. Surprisingly, economy-themed tweets did not lead during the week of the Democratic National Convention, nor during election week, which only saw four economy-related tweets. It is probable that the DNC shifted its focus during the later months of the year as the economy did in fact begin to recover and continue its pre-pandemic growth. Evidence of this assumption is supported by the fact that the highest months of economy-related discussion for the DNC occurred from May through August 2020, when the economy was at its lowest point (S&P 500 Index, 2021).

Democratic Focus on Healthcare

Healthcare was a consistent issue raised by the DNC (350 total tweets) and was markedly associated with pandemic-related discussion throughout the year; of total healthcare-related tweets, 25.7% included pandemic key terms. Specifically, pandemic-related healthcare tweets featured calls to protect the ACA from the Trump administration's threats to repeal it via the Supreme Court. This association with the pandemic started early during the COVID-19 outbreak when the DNC recognized the 10-year mark since the passing of the ACA and emphasized its vital importance during the pandemic in a series of tweets on March 23, 2020. In late June 2020, the DNC launched another Twitter blitz accusing Trump of breaking his promise to protect preexisting conditions following his and briefs filed by Republican attorneys general to the Supreme Court to end the ACA on June 25, 2020 (Flynn & Elfrink, 2020).

During July and August 2020, the DNC reduced healthcare-themed discussion, replacing it with an emphasis on the economy. Healthcare conversation ramped up after the death of U.S. Supreme Court Associate Justice Ruth Bader Ginsburg on September 18, 2020, with the DNC characterizing Amy Coney Barrett's impending nomination to the court as a critical threat to healthcare. By this point, the DNC was utilizing the "I Will Vote" campaign, which became increasingly associated with healthcare discussion the last two weeks of September 2020.

Party References to Opponents

The RNC targeted Biden and Harris in 14.7% of its tweets during the time range (1,059 total tweets). Among the RNC's tweets including Biden or Harris, 22.3% (242 total tweets) mentioned the economy, usually Biden's economic proposals and past economic decisions. The RNC characteristically claimed that Biden's proposed tax increases would cost American jobs and cited the Obama–Biden administration's perceived failure to produce consistent job creation.

More generally, RNC tweets focused on Biden's alleged incompetence by pushing rumors that former President Obama was not initially in favor of Biden's decision to run for president. An example includes a tweet from April 14, 2020, as primary results were showing Biden as the likely Democratic nominee, that stated, "Throughout the primary, Obama made clear he thought Dems could do better than Joe Biden. Obama's reluctant endorsement along with Bernie's own reluctance to support Biden shows that Dems know Biden is a weak candidate" (GOP, 2020c).

When excluding personalized voting campaign tweets, the DNC targeted Trump or Pence in 26% of its Twitter activity (1,038 total tweets). Volume for Trump/Pence attacks was particularly high during June and July 2020. The week of June 15, 2020, Trump-related tweets almost doubled, from 31 tweets the previous week to 61 tweets, as a result of Trump's rally in Tulsa, Oklahoma, held on June 20. Democrats blasted Trump for holding a rally in an enclosed arena with no social distancing and for scheduling the rally for June 20, one day after Juneteenth, which took on extra significance considering the Tulsa race massacre of June 1921. The following month, July 2020, was the highest-volume month for economy-related tweets mentioning Trump, which incidentally was when Biden launched the Build Back Better proposal to restore the economy.

Throughout the year, 51.6% of the DNC's economic tweets referred to Trump/Pence (253 total tweets) for the time range, a plurality of which included references to the pandemic (43.1%; 109 tweets). Just as striking, 50.8% of the DNC's pandemic tweets (444 total tweets) for the year referred to Trump/Pence, accusing Trump of placing higher priority on matters other than providing aid to Americans, particularly on petitioning the Supreme Court to overturn the ACA and, subsequently, for selecting a conservative justice to replace Justice Ginsburg. The DNC also took issue with Trump's knowledge concerning the severity of the virus as early as February 2020, as revealed in an interview with journalist Bob Woodward (Freking & Miller, 2020).

Conclusion

In 2020, the RNC's and DNC's social media posts on Twitter demonstrated that the parties use the platform differently from each other. After excluding personalized get-out-the-vote tweets made by the Democrats, the Republicans used the platform much more frequently than did the Democrats. The Republicans were more likely to have their content retweeted than were their opponents. The DNC used its platform to reach out to individual voters on

Twitter and get them to vote. The retweet counts suggest higher levels of engagement with the RNC tweets than the DNC tweets.

The issue-emphasis differences between the two camps were pronounced and demonstrate how the issues identified as important by voters were reflected in the parties' social media communication in what was a unique campaign year. More than 1 in 5 tweets from the DNC focused on the pandemic in some way, whereas a little over 1 in 10 RNC tweets did the same. Interestingly, some of the issue proportions were similar between the parties, but owing to the RNC's high volume, its message on those topics likely reached more people than did those by the DNC. The emphasis on some issues but not others at different points in time reflected the constraints and strategies that the parties faced.

Notes

1. Some keywords for the issue of economy were adapted from Hase et al. (2020).
2. Our indexing approach focused on keywords, such as coronavirus, COVID, and pandemic, and did not capture some of the tweets that were implicitly about the pandemic, such as "stepping up to the challenge" or "the outpouring from the private sector."

References

Borchers, C. (2017, October 4). Retweets ≠ endorsements? Oh, yes, they do, say the Hatch Act police. *The Washington Post.* https://www.washingtonpost.com/news/the-fix/wp/2017/10/04/retweets-endorsements-hatch-act/

Boxell, L., Gentzkow, M., & Shapiro, J. M. (2020, January). Cross-country trends in affective polarization. Working paper 26669. National Bureau of Economic Research. https://www.nber.org/system/files/working_papers/w26669/w26669.pdf

Bucktin, C. (2020, August 29). Donald Trump makes bold statement amid protests—"most important election." *Express.* https://www.express.co.uk/news/world/1328940/donald-trump-us-presidential-election-2020-joe-biden

Clausen, C. (2008, September 1). The most important election in history. *The American Scholar.* https://theamericanscholar.org/the-most-important-election/

Conway, B. A., Filer, C. R., Kenski, K., & Tsetsi, E. (2018). Reassessing Twitter's agenda-building power: An analysis of intermedia agenda-setting effects during the 2016 presidential primary season. *Social Science Computer Review, 36,* 469–483. https://doi.org/10.1177/0894439317715430

Conway, B. A., Kenski, K., & Wang, D. (2015). The rise of Twitter in the political campaign: Searching for intermedia agenda-setting effects in the presidential primary. *Journal of Computer-Mediated Communication, 20*(4), 363–380. https://doi.org/10.1111/jcc4.12124

Coronavirus in the U.S.: Latest map and cases. (n.d.). *New York Times.* https://www.nytimes.com/interactive/2021/us/covid-cases.html

Edelman, M. J. (1988). *Constructing the political spectacle.* Chicago, IL: University of Chicago Press.

Flynn, M., & Elfrink, T. (2020, June 26). Trump administration asks Supreme Court to strike down Obamacare. *The Washington Post.* https://www.washingtonpost.com/nation/2020/06/26/trump-obamacare-supreme-court-brief/

Freking, K. & Miller, Z. (2020, September 9). Book: Trump said of virus, "I wanted to always play it down." *Associated Press.* https://apnews.com/article/ap-travel-virus-outbreak-donald-trump-ap-top-news-bob-woodward-c9f35842f7bb355be72842d15a8f7c02

Giuliani: This election "most important." (2008, September 3). *UPI.* https://www.upi.com/Top_News/2008/09/03/Guliani-This-election-most-important/83841220500638/

GOP [@GOP]. (2020a, March 24). *In these times of emergency we need to hew to existing safeguards to ensure that only citizens are voting . . . only once & voting safely . . . Speaker Pelosi sees an opportunity & won't let patriotism or duty get in the way of partisan rent-seeking* [Tweet]. Twitter. https://twitter.com/gop/status/1242536471111892992.

GOP [@GOP]. (2020b, April 6). *Speaker Nancy Pelosi, D-Calif., & former VP Joe Biden say we must throw election integrity to the wayside in favor of an all-mail election. . . . The overhaul would vastly expand opportunities for fraud & weaken confidence in our elections* [Tweet]. Twitter. https://twitter.com/gop/status/1247190235575975945?lang=en

GOP [@GOP]. (2020c, April 14). *Throughout the primary, Obama made clear he thought Dems could do better than Joe Biden. Obama's reluctant endorsement along with Bernie's own reluctance to support Biden shows that Dems know Biden is a weak candidate* [Tweet]. Twitter. https://twitter.com/GOP/status/1250095043232305164

GOP [@GOP]. (2020d, June 2). *Joe Biden's record does not bring healing to our country: Less than two weeks ago, Biden insinuated that black people couldn't think for themselves when he said, "If you have a problem figuring out whether you're for me or Trump, then you ain't black"* [Tweet]. Twitter. https://twitter.com/GOP/status/1267870512509837313

GOP [@GOP]. (2020e, October 31). A vote for Biden and Harris is a vote to Ban Fracking, Ban Mining, and Completely Destroy Pennsylvania.—@realDonaldTrump [Tweet]. Twitter. https://twitter.com/gop/status/1322713033207095296?lang=en

GOP [@GOP]. (2020f, November 12). While Democrats fight amongst themselves, Republicans are going to hold the line against the Democrat Party's radical agenda of defunding the police, middle class tax hikes, the Green New Deal, and a government takeover of health care [Tweet]. Twitter. https://twitter.com/gop/status/1326983325005869057?lang=en

Hase, V., Engelke, K. M., & Kieslich, K. (2020). The things we fear. Combining automated and manual content analysis to uncover themes, topics and threats in fear-related news. *Journalism Studies, 21*(10), 1384–1402. https://doi.org/10.1080/1461670X.2020.1753092

McDaniel, R. [@GOPChairwoman]. (2020, December 11). *Also adding @realDonaldTrump and Operation Warp Speed for getting a vaccine ready in less than a year. Unprecedented leadership and results* [Tweet]. https://twitter.com/gopchairwoman/status/1337413148094107649

Metaxas, P. T., Mustafaraj, E., Wong, K., Zeng, L., O'Keefe, M., & Finn, S. (2015). What do retweets indicate? Results from user survey and meta-review of research. In *Proceedings of the International AAAI Conference on Web and Social Media, 9*(1), 658–661. https://ojs.aaai.org/index.php/ICWSM/article/view/14661

Pew Research Center. (2020, August 13). *Election 2020: Voters are highly engaged, but nearly half expect to have difficulties voting.* https://www.pewresearch.org/politics/2020/08/13/election-2020-voters-are-highly-engaged-but-nearly-half-expect-to-have-difficulties-voting/

Shearer, E. & Mitchell, A. (2021, January 21). News use across social media platforms in 2020. *Pew Research Center.* https://www.journalism.org/2021/01/12/news-use-across-social-media-platforms-in-2020/

S&P 500 Index. (n.d.). *MarketWatch.* https://www.marketwatch.com/investing/index/spx

Taylor, Jr., S. (1984, October 21). Whoever is elected, potential is great for change in high court's course. *The New York Times,* Section 1, Part 1, p. 30.

The Democrats [@TheDemocrats]. (2020, October 25). *Thanks for the ♥! We'll send you reminders to help with your plan to vote. It's going to take all of us to take back the White House. Don't forget to make your voting plan if you haven't already. Reply with #stop to opt out any time* [Tweet]. Twitter. https://twitter.com/TheDemocrats/status/1320557671527792640

Appendix: Some Major Issue Keywords

COVID-19 (Pandemic)

(coronavirus OR pandemic OR #covid OR #coronavirus OR covid OR #pandemic OR virus OR #virus OR pandemics OR #covid19 OR #testing OR #test OR test OR tests OR #tests OR testing OR #rapidtests OR mask OR masks OR #mask OR #masks OR vaccine OR #vaccine OR vaccines OR #vaccines OR fauci OR #fauci OR CDC OR social distancing OR invisible enemy OR #operationwarpspeed OR (crisis -("economic crisis" OR "climate crisis")) OR "public health" OR health crisis OR national emergency OR six feet apart OR FDA OR ventilator OR ventilators OR guidelines OR birx OR stay at home) -("border crisis" OR "drug crisis" OR "opioid crisis") -(retweets_of:joebiden)

Crime

(crime OR criminal OR criminals OR violence OR violent OR riot OR riots OR rioters OR loot OR looting OR looters OR looter OR theft OR vandalize OR vandalized OR vandals OR vandalism OR mob OR mobs OR trafficking OR gun reform OR peaceful protest OR anarchists OR antifa) -(retweets_of:joebiden)

Economy

(economy OR economies OR #economy OR economic OR deficit OR #deficit OR jobs OR #jobs OR unemployment OR #unemployment OR underemployment OR #underemployment OR stock OR stocks OR market OR markets OR investor OR investors OR inflation OR companies OR businesses OR industry OR bank OR banks OR financial OR tax OR taxes OR #tax OR #taxes OR budget OR costs OR small business OR small biz #heroesact OR stimulus OR #stimulus OR CARES act OR #caresact OR #ppp OR #paycheckprotectionprogram OR relief OR ((reopen OR reopening) -(schools))) -(retweets_of:joebiden)

Healthcare

(healthcare OR #healthcare OR health care OR ACA OR #ACA OR obamacare OR #obamacare OR health insurance OR #healthinsurance OR premium OR medical care OR medicare OR #medicare OR medicaid OR #medicaid OR prescription OR #protectourcare OR #medicareforall OR pre-existing) -(retweets_of:joebiden)

Race Relations

(race relations OR #blacklivesmatter OR black lives matter OR racial equality OR #racialequality OR race OR racism OR #racism OR racist OR

#racist OR racists OR #racists OR white supremacy OR white nationalism OR white supremacist OR white supremacists OR "white power" OR racial equity OR #racialequity OR racial disparity OR BLM OR #blm OR George Floyd OR Breonna Taylor OR Ahmaud Arbery OR floyd OR hispanic OR latino OR asian OR black OR "native american" OR african OR hispanics OR latinos OR asians OR blacks OR "native americans" OR "white americans") -("senate race" OR "congressional race" OR "governor race" OR run off OR #gapol OR url:secure.winred.com OR "commissioner race" OR "presidential race" OR congratulations OR "the race" OR "we race" OR "data race" OR "democrat race" OR "black friday" OR #stop OR "black ink" OR "white house")

Voting Campaign: Democrats (I Will Vote)
(happy election day OR url:iwillvote.com OR ballot OR ballots OR vote OR #vote OR voting OR voted OR voters OR voter OR #stop) -(retweets_of:joebiden) -(#stop OR "sorry to see")

Voting Campaign: Republicans (#HoldTheLine)
(election OR elections OR ballot OR ballots OR vote OR votes OR #vote OR voting OR voted OR voters OR voter OR #holdtheline OR url:vote.gop) -(fraud OR ballots OR signature verification OR corrupt election OR stolen OR election process OR election concerns OR mail-in vote OR vote absentee OR election lawsuit OR elections commission OR poll watchers OR fair election OR fair elections OR election officials OR tampering OR mail-in ballot OR ballot counting OR election interference OR legal transparency OR after election day OR ballot dumps OR mail in OR voting in person OR recounts OR recount OR lawful voter OR url:secure.winred.com OR legal vote OR legally cast vote OR universal mail in OR url:protectthevote.com OR ballot harvesting OR safeguards OR safeguard OR suppression OR irregularity OR irregularities OR election integrity OR elections integrity OR voting process OR polling stations OR counting OR landslide OR ballot security OR tip the scales OR full nine days OR confidence in their elections OR impeachment OR witch hunt OR overturn)

Voter Fraud Democrats
(fraud OR #votebymail OR voting access OR postmarked OR voter protection OR #supporttheusps OR election process OR mail-in vote OR vote absentee OR (election lawsuit) OR poll watchers OR fair elections OR election officials OR mail-in ballot OR ballot counting OR election interference OR legal transparency OR mail in OR fair election OR voting in person OR universal mail in OR safeguards OR safeguard OR suppression OR election integrity OR elections integrity OR voting process OR counting OR landslide OR ballot security OR poll observer OR vote-by-mail OR vote by mail OR

audits OR audit OR drop boxes OR absentee) -(url:iwillvote.com OR #stop OR return your OR "plan to vote" OR "vote early" OR "ballot tracking" OR #gapol OR url:votewarnock.com OR "your ballots" OR "your ballot" OR "voting plan" OR "your mail-in ballot" OR "our ballots" OR turn vote OR fill out OR filled out OR your voice OR "social security") -(retweets_of:joebiden)

Voter Fraud Republicans

(fraud OR ballots OR signature verification OR corrupt election OR stolen OR election process OR election concerns OR mail-in vote OR vote absentee OR election lawsuit OR elections commission OR poll watchers OR fair election OR fair elections OR election officials OR tampering OR mail-in ballot OR ballot counting OR election interference OR legal transparency OR after election day OR ballot dumps OR mail in OR voting in person OR recounts OR recount OR lawful voter OR legal vote OR legally cast OR universal mail in OR url:protectthevote.com OR ballot harvesting OR election safeguards OR election safeguard OR elections safeguards OR elections safeguard OR suppression OR irregularity OR irregularities OR election integrity OR elections integrity OR voting process OR polling stations OR ballot counting OR ballot security OR tip the scales OR full nine days OR confidence in their elections OR legal teams OR undermine election OR lawsuit pennsylvania OR transparency pennsylvania) -(impeachment OR witch hunt OR overturn)

CHAPTER SEVEN

Donald Trump and the COVID-19 Information Environment in Campaign 2020

Joshua M. Scacco, Jonathon Smith, and Kevin Coe

For a three-month period in the 2020 presidential election, cavernous arenas, school gymnasiums, and town squares that should have hosted boisterous campaign rallies remained empty. The coronavirus, or COVID-19, pandemic had disrupted a central organizing function for the major campaigns. After all but securing the Democratic Party's nomination, Joe Biden retreated to a makeshift broadcast studio in the basement of his Delaware home. President Donald Trump, who had held his first "Make America Great Again" rally only weeks after his inauguration and then made such rallies a staple of his public outreach, shifted gears to the White House briefing room and the panoply of platforms that would continue to give him a ubiquitous presence (Scacco & Coe, 2021). For a nearly 40-day stretch from mid-March to the end of April, Trump appeared almost daily in press conferences that addressed an eager news corps and millions of concerned Americans. His opportunity to shape the communicative reality of the pandemic, and thus the symbolic playing field of the campaign and his presidency, would be vast.

This chapter focuses on the contribution of the White House Coronavirus Task Force briefings to the COVID information environment and, by extension, the 2020 presidential campaign. Specifically, we consider the 41 briefings from late February to late April 2020 where Donald Trump appeared and spoke. As president and a candidate for reelection, Trump used these high-profile briefings to attempt to shape the broader information environment about COVID's origins, figurative "cures," and negative outcomes. We investigate how he did so and what contribution, if any, such briefings may have had on the knowledge acquisition of individuals in the key swing state of Florida. When considering this possibility of knowledge acquisition, we place Trump's potential contribution within the broader sociocultural environment in which COVID information, and misinformation, emerged and circulated.

Investigating the Trump COVID press conferences is important to understanding how the initial dynamics of the 2020 presidential campaign developed and ultimately solidified to place the incumbent president at a pronounced disadvantage. COVID, as an issue critical to the 2020 campaign and public health, created a hurdle for President Trump but also an opportunity. The press conferences were a strategic White House response to the burgeoning pandemic and the president's inability to hold large-scale rallies due to local and state restrictions (Colvin, 2020). By Election Day, exit polls indicated that COVID was an important factor in the vote choice for 60% of voters, including 23% who said it was the most important factor ("Exit polls," 2020). We investigate the initial contribution the White House's sprint of daily presidential press briefings had on the information environment that would set the stage for the heated campaign to follow.

The COVID Information Environment

Information Flows and Knowledge

The information and knowledge environment that characterized the early pandemic was complex, to put it mildly. Modern information flows are best understood as often contradictory and overlapping, with individual consumers operating amid a range of other forces in a process of targeting, filtering, and selection. Thorson and Wells (2016) aptly characterize this environment as one of "curated flows." As they explain it:

> Under conditions of many channels, a dissolving producer/consumer distinction, and networked flows of content, the number of ways in which individuals' media experiences vary has multiplied. There is no one dominant pattern of content "flow"; there are competing patterns based on individual interests, social networks, and the infrastructures of digital communication. (p. 310)

As the realities of the pandemic set in in the U.S. information environment in March and April 2020, news attention spiked (Mola, 2020). The five sets of "curating actors" that Thorson and Wells (2016) identify all played key roles in shaping the unfolding information environment. Journalists tried to get information to an unusually attentive public, relying on strategic communicators—some well-intentioned and some not—to understand the unfolding crisis. Individual media users navigated this information environment via their traditional means but also increased their attention to a broader array of sources, including public health officials and local news organizations (Shearer, 2020). All the while, social contacts and algorithms circulated and filtered information, including abundant misinformation (Mitchell et al., 2021). In some cases, it appears that the COVID-saturated information environment may have contributed to information overload and, ultimately, avoidance (Soroya et al., 2021).

It is within this complex milieu that the public's knowledge about COVID was generated, reinforced, and refined. Moments of national emergency can lead to public knowledge increases about the emergency itself or even to a broader array of related political issues, as was observed in the aftermath of the September 11 terrorist attacks (Prior, 2002). Certainly, a global pandemic has the potential to alter public motivation to become informed, particularly among individuals more vulnerable to negative outcomes. Absent such a catalyzing event, however, political and health knowledge among the U.S. public is low, at times misinformed, and shaped by the contours of one's curated information environment (Barabas et al., 2014; Bode & Vraga, 2018; Delli Carpini, & Keeter, 1996; De Vreese & Boomgaarden, 2006; Eveland & Hively, 2009). Such knowledge flows intersect with partisanship under any circumstances, but especially so during a campaign with stakes as high as the 2020 election. Predictably, both news coverage and public perceptions took on a partisan hue almost immediately as COVID took root in the United States (Hart et al., 2020; Van Green & Tyson, 2020). This outcome was perhaps inevitable, but was nonetheless fueled by President Trump's central role in the COVID information environment—a role he built early on via a series of press conferences.

Presidential Press Conferences

Presidents have long played a foundational role in the U.S. information environment. As the era of the "ubiquitous presidency" set in over the past several decades, the reach and variety of presidential communication have grown (Scacco & Coe, 2021). By means of access to a variety of platforms, as well as the staff to assist in adapting messages to a variety of audiences, presidents today create a nearly constant and highly visible presence. The presidential press conference is one means by which the chief executive can promote an agenda to journalists, as well as directly across multiple platforms when content is broadcast and then repurposed for social and digital media (Hart & Scacco, 2014). Although a strategic communications tool that emphasizes accessibility (for both the president and the press) and the public performance of executive leadership, press conferences also serve a critical accountability function in a democracy (Scacco & Wiemer, 2019).

For Donald Trump, the White House Coronavirus Task Force press conferences served multiple purposes. Trump began regularly hosting the press conferences on March 13, 2020, two days after cancelling his last campaign rally and immediately following a widely criticized primetime national address (Nicholas, 2020). Consistent with a modern ubiquitous presidency, Trump's appearances afforded him tremendous visibility. Nielsen ratings rivaled "Monday Night Football" audiences, with an average of 8.5 million viewers on cable news in March 2020 (Grynbaum, 2020). These ratings did not even include the viewership from network stations or their partnered streaming channels.

Trump appeared alongside experts and trusted figures in medicine and virology, but it was often the president's information—or misinformation— that made headlines. Among other items, Trump's appearances ignited conversations and controversy regarding three issues: the origins of the virus, miracle "cures," and COVID's evident life-and-death consequences. In the analysis that follows, we focus on these three issues. We do so for two reasons. First, as we will see in the ensuing analysis, each of these issues became an important theme in the information environment during our period of analysis. Second, we had access to a survey of Floridians that asked specific knowledge questions about each of these issues, along with questions about media use and attention to Trump's press conferences. This allowed us to explore both the content of Trump's press conferences and the possibility that these press conferences may have influenced knowledge acquisition in an electorally important state.

To investigate these issues, we ask the following research questions:

RQ1: What patterns emerged in how the White House press briefings discussed the origins, treatments, and negative outcomes of COVID?

RQ2: What factors predicted Floridians' knowledge about the origins, treatments, and negative outcomes of COVID?

Data and Analysis

Our analysis proceeded in two parts. First, we focused on the content of the White House Coronavirus Task Force press conferences where Donald Trump made an appearance. Forty-one transcripts for these press conferences (February 26, 2020–April 23, 2020) were gathered from the archived Trump White House website. The duration of each press conference was

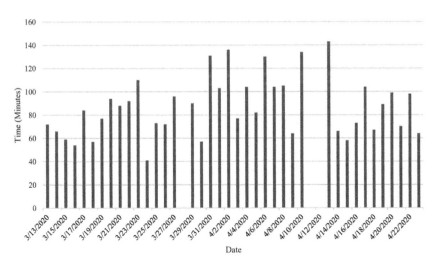

Figure 7.1   Occurrence and Time of Coronavirus Task Force Press Conferences with Trump

logged and appears in Figure 7.1 (M = 85 minutes, SD = 25.37 minutes, Range = 41 to 143 minutes). As the figure illustrates, these press briefings occupied significant portions of the White House's daily visibility in the crucial early stages of the pandemic in the United States.

An automated keyword search of each transcript located press conference mentions of the origins of the virus in China, unproven treatments for the virus, and COVID deaths. Keywords to capture the origin of the virus included China, Chinese, Wuhan, Asia, Asian, Chinese Virus, Wuhan Virus, Asia Virus, and Asian Virus. To locate "cures," we searched for variations of hydroxychloroquine (including hydrochloroquine [sic] or chloroquines in general). Keywords used for negative outcomes included variations of death and die. Three-day moving averages were calculated based on raw mentions of origins, cures, and deaths and then graphed to visualize trends. Finally, the keywords and visual trends assisted in identifying qualitative exemplars in the transcripts to assess emergent messaging patterns and provide descriptive value.[1]

The second part of the analysis included an assessment of public knowledge of the origins, treatments, and outcomes of COVID. To achieve a representative sample of data to answer the second research question, a statewide survey of 600 Floridians was fielded in April 2020. Participants were recruited via Prodege MR, a market research provider, to match the census demographics of the Florida population using stratified, quota sampling techniques. Respondents were required to be 18 years old and Florida residents.[2]

Three survey questions served as separate binary dependent variables to test COVID knowledge. The first asked respondents to identify the origins of the coronavirus ("China" was correct). The second asked respondents to agree or disagree with the statement that "there is no scientifically proven medication" capable of killing COVID ("agree" was correct). The third asked respondents to pinpoint the range of coronavirus-related deaths at the time the survey was fielded ("greater than 25,000 people" was correct). Survey participants then answered a series of questions about the frequency (1 = None to 4 = A Lot) with which COVID information was obtained from the president's press conferences, local and national newspapers, local and national television news, cable news (*CNN, MSNBC, Fox News*), and Facebook. Similar media usage patterns by local/national newspapers and television allowed for these measures to be combined for analysis; the same was true of center-left cable outlets (*CNN, MSNBC*).[3] Finally, respondents answered demographic questions regarding gender, education, age, race, ethnicity, and partisanship. Information acquisition, demographics, and partisanship were used as independent factors in explaining the likelihood that a respondent answered each of the knowledge questions related to origins, treatments, or outcomes correctly.

COVID Origins

As the pandemic unfolded in March and April 2020, COVID's origins garnered considerable attention. The virus' early spread in China and speculation that it emerged there created the possibility that some people would label the virus in location-based terms. In late February, however, the World Health Organization joined with UNICEF and the International Federation of Red Cross and Red Crescent Societies to put out guidelines warning of the stigma such labeling could create. In a section titled "Words Matter," these organizations urged people not to "attach locations or ethnicity to the disease," adding "this is not a 'Wuhan Virus', 'Chinese Virus' or 'Asian Virus'" (World Health Organization, 2020). The concern was not just that stigma would be attached to Chinese people but that such stigma might propagate a broader backlash against Asian people. As Ong and Lasco (2020) noted in early February, the risk was that "such dangerous narratives are encouraging racism and hate by portraying vulnerable populations as virulent carriers, rather than victims worthy of empathy and sympathy" (para. 4).[4]

Despite these warnings and concerns, Trump and his administration often referred to COVID in exactly these terms. For example, in a March 16 tweet, President Trump referred to COVID as "the Chinese Virus," a phrase he used several other times in various communications throughout the next week, defending the characterization as "not racist at all," even as concerns grew (Rogers et al., 2020). At the same time, stories circulated that a White

House official had used the racist phrase "Kung-Flu" in the presence of an Asian American journalist (Haltiwanger, 2020). In late March, the U.S. State Department tried to use the label "Wuhan virus" when drafting a statement on behalf of the Group of Seven, leading to disagreement and, ultimately, separate statements (Marquardt & Hansler, 2020). Major news organizations during this time often quoted Trump's use of "Chinese virus" and "China virus," as well as Secretary of State Mike Pompeo's use of "Wuhan virus" (Gaouette & Hansler, 2020; LaFranchi, 2020).

Such framing was deliberately used in the Coronavirus Task Force press briefings that the president attended. On March 19, for instance, a photo for Getty Images showed the president's briefing book with "corona" revised to read "Chinese" before the word virus (Yeung et al., 2020). Over the course of 40 days, President Trump and the White House press briefings devoted sustained attention to the origins of the coronavirus. Figure 7.2 shows this emphasis over time (via daily term frequency and the three-day moving average), highlighting two periods of emphasis on origins. The first occurs in mid-March and the second in early to mid-April.

The twin approaches of "othering" and responsibility deflection accompanied references to the "China virus," "Wuhan," "Asia," and more. In pointing to the original origins of COVID-19, Trump could construct the public health emergency as an external, foreign threat. Thinking of the nation as a metaphorical container—consistent with Trump's drive to build a physical border wall and reduce foreign migration—the president also employed

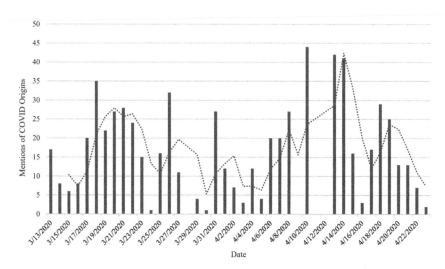

Figure 7.2 Mentions of COVID Origins in Coronavirus Task Force Press Conferences with Trump

national identity appeals. As he noted on April 21, 2020, "Great things were happening, except, all of a sudden, out of nowhere, came the invisible enemy. And we think we know where it came from, and we'll be talking about that probably a lot. But came—the invisible enemy. There's been nobody tougher than me on China." Trump referenced the travel "ban" a day later by again setting up the virus' origins. "If we didn't close our country to China, we would have been so infected, like nobody's ever seen." By the time Trump noted the travel ban's perceived reduction in infections from China, scientists had documented that the dominant COVID strain circulating in New York City had emerged in Europe (Zimmer, 2020). The European emergence went largely unaddressed by the president.

Such association of geography and people with the virus only served to heighten concerns about the marginalization of Asian Americans and Pacific Islanders. In the aftermath of the president's March 16, 2020, tweet, for instance, the use of the #chinesevirus hashtag increased significantly, and tweets using that hashtag were far more likely to include anti-Asian sentiment than were those that used the #covid19 hashtag (Hswen et al., 2021). "Kung Flu" first appeared in the news conferences in late March, with journalists raising questions at this time about potential hate crimes against individuals of Asian descent. Trump acknowledged concern for the community in his March 23, 2020, press conference by stating "It's very important that we totally protect our Asian American community in the United States and all around the world. They're amazing people, and the spreading of the virus is not their fault in any way, shape, or form" (Remarks by President Trump, 2020a). A journalist, however, noted that such a statement might contradict how the president's "Chinese virus" language could "contribute" to attacks on the community.

Focusing on the virus' origins also was an attempt to deflect presidential responsibility for its negative outcomes, including an initial federal response that allowed the virus to spread unimpeded. This crisis communication approach relied on both Trump distancing his administration from the virus and diminishing the amount of control he had over the situation (Coombs & Holladay, 2002). Constructing the foreign origins assisted with the geographical distancing Trump hoped to create. Moreover, he diminished his administrative control by claiming the virus as a surprise or unlucky occurrence. In a March 26 press conference he joined, Trump noted that, "Well, it's nobody's fault—certainly not in this country. Nobody's fault. We got very lucky when we made a decision not to allow people in from China at a very early date" (Remarks by President Trump, 2020b). Such claims were challenged later in September 2020 by the release of taped conversations Trump had with journalist Bob Woodward, in which the president admitted to "playing down" the situation during such public acknowledgments (Gangel et al., 2020).

The survey results from late April 2020 reveal that most Floridians—like the president—were quite familiar with the original origins of the virus. Of the 600 individuals surveyed, 93.6% correctly identified COVID's origin point. In a logistic regression model that estimated the likelihood an individual correctly identified COVID's origins, race was the only demographic factor that contributed to this knowledge.[5] Black or African American individuals were significantly less likely to know the virus's origins. Given that such information was frequently mentioned (in news sources and the press conferences), as well as known by the vast majority of Floridians, it is not surprising that no one information source emerged as a significant factor in acquisition of COVID's origins. Nonetheless, it is quite notable that a racial gap emerges here—potentially indicative of the broader equity-based challenges that emerged during the pandemic with infections, deaths, and ultimately vaccine access.

COVID "Cures"

The second issue we focused on is potential treatments for COVID. Health officials worked early in the pandemic to underscore the seriousness of the virus and the fact that there were, at that time, no treatments or vaccines. For example, in early February 2020, the Centers for Disease Control and Prevention (CDC) focused its *Morbidity and Mortality Weekly Report* on the "novel coronavirus outbreak," stating plainly that "no vaccine or specific treatment for 2019-nCoV infection is currently available" (Patel & Jernigan, 2020, para. 1). In this environment, news organizations and others with public sway were quick to promote new possibilities, even when speculative. The unproven potential of chloroquine and hydroxychloroquine quickly became a focal point. For example, on March 16, 2020, Tesla magnate Elon Musk tweeted to his more than 50 million followers a link to a paper suggesting the potential of chloroquine as a COVID treatment.[6] President Trump began to mention hydroxychloroquine just a few days later—often contradicting his own medical advisors. In a press briefing on March 20, 2020, for example, Dr. Anthony Fauci, director of the National Institute of Allergy and Infectious Diseases, stated unequivocally that there was no evidence to indicate hydroxychloroquine could effectively treat COVID. Trump disagreed: "I feel good about it. That's all it is. Just a feeling. You know, I'm a smart guy. I feel good about it" (Remarks at a White House Coronavirus Task Force, 2020a.)

Throughout late March, the potential of chloroquine and hydroxychloroquine as COVID treatments made headlines. This coverage became even more intense when, on March 28, 2020, the Food and Drug Administration (FDA) issued emergency authorization for the use of chloroquine and hydroxychloroquine to treat patients hospitalized with COVID (Baker et al., 2020). But just as quickly as this speculation arose, it faded. By April 24, *The*

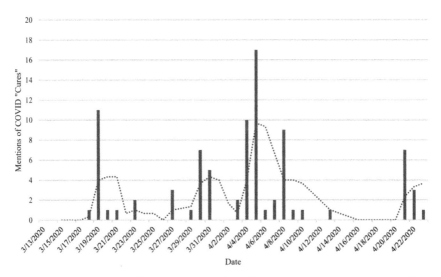

Figure 7.3   Mentions of COVID "Cures" in Coronavirus Task Force Press Conferences with Trump

Washington Post was already analyzing "The Rise and Fall of Trump's Obsession with Hydroxychloroquine" (Bump, 2020).

During the president's 40 days of press briefings with the White House Task Force, attention to hydroxychloroquine was lower and more variable compared to the focus on COVID's origins. Figure 7.3 visually illustrates these trends.

Attention began to grow in late March 2020, a period that coincided with the FDA's emergency use authorization of the drug, as well as focus on the "curative" properties in conservative media. On March 27, Trump was asked in the briefing room about his advocacy of chloroquines as a "cure." He responded by noting his divergence from medical experts, but the potential necessity given mounting deaths. "There's reason to believe that it could be successful here. Now, the reason I disagree with you—and I think Tony [Dr. Anthony Fauci] would disagree with me—but the reason I disagree with you is that we have a pandemic. We have people dying now" (Remarks by President Trump, 2020c). The White House's advocacy followed extensive coverage of the drug on conservative outlet *Fox News*, including host Sean Hannity's focus on the (questionable) claims of Dr. Vladimir Zelenko, as well as extensive social media boosting by some of the president's key allies (Roose & Rosenberg, 2020).[7] The conservative media ecosystem's promotion had created a feedback loop with the White House, as became common during the Trump campaign and administration (Benkler et al., 2018).

Raw mentions of the medicine peaked in early April 2020. On April 4, the president promoted the drug, FDA authorization, and distribution through the federal stockpile in his opening statement. Dr. Fauci was in attendance but did not advocate for, or even mention, the drug. Trump cycled to the phrase "What do you have to lose?" four times in reference to the drug. "And I hope they use the hydroxychloroquine, and they can also do it with Z-Pak, subject to your doctor's approval, and all of that. But I hope they use it because I'll tell you what: What do you have to lose? In some cases, they're in bad shape. What do you have to lose?" (Remarks by President Trump, 2020d). The following day, the president was asked by a journalist about his enthusiasm for the drug given the lack of evidence of its effectiveness. The journalist noted, "Your words carry enormous weight in this country and around the world. And while you acknowledge you're not a physician, you do promote these medicines extensively here" (Remarks by President Trump, 2020e). The president responded by pivoting to his desire to keep people from dying. "Because I want people to live and I'm seeing people dying. And I see people that are going to die without it. And you know the expression. When that's happening, they should do it. What really do we have to lose?" (Remarks by President Trump, 2020e). The president repeated the gambling-related phrase five times during this press conference and proceeded to interrupt Dr. Fauci from answering a press question about the drug.

By the time we entered the field with the April 2020 COVID survey of Floridians, mentions of hydroxychloroquine had ebbed during the press conferences. Yet the spread of such misinformation was detectable in the sample. Although the vast majority of Floridians were informed of a lack of COVID cures in mid-to-late April 2020, almost one in five (17.1%) either disagreed with the statement or did not know that there was "no scientifically proven medication" for killing COVID. When we assess the likelihood of responding to this statement correctly using a logistic regression model that controls for demographic, political, and information environment factors, a few trends emerge.[8] Demographically, older individuals were more likely to answer correctly and Black or African American Floridians were less likely to answer correctly. Republicans were significantly less likely to answer this question correctly as well. In regard to the information environment, obtaining COVID-related information from newspapers, television, and center-left cable news (*CNN, MSNBC*) all increased the likelihood that one answered correctly. In this sample, attendance to the president's press conferences, *Fox News*, or Facebook did not have significant effects on knowledge.

We see with the COVID "cure" several of the important trends that would define the pandemic. First, and related to knowledge of COVID origins, a race gap emerges. Such equity issues would tragically continue throughout the waves of the pandemic. Second, politicization of information emerges in how Republicans were more likely to subscribe to false beliefs about a miracle cure for the coronavirus. Although our data do not reveal the contributing factors for these beliefs, it seems likely that aspects of curated partisan information flows not accounted for in our survey were a contributing factor. Finally, we do find that elements of the information environment mattered for information acquisition. Attention to more traditional news sources (local and national newspapers; local and national television), as well as *CNN* and *MSNBC* all served to bolster knowledge about a lack of COVID-related "cures."

For a small number of individuals, false beliefs about possible "cures"—concurrently echoed by the president and some conservative media sources—took a toll. On March 24, 2020, a man died after attempting to preventatively self-medicate by ingesting chloroquine phosphate, which he saw as an ingredient in a parasite treatment for fish and mistook for the medical form of chloroquine. The man's wife, who had also ingested the chloroquine phosphate but survived, said that she and her husband had heard about chloroquine by viewing Trump's briefings (Edwards & Hillyard, 2020). While such events clearly are the exception, they nonetheless illustrate the presidential pull Trump's words had for some individuals.

COVID Deaths

Finally, we considered an issue that quickly became an all-too-familiar element of the COVID information environment: death tolls. Amid already tragic numbers of international casualties, the U.S. death toll began to escalate dramatically in March. Consider that on March 1, 2020, the seven-day daily average of reported COVID deaths across the United States was just four. By the end of the month, it was 520. In mid-April, as the United States reached its first peak, this daily average routinely surpassed 2,200 deaths ("Tracking U.S. covid-19 cases," n.d.). As the Florida survey went into the field around this time, the total death toll in the United States had climbed above 20,000. News organizations marked this tragic milestone with headlines such as "US surpasses 20,000 coronavirus deaths, the highest national death toll" (Torres & Mansell, 2020).

The information environment, including news and government officials such as President Trump, took different approaches to covering the negative outcomes. National and cable news outlets widely reported cases and deaths with graphics and chyrons. Communities reported their first local deaths, as Cleveland.com (*Plain Dealer*) did on March 21, KUTV Salt Lake City did on March 22, and the *Tampa Bay Times* did on March 24 (Christ, 2020; McNeill & Sampson, 2020; Roberts, 2020). Major news organizations also were observing the contrast between Trump's unwarranted optimism and the emerging projections that COVID would likely kill many Americans (Collinson, 2020). In the White House in February and March, President

Trump compared the deaths to the seasonal flu, pushed back against the mortality rate, and diminished the scope of the effects (Kiely et al. , 2020). For instance, the president toured the CDC on March 6, 2020, and his remarks (alongside those in his administration) referenced the flu 15 times. "We've had 11 deaths, and they've been largely old people who are—who were susceptible to what's happening. Now, that would be the case, I assume, with a regular flu too. If somebody is old and in a weakened state or ill, they're susceptible to the common flu too" (Remarks by President Trump after tour, 2020). Such actions served to compartmentalize the most severe effects to older individuals while falsely equating COVID outcomes to the flu.

When we assess the 40-day period of press briefings the president gave alongside the White House Coronavirus Task Force (see Figure 7.4), we see that mentions of deaths initially tracked with negative COVID outcomes. Discussions first begin to rise in late March 2020, corresponding to local news stories about community deaths and a mounting national mortality toll.

The press conferences are an important artifact to assess communication regarding COVID deaths because the president showed little interest in talking about negative health outcomes. However, as an accountability forum, journalists' briefing questions required some administration acknowledgment of the morbid reality—even if the president still attempted to downplay that reality. For example, in a March 31 press briefing, journalist Steve Holland of Reuters asked the president to project the final COVID death toll in the United States, assuming people were "reasonably good at following these mitigation measures" (Remarks at a White House Coronavirus Task

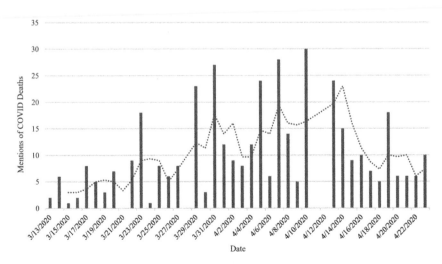

Figure 7.4 Mentions of COVID Deaths in Coronavirus Task Force Press Conferences with Trump

Force, 2020b). Trump responded, "Well, if they're reasonably good, I guess we could say that—I'd like to have maybe Dr. Fauci or Deb come up and say. I mean, I have numbers, but I'd rather have them say the numbers, if you don't mind. It's a big question." Ultimately, Dr. Deborah Birx indicated that the final projection was 100,000 to 200,000 deaths—an astoundingly optimistic figure in retrospect.

By Easter Sunday (April 12, 2020)—a day by which the president had, only weeks before, projected the nation would be "opened up"—more than 2,000 Americans were dying a day of COVID-related complications and the first viral wave had yet to crest (Liptak et al., 2020; "Tracking U.S. covid-19 cases," n.d.). The press conferences contained some of the greatest raw frequencies of death mentions. Scripted parts of the briefings show the president expressing some sympathy for the victims. Unscripted parts of the briefings show Trump diminishing the negative outcomes or again attempting equivalencies (as he did in March 2020 with the flu). Only two days prior, the president conceded that opening up the country "could lead to death" while simultaneously claiming that "staying at home leads to death also. And it's very traumatic for this country. But staying at home—if you look at numbers—that leads to a different kind of death, perhaps, but it leads to death also" (Remarks by President Trump, 2020f). By the Monday following Easter in 2020, the president chose to highlight "the success we're having" and played a video of Democratic governors praising the federal response (Remarks by President Trump, 2020g). CNN White House correspondent Jim Acosta challenged the president on his "sizzle reel" and pushed him on federal preparations following the China travel ban. Acosta said, "Twenty million people are unemployed, tens of thousands of Americans dead" (Blitzer, 2020). In response, the president called CNN "fake news," said his administration did "a lot" in February without providing details and referenced then-presumptive Democratic presidential nominee Joe Biden's opposition to the travel ban.

The Florida survey entered the field in the midst of the first national virus wave, an important moment to assess whether individuals knew of the death toll at that moment. A majority of Floridians surveyed (56%) correctly identified that more than 25,000 Americans had died of the novel coronavirus by mid-April. Analyzing the predictors of knowing this fact revealed a pattern somewhat similar to knowledge of COVID "cures."[9] Older and more educated Floridians were more likely to know the death toll, while Latinx and Hispanic Floridians were less likely to answer correctly. Attention to center-left cable news (CNN and MSNBC), with its prominent focus on negative outcomes, increased the likelihood of correctly identifying the death toll. Importantly, Facebook emerged as a depressive influence on knowledge such that greater use of the social media platform for finding COVID information reduced the likelihood of knowing the number of deaths. No other information environment elements, including the president's press conferences, had a direct influence on mortality knowledge.

Conclusion

The coronavirus pandemic presented a significant challenge to the Trump presidency and the 2020 campaign. Yet presidential communication can help to shape broader realities. Trump seized opportunities to respond to the public health challenges with regular White House press briefings in March and April 2020. The venue served as an important visibility tool for the president and presented vast possibilities to shape the information environment.

Our findings in this chapter, pertaining to how the Trump White House used the daily press conferences, as well as their limited influence on some knowledge items, present three key takeaways. First, while the almost-daily presidential press conference occupied journalists' and the public's time and attention in March and April 2020, it had little independent influence among Floridians surveyed on the knowledge items tracked. Given the ways that presidential content is repurposed across news, digital, and social media platforms, we cannot discount the possibility of an indirect influence of the briefings. Nevertheless, these findings do provide general support for the difficulty presidents have in moving some indicators of public opinion.[10] Second, the emergence of race and ethnicity gaps in some knowledge items pinpoints one harbinger of the inequities that would emerge with regard to COVID-related health outcomes and access issues (Artiga et al., 2020). Understanding the systemic inequities that would create such knowledge gaps in the first place is of the utmost importance to eliminating health disparities. Finally, the broader information environment mattered for acquisition of COVID (mis)information. Center-left cable, despite its focus on anti-Trump appeals at times, nonetheless played a role in educating segments of the public. Conversely, the results that Facebook attention reduced the likelihood of identifying the correct number of COVID-related deaths illustrates an early challenge the platform confronted: the rampant spread of misinformation across its networks (Brennen et al., 2020). Although platforms like Facebook attempted to respond and eliminate such content, the space was an important facilitator for the spread of pandemic-related misinformation and disinformation.

The findings in this chapter represent one snapshot at the beginning of what would become an arduous and lengthy public health crisis. Accordingly, we note two realities related to the data we examined. First, an automated keyword search of the transcripts allowed for a general assessment of trends and messaging related to COVID from the White House in March and April 2020. More systematic assessments that place the words in the interpretive context of the issues assessed would require broader content analytic techniques, a fruitful avenue for future research. We also are open to the possibility that some of these messages, particularly on treatments, evolved as the health situation changed. Second, the cross-sectional survey data were collected (and weighted) to be representative of the population of Florida as it existed in April 2020. The results are not generalizable to the United States as a whole and should be interpreted cautiously beyond the period assessed. A rapidly evolving public health situation, in addition to regular changes in the information environment, would continue to alter COVID knowledge and attitudes as 2020 progressed.

Notes

1. On the necessity of such description, see Gerring, J. (2012). Mere description. *British Journal of Political Science, 42*(4), 721–746. https://doi.org/10.1017/S0007123412000130

2. Demographically, greater than half of the sample identified as female (51.3%), one-quarter as Hispanic or Latinx (25.4%), just over three-quarters (77.5%) as White/Caucasian, and one-sixth (16.5%) as Black/African American. The average age was 48.1 years ($SD = 17.76$). A majority of the sample reported earning a college degree or more (41.4%) or having some post high school education but no college degree (39.8%), while a fifth of the sample claimed a high school degree or less (18.8%). Politically, a plurality identified as Democrats (43.4%), with Republicans (30.5%) and independents (26.1%) making up smaller portions of the sample. The authors thank Nielsen Holdings for their partnership with the University of South Florida in financially supporting data collection as part of the Sunshine State Survey. Analysis and interpretation are the sole responsibility of this chapter's authors. Analyses are weighted to population parameters.

3. Usage patterns were determined based on two-tailed Pearson's correlation coefficients for the following measures: Local and national newspapers ($r = 0.63$, $p < 0.001$; $M = 2.20$, $SD = 1.06$); Local and national television news ($r = 0.60$, $p < 0.001$; $M = 3.10$, $SD = 0.93$); Center-left cable news ($r = 0.60$, $p < 0.001$; $M = 2.26$, $SD = 1.09$). The means and standard deviations for the other information and media use measures include presidential press conferences ($M = 2.86$, $SD = 1.02$), *Fox News* ($M = 2.31$, $SD = 1.26$), and Facebook ($M = 2.28$, $SD = 1.16$).

4. See also Marcelo, P. (2020, March 12). Asian-American leaders decry racism amid global pandemic. *The Associated Press.* https://apnews.com/article/0fc3786c7580ad5a19123cb47cc47a2a; Vazquez, M. (2020, March 12). Calling COVID-19 the "Wuhan Virus" or "China Virus" is inaccurate and xenophobic. (2020, March 12). Yale School of Medicine. https://medicine.yale.edu/news-article/calling-covid-19-the-wuhan-virus-or-china-virus-is-inaccurate-and-xenophobic/

5. To examine this, we regressed each individual's answer to the COVID origin question (1 = correct, 0 = incorrect) by demographic and information

environment factors. Information environment factors (attendance to news sources and the presidential press conferences) were eliminated due to nonsignificance and poor model fit, as indicated by the Hosmer-Lemeshow test. A simpler logistic regression model with demographic and political factors was used. The model predicted approximately 3% of the variance in knowledge using the Cox and Snell pseudo R-square [$\chi^2(7)$ = 19.24, p < 0.01]. The following variables were included in the model: **Constant (***B* **=3.14,** *SE* **=0.85,** *p* **< 0.001)**, Age (*B* = 0.002, *SE* = 0.12, *p* = 0.83), Female (*B* = –0.33, *SE* = 0.39, *p* = 0.39), **Black/AA (***B* **= –1.66,** *SE* **= 0.44,** *p* **< 0.001)**, Latinx/Hispanic (*B* = –0.42, *SE* = 0.47, *p* = 0.37), Education (*B* = 0.02, *SE* = 0.25, *p* = 0.93), Democrat (*B* = 0.33, *SE* = 0.40, *p* = 0.41), Republican (*B* = 0.44, *SE* = 0.56, *p* = 0.43). Bolded variables are significant using conventional standards.

6. For the text of the tweet, see: https://twitter.com/elonmusk/status /1239650597906898947

7. Progressive research nonprofit Media Matters found that *Fox News* promoted usage of hydroxychloroquine 146 times from March 23–29, 2020.

8. To examine this, we regressed each individual's answer to the COVID cure/medicine statement (1 = correct, 0 = incorrect) by demographic, political, and information environment factors. The model exhibited good fit as indicated by the Hosmer-Lemeshow test. The model predicted approximately 7% of the variance in knowledge using the Cox and Snell pseudo R-square [$\chi^2(13)$ = 45, p < 0.001]. The following variables were included in the model: Constant (*B* = –0.09, *SE* = 0.70, *p* = 0.90), **Age (***B* **= 0.02,** *SE* **= 0.01,** *p* **< 0.05)**, Female (*B* = 0.20, *SE* = 0.25, *p* = 0.42), **Black/AA (***B* **= –0.92,** *SE* **= 0.34,** *p* **< 0.01)**, Latinx/ Hispanic (*B* = 0.001, *SE* = 0.30, *p* = 0.997), Education (*B* = –0.06, *SE* = 0.17, *p* = 0.71), Democrat (*B* = –0.52, *SE* = 0.31, *p* = 0.09), **Republican (***B* **= –0.79,** *SE* **= 0.35,** *p* **< 0.05)**, President's Press Conferences (*B* = –0.05, *SE* = 0.14, *p* = 0.73), **Newspapers (***B* **= 0.31,** *SE* **= 0.14,** *p* **< 0.05)**, **Television (***B* **= 0.30,** *SE* **= 0.14,** *p* **< .05)**, **Center-Left Cable (***B* **= 0.32,** *SE* **= 0.15,** *p* **< 0.05)**, *Fox News* (*B* = –0.05, *SE* = 0.12, *p* = 0.69), Facebook (*B* = –0.15, *SE* = 0.11, *p* = 0.19). Bolded variables are significant using conventional standards.

9. To examine this, we regressed each individual's answer to the number of COVID deaths (1 = correct, 0 = incorrect) by demographic, political, and information environment factors. The model exhibited good fit as indicated by the Hosmer-Lemeshow test. The model predicted approximately 12% of the variance in knowledge using the Cox and Snell pseudo R-square [$\chi^2(13)$ = 71.54, p < 0.001]. The following variables were included in the model: **Constant (***B* **= –1.89,** *SE* **= 0.57,** *p* **< 0.01)**, **Age (***B* **= 0.01,** *SE* **= 0.01,** *p* **< 0.05)**, Female (*B* = 0.23, *SE* = 0.19, *p* = 0.23), Black/AA (*B* = –0.35, *SE* = 0.27, *p* = 0.20), **Latinx/Hispanic (***B* **= –0.44,** *SE* **= 0.23,** *p* **= 0.05)**, **Education (***B* **= 0.51,** *SE* **= 0.13,** *p* **< 0.001)**, Democrat (*B* = 0.02, *SE* = 0.23, *p* = 0.93), Republican (*B* = –0.10, *SE* = 0.26, *p* = 0.70), President's Press Conferences (*B* = 0.11, *SE* = 0.11, *p* = 0.28), Newspapers (*B* = –0.13, *SE* = 0.10, *p* = 0.19), Television (*B* = 0.14, *SE* = 0.11, *p* = 0.21), **Center-Left Cable (***B* **= 0.36,** *SE* **= 0.11,** *p* **< 0.01)**, *Fox News* (*B* = 0.02, *SE* = 0.09,

p = 0.79), **Facebook (*B* = −0.38, *SE* = 0.09, *p* < 0.001)**. Bolded variables are significant using conventional standards.

10. See, for instance, Rottinghaus, B. (2010). *The provisional pulpit: Modern presidential leadership of public opinion*. College Station, TX: Texas A&M University Press.

References

Artiga, S., Corallo, B., & Pham, O. (2020, August 17). Racial disparities in COVID-19: Key findings from available data and analysis. *Kaiser Family Foundation*. https://www.kff.org/racial-equity-and-health-policy/issue-brief/racial-disparities-covid-19-key-findings-available-data-analysis/

Baker, P., Rogers, K., Enrich, D., & Haberman, M. (2020, April 6). Trump's aggressive advocacy of malaria drug for treating coronavirus divides medical community. *The New York Times*. https://www.nytimes.com/2020/04/06/us/politics/coronavirus-trump-malaria-drug.html

Barabas, J., Jerit, J., Pollock, W., & Rainey, C. (2014). The question (s) of political knowledge. *American Political Science Review, 108*(4), 840–855. https://doi.org/10.1017/S0003055414000392

Benkler, Y., Faris, R., & Roberts, H. (2018). *Network propaganda: Manipulation, disinformation, and radicalization in American politics*. New York, NY: Oxford University Press.

Blitzer, W. (Host) (2020, April 13). The Situation Room. [Television Program]. Washington, D.C.: *CNN*. http://transcripts.cnn.com/TRANSCRIPTS/2004/13/sitroom.02.html

Bode, L. & Vraga, E. K. (2018). See something, say something: Correction of global health misinformation on social media. *Health Communication, 33*(9), 1131–1140. https://doi.org/10.1080/10410236.2017.1331312

Brennen, J. S., Simon, F. M., Howard, P. N., & Nielsen, R. K. (2020, April). Types, sources, and claims of COVID-19 misinformation. *Reuters Institute for the Study of Journalism*. https://reutersinstitute.politics.ox.ac.uk/sites/default/files/2020-04/Brennen%20-%20COVID%2019%20Misinformation%20FINAL%20(3).pdf

Bump, P. (2020, April 24). The rise and fall of Trump's obsession with hydroxychloroquine. *The Washington Post*. https://www.washingtonpost.com/politics/2020/04/24/rise-fall-trumps-obsession-with-hydroxychloroquine/

Christ, G. (2020, March 21). First coronavirus-related death in Cuyahoga County reported. *Cleveland.com*. https://www.cleveland.com/business/2020/03/first-coronavirus-related-death-in-cuyahoga-county-reported.html

Collinson, S. (2020, February 26). Jarring contradictions cast doubts on Trump's ability to handle coronavirus. *CNN*. https://www.cnn.com/2020/02/26/politics/coronavirus-donald-trump-politics-us-health/index.html

Colvin, J. (2020, March 25). Coronavirus briefings are the new campaign rallies for Trump. *Associated Press.* https://apnews.com/article/969eafc8f5cb01e9b3e8fe941b3264eb

Coombs, W. T. & Holladay, S. J. (2002). Helping crisis managers protect reputational assets: Initial tests of the situational crisis communication theory. *Management Communication Quarterly, 16,* 165–186. https://doi.org/10.1177/089331802237233

Delli Carpini, M. X. & Keeter, S. (1996). *What Americans know about politics and why it matters.* New Haven, CT: Yale University Press.

De Vreese, C. H. & Boomgaarden, H. (2006). News, political knowledge and participation: The differential effects of news media exposure on political knowledge and participation. *Acta Politica, 41*(4), 317–341. https://doi.org/10.1057/palgrave.ap.5500164

Edwards, E. & Hillyard, V. (2020, March 23). Man dies after taking chloroquine in an attempt to prevent coronavirus. *NBC News.* https://www.nbcnews.com/health/health-news/man-dies-after-ingesting-chloroquine-attempt-prevent-coronavirus-n1167166

Eveland Jr, W. P. & Hively, M. H. (2009). Political discussion frequency, network size, and "heterogeneity" of discussion as predictors of political knowledge and participation. *Journal of Communication, 59*(2), 205–224. https://doi.org/10.1111/j.1460-2466.2009.01412.x

Exit polls (2020). *CNN.* https://www.cnn.com/election/2020/exit-polls/president/national-resultsGangel, J., Herb, J., & Stuart, E. (2020, September 9). "Play it down:" Trump admits to concealing the true threat of coronavirus in new Woodward book. *CNN.* https://www.cnn.com/2020/09/09/politics/bob-woodward-rage-book-trump-coronavirus/index.html

Gaouette, N. & Hansler, J. (2020, March 18). Pompeo says State Department employees tested positive for coronavirus as he blasts Iran and China over "disinformation." *CNN.* https://www.cnn.com/2020/03/17/politics/pompeo-coronavirus-presser/index.html;

Grynbaum, M. M. (2020, March 25). Trump's briefings are a ratings hit. Should networks cover them live? *The New York Times.* https://www.nytimes.com/2020/03/25/business/media/trump-coronavirus-briefings-ratings.html

Haltiwanger, J. (2020, March 17). A White House official called coronavirus the "Kung-Flu" to an Asian-American reporter's face. *Business Insider.* https://www.businessinsider.com/reporter-says-trump-official-called-coronavirus-the-kung-flu-2020-3

Hart, P. S., Chinn, S., & Soroka, S. (2020). Politicization and polarization in COVID-19 news coverage. *Science Communication, 42*(5), 679–697. https://doi.org/10.1177%2F1075547020950735

Hart, R. P., & Scacco, J. M. (2014). Rhetorical negotiation and the presidential press conference. In R. P. Hart (Ed.), *Communication and language analysis in the public sphere* (pp. 59–80). Hershey, PA: IGI Global. https://doi.org/10.4018/978-1-4666-5003-9.ch004

Hswen, Y., Xu, X., Hing, A., Hawkins, J., Brownstein, J. S., & Gee, G. C. (2021). Association of "#covid19" versus "#chinesevirus" with Anti-Asian sentiments on Twitter: March 9–23, 2020. *American Journal of Public Health, 111*(5), 956–964. https://doi.org/10.2105/AJPH.2021.306154

Kiely, E., Roberston, L., Rieder, R., & Gore, D. (2020, October 2). Timeline of Trump's COVID-19 comments. *FactCheck.org.* https://www.factcheck.org/2020/10/timeline-of-trumps-covid-19-comments/

LaFranchi, H. (2020, March 30). Containing coronavirus: Why US, China compete about that, too. *The Christian Science Monitor.* https://www.csmonitor.com/USA/Foreign-Policy/2020/0330/Containing-coronavirus-Why-US-China-compete-about-that-too

Liptak, K., Vazquez, M., Valencia, N., & Acosta, J. (2020, March 24). Trump says he wants the country 'opened up and just raring to go by Easter,' despite health experts' warnings. *CNN.* https://www.cnn.com/2020/03/24/politics/trump-easter-economy-coronavirus/index.html

Marquardt, A. & Hansler, J. (2020, March 26). US push to include "Wuhan virus" language in G7 joint statement fractures alliance. *CNN.* https://www.cnn.com/2020/03/25/politics/g7-coronavirus-statement/index.html

McNeill, C. & Sampson, Z. T. (2020, March 24). Tampa Bay has its first coronavirus death. This time, the state says it's for real. *Tampa Bay Times.* https://www.tampabay.com/news/health/2020/03/24/florida-coronavirus-cases-top-1400-as-tests-expand-south-florida-sees-jump/

Mitchell, A., Jurkowitz, M., Oliphant, J. B., & Shearer, E. (2021, February 22). How Americans navigated the news in 2020: A tumultuous year in review. *Pew Research Center.* https://www.journalism.org/2021/02/22/misinformation-and-competing-views-of-reality-abounded-throughout-2020

Mola, R. (2020, March 17). It's not just you. Everybody is reading the news more because of coronavirus. *Vox.* https://www.vox.com/recode/2020/3/17/21182770/news-consumption-coronavirus-traffic-views

Nicholas, P. (2020, April 7). The real point of Trump's coronavirus press conferences. *The Atlantic.* https://www.theatlantic.com/politics/archive/2020/04/trump-coronavirus-bully-pulpit/609565/

Ong, J. C., & Lasco, G. (2020, February 4). The epidemic of racism in news coverage of the coronavirus and the public response. *The London School of Economics.* https://blogs.lse.ac.uk/medialse/2020/02/04/the-epidemic-of-racism-in-news-coverage-of-the-coronavirus-and-the-public-response/

Patel A., & Jernigan, D. B. (2020, February 7). Initial public health response and interim clinical guidance for the 2019 novel coronavirus outbreak — United States, December 31, 2019–February 4, 2020. *Morbidity and Mortality Weekly Report, 69*(5), 140–146. http://dx.doi.org/10.15585/mmwr.mm6905e1external icon.

Prior, M. (2002). Political knowledge after September 11. *PS: Political Science and Politics, 35*(3), 523–529. https://www.jstor.org/stable/1554681

Remarks at a White House Coronavirus Task Force press briefing. (2020a, March 20). *The American Presidency Project.* https://www.presidency .ucsb.edu/documents/remarks-white-house-coronavirus-task-force -press-briefing-6

Remarks at a White House Coronavirus Task Force Press Briefing. (2020b, March 31). *American Presidency Project.* https://www.presidency.ucsb.edu /documents/remarks-white-house-coronavirus-task-force-press-briefing-16

Remarks by President Trump after tour of the Centers for Disease Control and Prevention, Atlanta, GA. (2020, March 7). *The White House.* https://trumpwhitehouse.archives.gov/briefings-statements/remarks -president-trump-tour centers-disease-control-prevention-atlanta-ga/

Remarks by President Trump, Vice President Pence, and Members of the Coronavirus Task Force in Press Briefing. (2020a, March 23). *The White House.* https://trumpwhitehouse.archives.gov/briefings-statements/remarks -president-trump-vice-president-pence-members-coronavirus-task -force-press-briefing-9/

Remarks by President Trump, Vice President Pence, and Members of the Coronavirus Task Force in Press Briefing. (2020b, March 26). *The White House.* https://trumpwhitehouse.archives.gov/briefings-statements/remarks -president-trump-vice-president-pence-members-coronavirus-task -force-press-briefing-12/

Remarks by President Trump, Vice President Pence, and Members of the Coronavirus Task Force in Press Briefing. (2020c, March 27). *The White House.* https://trumpwhitehouse.archives.gov/briefings-statements/remarks -president-trump-vice-president-pence-members-coronavirus-task -force-press-briefing-13/

Remarks by President Trump, Vice President Pence, and Members of the Coronavirus Task Force in Press Briefing. (2020d, April 4). *The White House.* https://trumpwhitehouse.archives.gov/briefings-statements/remarks -president-trump-vice-president-pence-members-coronavirus-task -force-press-briefing-19/

Remarks by President Trump, Vice President Pence, and Members of the Coronavirus Task Force in Press Briefing. (2020e, April 5). *The White House.* https://trumpwhitehouse.archives.gov/briefings-statements/remarks -president-trump-vice-president-pence-members-coronavirus-task -force-press-briefing-20/

Remarks by President Trump, Vice President Pence, and Members of the Coronavirus Task Force in Press Briefing. (2020f, April 10). *The White House.* https://trumpwhitehouse.archives.gov/briefings-statements/remarks -president-trump-vice-president-pence-members-coronavirus-task -force-press-briefing-24/

Remarks by President Trump, Vice President Pence, and Members of the Coronavirus Task Force in Press Briefing. (2020g, April 13). *The White House.* https://trumpwhitehouse.archives.gov/briefings-statements/remarks

-president-trump-vice-president-pence-members-coronavirus-task
-force-press-briefing-25/

Roberts, A. (2020, March 22). First person in Utah dies from coronavirus, one day after testing positive. *KUTV*. https://kutv.com/news/coronavirus /first-person-in-utah-dies-from-coronavirus

Rogers, K., Jakes, L., & Swanson, A. (2020, March 18). Trump defends using "China Virus" label, ignoring growing criticism. *The New York Times*. https://www.nytimes.com/2020/03/18/us/politics/china-virus.html

Roose, K. & Rosenberg, M. (2020, April 2). How a "simple country doctor's" claims of a coronavirus cure made it all the way to Trump and turned him into a right-wing star. *Chicago Tribune*. https://www.chicagotribune.com/coronavirus /ct-nw-nyt-coronavirus-vladimir-zelenko-hydroxychloroquine-cure -20200402-s4rwdsfi5ncx7oyxoiwgmoml7y-story.html

Scacco, J. M. & Coe, K. (2021). *The ubiquitous presidency: Presidential communication and digital democracy in tumultuous times*. New York, NY: Oxford University Press.

Scacco, J. M., & Wiemer, E. C. (2019). Press conferences. In T. P. Vos, F. Hanusch, D. Dimitrakopoulou, M. Geertsema-Sligh & A. Sehl (Eds.), *The international encyclopedia of journalism studies*. Hoboken, NJ: Wiley. https://doi .org/10.1002/9781118841570.iejs0264

Shearer, E. (2020, July 2). Local news is playing an important role for Americans during COVID-19 outbreak. *Pew Research Center*. https://www .pewresearch.org/fact-tank/2020/07/02/local-news-is-playing-an -important-role-for-americans-during-covid-19-outbreak/

Soroya, S. H., Farooq, A., Mahmood, K., Isoaho, J., Zara, S. (2021). From information seeking to information avoidance: Understanding the health information behavior during a global health crisis. *Information Processing & Management, 58*(2), 1–16. https://doi.org/10.1016/j.ipm.2020.102440

Thorson, K. & Wells, C. (2016). Curated flows: A framework for mapping media exposure in the digital age. *Communication Theory, 26*, 309–328. https://doi .org/10.1111/comt.12087

Torres, E. & Mansell, W. (2020, April 12). US surpasses 20,000 coronavirus deaths, the highest national death toll. *ABC News*. https://abcnews .go.com/US/coronavirus-updates-michael-avenatti-granted-temporary -release-prison/story?id=70098434

Tracking U.S. covid-19 cases, deaths and other metrics by state. (n.d.). *The Washington Post*. https://www.washingtonpost.com/graphics/2020/national /coronavirus-us-cases-deaths/?itid=hp_pandemic%20test

Van Green, T. & Tyson, A. (2020, April 2). 5 facts about partisan reactions to COVID-19 in the U.S. *Pew Research Center*. https://www.pewresearch.org /fact-tank/2020/04/02/5-facts-about-partisan-reactions-to-covid-19-in -the-u-s/

World Health Organization. (2020, February). *Social stigma associated with COVID-19*. https://www.who.int/docs/default-source/coronaviruse/covid19 -stigma-guide.pdf

Yeung, J., Regan, H., Renton, A., Reynolds, E., & Alfonso III, F. (2020, March 19). March 19 coronavirus news. *CNN.* https://edition.cnn.com/world/live -news/coronavirus-outbreak-03-19-20-intl-hnk/h_21c623966aa148dbe ed242de4e94943e

Zimmer, C. (2020, April 8). Most New York coronavirus cases came from Europe, genomes show. *The New York Times.* https://www.nytimes.com /2020/04/08/science/new-york-coronavirus-cases-europe-genomes.html

Forced Online: The Promise and Challenge of Relational Organizing Technology in a 2020 State-Level Campaign

Ashley Muddiman and Cameron W. Piercy

In spring 2020, cities, schools, businesses, and colleges across the United States shut down to prevent the spread of COVID-19. Political campaigns faced the same choice. Should candidates campaign in person—knock on doors, hold rallies, and meet with voters face to face—but risk the health of their supporters? Or should they follow safety guidelines and stay at home but risk losing relationships with potential voters? Democratic presidential candidate Joe Biden ran a largely mediated campaign from his home in Delaware (much to the enjoyment of Republicans). Many down-ballot Democratic candidates followed his lead but consistently faced the question of whether "traditional" organizing methods might better connect with their voters.

Candidates who made the decision to run virtual campaigns faced substantial challenges. Down-ballot candidates, including those running for state legislature, often have districts that are too small to justify costly advertising buys. Instead, they rely heavily on personal contact with voters through house parties, door-to-door canvassing, and other in-person events.

The unique COVID-19 context of the 2020 election created an opportunity to ask: How can a down-ballot campaign build relationships with supporters and potential voters using digital technology?

Research findings are clear and well-known to experienced campaign managers: Relative to mass messages, personal contact generates significantly higher voter engagement (Gerber & Green, 2017). But building a relationship with supporters is challenging—especially when face-to-face contact is limited. Personal contact has taken on a new persona in recent years through a process called relational organizing. *Relational organizing* refers to deliberate relationship building "for the purpose of finding common ground for political action" (Warren, 1998, p. 87). Formally, we borrow the National Association for the Advancement of Colored People's (NAACP's) definition of relational organizing: "talking to people you know personally and persuading them to take an action on something" (Mbonu, 2020, para. 1). While this definition certainly includes door-to-door canvasing (Gerber & Green, 2017), it also increasingly means person-to-person mediated communication (Cormack, 2019).

Relational organizing has become a buzzword and practice in recent years in both politics (Cormack, 2019) and labor union organizing (Tapia, 2019). While the concept is not new, it is affected by the "nuances, mechanisms, and complexities" of new media platforms (Tsatsou, 2018, p. 2). Further, ubiquitous data encourage campaigns to continue to quantify voter engagement, but through the lens of peer-to-peer networking. Relational organizing is helpful (Gerber & Green, 2017), but the logic of building personal relationships in political campaigns also runs contrary to traditional organizing processes that often focus on numbers of interactions: doors knocked, calls made, or texts sent (Edelman, 2020). As Stromer-Galley (2014) demonstrates, digital communication technology offers a pretense of interactivity, while in reality providing political campaigns control over many of their supporters' behaviors and messages. The question is, can technology designed specifically for relational organizing generate interaction that is both meaningful and quantifiable?

The COVID-19 pandemic's disruption of typical campaign practices in 2020 offered the opportunity for campaigns to experiment with and adopt creative new digital technologies to build relationships with supporters and voters with whom the campaign could not interact in person. We joined a state-level Senate campaign in a midwestern state to investigate whether the opportunity to engage in relational organizing via technology was realized. Beyond exploring a campaign in the unprecedented pandemic election, our research also extends prior work on political campaigns by centering on a down-ballot, rather than presidential or congressional, election. First, we overview the campaign context and method of the study. Next, we present intersubjective examples from the data to illustrate the challenges and promises of relational organizing technology, as well as the campaign's data-driven approach to relationships. In all, our findings reveal a tension in the campaign between building and controlling relationships.

Campaign Context and Method

We were invited to join a state-level Senate race in a small midwestern state as the campaign transitioned to online canvassing. In April 2020, the candidate made the decision to run the campaign virtually and other than conducting some in-person literature drops and door-to-door canvassing very late in the campaign, conducted the entire campaign using digital tools ranging from Zoom, to text banking, to a relational organizing tool called Outreach Circle (ORC). The candidate ran as a Democrat in a historically Republican district. Although she ultimately lost the race, she improved the Democrats' percentage of the vote by more than 10% compared to the previous election cycle. To protect the privacy of the participants, we use pseudonyms throughout the chapter.

These data were collected as part of a larger project. We began attending, recording, and memoing meetings in May 2020. With human subjects approval and consent of participants, we engaged as participant-observers in weekly meetings from May 2020 until the conclusion of the campaign in November 2020. In all, one or both authors attended each of 27 weekly meetings. Across meetings, between 6 and 16 people attended. We only include as participants the attendees who completed the consent process, including the candidate (Julie), two paid staff members who developed campaign strategy (Tim and Chase), an unpaid campaign coordinator (Mary), and up to 12 volunteers. Each participant was in charge of such things as training supporters, running phone and text banks, posting to social media, purchasing digital advertising, and other tactical outreach to top supporters and potential voters. Because the candidate, paid staffers, and campaign coordinator spoke most frequently in the meetings, we often use direct quotations from these participants. Meetings lasted from 43 minutes to 1 hour and 51 minutes (M = 71 minutes, SD = 21 minutes). Our memos generated 22 single-spaced pages, and meeting transcripts, created by Zoom's automatic artificial intelligence, yielded 1,656 single-spaced pages. We also interviewed meeting participants, which informs how we see the context, but we do not report any verbatim interview findings here.

Data analysis was conducted by using a constant comparison approach (Lindlof & Taylor, 2011). This analytic approach is valuable because it allows us to incorporate both the verbatim meeting transcripts and our ethnographic observations to generate intersubjective understanding of the context. The goal of a constant comparative method is to progress logically through a series of coding steps in order to better understand a phenomena

(Charmaz, 2006). The constant comparative approach offers a systematic set of coding steps that we followed to inductively reason, verify the data, and repeat the process by "induction via ongoing data comparisons" (Heath & Cowley, 2004, p. 145).

This method allowed for analysis of meeting transcripts, dialogue exchanged among meeting attendees, and our memos about the process. Given the breadth of this corpus of data, for this chapter we focused on meeting interactions during two major technology adoption phases: (1) the adoption of ORC at the beginning of the campaign and (2) the adoption of ThruText as a mass messaging platform near the end of the campaign (especially in September and October). Initially, each author began coding in separate meetings. During this initial coding phase, we read through meetings and coded utterance by utterance to generate an understanding of our data. Next, we met to compare notes, consider overlap/agreements, and resolve disagreements. At this stage we also visited literature on online campaign processes and generated research questions. Then, the data were axially coded by systematically comparing each successive code to prior codes so that codes could be collapsed into major categories and ordered hierarchically as appropriate. Throughout this process, the authors regularly communicated and reconciled the dataset to reach agreement about our shared interpretations (Walker & Myrick, 2006).

As we coded, we incorporated two major literatures to help organize our coding process: McGregor's (2020) political campaign social media framework and Stromer-Galley's (2014) controlled interactivity. After interviewing U.S. presidential campaign professionals, McGregor (2020) proposed "a model for how campaigns use social media as public opinion" (p. 252). McGregor's framework emphasizes a two-dimensional approach. The first dimension is a focus on *qualitative* (i.e., "drawn from individuals' conversations"; p. 238) versus *quantitative* (i.e., data aggregated from online platforms). The second dimension, derived from Herbst (1993), is *instrumental* (campaigns' efforts to collect and understand data) and *symbolic* (campaigns' ability to present their view of information). In a state campaign, understanding (and at times influencing) public opinion is important, but little data is available about voters. Thus, we apply this framework to any data—from social media or from other sources—the campaign used to understand or influence voters. Second, Freelon (2017) summarizes controlled interactivity well: it is when a campaign "attempts to leverage citizens' online behavior toward the goal of electing the candidate" (p. 168). As with McGregor's framework, controlled interactivity has primarily been applied to federal or presidential campaigns. By applying these frameworks to the decisions made by a state-level campaign, we explore the extent to which a down-ballot campaign follows similar (or distinct) logics.

Findings

The Promise of Digital Relational Organizing

Decades of political campaign research suggest that a relational approach can be powerful (Gerber & Green, 2017), increasing turnout by as much as 8.3% in a large-scale study (Schein et al., 2021). This body of research suggests that campaigns should be able to take advantage of their supporters' social connections to increase votes in elections.

Several members of the campaign, especially the candidate and paid staff, also believed in the promise of relational organizing during a digital campaign. The campaign decided to use a platform called ORC, which describes itself as a relational organizing platform for web, iPhone, and Android that is designed to let "Friends reach out to Friends via email, text, or social media" (Peruri, 2020, para. 19). The platform was designed to allow campaigns to identify and recruit supporters who would use the platform to reach out to their own personal networks via their (phone) contact list.

Campaign decision makers offered the platform as a replacement to door-to-door canvassing early in the primary period of the campaign. For instance, in May 2020, the candidate explained:

> *Julie*: Right now I'd be spending four hours a day knocking on doors. And I can't do that. So, we've got to find some way to reach out to people and say, "Hey, will you introduce me to your neighbors?" And that's what ORC is. (May 13, 2020)

In her justification of relational organizing technology, the candidate emphasized the use of a person's network (here, by asking a hypothetical contact to introduce the candidate to the contact's neighbors) to build out the relationships made by the campaign.

Later in May and June, the campaign manager overviewed the goals of the campaign's digital outreach and offered a similar perspective. To him, the benefit of both canvassing and relational organizing technology was to help the campaign build connections and trust between campaign decision makers and the campaign's supporters:

> *Tim*: I believe canvassing works . . . it gives people a personal connection to the politics and the campaign that is otherwise difficult to create. So, when we connect with the voter, a lot of the time, the hardest part is getting them convinced that politics isn't meaningless to their life. And the good thing about ORC is it's going to connect us on a personal level with people who might otherwise feel disconnected . . . the fact that Julie is connected with our volunteers, which makes her credible, which means that they can effectively create a relationship of trust in a rapid

manner is still going to apply. We're just going to have to do it digitally, not at the door. (May 20, 2020)

A second level of trust between the campaign's supporters and those supporters' personal connections was crucial to the campaign manager as well:

> *Tim:* We're going to be doing something that's organic and something that is through trust channels that [the opposing candidate] can't access and the net result is going to be that people will believe that we need them. They'll understand that we need them in order to get this job done . . . it seems like a lot of work building trust, but the end result of it is going to be that we will be able to deliver our message better than [our opponent] can. (June 17, 2020)

Perhaps the campaign manager conveys the nature of relational organizing better than researchers have. He acknowledges that the trust between the supporters and those supporters' friends, family members, and acquaintances is stronger than any direct connection a candidate could make with voters in a short time period. And digital technology—in this case ORC—was perceived by campaign decision makers as a key component of relationship building.

The campaign team valued relational organizing and emphasized the importance of building a network of relationships that they could lean on during the general election. They discussed relationship building, connections, personal relationships, and trust and advocated for the use of ORC as a digital platform for building those relationships with supporters. The campaign believed so deeply in the value of relational organizing that from May through early September 2020, all onboarding efforts centered on getting volunteers to use ORC. However, as we detail next, the promise of digital relationship building was also met with significant challenges.

The Challenges of Digital Relational Organizing

While the campaign decision makers advocated for relational organizing technologies as the campaign moved to a digital approach, paid staffers and volunteer campaign members also voiced concerns with digital relational organizing. The challenges they faced were wide ranging. For instance, according to the candidate, the technology itself presented a hurdle to campaign supporters, especially those who were older. As Julie explained, "A lot of my followers are 50 and over. That's a challenge because they're not the most likely to adopt a new technology quickly" (May 13, 2020).

The technical issues were not fully addressed by regular, weekly trainings held throughout the campaign. According to campaign staffer Chase, after working an onboarding event, "if any of my people were a little on the older side and having problems, then it slowed down the whole group" (September 9, 2020). Even as Chase described a training that "went pretty well," he also mentioned that the attendees needed "individualized one-on-one with the breakout rooms"—which required the time of several campaign members—and faced problems "because, for some reason, people have a really hard time typing in the URL" to access the platform (June 3, 2020).

Beyond technical problems, members of the campaign viewed supporter privacy concerns as a major hurdle. When supporters joined the platform, ORC encouraged them to upload their phones' contact lists so that the platform could cross-reference those contacts with the Democratic Party's voter database and identify the contacts who had the same party affiliation and lived in the candidate's district. Although the personal contact information of those contacts was not shared with the campaign or the platform, members of the campaign viewed the request to upload contacts as a major hurdle:

> *Julie*: And then there's this other issue of sharing contacts, which people get really leery. . . . This has been the main reason that some of the Democrats in [the] county have not wanted to use this vehicle because they don't understand . . . they worry that we're asking our supporters to give up their contacts. This, to me, is a huge barrier. (May 13, 2020)

Supporter and voter burnout was also a concern throughout the campaign. Early in the primary period, Tim identified this potential problem: "We don't necessarily want to burn out our 10 strongest volunteers or rather burn out their contact list by pushing too much effort through those 10 people" (May 20, 2020). Relational organizing is difficult, and relying on a few very active supporters using the platform could overload those supporters' contacts. Later in the campaign, the candidate made a similar point, focusing on the campaign supporters: "I would like to remove people who don't wanna participate because I don't want to upset or burnout people who don't want to be doing this" (September 2, 2020).

Participation in online events waned as the campaign progressed. Everyone was tired. By October 2020, as the campaign entered the final push, the day before an event with a prominent health researcher and the state's lieutenant governor, only three people had signed up for an event—and two of the sign-ups were campaign volunteers. The candidate reflected: "People are just burnt—burnt out, they're tired" (October 7, 2020). So were the campaign volunteers and staff, as reflected in the following conversation:

> *Tim*: I think that there is a lot of exhaustion and cynicism and then there's also a lot of depression and mental health stuff going on. I literally am talking to people who are Democrats who are hardcore who are like, I'm thinking about moving to Central America...
>
> *Julie*: I know a lot of people like that. I'm telling you. (September 16, 2020)

At another point, the candidate said, "I'm giving all technology up when this is over. I am going off the grid." Andrew, a volunteer, replied, "I was looking at Airbnb in Colorado today for the week after the election. Yep." Julie: "Yeah, I'm ready to escape!" (September 23, 2020).

In October, technological fatigue had only grown. The team continued to push ORC onboarding. Chase explained, "If they are coming through your page on your website that says they want to volunteer . . . they're getting a message being asked if they'd like to be on ORC" (October 7, 2020). While some had signed up for ORC, few were actively using the platform:

> *Mary*: Nobody signed up for [the digital canvassing event] last night, and we have two in the morning.
>
> *Chase*: Julie, were you going to text everybody?
>
> *Julie*: I texted everybody on ORC. I got a few people that texted back and said "I, you know, I can't do anything right now I'm—I'm off on this project," or, you know, "I've got this commitment." So, I think people are now consumed with life. And so, it's a lot harder to get them to follow through. So, I think these last couple of weeks are really gonna fall to us to just push through it. (October 21, 2020)

Campaign members brainstormed solutions to get people engaged online, for instance, suggesting that the campaign include a message on ORC that addressed potential concerns, send a text with important information to supporters prior to training events, share step-by-step instructions for how to use ORC, and remove supporters from the relational organizing platform who were not active in sharing campaign messages. The challenges that emerged were significant and appeared in many conversations throughout the campaign.

Balancing Relational and Controlled Interactivity

In July 2020, the campaign began experimenting with a new use of ORC: "affinity texting." This practice used voter data from the party database to identify voters who were reasonably likely to support the candidate (via voter "propensity scores") and asked volunteers to text those voters through the relational organizing platform. This approach differed from ORC's main purpose, which was to help supporters reach out to people they individually knew, and the campaign faced major difficulties in using the platform this way (i.e., a limit of texting 200 people at a time on ORC [July 1, 2020]; supporters did not like using their own phone number and were at times blacklisted by cellular carriers [September 16, 2020]; and because these were personal messages from personal numbers, it was not possible to opt people out of texting if they requested it [September 16, 2020]). So, on September 9, 2020, the campaign began the adoption of a mass texting tool called Thru-Text designed for a few supporters to reach out to many potential voters who were not personal contacts. Although the campaign still used ORC, the focus on this tool was reduced during many campaign meetings. By September 23, 2020, Chase explained, "We're kind of replacing a portion of ORC with ThruText."

For the remainder of the campaign, many more messages were sent via ThruText. On October 21, after just over a month of active use, the group estimated they had sent 47,000 text messages. In contrast, in August, after three months of use, "250 [ORC] supporters ha[d] sent around 6,000 emails, texts, and app messages" (August 12, 2020). In terms of messaging, the team ultimately sent far fewer messages through the relational organizing platform than they did through mass texting campaigns, phone banking, and other means.

The decision to adopt ThruText was a significant turning point in the campaign's outreach for several reasons. First, ThruText gave the campaign more control over messaging compared to ORC. On October 14, 2020, campaign team members revisited a potential ORC task that involved supporters sending text messages to their personal connections asking whether those connections were "familiar with" the candidate. Campaign staffer Chase then explained, "in the Google Doc, I'll . . . [give] a couple potential responses that people might get so they can just copy and paste" a reply (October 14, 2020). ORC's technological design made it difficult for the campaign to provide these types of follow-up messages because the messages needed to be saved in a Google Doc file outside of ORC. Supporters had to click a link to find the instructions and then needed to sort through two types of messages based on whether a personal contact said they were or were not familiar with Julie. Yet despite these technical difficulties, the campaign still worked to control the messaging.

With the mass texting platform, campaign staffers were more easily able to input messages that volunteers could use as a first text and a series of possible second messages based on how text recipients responded. As Mary explained, in ThruText:

> There are suggested replies . . . just like setting up the initial text on ORC that the people send out. So, I think [we may] want to learn to do it. There are what are called "global" replies, like put in there an opt out or wrong number. And somebody can just click on a reply unlike ORC where you have to type out your reply to the person. (September 9, 2020)

Compared to the issues the campaign faced with their "affinity" texting approach via ORC, ThruText's bulk approach offered much more efficient, albeit controlled, messaging.

Second, the focus shifted from more individual, personal connections with ORC to mass, anonymous connections with ThruText. When asked how long it would take to send texts out to 10,000 people in the candidate's district, Mary, the campaign coordinator, explained, "Most [of] the time they can pick 100 at a time, it really only takes about five minutes to send them out. You just click, click, click, click, click." She admitted that it takes "a little bit more time" because the volunteers have to also respond to replies, but there are "not that many replies" (September 9, 2020). At the next week's meeting, she provided a review of the text bank they ran: "we sent 4,000 texts in two days and we couldn't have done that [with ORC]. And that was only I think six or seven volunteers at most" (September 16, 2020). Thus, the switch to ThruText allowed the campaign to reach large numbers of people very quickly with fewer volunteers.

After the adoption of ThruText, there was still some talk emphasizing the value of relational organizing. The candidate, for instance, argued, regarding getting people to use ORC, that maybe a personal message was needed, saying, "Click some buttons, show up for 30 minutes and we'll help you help us" (October 7, 2020). But as the examples earlier demonstrate, the relational and controlled dimensions were, in practice, often in tension.

Thus, whereas the campaign originally set out to use ORC as a replacement for door-to-door canvassing, it briefly became a tool for one-to-many communication through "affinity messaging" and was at times relegated to the background when the campaign shifted to get-out-the-vote efforts. The team even resumed door-to-door canvassing using lists of voters derived from the national database in mid-September 2020. Although the campaign members continued to espouse the value of relational organizing, they also recognized the significant burden and reduced control that came along with it.

Data-Driven Organizing Decisions

Digital technologies have long promised campaigns access to immense amounts of data and, at least in theory, more control over potential voters they reach. Howard (2006), for instance, argued that electoral and issue campaigns manage citizens based on the trace data they leave in digital settings. Work by Stromer-Galley (2014) and Kreiss (2012) also uncovered a growing reliance on sophisticated party voter databases, experimental A/B testing of messages, and other digital trace data. Baldwin-Philippi (2015) and McGregor (2020) find that some campaigns take a different approach by also encouraging their supporters to share campaign-generated messages on social media platforms. Thus, in addition to microtargeting specific people by parsing large amounts of data, these campaigns tried to increase their reach to anyone in their supporters' social networks. The campaign we followed used various data types to make decisions about their digital relational organizing as well.

Quantitative Data

Throughout the campaign, team members discussed digital relationship building in terms of data—especially quantitative data emphasizing metrics and reach. Even early in the campaign, decision makers discussed relational organizing through a quantitative lens. The candidate justified the use of ORC in part because it would let them reach a large number of people:

> *Julie*: It's a relational organizing platform that allows you to reach out to people who are your key influencers, and you send out a message and then they send the message out to their social network. And by extrapolation, you have the opportunity to reach lots and lots of people over time . . . I want to see big numbers. I want to see us reach 10,000 reaches, 10,000 people. By June 1. And if we're not going to get there maybe by June 15, but only if we figure out how to get people onboard and activated. (May 13, 2020)

The campaign manager made a similar case for ORC, explaining, "once we activate the people who are already supporting us, then it will [have] 10 times the reach of any campaign we do" (May 20, 2020). But by the end of the campaign, just over 300 supporters had signed up for ORC and far fewer had used the platform. The team persistently discussed the number of messages, number of supporters, and especially the number of likes or views as a form of quantitative reasoning. As explained earlier, ThruText allowed for a greater reach than ORC. Despite the campaign's hope that digital relational organizing would have exponential growth, the more controlled and less personal technology better met their quantitative goals.

Qualitative Data

Qualitative data informed the campaign's decisions about relational organizing as well, but, unlike in McGregor's (2020) study, the campaign relied less on qualitative messages and comments posted to social media and more on the qualitative opinions shared by volunteers/voters and the state party. On May 6, 2020, Cameron memoed: "I stuck around after the meeting to have a conversation with Julie, she told me she faced resistance from 'old-school Dems groups' that were generally resistant to change in the state. She shared many folks thought she was 'off track' and had 'lost her mind' because she was spending so much time on ORC." The views of the state and county party were coded in nearly all meetings.

As the campaign progressed, volunteer and party narratives persisted: Julie stated in the October 7, 2020, meeting that the state Democratic Party had advised the campaign to use bulk uploads of state data to target voters on social media. The state party also contracted with ThruText. In two consecutive September meetings, Julie opened the meeting by sharing how supporters' stories influenced her thinking. For instance, on September 9, Julie shared about contacting a long-time party supporter and asking if she was interested in canvassing in person. The volunteer replied: "Well, I'm glad to see you're taking this election seriously." Another story focused on an annoyed voter who called the candidate to complain that they were texting on a Jewish holiday—the conversation concluded with a back-and-forth about how he would not be voting for Julie. As with the quantitative data, the qualitative feedback uncovered challenges with the campaign's focus on digital outreach.

Symbolic and Instrumental Dynamics

The quantitative and qualitative data collected were used instrumentally by the campaign in the decision to back away from the original focus on digital relational organizing. Discussion of symbolic and instrumental data use also emerged together in debates about how the campaign should use voter and supporter outreach platforms. In the August 26, 2020, meeting, Julie asked the team if they should create a survey for supporters to send to their friends about relevant issues in late September or early October. Julie suggested they would link to the voter database by having an "activist code rather than starting a conversation to kinda measure what people are thinking." Mary replied, "Do you want this for personal reassurance or GOTV (get-out-the-vote)?" The answer was both—the campaign was struggling to know where they stood with voters. After some discussion, Tim concluded, "I think we need to inform more than we need to poll at this point." In McGregor's (2020) typology, the campaign acknowledged that instrumental data are good but also that symbolic actions were more logical for the team to pursue.

A similar conversation occurred when Tim argued that ORC, as a relational organizing platform, had a different role to play than mass texting: "ORC is a persuasion tool, ThruText is a turnout tool" (September 16, 2020). The implication is that people could use ORC to send text messages to friends or share campaign-created Facebook posts and change the minds of their personal connections, a symbolic approach. Alternatively, mass texting offered an instrumental approach—the campaign could target texts to likely supporters identified via the Democratic voter database (e.g., asking likely supporters about their voting plans).

Disagreements arose on how to use each platform, however. Mary, who set up and worked the text banks, provided the perspective that, while rare, potential voters who responded to the mass texts provided an opportunity to change minds:

> *Mary*: I actually think that ThruText can work some on persuasion. . . . I said, "Julie wants to be your Midwest State Senator and what's your top issue?" and we did get some interaction with people who did not know anything about Julie. And yet they will now vote for her, and they might have done it on their own, but they just hadn't done any research yet. (September 16, 2020)

Mary used qualitative responses from potential voters to argue that even mass texting offers a way to change public opinion through deeper relationship building. Thus, even as a state campaign with less data access than is typically available in a national campaign, the campaign used quantitative and qualitative data to make decisions and engaged in both symbolic and instrumental approaches to information.

Discussion and Conclusion

Overall, even during a pandemic-era campaign that required a down-ballot Democratic candidate to campaign virtually, the campaign faced pressures to return to tried-and-true methods of controlled interactivity. Although the campaign studied here clearly recognized the value of relational organizing practice, they struggled to stick with this approach when offered easy-to-use mass communication options and quantified scores regarding voters. This campaign was well funded, with more than $200,000 in cash contributions across the election cycle. Although they lost, the team was undeniably successful with a more than 10% increase in votes relative to their predecessor. The campaign team valued relational organizing, but they struggled to keep the campaign–constituent relationships relational as they proceeded through the campaign. We conclude our chapter discussing theoretical and practical implications.

Theoretical Contribution

Relational Organizing

Research suggests relational contact is a more powerful motivator than mass messaging (Gerber & Green, 2017). But when direct contact is coupled with technological tools to scale-up efforts, the results are complex. Although relational organizing is undeniably helpful to campaigns, it is not surprising that even a campaign highly committed to relational organizing might face pressure to engage in quantified forms of controlled interactivity.

Warren (1998) argued, "The relational strategy works best, then, when the institutional context of the organizing network allows for discussions among diverse communities and with participants at many different levels" (p. 87). But this campaign, like many (McGregor, 2020), relied heavily on quantitative and qualitative data from the Democratic Party, stories from party members, and feedback via already committed supporters. In reality, contact across political divides coupled with relational organizing practices seems unlikely, especially given the potential for burnout as the messaging gets repeatedly pushed to overlapping audiences through a relational tool. Add in the heavily mediated pandemic environment, and relational organizing technologies faced major challenges. Still, we point out the significant strides this campaign made in terms of fundraising and improving votes for a Democratic candidate in a Republican stronghold. In all, this evidence suggests that relational organizing can work—but also that it comes at a great cost relative to mass communication tools.

Controlled Interactivity

Freelon (2017) argues few studies "have systematically analyzed the substance of controlled interactivity to ascertain just how much control campaigns are able to exercise" (p. 170). We use an intersubjective analysis to reveal the tension for a down-ballot campaign, which was highly invested in relational organizing, forced to engage in controlled interactivity practices. Stromer-Galley's (2000, 2014) conclusion holds in our research: technological spaces "provide a façade of campaign and candidate interaction through media interaction" (p. 127). Our project adds to this line of research, finding that, for some supporters, maybe a façade is enough.

The difficulty supporters had getting on the relational organizing platform, staying on the relational organizing platform, and remaining motivated to have conversations with others speaks to the value of controlled interactivity. As Ashley memoed on September 9, 2020, in the campaign team's view, ThruText "is easier (user friendly, supporters don't have to use their own phone numbers, responses are programmed into the system)." In May, the campaign knew they would have to wait to roll out major asks of the volunteers—by October everyone was out of steam. Controlled interactivity may make life easier for volunteers (e.g., with auto-replies) and campaigns (e.g., simpler and more controlled interfaces). The key to leveraging ubiquitous evidence that relational organizing works may be finding a way to scale relational practices for the benefit of every party involved.

Practical Implications

In a team document from August 12, 2020, summarizing ORC successes and suggestions for improvement, the team noted that the first improvement was "keeping the action feed small" in ORC. The group learned early that there was a fine balance between not enough and too many posts on ORC. Volunteers and supporters grumbled too, so attending to issues of fatigue and burnout is important as campaigns consider digital relational organizing processes. Campaigns ought to balance relational techniques with easy-to-use technologies.

The findings paint a compelling picture: This campaign was dedicated to relational organizing values. The campaign also felt strong pressure to collect instrumental data, use and generate symbolic and qualitative evidence, and, especially, quantify when they could. This challenge may not be unique to the pandemic, as a *Wired* article on the 2016 campaign and relational organizing succinctly describes: "There was no way to get credit for having volunteers reach out to their personal networks. The existing campaign technology wasn't designed to take advantage of relationships" (Edelman, 2020, para. 4). Campaigns may be willing to take risks—but those running campaigns also want the security of what they know works. Implementing relational tactics is a challenge for campaigns and technologies.

Our conclusion is relational organizing can work (see Gerber & Green, 2017; Schein et al., 2021), but experimenting and succeeding with relational organizing requires commitment, investment, and substantial effort from the campaign and the campaign's supporters. Further, we suspect that campaigns will continually face a tension to turn to more tangible or quantifiable metrics for understanding voters (e.g., propensity scores, social media metrics). We do not consider this a fault of relational organizing software, like ORC. Instead, this is a challenge for campaigns to take on the difficult work of building relationships. Future campaigns will benefit from a strong commitment to relational organizing technology with a well-balanced approach to volunteers, staff, and voter fatigue and ability.

References

Baldwin-Philippi, J. (2015). *Using technology, building democracy: Digital campaigning and the construction of citizenship.* New York, NY: Oxford University Press.

Charmaz, K. (2006). *Constructing grounded theory: A practical guide through qualitative analysis.* Thousand Oaks, CA: SAGE Publishing.

Cormack, L. (2019). Leveraging peer-to-peer connections to increase voter participation in local elections. *Politics & Policy, 47,* 248–266. https://doi.org/10.1111/polp.12297

Edelman, G. (2020). The next campaign text you get may be from a friend. *Wired.com*. https://www.wired.com/story/relational-organizing-apps-2020-campaign/

Freelon, D. (2017). Campaigns in control: Analyzing controlled interactivity and message discipline on Facebook. *Journal of Information Technology & Politics, 14*(2), 168–181. https://doi.org/10.1080/19331681.2017.1309309

Gerber, A. S. & Green, D. P. (2017). Field experiments on voter mobilization: An overview of a burgeoning literature. In A. V. Banerjee & E. Duflo (Eds.), *Handbook of economic field experiments, Vol. 1*, (pp. 395–438). Amsterdam, NL: Elsevier. https://doi.org/10.1016/bs.hefe.2016.09.002

Heath, H. & Cowley, S. (2004). Developing a grounded theory approach: A comparison of Glaser and Strauss. *International Journal of Nursing Studies, 41*, 141–150. https://doi.org/10.1016/S0020-7489(03)00113-5

Herbst, S. (1993). *Numbered voices: How opinion polling has shaped American politics*. Chicago, IL: University of Chicago Press.

Howard, P. N. (2006). *New media campaigns and the managed citizen*. New York, NY: Cambridge University Press.

Kreiss, D. (2012). *Taking our country back: The crafting of networked politics from Howard Dean to Barack Obama*. New York, NY: Oxford University Press.

Lindlof, T. R. & Taylor, B. C. (2011). *Qualitative communication research methods*. Thousand Oaks, CA: SAGE Publishing.

Mbonu, V. (2020, March 2). How to be a relational organizer. *NAACP*. https://naacp.org/articles/how-be-relational-organizer

McGregor, S. C. (2020). "Taking the temperature of the room": How political campaigns use social media to understand and represent public opinion. *Public Opinion Quarterly, 84*(S1), 236–256. https://doi.org/10.1093/poq/nfaa012

Peruri, S. (2020, March 16). Organizing with social distance. *Outreach Circle*. https://blog.outreachcircle.com/2020/03/16/organizing-with-social-distance/

Schein, A., Vafa, K., Sridhar, D., Veitch, V., Quinn, J., Moffet, J., Blei, D. M., & Green, D. P. (2021). Assessing the effects of friend-to-friend texting on turnout in the 2018 US midterm elections. In J. Leskovec, M. Grobelnik, M. Najork, J. Tang, & L. Zia (Eds.) *WWW 21: Proceedings of the Web Conference 2021*, (pp. 2025–2036). Ljubljana, Slovenia: Association for Computing Machinery. https://doi.org/10.1145/3442381.3449800

Stromer-Galley, J. (2000). On-line interaction and why candidates avoid it. *Journal of Communication, 50*(4), 111–132. https://doi.org/10.1111/j.1460-2466.2000.tb02865.x

Stromer-Galley, J. (2014). *Presidential campaigning in the Internet age*. New York, NY: Oxford University Press.

Tapia, M. (2019). "Not fissures but moments of crises that can be overcome": Building a relational organizing culture in community organizations and trade unions. *Industrial Relations: A Journal of Economy and Society, 58*, 229–250. https://doi.org/10.1111/irel.12229

Tsatsou, P. (2018). Social media and informal organisation of citizen activism: Lessons from the use of Facebook in the Sunflower Movement. *Social Media + Society, 4*(1). https://doi.org/10.1177/2056305117751384

Walker, D. & Myrick, F. (2006). Grounded theory: An exploration of process and procedure. *Qualitative Health Research, 16*, 547–559. https://doi.org /10.1177/1049732305285972

Warren, M. R. (1998). Community building and political power: A community organizing approach to democratic renewal. *American Behavioral Scientist, 42*, 78–92. https://doi.org/10.1177/0002764298042001007

"The SPN Family Votes!": Celebrity Endorsements in Online Fan Communities

Ashley A. Hinck

During the run-up to voting on Super Tuesday on March 3, 2020, Misha Collins, one of the stars of the CW show *Supernatural* (2005–2020) endorsed Joe Biden for president. In a video posted to Twitter, Collins (2020a) said, "I believe Joe Biden is the candidate who has the best chances of beating Donald Trump. . . . Joe Biden is bringing to the table a legacy of success." At the end of his video, Collins invited *Supernatural* fans to discuss the candidates with him. A few months later, Biden won another *Supernatural* endorsement—this time from the main characters in *Supernatural,* Sam and Dean. Eric Kripke, *Supernatural* creator and writer, tweeted: "If you're in a Midwest state (I'm proudly from Toledo, Ohio) & a fan of #SPN [Supernatural], know this: I created Sam & Dean, so I know that they'd vote for @JoeBiden. For whatever that's worth" (2020).

These weren't passing one-off endorsements. Collins and Kripke returned to issues at the center of the 2020 presidential election over and over again. They hosted a phone banking livestream and a *Supernatural* watch party that called fans to make pledges to vote and a "get-out-the-vote" watch party. During these Zoom videoconferencing events, big-name Democrats like U.S. Senator Cory Booker and businessperson Andrew Yang—both of whom sought the Democratic nomination for president in 2020—joined

Supernatural stars like Felicia Day and Jared Padalecki for conversations about Midwest values, the COVID-19 pandemic, political polarization, economic stimulus, and more.

The scholarly literature on celebrity endorsements often imagines celebrity endorsements as taking place within a mass media context. Yet, today celebrity endorsements, like the ones that occurred in the *Supernatural* fandom, emerge almost entirely in a social media environment with significant implications for political communication. Networked media has resulted in fragmented audiences and personalized celebrities. In this chapter, I re-examine celebrity endorsements in an era of social media to show how fragmented audiences demand increased use of case studies to analyze niche audiences. I argue that personalizing popular culture celebrities transforms celebrities from a cultural elite to a friend and fellow citizen, while the personalization of political surrogates transforms surrogates from a political elite to a fellow fan. Ultimately, the personalization of politicians and popular culture celebrities makes fandom a significant location for political campaigning.

I make this argument by first turning to the literature on celebrity endorsements and audience fragmentation. I make the case that audience fragmentation requires political communication scholars to visit the audiences that campaigns visit—audiences like the *Supernatural* fandom. My analysis proceeds in two parts. First, I examine the personalization of popular culture celebrities. I argue that *Supernatural* celebrities used two different strategies for their celebrity endorsements: Kripke linked *Supernatural* fan values with Midwestern values and the values of the Biden–Harris campaign. Collins surrounded his endorsement of Biden with enactments of civic practices, imbuing them with cultural importance for *Supernatural* fans. Second, I examine the personalization of politicians. I argue that the speeches of Booker, Stacey Abrams, and MJ Hegar to the *Supernatural* fan community largely mirrored the celebrity endorsements made by *Supernatural*'s popular culture celebrities. The line between popular cultural celebrity and political elite is blurred when both adopt the same rhetorical strategies.

Celebrity Endorsements in Mass Media and Social Media

Political communication scholars have sought to explain celebrity endorsements of politicians by looking at the research on celebrity endorsements of products conducted by advertising and marketing researchers over the past 50 years. Advertising and marketing research has taken up four theoretical models to explain celebrity endorsements: the source credibility model, the source attractiveness model, the match-up hypothesis, and the cultural transfer model. Schimmelpfennig and Hunt (2020) argue that scholars must integrate these models into one overarching framework, positing that celebrity endorsements work when all elements in the four models are present: celebrities must be credible, attractive, and familiar; celebrity brands must match up with product brands; and celebrities must successfully transfer cultural meanings to an endorsed product. In a meta-analysis of advertising and marketing studies of celebrity endorsements, Knoll and Matthes (2017) found strong positive and negative effects for celebrity endorsements across a total of more than 10,000 participants.

Scholars have found similar support for celebrity endorsements of political candidates. Garthwaite and Moore (2013) advance what is perhaps some of the most convincing findings. They examine Oprah Winfrey's endorsement of Barack Obama during the Democratic Party's primaries leading up to the 2008 presidential election. Using her book club sales as a proxy for fandom, they estimate that Winfrey's endorsement earned Obama 1 million additional votes over Hillary Clinton. The effects of celebrity endorsements are strongest in primary elections, like the one Garthwaite and Moore studied, on low-salience policy issues (Atkinson & DeWitt, 2016; Veer et al., 2010) and with independent voters (Chou, 2014).

Other research has shown mixed results (Agina & Ekwevugbe, 2017; Brubaker, 2011; Friedrich & Nitsch, 2019). For example, Friedrich and Nitsch (2019) find "there is no conclusive evidence for celebrity endorsement effects in Europe" (p. 4888). One explanation for these mixed results is an assumption that most studies of celebrity endorsements of politicians take place within a mass media context. Studies focus on celebrity endorsements conveyed to a national audience through television and print advertisements and quotes from celebrities in newspapers and magazines. Further, they assume a celebrity–fan relationship that takes place in mass media: We read magazine feature articles about our favorite celebrities, tune in for an intimate interview with a reporter, and check out the latest paparazzi pictures (Turner, 2014). Yet the media environment in which today's endorsements take place includes social media. Chadwick (2013) calls this a hybrid media system and asks political communication scholars to examine how mass media and social media logics function together. Here, I aim to do that by considering how social media has caused two important changes in how celebrity endorsements work through (1) audience fragmentation and (2) personalization.

Social Media and Audience Fragmentation

Networked media like social media platforms have introduced significant media fragmentation. Media fragmentation, combined with the networking capabilities of the Internet, has led to the growth of fan communities in recent decades (Gray et al., 2007). The *Supernatural* fandom is a prime example of this shift. *Supernatural* was a fantasy television show that aired on the CW for 15 years. Not likely to be a mainstream, national hit like the popular sitcom *Friends*, *Supernatural* nevertheless managed to develop a deep, strong, and highly dedicated fan community. In an environment of audience fragmentation, fan communities are segmented and siloed but highly active, dedicated, and loyal.

Audience fragmentation has not only transformed popular culture fan audiences but also political communication audiences as well. Scacco and Coe (2021) argue that media fragmentation has helped to transform the rhetorical presidency into the ubiquitous presidency, in which a president's communication is everywhere—not a once-a-year speech to millions through mass media, but rather a daily communication achieved through targeted (often social) media. Rather than targeting national audiences through mass media in special-occasion speeches, celebrity endorsements target niche audiences through social media in frequent and ubiquitous ways. Media fragmentation has transformed the audience for both presidential candidates and celebrities.

Media fragmentation may mean that celebrity endorsements are less likely to be effective for national audiences through mass media and more likely to be effective for niche audiences through social media. In their study of celebrity endorsements, Friedrich and Nitsch (2019) suggest that "audience fragmentation might restrict the cultural significance of stars. Celebrities might nowadays share 'fundamental cultural orientations and values' (Choi et al., 2005, p. 86) only with specific fan communities, but not necessarily with a society at large" (p. 4890).

Media fragmentation might also help explain the strong third-person effect found in the celebrity endorsement literature. In this research, participants report that other people may vote for particular politicians because of a celebrity endorsement but state that they wouldn't stoop so low themselves (Agina & Ekwevugbe, 2017; Brubaker, 2011). For someone who isn't a Lady Gaga fan who trusts her and shares her values, it may be easy to ignore or dismiss her endorsement. This third-person effect emerges because celebrity endorsements are culturally devalued civic behaviors. Celebrity endorsements are often imagined as empty: celebrities don't speak from policy expertise (celebrities are good actors, musicians, etc., but not policy experts); celebrity endorsements don't rely on evidence (the celebrity discloses which politician they support without making an argument as to why); and fans are swayed by their own feelings about celebrities, rather than policy arguments (Hunting & Hinck, 2017). Such stigma might be highest when citizens don't feel a close connection to the particular celebrity used in research studies. Celebrities may be significant or persuasive only for members of those particular fan communities, rather than a broad national audience.

Social Media and the Personalization of Celebrities: Close, Intimate Friends

Social media has not only increased media fragmentation but also introduced the personalization of celebrities. Popular culture celebrities use social media to share personal aspects of their lives, giving fans a glimpse into the "backstage" (Marwick & boyd, 2011). On social media, fans can interact directly with celebrities, without an intervening interviewer or journalist, creating a sense of proximity or closeness (Bennett, 2014). The line between celebrity and friend is blurred as our social media feeds are filled with posts from both friends and celebrities (Baym, 2012). We read Beyonce's tweet right next to our best friend's. Put simply, celebrities are now personalized, transforming the relationship between celebrities and their fans.

This new celebrity–fan relationship affects how celebrity endorsements work by reducing the social distance between celebrity and fan. Researchers in advertising, marketing, and public relations have begun to study how influencers endorse and sell products across social media platforms like YouTube and Instagram. In a study of YouTube beauty vloggers, Rasmussen (2018) finds that the close relationship fans feel with a social media celebrity increases their willingness to buy an endorsed product. Rasmussen (2018) writes, "The interaction goes beyond product placement and branded entertainment; instead viewers socialize with YouTube celebrities who may also serve as product ambassadors. In a sense YouTube celebrities become friends sharing their opinion" (p. 281). On social media, celebrities are personalized as friends, transforming a celebrity endorsement into a friend's recommendation.

Methods and Texts

In this chapter, I attend to audience fragmentation and celebrity personalization by taking a case study approach. Rather than utilizing a national survey or experimental design in which participants might have a wide range of favorite celebrities, I focus on one fan community, overcoming the challenges identified by Friedrich and Nitsch (2019). Adopting a case study approach allows me to examine the particular kind of relationships celebrities build with their fans, the specific values a fan community holds, and the longer history of the fandom that serves as a foundation for effective endorsements. All of these affect the rhetorical resources at the disposal of celebrities and politicians addressing an audience of fans.

To understand celebrity endorsements in the *Supernatural* fandom, I archived the two tweets from Misha Collins and Eric Kripke that announced their endorsements of Joe Biden. I also downloaded and transcribed 14 YouTube videos uploaded by Collins to his YouTube channel between August 11, 2020, and December 15, 2020. These videos extended Collins's and Kripke's endorsements and featured conversations between Democratic candidates, Biden–Harris surrogates, and *Supernatural* cast members. The videos were originally livestreamed on Zoom and YouTube and later uploaded to You-Tube. Eleven of the archived videos occurred before the 2020 Election Day on November 3, 2020. Three videos occurred after Election Day on December 8, 2020, December 15, 2020, and December 16, 2020. I include these three videos in my analysis because they discussed the Georgia U.S. Senate run-off election featuring Democratic candidates Jon Ossoff and Raphael Warnock in races that originally took place on the November 3, 2020, ballot but which required additional run-off elections because the votes were so close. Many of these videos were a part of the official #TeamJoeTalks project, which recruited celebrities and influencers to host discussions with Biden campaign staff and surrogates on Facebook, Instagram, Zoom, and YouTube (Gardner, 2020; Jacobs, 2020; Nichols, 2020). Celebrities included actor Alyssa Milano, rapper Killer Mike, and *American Idol* runner-up Adam Lambert.

In many ways, *Supernatural* is a particularly rich case study to understand new possibilities for celebrity endorsements. Collins utilized official campaign channels through the #TeamJoeTalks project, making *Supernatural* celebrity endorsements and surrogate speeches an official, purposeful, and carefully orchestrated part of the Biden–Harris campaign. Additionally, the *Supernatural* fandom has a long history of political action, including activism around mental health, Black Lives Matter, and Internet privacy. The 2020 *Supernatural* celebrity endorsements took place in a fandom accustomed to organized political action.

Kripke's Endorsement and the Application of Fan Values to Civic Actions

The celebrity endorsements in the *Supernatural* fandom were enabled by both the fragmentation of media audiences and the personalization of celebrities. In this section, I argue that Kripke and Collins's celebrity endorsements of Biden utilize two different rhetorical strategies to build out civically rich and rhetorically substantive endorsements. Kripke made his endorsement through fan values developed in a deep, niche, and highly committed fandom enabled by media fragmentation. Collins relied on the personalization of his celebrity–fan relationship for his endorsement, framing and enacting a close, intimate friendship with his followers, even as he shifted from topics of popular culture to American politics.

Kripke anchored his endorsement in a value from *Supernatural*, transforming what was once a fan value into a civic value. Fans often work to extrapolate lessons, ethics, and values from their fan object. Of course, popular culture objects like television shows, books, and movies can have multiple interpretations—many different (and sometimes contradictory) values might emerge (Hinck, 2016). Fan communities function as interpretive communities, generating broad agreement on the best interpretations and most important values (Busse & Gray, 2011). Fan communities often draw on these fan values to ground their political activism (Bennett, 2012, 2014; Jones, 2012). For example, Harry Potter fans supported fair trade through a boycott because Harry Potter represented equality (Hinck, 2016). In the case of the *Supernatural* fandom, we see this rhetorical move taken up by celebrities during an election campaign. This is a significant departure from what celebrity endorsements sometimes look like: not simply an empty proclamation of who that celebrity may vote for, but rather an argument anchored in values from a fan community.

One of the primary values/ethics of the *Supernatural* fandom is family (Casper, 2014; Xanthoudakis, 2020). In *Supernatural*, the main characters, brothers Sam and Dean, lost their mother to a demon when they were young children and lost their father to demon hunting as young adults—these are losses they feel deeply and struggle with across the series. Sam and Dean make friends with fellow demon hunters. These friends come to function as a kind of surrogate family. Speaking to this kind of close relationship, Bobby Singer, a close friend of Sam and Dean's father, tells Sam and Dean that "family don't end with blood." Casper (2014) writes, "It's this unshakeable commitment to family, regardless of circumstance, that resonates with fans and creates the fandom's underlying personality" (p. 79).

Kripke's endorsement of Biden was grounded in the *Supernatural* fandom's value of family. In a tweet on October 22, 2020, Kripke asserted that the main characters of *Supernatural*, Sam and Dean, would vote for Biden. He wrote, "OK, look. If you're in a Midwest state (I'm proudly from Toledo, Ohio) & a fan of #SPN, know this: I created Sam & Dean, so I know that they'd vote for @JoeBiden. For whatever that's worth. #SPNFamily @jarpad @JensenAckles @realGpad #TheBoys" (Kripke, 2020). In one of Collins's Zoom calls with Barbara Bollier, a Democratic U.S. Senate candidate in Kansas, and Michelle de la Isla, a Democratic candidate for the U.S. House of Representatives in Kansas, Kripke expanded his argument for why Sam and Dean would vote for Biden. For Kripke, it comes down to what he repeatedly calls "Midwestern values." He defines Midwestern values this way:

> I'm a moderate guy but it's about family and it's about common sense. And being down to earth and treating people with respect and not intentionally trying to create divisiveness and drama and chaos, like it's embarrassing to me as a Midwesterner, that that, all that craziness. And you just like, no, you take care of your neighbor and you speak rationally and calmly. (Collins, 2020d)

Kripke then links the values of the Midwest, the values of Biden's campaign, and the values of Sam and Dean: "To me, that's what the Midwest signifies, and why I think what Joe signifies, I think what the ladies on this call are signifying, and I don't see that on the other side. So that is why to me, Sam and Dean would be, would be voting Democrat this, this election cycle" (Collins, 2020d).

Kripke's emphasis on Midwestern values and his own performance of a Midwestern identity helped target Midwestern swing states like Ohio, Michigan, and Wisconsin. But it also worked to connect *Supernatural* fan values to civic values already established in the Midwest. For Kripke, the Democratic Party is defined by family, care, and common sense—exactly the civic values at the heart of the Midwest and exactly the values at the heart of *Supernatural*. For fans who love *Supernatural*, Kripke presents a powerful argument: If you love Sam and Dean and believe in what they stand for (family), then you should vote for Biden. In his endorsements, Kripke transforms fan values into civic values, which then come to function as warrants for arguments about who to vote for in the 2020 presidential election.

Collins's Endorsement and the Enactment of Civic Practices

While Kripke anchored his endorsement of Biden in a key fan value, Collins utilized a different strategy. Collins's endorsement drew upon his personalization as a celebrity. His endorsement functioned not as an endorsement from a cultural elite, but rather as an endorsement from a fellow citizen. Alex Xanthoudakis (2020) argues that Collins has developed an intimate relationship with his fans. He has organized elaborate games and projects like GISH, the Greatest International Scavenger Hunt; shown his backstage life through social media posts like YouTube videos cooking with his kids and vulnerable aspects of his life such as his periodic childhood homelessness; and enacted the same kind of social support for fans that fans enact for each other.

In building that intimacy with *Supernatural* fans, Collins is enacting the fandom's value of "family." Fans have come to refer to the *Supernatural* fandom as family, shortened as the "SPN family." Early on, Jared Padalecki, the actor who plays Sam Winchester, called fans his "third family." He said, "I have my family, my on-set family, and then our '*Supernatural*' family" (Casper, 2014). Padalecki's definition of the fandom as a family resonated with fans, and fans and other *Supernatural* celebrities soon took up the phrase. Indeed, *Supernatural* fans are fiercely protective of their "*Supernatural* family," protecting each other in the same way Sam and Dean protect each other in the television series. The *Supernatural* celebrities (like Padalecki, Jensen Ackles, and Collins) are included as a part of that *Supernatural* family and can be as fiercely protective of that family as fans are.

This defines Collins and other *Supernatural* celebrities as close family members, rather than as distant strangers. This close, intimate relationship transforms Collins's endorsement of Biden. Instead of functioning as an endorsement of a distant celebrity who a fan might never meet, Collins's endorsement functions more like an endorsement from a close friend than a distant cultural elite. This aligns Collins's endorsement of Biden with the endorsements fans might receive from their other friends, other people they know well, respect, and trust.

Collins further built on this sense of "endorsement from a friend" by enacting civic practices that fellow citizens might enact together, including deliberation, phone banking, and information gathering. In the text of his tweet, Collins (2020a) framed his endorsement as an invitation to a conversation: "This is who I'm supporting. Who are you voting for? Text me at 'VOTING4' and let's have a civic conversation about it." Collins (2020a) emphasized this invitation again in the video uploaded as part of his tweet, saying, "I'm gonna share with you who I'm voting for, the candidate who I think is best positioned to beat Donald Trump, and I'd love to hear from you who you are voting for and why." At the end of the video, Collins (2020a) articulates the kind of conversations he hopes will emerge: "Please share with me your thoughts. I'd love to have a conversation—a CIVIL conversation, where we can actually share ideas and hopefully improve one another's understanding of the world and our place in it."

Many fans took up Collins's invitation by not only texting the phone number but also replying to his tweet publicly. A largely civil conversation emerged on Twitter, filled with some fans agreeing with Collins's choice of Biden, some fans expressing support for U.S. Senators Bernie Sanders and Elizabeth Warren instead, and others still deciding. Fans talked with each other, referencing issues, analyzing candidate characteristics, and debating the best political strategies for the primary. Collins's endorsement did not dupe fans into voting for a candidate—it enacted deliberation as a civic practice.

After his initial endorsement, Collins continued to enact civic practices along with *Supernatural* fans. In later videos, he enacted information gathering and phone banking. In October 2020, Collins organized a phone-banking effort targeting voters in Nevada (Collins, 2020c). Fourteen *Supernatural* cast members appeared via Zoom and made phone-banking calls alongside *Supernatural* fans. More than 1,500 fans logged in to Zoom to watch the phone-banking effort live. During the Zoom call, the *Supernatural* celebrities defined what phone banking was and talked about how to phone bank: The cast members asked each other and the Biden representative on the call questions like, "What do we do if someone doesn't answer?" The cast also fielded audience questions about how to phone bank posted in the Zoom chat. The *Supernatural* cast took turns unmuting themselves and sharing their phone-banking calls live on the Zoom video. Here, *Supernatural* celebrities were enacting the same kinds of civic practices that regular citizens enact.

Collins went on to record more than 10 other videos that featured conversations with Biden–Harris surrogates and other Democratic candidates. In these videos, Collins discussed major issues, like Medicaid, education, a universal basic income, and many others. In doing so, he modeled civil discussion and provided important political information to fans.

Enacting deliberation with celebrities or political elites would not have been possible if the celebrity endorsements had occurred via mass media. Scacco and Coe (2021) explain, "Traditional mass media forms primarily permitted a unidirectional flow of information, often from political elites to individuals. In contrast, digital and social media forms allow for a multidirectional flow of information and the establishment of possible feedback loops" (p. 15) Whereas two-directional conversation or deliberation was limited to citizen to citizen in an era of mass media, two-directional conversation and deliberation can now occur not only between citizens but also between citizens and political and cultural elites, who may feel like fellow citizens.

While Collins may function as a close friend or family member, he still carries significant power as a celebrity. Although some may worry that the power celebrities wield may lead to duping fans into voting a particular way, I argue that celebrities' power might better be understood as attributing value to particular practices. Collins's enactments of civic practices imbued these civic practices with value, importance, and prestige. While some Americans may believe their political opinions don't matter,[1] Collins told his fans that their opinions do matter—their political opinions matter deeply to him and should matter deeply to each other. Collins's enactment of these civic practices makes them valuable and important. Collins uses his celebrity to extend cultural value to practices that are often a difficult or boring part of our democracy. Ultimately, Collins's endorsement is anything but an empty call to vote for Biden. Rather, Collins engages fans as fellow citizens in civic practices.

Politicians Performing Fandom

Democratic politicians and Biden–Harris surrogates often appeared on these Zoom calls and YouTube videos alongside *Supernatural* celebrities. For example, actors Collins and Ackles appeared with politicians such as Yang and Booker. While celebrity endorsements and campaign surrogate speeches are often conceptualized as very different genres of communication, the communicative work going on in the *Supernatural* fandom during the 2020 presidential election demonstrates that these communication practices might be remarkably similar in a social media–inflected environment. The personalization of both politicians and popular culture celebrities means that celebrity endorsements and political surrogates may use the same rhetorical strategies to persuade fans. In the next section, I trace how surrogates for the

Biden–Harris campaign performed their *Supernatural* fandom and anchored their calls to action in fan values, connecting *Supernatural* to the 2020 presidential election.

Social Media and Personalization of Politicians: Politicians as Fans

Personalization has not only occurred among popular culture celebrities but also among politicians. Scacco and Coe (2021) argue that "presidents and other political figures in the mid- to late 20th century began to adopt a more interpersonally oriented style of communication" (p. 15). Presidents began to share the same kind of "behind the scenes" information and stories that Marwick and boyd (2011) find popular culture celebrities sharing. While Scacco and Coe point to examples like Bill Clinton on *The Arsenio Hall Show* and George W. Bush on *The Late Show with David Letterman*, I argue that popular culture fandom is another way in which politicians engage in the personalization demanded by the ubiquitous presidency. For example, Democratic presidential candidate Clinton performed his Elvis fandom during the 1992 presidential election (Marcus, 2004) and U.S. Senator Ted Cruz of Texas performed his Star Wars fandom during the Republican Party primaries ahead of the 2016 presidential election (Booth et al., 2018). In both cases, fandom performances aligned the candidate with voters who were also fans, inviting identification and framing the candidate as attractive to additional blocs of voters.

Such personalization opens up opportunities to make political arguments grounded in fan values and identity (like Kripke did). However, candidates have largely refrained from making these arguments themselves, leaving the arguments implied or relying on fans and political action committees (PACs) to make the arguments explicitly. During the 2008 presidential election, Nerds for Obama argued that fans ought to vote for Obama with t-shirts and buttons with phrases like, "Gryffindors for Obama" for Harry Potter fans and "Timelords for Obama" for Doctor Who fans (Hinck, 2016, 2019). The Obama campaign tacitly allowed Nerds for Obama to sell merchandise but didn't integrate the arguments or merchandise into their own campaign.

Similarly, in 2017 a PAC in Georgia argued that the *Star Wars* fandom of Jon Ossoff—then the Democratic candidate in a special election to represent Georgia in the U.S. House of Representatives—was a desirable characteristic and aligned Ossoff with Obi-Wan Kenobi as the "new hope" for the state's Sixth Congressional District (Booth et al., 2018). Ossoff played with the association, taking pictures with light sabers at a rally, but his campaign refrained from explicitly making the fan-based argument itself.

In the case of the endorsements in the *Supernatural* fandom, politicians made these fan-based arguments themselves. They engaged in deep personalization, revealing their own fandom, and explicitly integrating that fandom into their stump speeches. Rather than implicitly inviting fans to make those connections or leaving those arguments at the level of enthymeme, these politicians explicitly argued that their popular culture fandom demanded particular political actions.

Biden–Harris Political Surrogates Perform *Supernatural* Fandom

Surrogates from the Biden–Harris campaign performed their *Supernatural* fandom in deep and meaningful ways on Collins's Zoom calls and YouTube videos. In doing so, these politicians became *Supernatural* fans who endorsed Biden. These performances invited *Supernatural* fans to see themselves in the Democratic Party broadly and Biden–Harris supporters specifically. This is an extension of a common strategy politicians use—drawing on their biography to create identification between themselves and their audiences. While politicians often invoke characteristics like small-town origin, growing up middle or working class, business owner, etc., in this case, politicians invoke fandom as a recognizable and politically useful identity, seeking to connect with *Supernatural* fans in the same ways they might seek to connect with teachers, families, or business owners (Booth et al., 2018).

Democrats Booker, MJ Hegar, and Stacey Abrams showed their love of *Supernatural*, a key part of performing fandom. At the core of fandom is an affective tie to the fan object—a deeply felt love for the fan object (Abercrombie & Longhurst, 1998; Hills, 2002; Sandvoss, 2005). Fans often openly admit and show their love for and connection with fan objects, particularly along with other fans. In a video on October 8, 2020, U.S. Senator Booker showed his love for *Supernatural* clearly, "You [*Supernatural* writers and actors] have so enriched my life. I love, love this show" (Collins, 2020b). He goes on to praise the show: "I am honored tonight to be on with what is truly one of my greatest pleasures over the last 15 years, with folks who have shown the power of American creativity and artistry to inspire, to nourish, to sustain, occasionally scare, often make laugh. This show has been a great gift" (Collins, 2020b).

Hegar, a Democratic candidate running in Texas for the U.S. Senate in 2020, performed her fandom too. She described her love of the show using the term, "fangirl," a verb that describes the act of excited, passionate love for a show: "I cannot believe how lucky I am to be able to fangirl, my favorite cast and crew," she said. (Collins, 2020b). Voting rights activist Abrams, a Democrat who ran for governor of Georgia in 2018, also explicitly identified herself as "a fan for life" (Collins, 2020e).

These politicians not only demonstrated a love of *Supernatural*, but they also performed key fan practices, recognizable to the *Supernatural* fan audience. At the start of the "get-out-the-vote" event, Booker joked, "I thought this was for me to come on and give my list of grievances with the series

I've been dedicated to for 15 years" (Collins, 2020b). Many fans feel so passionately about their favorite shows that they also have strong opinions about what they would have changed themselves. Booker enacts this common fan practice, while emphasizing the length of his fandom (15 years). Abrams tells the audience about how she, like so many of them, also binge-watched *Supernatural*: "And over the next year I watched all, like binge watched 11 seasons because you were the thing I watched when I traveled, you were the way I found the respite when I was tired" (Collins, 2020e).

Hegar shows her deep fan knowledge in referencing the characters' back stories while talking about the ways the show mattered greatly to her for the past 15 years. She explains that she fell in love with the show when it debuted while she was in pilot training with the U.S. Air Force. When her helicopter was shot down by the Taliban in 2009, she tried to protect her crew on the ground, saying, "I'm channeling, I'm channeling the Winchester boys. We're going to get out of this just like y'all got out of every bind. Well, maybe not every bind. A couple of years, a couple, a couple of centuries in hell I'm sure didn't feel good, but I felt like I could overcome" (Collins, 2020b). Hegar says that *Supernatural* guided her in one of the most difficult and significant events of her life. She doesn't waffle, hide, or minimize her fandom—she admits fully the important role it played in her life. In performing their *Supernatural* fandom while endorsing Biden, the Biden political surrogates argue that *Supernatural* fans can see themselves in the Biden–Harris campaign.

Like Kripke, these campaign surrogates offered endorsements of Biden anchored in *Supernatural* fan values, utilizing the same rhetorical strategy and blurring the boundaries between celebrity endorsement and campaign surrogate speech. Both Hegar and Abrams anchor their political arguments in the *Supernatural* fan value of an "obligation to fight." Hegar, who had long been a fan of *Supernatural*, said she felt like Sam and Dean, a regular person who was working to protect people like her family, even against great odds:

> And y'all were, especially in those early seasons, taking on people with superpowers. And that's how I feel all the time that I am a regular Texan taking on some very powerful forces in DC and, and, very powerful, rich, wealthy, special interests. I am fighting for regular people, and I'm fighting for my family. I watched you guys fight for your family. (Collins, 2020b)

In *Supernatural*, Sam and Dean take on the worst demons and most powerful threats to humanity, despite being regular people themselves. They are part of a group of demon hunters, regular humans who share information about hidden threats like vampires, werewolves, ghosts, ghouls, and Lucifer. Sam and Dean find themselves obligated to protect others—how could they turn away knowing what they know? Hegar connects this explicitly to politics near the end of her speech, "And the future of our democracy is in the hands of regular people like the Winchester boys" (Collins, 2020b). Here, Hegar asserts that *Supernatural* offers values that are applicable to political action.

Both Hegar and Abrams argue that *Supernatural* shouldn't just guide their political actions and views. It should guide other *Supernatural* fans' political actions as well. Hegar specifically called on *Supernatural* fans to extend the show's story by participating in politics. In the fall of 2020, *Supernatural* was entering its 15th and final season, and fans were feeling sad about the show's impending end. Across fandoms, fans often look for ways to extend their favorite shows through practices like fanfiction (writing stories about their favorite characters and settings), conventions (face-to-face events featuring panels and activities with other fans), and cosplay (the creation of costumes). Hegar's call to action responds to that fannish impulse to extend the story. She said:

> So for those of you out there that feel the same way, that feel empowered by this show and feel like you don't want it to come to an end, it doesn't have to come to an end. Get into connection with that place in you, that this show has touched, that says you are powerful. You're a human being. You don't have superpowers, but you do have angels like Misha on your side.[2] You do have fate and destiny on your side, and you can do extraordinary things. (Collins, 2020b)

On his YouTube channel, Collins titled the recording of this Zoom video "Be Like Sam & Dean," reinforcing Hegar's explicit call to enact Sam and Dean's values from the fictional television show in the real life 2020 presidential campaign.

Abrams makes a similar argument during one of Collins's livestreamed YouTube videos ahead of the run-off elections for Georgia's two U.S. Senate seats in January 2021. The Zoom event raised more than $250,000 for Fair Fight, the voting rights organization founded by Abrams. During the event, Abrams argued that she felt the same obligation to fight to save the world that Sam and Dean did. She explained:

> But there's this moment where you two [Sam and Dean] are in baby [the car], and you're having this conversation about just how hard it is to live— the life you've been told to live but that you don't have a choice. You've got to do it anyway, because I think it was you, Jensen [Ackles], you were like, 'Who else is going to do it?" But it was this moment of "We've got to stick with this because there are monsters out there and no one else understands it. No one else believes it. And even, even if it's hard for us, we can't stop." I got into politics because I grew up poor in Mississippi, and I know there are monsters. And I know that when people have the chance to vote

and to pick leaders who see them, who understand them, that that's their best opportunity for success. (Collins, 2020e)

For *Supernatural* fans like Abrams, when you see bad things happening, you are obligated to fight back. Abrams says that is what she is doing in her work to ensure voting rights throughout the United States. This argument is reinforced visually by the title slide and preview image for the video. The image showed the three main characters of the show—Sam, Dean, and Cas— alongside Abrams. In doing so, the image positioned Abrams as a fourth hero of *Supernatural*, working with Sam, Dean, and Cas to save the world.

The endorsements that occurred within the *Supernatural* fan community blur the boundaries between celebrity endorsements and campaign surrogate speeches. Abrams's, Hegar's, and Booker's addresses to the *Supernatural* fan community on Zoom illustrate that fan communities function as key locations for presidential campaigning. The political communication strategies required for audiences of fans look much like the political communication strategies used during celebrity endorsements.

Conclusion

While celebrity endorsements are sometimes ignored or criticized as unimportant, silly, or unproductive civic actions, the case of *Supernatural* endorsements demonstrates that celebrity endorsements can be rhetorically rich and civically robust. In an era of media fragmentation and celebrity and politician personalization, celebrities and fans are playing an increasingly important role in political communication. During the 2020 presidential election, *Supernatural* celebrities endorsed Biden using two rhetorical strategies: Eric Kripke anchored his Biden–Harris endorsements in the fan value of "family," while Misha Collins enacted his endorsement alongside civic practices like deliberation and information gathering.

These celebrity endorsements took place alongside official surrogate speeches. The politicians largely adopted the same strategies *Supernatural* celebrities did, performing their own *Supernatural* fandom and grounding their civic arguments in fan values. The case of *Supernatural* endorsements illustrates both how celebrity endorsements might be productive for democracy and how the line between popular culture celebrity endorsement and campaign surrogate speech is blurring. *Supernatural* demonstrates that celebrity endorsements don't have to be empty proclamations, devoid of civic value. Rather, they can function as sites of civic practices and audience engagement. Indeed, *Supernatural* offers important lessons for any future campaigns willing to listen: Celebrity endorsements on mass media may not be enough to convince fans to vote for your candidate. Taking celebrity and social media seriously means engaging online audiences where they are—in fandoms.

Notes

1. The Pew Research Center (2018) found that more than 75% of Americans believe that the government is run for the benefit of a few big interests rather than for the benefit of all citizens. Only 52% of Americans believe ordinary citizens can affect government action.

2. Misha Collins is the actor who plays Castiel (known as Cas), an angel on *Supernatural*.

References

Abercrombie, N. & Longhurst, B. (1998). *Audiences: A sociological theory of performance and imagination*. Thousand Oaks, CA: SAGE Publishing.

Agina, A. & Ekwevugbe, A. (2017). Celebrity endorsement of political aspirants and its effects on college students in Lagos. *Journal of African Media Studies, 9*(3), 487–505. https://doi.org/10.1386/jams.9.3.487_1

Atkinson, M. D. & DeWitt, D. (2016). Celebrity political endorsements matter. *Celebrity Studies, 7*(1), 119–121. https://doi.org/10.1080/19392397.2016.1131014

Baym, N. (2012). Fans or friends?: Seeing social media audiences as musicians do. *Participations: Journal of Audience & Reception Studies, 9*(2), 286–316. https://www.participations.org/Volume%209/Issue%202/17%20Baym.pdf

Bennett, L. (2012). Fan activism for social mobilization: A critical review of the literature. *Transformative Works and Cultures, 10*. https://doi.org/10.3983/twc.2012.0346

Bennett, L. (2014). 'If we stick together we can do anything': Lady Gaga fandom, philanthropy and activism through social media. *Celebrity Studies, 5*(1–2), 138–152. https://doi.org/10.1080/19392397.2013.813778

Booth, P., Davisson, A., Hess, A., & Hinck, A. (2018). *Poaching politics: Online communication during the 2016 US presidential election*. New York, NY: Peter Lang.

Brubaker, J. (2011). It doesn't affect my vote: Third-person effects of celebrity endorsements on college voters in the 2004 and 2008 presidential elections. *American Communication Journal, 13*(2), 4–22. http://ac-journal.org/journal/pubs/2011/summer/brubaker_Proof.pdf

Busse, K. & Gray, J. (2011). Fan cultures and fan communities. In V. Nightingale (Ed.), *The handbook of media audiences* (pp. 425–553). Hoboken, NJ: Wiley-Blackwell.

Casper, M. F. (2014). Family don't end with blood: Building the Supernatural family. In L. S. Zubernis & K. Larsen (Eds.), *Fan phenomena: Supernatural* (pp. 77–87). Bristol, UK: Intellect.

Chadwick, A. (2013). *The hybrid media system: Politics and power*. New York, NY: Oxford University Press.

Choi, S. M., Lee, W-N, & Kim, H-J. (2005). Lessons from the rich and famous: A cross-cultural comparison of celebrity endorsement in advertising. *Journal of Advertising, 34*(2), 85–98. http://www.jstor.org/stable/4189299

Chou, H.-Y. (2014). Effects of endorser types in political endorsement advertising. *International Journal of Advertising, 33*(2), 391–414. https://doi.org /10.2501/IJA-33-2-391-414

Collins, M. [@mishacollins]. (2020a, March 3). *Today is Super Tuesday, I'm on the Supernatural set & it's super important that we all vote in the primaries. This is who I'm supporting.* [Tweet]. Twitter. https://twitter.com/mishacollins/status /1234938953922314241

Collins, M. (2020b, October 8). *#SPNVotes Watch Party* [Video]. YouTube. https:// www.youtube.com/watch?v=ZTGbFX-B-Cc

Collins, M. (2020c, October 29). *SPN Phone Banking!* [Video]. YouTube. https:// www.youtube.com/watch?v=MEnsZZAeILI

Collins, M. (2020d, November 2). *Be like Sam & Dean* [Video]. YouTube. https:// www.youtube.com/watch?v=dpPJT3JEAc8

Collins, M. (2020e, December 8). *Supernatural Fights On!* [Video]. YouTube. https://www.youtube.com/watch?v=3DppFG4S8RA&t=14s

Friedrich, K. & Nitsch, C. (2019). Celebrity political endorsement and young voters in Europe: A five-country comparison on celebrity support effectiveness in the European elections. *International Journal of Communication, 13,* 4874–4894. https://ijoc.org/index.php/ijoc/article/view /11100/2816

Gardner, A. (2020, April 14). A guide to all the celebrity endorsements for the 2020 presidential election. *Glamour.* https://www.glamour.com/gallery /celebrity-endorsements-2020-presidential-election

Garthwaite, C. & Moore, T. J. (2013). Can celebrity endorsements affect political outcomes? Evidence from the 2008 US Democratic presidential primary. *Journal of Law, Economics, and Organization, 29*(2), 355–384. https://doi.org /10.1093/jleo/ewr031

Gray, J., Sandvoss, C., & Harrington, C. L. (2007). Introduction: Why study fans? In J. Gray, C. Sandvoss, & C. L. Harrington (Eds.), *Fandom: Identities and communities in a mediated world* (pp. 1–18). New York, NY: New York University Press.

Hills, M. (2002). *Fan cultures.* New York, NY: Routledge.

Hinck, A. (2016). Ethical frameworks and ethical modalities: Theorizing communication and citizenship in a fluid world. *Communication Theory, 26*(1), 1–20. https://doi.org/10.1111/comt.12062

Hinck, A. (2019). *Politics for the love of fandom: Fan-based citizenship in a digital age.* Baton Rouge, LA: LSU Press.

Hunting, K. & Hinck, A. (2017). "I'll see you in Mystic Falls": Intimacy, feelings, and public issues in Ian Somerhalder's celebrity activism. *Critical Studies in Media Communication, 34*(5), 432–448. https://doi.org/10.1080/152950 36.2017.1348613

Jacobs, E. (2020, July 6). Joe Biden turning to Instagram Live, celebrity chats to engage voters. *New York Post*. https://nypost.com/2020/07/06/joe-biden-turning-to-instagram-live-for-help-engaging-voters/

Jones, B. (2012). Being of service: "X-Files" fans and social engagement. *Transformative Works and Cultures, 10*. https://doi.org/10.3983/twc.2012.0309

Knoll, J. & Matthes, J. (2017). The effectiveness of celebrity endorsements: A meta-analysis. *Journal of the Academy of Marketing Science, 45*(1), 55–75. https://doi.org/10.1007/s11747-016-0503-8

Kripke, E. [@therealKripke]. (2020, October 23). *Ok, look. If you're in a midwest state (I'm proudly from Toledo, Ohio) & a fan of #SPN, know this: I created Sam & Dean, so I know that they'd vote for @JoeBiden. For whatever that's worth. #SPNFamily @jarpad @JensenAckles @realGpad #TheBoys* [Tweet]. Twitter, https://twitter.com/therealKripke/status/1319477140140650497

Marcus, D. (2004). *Happy days and wonder years: The fifties and the sixties in contemporary cultural politics*. New Brunswick, NJ: Rutgers University Press.

Marwick, A., & boyd, d. (2011). To see and be seen: Celebrity practice on Twitter. *Convergence: The International Journal of Research into New Media Technologies, 17*(2), 139–158. https://doi.org/10.1177/1354856510394539

Nichols, H. (2020, July 6). Biden campaign using Instagram to mobilize celebrity supporters. *Axios*. https://www.axios.com/biden-campaign-instagram-celebrity-supporters-56d15c93-6ae4-434f-99e7-1c6c9e3397da.html

Pew Research Center. (2018, April 26). The public, the political system and American democracy. https://www.pewresearch.org/politics/2018/04/26/the-public-the-political-system-and-american-democracy/

Rasmussen, L. (2018). Parasocial interaction in the digital age: An examination of relationship building and the effectiveness of YouTube celebrities. *The Journal of Social Media in Society, 7*(1), 280–294. https://thejsms.org/index.php/JSMS/article/view/364

Sandvoss, C. (2005). *Fans: The mirror of consumption*. Hoboken, NJ: Wiley.

Scacco, J. M. & Coe, K. (2021). *The ubiquitous presidency: Presidential communication and digital democracy in tumultuous times*. New York, NY: Oxford University Press.

Schimmelpfennig, C. & Hunt, J. B. (2020). Fifty years of celebrity endorser research: Support for a comprehensive celebrity endorsement strategy framework. *Psychology & Marketing, 37*(3), 488–505. https://doi.org/10.1002/mar.21315

Turner, G. (2014). *Understanding celebrity* (2nd ed.). Thousand Oaks, CA: SAGE Publishing

Veer, E., Becirovic, I., & Martin, B. A. S. (2010). If Kate voted Conservative, would you?: The role of celebrity endorsements in political party advertising. *European Journal of Marketing, 44*(3/4), 436–450. https://doi.org/10.1108/03090561011020516

Xanthoudakis, A. (2020). Mobilizing minions: Fan activism efficacy of Misha Collins fans in Supernatural fandom. *Transformative Works and Cultures, 32*. https://doi.org/10.3983/twc.2020.1827

CHAPTER TEN

Hope and Fear in a Pandemic: Videostyle in 2020 Presidential Advertising

Kelly L. Winfrey

If one were to watch all the federal political ads aired each time they aired in Phoenix, Arizona, it would take more than two months. That is more than 60 days, 24 hours a day, of advertising. The Phoenix media market had the greatest number of federal ad airings of any media market, but advertising was greater in 2020 across the board (Ridout et al., 2021). Advertising was perhaps more important in 2020 than any election in recent history. The coronavirus pandemic limited in-person campaigning, particularly from Democrats, and increased the importance of advertising to reach voters. The presidential race was expected to be close, and the fate of both chambers of Congress was at stake. Presidential ad airings more than doubled in 2020 compared to 2016, with 2.35 million airings during the full election cycle and 804,000 airings from September 1 to Election Day (Ridout et al., 2021). These numbers reflect an increase in both candidate-sponsored ads and ads from outside groups with more than $1.7 billion spent. The increase in advertising occurred down-ballot as well with U.S. House and Senate candidates airing ads and spending more on advertising than the previous three election cycles.

There is no doubt that candidates and outside groups saw advertising as essential in 2020. It was a unique election cycle for multiple reasons, and this chapter examines how the presidential candidates, Donald Trump and Joe Biden, navigated this unique cycle through their television advertising. The deep divisions in the country, a pandemic and its ripples, and renewed protests for racial justice in the wake of another murder of a Black person by police set the stage for a campaign unlike any other. Biden's selection of Kamala Harris as his running mate—the first Black and first South Asian woman vice presidential candidate—created another unique variable in 2020. By examining the advertising created by each campaign, one can better understand the strategic decisions and priorities of each candidate. This chapter analyzes the videostyle of candidate-sponsored television ads to better understand the messaging of the Biden and Trump campaigns and provide insights into the outcome of the election, as well as the varied opinions of American voters.

The Effects of Political Advertising

While many voters will say they dislike political ads, research has demonstrated that they can be effective. Advertising can reach potential voters that debates, speeches, and even news media coverage may not because it finds them where they already are—be it during local news or an episode of *Grey's Anatomy* (Benoit, 2016). Political ads can increase knowledge of candidates and issues, so even the least-informed voter has access to basic information about the candidates and where they stand on key issues (Kaid et al., 2007; Valentino et al., 2004). In fact, negative ads, perhaps the most disliked type, have been found to increase attention, increase knowledge on issues, decrease favorability of the focus of the attack, and have a positive effect on turnout (Freedman & Goldstein, 1999; Pinkleton, 1997).

Furthermore, political advertising can influence vote choices and election outcomes (Atkin & Heald, 1976; Gordon & Hartmann, 2012; Huber & Arceneaux, 2007; Kahn & Geer, 1994; Kaid, 1997; Kaid et al., 1992; Kaid et al., 2011; Tedesco, 2002; Tedesco & Kaid, 2003; Valentino et al., 2004). For example, one field experiment during Rick Perry's campaign for Texas governor found as much as a 6-point increase from television advertising (Gerber et al., 2011). Other studies have estimated a smaller yet significant advantage in vote share based on ad advantage (Franz & Ridout, 2010; Spenkuch & Toniatti, 2018). For example, Ridout et al. (2021) estimate that Biden's ad advantage in the Philadelphia media market could have gained him 3.1 to 6.2 percentage points, a significant difference given the close finish in Pennsylvania.

Modern political advertising, across a variety of channels and devices, also offers the ability to target messages to specific voters based on location and identity, among other factors. For example, Ridout et al. (2012) found Democratic and Republican presidential candidates in 2000, 2004, and 2008 advertised across different types of programs in efforts to reach specific voters. Democratic candidates tended to target women and Spanish-language programing with ads during telenovelas, daytime dramas, and daytime talk shows. George W. Bush aired more advertising during live sports, and John McCain attempted to appeal to moderate and Democratic-leaning audiences during daytime talk shows and game shows.

Location is also an important element in presidential advertising strategy. In 2020, advertising was higher in battleground states like Florida, Pennsylvania, and Wisconsin (Ridout et al., 2021). Candidate and group-sponsored presidential advertising skewed to Biden's advantage. That advantage was greatest in the "blue wall" of Wisconsin, Michigan, and Pennsylvania, which Democratic presidential candidate Hillary Clinton lost in 2016. Biden also had a significant advantage in Florida, Arizona, and Nevada (Ridout et al., 2021). The decision to advertise heavily in these areas is noteworthy because these states were essential to Biden's victory and won by slim margins. In addition to the standard use of traditional television (e.g., broadcast, cable, satellite), 2020 saw a significant amount of money poured into digital advertising—which constituted about 24% of ad spending related to the presidential race. With the ability to macrotarget ads to audiences watching specific programs, in specific locations, on traditional TV or streaming services, candidates can create advertising content aimed at persuading key voting groups.

However, simply creating and airing ads does not garner an advantage. The content of the ads must persuade voters to support (or not support) a candidate. One of the advantages of studying advertisements is that they often encapsulate a campaign's major themes in 30 to 60 seconds. Ads require campaigns to distill complicated issues and to shape a candidate's image in a short amount of time. The content of political advertisements reflects the larger strategy of campaigns and reveals its priorities and goals.

Videostyle: Understanding Advertising Content

Videostyle was developed by Kaid and Davidson (1986) as a theoretical lens and method for understanding the content of television political advertisements. This approach examines common elements of political communication—such as types of appeals and issues and image characteristics emphasized—but also allows for an examination of how these elements are communicated through the specific medium of television. Citing research by Norton and Brenders (1996), Kaid and Johnston (2001) argued, "Presentation of style is very important because it reveals something more than the content of the message; it reveals the context that one should use to interpret the content" (p. 27). Videostyle examines three primary components of political advertisements—verbal, nonverbal, and production elements.

Verbal Components

The verbal elements of videostyle include the issues and image qualities mentioned, whether the ad is positive or negative, the types of appeals
made, and the strategies used. In the most extensive study of videostyle in
presidential campaign advertising, Kaid and Johnston (2001) examined ads
sponsored by general election presidential candidates from 1952 to 1996,
and Johnston and Kaid (2002) expanded this to include the 2000 election.
Their studies found that more than 60% of ads had a positive focus, and
negative ads emphasized issues more often than image. However, negative
ads consisted of a much greater proportion of ads in the 1990s than in earlier
elections (Kaid, 2004). Later research found positive ads were more prevalent in 2004 (Kaid & Dimitrova, 2005), but that changed again in 2008.
Both McCain and Barack Obama in 2008 had more negative ads, with about
three-quarters being attack ads, but the two candidates used different attack
strategies, with McCain making more character attacks and Obama making
more attacks on group affiliations (Kaid, 2009).

Negative advertising was a defining characteristic of the 2012 presidential
election, constituting 64% of ads from all sponsors and 54% of candidate-
sponsored ads (Franklin Fowler & Ridout, 2013). The 2016 presidential election was slightly less negative than 2012, but about half of both Clinton's and
Trump's ads made an attack. The primary difference was that Trump ran
more contrast spots that attacked Clinton while also making positive statements about Trump; Clinton ran more straight negative ads (Franklin Fowler
et al., 2017).

Despite the rising negativity in presidential advertising, studies have consistently found issues to be the dominant focus of ads rather than image
qualities, but most ads contain some mention of both issues and image
(Airne & Benoit, 2005; Kaid, 2004; Kaid, 2009; Kaid & Dimitrova, 2005;
Kaid & Johnston, 2001). The ratio of issue and image focus has also varied
across elections and between candidates. For example, in 2008, McCain and
Obama both ran more positive than negative ads, but overall, their advertising was more negative than the 2004 candidates. Additionally, McCain's ads
were relatively evenly split between issue and image, with slightly more issue
ads, but 60% of Obama's ads made issues the dominant focus (Kaid, 2009).
Issue-dominant ads also vary in content, with most articulating the candidates' general concerns rather than policy preferences or proposals (Kaid &
Johnston, 2001).

Another variable in verbal content is the type of appeal made. Drawing
from Aristotle's three forms of proof—logos, pathos, and ethos—videostyle
analysis has examined the frequency of logical, emotional, and ethical or
credibility appeals. Interestingly, it is not logical appeals that dominate either
issue or image ads. Emotional appeals are the most common overall, are most

often the dominant type of appeal, and are most common in issue-focused ads specifically (Kaid & Johnston, 2001). For example, Obama's 2008 ads, which were about 60% issue focused, relied mostly on emotional appeals. McCain's ads, which were more image based, relied most heavily on ethical or credibility appeals—often using endorsements from other political figures (Kaid, 2009). Additionally, fear appeals have been commonly used through presidential advertising history, with peaks in 1964, 1992, and 1996 (Kaid & Johnston, 2001), with Lyndon Johnson's 1964 "Daisy Girl" ad being a well-known example.

How candidates present themselves and the issues they prioritize make up additional components of verbal videostyle. Candidates from 1952 to 1996 most frequently emphasized traits of aggression and competence but did not often express warmth and compassion (Kaid & Johnston, 2001). The exceptions were Jimmy Carter, who emphasized warmth and compassion in 21% of his ads in 1980, and Bill Clinton with 44% in 1996. Kaid and Johnston (2001) note that Clinton had a more balanced strategy of emphasizing strength, aggression, and compassion in about equal frequency. It is relatively common today for ads to portray candidates as honest and trustworthy, but it has been a relatively recent phenomenon. Prior to the 1990s, no candidate mentioned this trait in more than 15% of their ads. But in 1996, Clinton emphasized these traits in 21% of his ads and Robert Dole in 30% of his (Kaid & Johnston, 2001). In Obama's 2008 ads, honesty was the second most frequently mentioned trait (following competence), but it did not make the top three for McCain, who focused more on competence, qualifications, and strength (Kaid, 2009).

The traits presidential candidates emphasize are directly related to what voters are seeking. Numerous studies have found voters seek presidential candidates who demonstrate stereotypically masculine traits like being a strong leader, action oriented, and assertive (Dolan, 2005; Godbole et al., 2019; Huddy & Terkildsen, 1993). Additionally, the increase in presidential candidates highlighting honesty and compassion likely relates to the fact that voters find those qualities to be important (Trent et al., 2010; Winfrey, 2018).

The issues emphasized by presidential candidates in their advertising have been both consistent and election specific. Kaid and Johnston (2001) found that economic issues, taxes, international affairs, and military spending have been common topics since the beginning of political television advertising, but other issues like crime, education, and senior citizens' issues have varied based on the electoral context. For example, in 2004, post 9/11 and during the wars in Iraq and Afghanistan, Bush's ads focused on national security and defense. These are not uncommon historically but were certainly context specific in that election. John Kerry, however, focused on the economy and healthcare (Kaid & Dimitrova, 2005). In 2008, as the Great Recession hit under a second-term Republican president, both candidates emphasized the economy and taxes, but Obama, a Democrat, mentioned the economy more than McCain. McCain, a Republican with strong national security and military credentials, mentioned terrorism more (Kaid, 2009).

The rhetorical strategies employed in ads constitute another component of videostyle. Trent and Friedenberg (1995) identified several strategies they categorized as incumbent and challenger. Incumbent strategies include using the office and their incumbency to establish legitimacy, emphasizing accomplishments, using endorsements, having surrogates speak, and taking an "above the trenches" position. Challenger strategies include calling for change, taking the offensive position on issues, attacking the record of the opponent, speaking to traditional values, representing the philosophical center of the party, and emphasizing hope for the future. Overall, incumbent strategies are more often used by incumbents and challenger strategies by challengers, but many are used by both to some degree. For example, incumbents often speak to traditional values, emphasize hope, and attack opponents. Challengers also commonly use the office they hold (other than the presidency) to establish their competence, depend on surrogates, and emphasize accomplishments (Kaid & Johnston, 2001).

Johnston and Kaid (2002) also found that image-focused ads often used the strategies promoting competency and using surrogates, while issue ads more often called for change, took the offense on issues, and attacked opponents' records. Bystrom et al. (2004) also analyzed videostyle with a gender focus and, based on the rhetorical work of Campbell (1989), identified some additional strategies categorized as masculine and feminine based on their relationship to traditional gender stereotypes and expectations. Masculine strategies include the use of statistics and expert authorities to support positions. Feminine strategies include using a personal tone, addressing viewers as peers, using personal experience to support positions, and identifying with the experience of others. Feminine strategies are particularly useful when trying to connect with voters through the medium of television.

Nonverbal Components

The nonverbal elements of videostyle include visuals and sounds, give context to the verbal content, and shape how the message is interpreted. Nonverbals can also convey meaning not explicitly stated verbally, such as showing a candidate with specific constituents or using music to evoke emotion. The nonverbal components include aspects of the performance like the people pictured, clothing, body movement, eye contact, and setting (Kaid & Davidson, 1986; Kaid & Johnston, 2001).

Candidates appeared in about 60% of the ads studied by Kaid and Johnston (2001), with other ads featuring a mix of supporters, surrogates, and opponents. The dominant speaker in presidential ads was most frequently an anonymous announcer (40%) followed by the candidate (37%). Candidates spoke for themselves most frequently in image ads (Johnston & Kaid, 2002). However, the frequency of ads featuring the candidate as the dominant speaker has decreased over time (Kaid & Johnston, 2001). For example, the 2008 cycle featured an anonymous announcer in a large majority of ads (Kaid, 2009). The increase in ads using an anonymous announcer corresponds to an increase in ads that attack an opponent; an anonymous speaker distances the sponsoring candidate from the attack.

Additionally, candidates need to appear professional yet likable. In doing this, candidates make eye contact with the viewer (camera) in nearly half of the ads, use a moderate amount of body movement, often have a serious or attentive facial expression, and usually appear formally dressed and in formal settings (Johnston & Kaid, 2002; Kaid & Johnston, 2001).

Production Components

The production elements are unique to mediated communication like television ads and, more recently, Internet ads. Like nonverbals, production elements also provide context and create meaning (Kaid & Johnston, 2001). They include format, production styles, camera angles, lighting, sound, and use of special effects. These elements can create emotions, link ideas, distort images or ideas, and shape viewers' interpretation.

In their analysis of presidential advertisements from 1952 to 2000 Kaid and Johnston (2001) found the most common formats were introspective, where a candidate reflects on a concern, and opposition-focused ads, which include negative and comparative spots. Additionally, cinema verité, candidate head-on, and voice-over with slides were the most frequently used production styles. Johnston and Kaid (2002) examined differences between image- and issue-focused spots and found image ads tended to use a testimonial format and used a person other than the candidate speaking directly to the camera. Issue ads tended to be more introspection and opposition focused and use cinema verité and candidate head-on styles. For example, in 2008, Obama used the introspective style more than McCain, and more of his ads were issue focused (Kaid, 2009). Special effects like computer graphics, superimposition, and slow and fast motion are also commonly used in presidential spots (Johnston & Kaid, 2002; Kaid, 2009; Kaid et al., 1992; Kaid & Johnston, 2001).

Videostyle provides a framework for examining the content and strategic choices in political advertising. The coronavirus pandemic increased the reliance on political advertising in the 2020 election, which is reflected in the number of ads aired and dollars spent. The close outcome, complete with recounts and protests, warrant investigation into the messages communicated to voters. The close outcome in several key states coupled with research showing advertising can influence vote choice suggest that TV ads may have swung the election in Biden's favor. To examine the strategy of each candidate, two guiding questions are explored:

- What was the videostyle of Biden and Trump in the 2020 election?
- How were the videostyles of Biden and Trump different and similar?

Method

This study examined the videostyle of candidate-sponsored advertisements for Biden and Trump during the 2020 general election. All advertisements were collected from the candidates' official YouTube pages. The YouTube pages of both candidates contained hundreds of videos, but only videos that were labeled as an advertisement, conformed to the typical length (e.g., 15 seconds, 30 seconds, 1 minute) or included a candidate approval statement were included in the sample. A total of 253 ads were downloaded: 177 from Biden and 76 from Trump. Given the limitations of coders, the set was then narrowed to include only English-language ads, leaving a total of 218.

Ads were coded for their verbal, nonverbal, and production elements as outlined earlier and in previous research (e.g. Bystrom et al., 2004; Kaid & Johnston, 2001). Three independent coders were trained using presidential advertisements from previous election cycles. Coders then independently coded a random sample of the study's ad set (10%, $n = 23$). Intercoder reliability was calculated using Holsti's formula (North et al., 1963) across all categories and was strong at 0.96. Intercoder reliability was also calculated across each category: verbal = 0.96, nonverbal = 0.96, and production = 0.90. Significant differences between the candidates' use of each videostyle variable was tested using chi-square analysis with significance established at $p \leq 0.05$.

Results

Verbal Elements

Consistent with prior research on presidential advertising (e.g., Kaid & Johnston, 2001; Kaid, 2009), a majority of ads from both candidates were issue focused, with 63.7% of Biden's ads and 56.9% of Trump's focusing primarily on issues. Emotional appeals were again the dominant type of appeal used by both candidates, although Biden used them in 96.3% of his ads and Trump in 83.1%, a statistically significant difference. Trump used logical appeals more often than Biden, 42.4% to 11%. Biden (19.9%) used more source credibility appeals than Trump (5.1%). Trump (29.3%) also used fear appeals significantly more often than Biden (11.9%). Biden's ads were significantly more positive than Trump's. Biden's ads had a positive focus 62.2% of the time, and Trump had a negative focus in 81.4% of his ads. Additionally, significantly more of Trump's (59.3%) than Biden's (12.7%) ads ended with a negative statement. Significantly more of Trump's (89.3%) than Biden's (51.9%) ads made an attack.

Of the ads that made an attack, both candidates relied most heavily on direct attacks against their opponent. Trump's attack ads used this strategy 98.1% of the time and Biden in 94.3%. However, Trump also made direct attacks against other politicians (15.1%) and direct attacks against the opposing party (11.3%) significantly more often than Biden (whose ads attacked another politician 1.4% and the other party 0%). Both candidates most frequently made attacks on issue stands, but Trump's ads more often attacked Biden's group affiliations; 43.4% of Trump's ads and 2.9% of Biden's ads used this strategy. Biden attacked Trump's past performance in 28.6% of his attack ads, and Trump did this in only 11.3% of his ads.

Both candidates most frequently used the strategy of associating the opponent with undesirable actions, but Biden (91.4%) used it significantly more often than Trump (79.2%). Trump also used a guilt-by-association strategy in 39.6% of his ads, and Biden used this in only 1.4%, a significant difference. The last significant difference related to attacks is who made the attack. As is common in attack ads, an anonymous announcer made the attack in 83% of Trump's ads, and 21.4% of Biden's. However, Biden's ads differed by featuring a voter or citizen making attacks in 64.3% of ads, while Trump only used this approach in 9.4% of his attacks.

Biden's spots most frequently focused on issues falling into the category of compassion issues, with the pandemic and coronavirus mentioned most frequently, followed by racial justice and inequality and healthcare. Biden mentioned each of these issues significantly more often than Trump. Biden's ads also addressed education and voting more often. Trump focused most on issues related to military, security, and crime. His ads most frequently addressed issues related to policing and crime. Compared to Biden, Trump's ads more often mentioned employment, taxes, international issues, immigration, national security, energy, and the Supreme Court. See Table 10.1 for the full list of issues and issue categories covered.

Mentions of image qualities of the sponsoring candidates were analyzed individually and by the masculine and feminine categories used by Bystrom et al. (2004). Both candidates mentioned masculine traits more frequently than feminine traits. Trump's ads most frequently characterized him as tough, a leader, competent, and action oriented. Emphasis on masculine traits is not surprising given that they are most often associated with presidential leadership (Dolan, 2005; Godbole, et al., 2019; Huddy & Terkildsen, 1993). It is important to note that Biden ran more candidate-positive focused ads, and

Table 10.1   Frequency of Ads Mentioning Issues

	Biden	Trump
No issues mentioned	7.4%	8.5%
Compassion issues*	61.8%	27.1%
Racial justice/inequality*	21.3%	6.8%
Education*	7.4%	0%
College education/debt	1.5%	0%
Coronavirus, pandemic*	36%	10.2%
Healthcare*	18.4%	6.8%
Poverty, hunger, homeless	0.7%	3.4%
Senior citizen issues	5.1%	3.4%
Women's issues	1.5%	1.7%
Economic issues*	25%	39%
Econ general	9.6%	11.9%
Income inequality	3.7%	0%
Employment*	11.8%	25.4%
Taxes*	7.4%	22%
Trade deficit*	0%	3.4%
Military/security/crime*	8.8%	55.9%
Immigration*	0%	15.3%
International issues*	0%	20.3%
National security*	1.5%	6.8%
Crime and police*	7.4%	27.1%
Neutral issues	33.1%	13.6%
Agriculture/farming	2.9%	0%
Energy*	0%	3.4%
Climate change	4.4%	0%
Dissatisfaction with government	5.1%	0%
Ethics, moral decline	2.2%	0%
Gun control/rights	0%	1.7%
Voting*	18.4%	0%
Supreme Court*	0%	3.4%
Veterans	6.5%	5.1%

Note: * Indicates a significant difference in frequency between candidates, $p < 0.05$. Issues coded but mentioned in less than 1% of ads by both candidates were drugs, childcare, welfare/food programs, federal budget, and recession/depression.

Table 10.2   Frequency of Traits Associated with Sponsoring Candidate

	Biden	Trump
No Traits*	25%	50.8%
Masculine Traits*	60.3%	35.6%
Toughness/strength	10.3%	13.6%
Aggressive/fighter	25%	16.9%
Competency	17.6%	8.5%
Past performance	5.9%	3.4%
Action oriented*	25%	6.8%
Leadership*	25.7%	11.9%
Qualified	0.7%	1.7%
Experience in politics	3.7%	0%
Knowledge/intelligent	6.6%	3.4%
Feminine traits*	52.2%	10.2%
Trustworthy/honest*	9.6%	1.7%
Unifier*	18.4%	0%
Cooperation	8.8%	3.4%
Sensitive/understanding*	32.4%	5.1%
Of the people*	8.8%	0%

Note: * Indicates a significant difference in frequency between candidates, $p < 0.05$. The trait "Washington outsider" was coded but mentioned in no ads.

only sponsoring candidate's traits were coded. About half of Trump's ads did not mention any traits about himself. Biden's ads most frequently characterized him as sensitive and understanding, a leader, as aggressive or a fighter, action oriented, and as a unifier. Biden's ads took a more balanced approach that demonstrated both masculine leadership traits and feminine traits that are often seen as desirable in leaders. See Table 10.2 for a full list of the image qualities associated with each candidate.

Interestingly, both candidates relied most heavily on challenger strategies, but there were some significant differences among the challenger strategies they used. Biden most frequently, and more than Trump, called for change and emphasized optimism for the future. Trump more often attacked his opponent's stands, record, and personal qualities. Generally, incumbents have engaged in less of these challenger strategies, but given the proportion of Trump's ads that were opponent focused, these strategies make sense. Using a more traditional incumbent tactic, Trump's ads frequently emphasized his accomplishments and did so more than Biden. Biden used the feminine strategies of personal tone, emphasizing personal experience, addressing viewers as peers, and inviting viewer participation significantly more than Trump. Again, these strategies are in line with other elements of Biden's verbal videostyle that was more positive and appealed more to emotions. Table 10.3 displays the frequencies in which ads employed each strategy.

Table 10.3   Frequency of Strategies Used

	Biden	Trump
Incumbent strategies	19.1%	15.3%
Incumbency means legitimacy*	0%	3.4%
Using endorsements of political leaders	5.1%	1.7%
Emphasizing accomplishments*	2.9%	10.2%
Above the trenches	13.2%	5.1%
Challenger strategies	87.5%	88.1%
Call for change*	49.6%	0%
Emphasizing optimism/hope for the future*	46.3%	8.5%
Reinforcing/promoting traditional values*	11%	0%
Attack record of opponent	15.4%	25.4%
Attack opponent personal qualities*	11.0%	40.7%
Attack opponent stands*	22.8%	44.1%
Compare candidate stands with opponent	5.9%	6.8%
Compare candidate personal qualities with opponent	4.4%	0%
Voice of state	0.7%	1.7%
Yearning for the past	1.5%	1.7%
Masculine strategies	2.9%	5.1%
Use of statistics	2.9%	3.4%
Use of expert authorities	0%	1.7%
Feminine strategies*	82.4%	22%
Personal tone*	42.6%	5.1%
Address viewers as peers*	29.4%	8.5%
Invite viewer participation*	24.3%	5.1%
Using personal experience*	39.0%	8.5%
Identifying with experience of others	3.7%	0%

Note: *Indicates a significant difference in frequency between candidates, $p < 0.05$. Strategies coded but mentioned in less than 1% of ads by both candidates were representing the philosophical center of party and taking the offense on issues.

Nonverbal Elements

Kaid and Johnston (2001) found that presidential candidates have appeared in about 60% of their ads, and Biden's ads conformed to this norm, with him appearing in 61.5% of his ads. Trump appeared in significantly less, 42.4%, of his ads. Trump's ads most often, and more than Biden, pictured only the opponent. This likely reflects the more negative and opponent focus of Trump's ads. Biden's ads varied more by picturing a mix of Biden, other people, and the opponent. Biden's ads pictured racially diverse groups, senior citizens, children, and veterans more often than Trump. Table 10.4 shows the frequencies with which various people or groups appeared in ads.

The dominant speaker in ads also varied significantly. An anonymous announcer was used in 66.1% of Trump's ads and 17.8% of Biden's. This—coupled with who was pictured in Trump's ads—reflects an opponent-centered strategy that distanced the candidate from his ads. On the other hand, a citizen or average person was featured as the dominant speaker in 50.4% of Biden's ads, but only 8.5% of Trump's. Biden was the dominant speaker in 17.8% of his ads, while Trump was the dominant speaker in only 1.7% of his ads. The dominant speakers and people pictured reflect the mix of opponent- and candidate-focused ads from Biden, as well as a greater quantity of ads.

Table 10.4   People and Groups Pictured

	Biden	Trump
Opponent and other people only*	5.9%	44.1%
Candidate, opponent, and other people*	33.9%	19.9%
Candidate and other people*	39%	11.9%
Only people other than the candidates*	30.9%	3.4%
Opponent only*	0%	3.4%
Candidate only	1.5%	1.7%
No people are pictured	2.9%	1.7%
Identity groups		
Racially diverse groups*	86%	61%
Senior citizens*	46.3%	18.6%
Children*	39.7%	15.3%
Veterans*	19.9%	8.5%

Note: *Indicates a significant difference in frequency between candidates, $p < 0.05$.

In most ads where the sponsoring candidate was pictured, the candidates did not make eye contact with the viewer—96% of Trump's and 78.3% of Biden's ads. However, Biden always or almost always made eye contact in 13.2% of his ads, but Trump's eye contact never fell into those categories. Trump and Biden were both most often shown with an attentive or serious facial expression, never or sometimes using gestures, compact body movement, and in formal dress. However, Biden was pictured wearing a face mask in 68.8% of his ads, significantly more than the 8.3% of Trump's ads that pictured him with a face mask. Biden was also pictured touching others in 71.1% of his ads, while Trump was pictured touching others in 32% of ads. Biden's ads pictured his vice presidential candidate, Kamala Harris, in 16.3% of ads, while Trump ads pictured Mike Pence in 11.9% of ads.

Production Elements

The dominant camera angle used in about 96% of ads for both candidates was a straight-on shot. Most shots of Biden (84.3%) and Trump (72%) were waist up, although the dominant shot for Trump was full length in 24% of ads, compared to only 7.2% of Biden's. Both candidates relied heavily on the production style of using photos or short videos with voice- overs. This style was used in 51.7% of Trump's and 48.9% of Biden's ads. However, Biden used a cinema verité style in 21.5% of ads, compared to 3.4% of Trump's ads, and the majority of both candidates' cinema verité ads used a "person on the street" style. Both candidates used still images in about 45% of their ads. They also used montages of still photos or short videos often, Biden in 58.1% and Trump in 49.2%. There were some statically significant differences in the use of special effects. Trump used computer graphics in 86.4% of ads, while Biden used them in 43.4% of ads. Computer alteration or morphing was used in 13.6% of Trump's ads and 5.1% of Biden's. Superimposition was used in 30.5% of Trump's and 0.7% of Biden's ads. Biden used slow motion in 61.8% of ads compared to Trump's use in 30.5%. Some of these differences are likely tied to ad focus and strategy. Negative ads tend to use more special effects, and Trump ran more negative ads.

Discussion

The videostyle analysis of Trump and Biden provide a quantitatively supported picture of each candidate's strategies. Taken together, the videostyle elements analyzed here reveal Trump and Biden had fundamentally different strategies. Some of this may have been informed by the successes and mistakes of 2016, and some were related to the unique context of the 2020 election. The following section discusses strategies and themes in 2020 advertising.

Trump's Strategy

Trump's advertising strategy involved little Trump and a lot of Biden. It was opponent-focused and negative. Nearly 90% of Trump's ads made an attack, and it's noteworthy that an incumbent president heavily utilized the challenger strategies of attacking the opponent's stands and personal qualities. Trump himself was distant from much of his advertising. He only appeared in one-quarter of his ads, and in those never made eye contact with the viewer and was the dominant speaker in only 1.7%. Instead, Trump's ads focused on his opponent; relied on anonymous announcers; were set in nondescript places; and relied on special production effects like computer graphics, alterations, and superimposition. Trump also frequently attacked other politicians and the Democratic Party and used the guilt-by-association strategy to attack Biden.

Before jumping into examples and sharing the titles of some of these ads, it is worth noting that Trump's ads were titled untraditionally. Perhaps related to his heavy use of social media, the ads were often titled as an argument. An example of both the titling and the use of attacks and computer graphics is "Joe Biden is a Trojan Horse for the Radical Left" (Trump, 2020f). The ad opens with what looks like a yellow tinged, old book with an image of a Trojan horse. Biden's head has been superimposed onto the horse along with a Democratic logo and Soviet hammer and sickle. Pages are turned in the book to show altered, superimposed images of Biden. The ad goes on to call him a socialist and attack him on tax policy. An anonymous announcer also uses the guilt-by-association strategy by associating him with "crooked" Hillary, Bernie Sanders "and his comrades," Alexandria Ocasio-Cortez, and the "radical left."

The ad "Dangerous" (Trump, 2020a) epitomizes Trump's personal attacks on Biden that framed him as mentally unstable and having diminished capacity. The ad shows Biden yelling at a reporter, forgetting an answer to a question, and making confused faces. The ad also associates Biden with negative actions related to China, saying with text that "BIDEN STANDS UP FOR CHINA" and an anonymous announcer verbally attacked Biden's opposition to travel restrictions on China and Biden's son's business dealings in China.

The personal attacks on Biden largely centered on portraying him as mentally or physically unwell. This was similar to attacks made by the Trump campaign against Hillary Clinton in 2016. Dunn and Tedesco (2017) pointed out a 2016 Trump ad, also titled "Dangerous," that attacked Clinton on foreign affairs issues and stated "Hillary Clinton doesn't have the fortitude, strength, or stamina to lead in our world" coupled with an image of Clinton collapsing (p. 111). In the 2020 ad "Joe Biden is Lost" (Trump, 2020l), text mirrors an anonymous announcer stating Joe Biden has "lost" "For 5 Decades." The ad mentions losing manufacturing jobs, veterans' lives, and Americans' trust and respect. These attacks are coupled with images of Biden looking down, yelling, and appearing confused. The ad concludes with text and the announcer saying, "JOE BIDEN'S LOST IT."

Trump's ads also regularly characterized Biden as untrustworthy, often in connection to his son Hunter's business dealings, as in the ad "Biden Lied" (Trump 2020h). This strategy was rather successful for Trump in 2016 when he attacked Clinton's honesty, often related to her use of a personal email server. However, whether it was because Biden was more liked and trusted than Clinton or that the Hunter Biden scandal did not have the legs of Clinton's emails, these attacks seemed less successful in 2020.

While both candidates relied heavily on emotional appeals, Trump relied more on fear appeals. Ads characterized Biden's mental capacity and alleged dishonesty as something to fear. Other ads created fear around the protests tied to racial justice and the murder of George Floyd. In the ad "Lawless-Kenosha," an anonymous announcer states "as lawless criminals terrorize Kenosha Joe Biden takes a knee" (Trump, 2020c). "Chaos and violence" are blamed on Democrats' "weak response," and viewers are threatened that Biden would defund police and make things worse. This issue and fear appeal were used in several ads, and ads like "Joe Biden Does Not Have the Backs of Police Officers" used testimonials from what appear to be police officers. They claim (with text mirroring their words) that Biden will empower "these people" to commit more crime and that "In Joe Biden's America, we will all be in danger" (Trump, 2020e). Another says, "If you support the police and want to be safe in your home and you want your children safe, support Donald Trump."

Economic issues, international issues, and issues related to crime and policing were among the most common areas of attack. As was already mentioned, China and Ukraine were common topics in Trump's attacks. Economic issues, such as employment and taxes, were frequently mentioned, and these were also tied to fear appeals about immigration. "The Real Biden Plan" (Trump, 2020i) claims Biden will raise taxes for 82% of Americans and then goes on to associate that with granting amnesty and providing healthcare to undocumented immigrants. "For You" makes similar claims that Biden will raise taxes and create higher gas prices, utility bills, and medical bills with claims that "You'll compete with illegal immigrants to keep your job" (Trump, 2020d). The ad then touts Trump's accomplishments related to employment.

Trump ran fewer ads than Biden and fewer candidate-positive focused ads, providing limited opportunities to shape Trump's image. He was generally characterized as possessing masculine traits such as being a tough, action-oriented leader. For example, the ad "Lawless-Kenosha" claims Trump was stopping violent protests and providing "strong leadership when America needs it" (Trump 2020c). Trump's positive ads focused largely on the economy, security, and foreign affairs. For example, an anonymous announcer claims "America is stronger, safer and more prosperous" in an ad bearing that title and highlights economic growth and employment numbers. (Trump, 2020k). "President Trump by the Numbers," an ad with no voice content that relied on computer-generated graphics and superimposed faces to tell the story, emphasized Trump's accomplishments on the economy, jobs, Middle East peace, and the military, among other issues (Trump, 2020j).

In short, Trump's advertising strategy was primarily to attack his opponent on issue stances and personal qualities. That strategy was supplemented with highlighting Trump's accomplishments and his masculine leadership traits. Comparing Trump's videostyle in 2020 to the themes identified by Dunn and Tedesco (2017) in their study of television advertising aired in the 2016 presidential campaign reveals similar approaches. In 2016, Trump attempted to portray Clinton as dishonest, unhealthy, and disconnected from voters. In 2020, Trump homed in on an alleged scandal involving Joe Biden's son, but there was little evidence to support any wrongdoing. And unlike Clinton's 2016 email scandal, there was no FBI investigation to keep the Hunter Biden story in the headlines. Attacks on Biden's mental health were frequently incorporated into Trump's negative ads and may have been persuasive to some, particularly those who did not like his vice presidential candidate. However, Trump was only three years younger than Biden and there were questions about his mental and physical health as well.

Biden's Strategy

Biden's advertising strategy was more diversified than Trump's, evident both in the greater number of spots and the various strategies, issues, and image qualities mentioned. Biden also had considerably more ads with a one-minute runtime; 58% of Biden's ads were one minute compared to 15% of Trump's. The longer runtime made it possible to address more topics in varied ways. Biden's overall strategy was focused on making Biden likable and relatable. He had more positive than negative ads, and he was characterized as a sensitive and understanding leader that could unify the country and get things done. Nonverbals also supported this by showing Biden talking informally to people from a variety of identity groups and touching people by shaking hands, touching shoulders, and giving high-fives. For example, in the one-minute ad "Make Life Better," Biden is shown talking with people of different races and ages, shaking hands, and giving fist bumps. An announcer's voice plays over the video:

> America is a place for everyone. Those who chose this country. Those who fought for it. Some Republicans. Some Democrats. And most just somewhere in between. All looking for the same thing. Someone who

understands their hopes, their dreams, their pain. To listen. To bring people together. To get up every day and work to make life better for families like yours. To look you in the eye, treat you with respect, and tell you the truth. To work just as hard for the people who voted for him as those who didn't. To be a president for all Americans. (Biden, 2020h)

"Keep Up" is an example of an ad depicting Biden as action-oriented and someone who gets things done and provides a counter to Trump's attacks on Biden's mental and physical health. This two-minute spot ran prior to Trump's speech at the Republican National Convention, and its longer format gives a more complete picture of Biden's strategy. It starts with the announcer saying "Some people are always in a hurry. They run when they could walk. Race up steps when others take it slow." The words are matched with images of Biden running and of Trump slowly, and somewhat shakily, walking down steps. It goes on to say "we won't have to wait" for Biden to address issues like COVID-19 and economic issues of working families (Biden, 2020c).

This ad also demonstrates the Biden campaign's strategic balance of calling for change and optimism for the future. The second minute of the ad is Biden's voice-over, taken from speeches. He says, "America is an idea, an idea stronger than any army, more powerful than any dictator or tyrant. It gives hope to the most desperate people on earth." He then says this idea "beats in the heart of the people in this country," regardless of race, ethnicity, sexual orientation, gender identity, religion, or immigration status. He finishes by showing hope for the future, using personal tone, addressing viewers as peers, and inviting their participation, saying:

In times as challenging as these I believe there's only one way forward, as a united America. United in our dream of a better future for us and for our children. This is our moment. This is our mission, and we'll do it together. (Biden, 2020c)

The elements of this longer spot are replicated in many shorter ads. This is particularly true for ads focused on racial justice. The ad "Powerful Voices" begins with a clip of Biden from a speech saying, "There have been powerful voices for justice in recent weeks and months" (Biden, 2020g). The ad mentions the violence and discrimination Black Americans face and cuts between images of Biden speaking, images of contemporary Black Americans, and historical footage of civil rights rallies. Similarly, "Better America" features the voice of an anonymous woman announcer, over contemporary and historical images, equating standing up to Trump and racism to the Civil Rights Movement (Biden, 2020a). The ad makes a clear call for change and invites viewers to be part of a movement for a better future.

Biden's spots also used citizen speakers and the "person on the street" production format regularly. The ad "Building Back Small Businesses" features a

Black woman who owns a salon. She criticizes the Trump administration on the pandemic and its effect on her and other small businesses. She then says Biden's plan can "get the job done" (Biden, 2020k). Likewise, "What It Means to Serve" features Cedric, a Black veteran who lost his leg in combat. Cedric tells his story, then attacks Trump for calling soldiers "suckers" and "losers" and ends by saying Biden knows what it means to serve (Biden, 2020e). These ads also demonstrate the primary mode of attack in Biden's ads. His negative ads were predominantly focused on attacking Trump directly, often on issues. He relied most heavily on citizens making the attack. Ads featured business owners, veterans, students, seniors, people of color, and women making attacks on Trump's position, record, and words. This strategy is more relatable to the viewer than attacks made by an anonymous announcer. Viewers can better relate to ads featuring citizens who look like them or have shared experiences.

Biden's ads addressed a variety of issues, but the greatest number mentioned the coronavirus pandemic, racial inequality, and healthcare. The pandemic and racial inequality will be addressed in more depth later, given their unique importance in the 2020 election. Healthcare is not a new topic for presidential campaigns, but it was a central part of the Democratic primary campaigns and the general election. Biden's healthcare proposal was far more moderate than many of his Democratic opponents, but the Republican narrative was that Biden's plan would raise taxes and constituted socialism. In many of Biden's ads that mentioned healthcare, it was included among a list of other issues like social security and jobs. In some cases, the ads preempted the Republican argument by saying that only the taxes of the very wealthy would increase. Biden also built on the success of the Affordable Care Act (ACA). For example, in "Healthcare Is a Right," a woman tells the story of how the ACA helped her catch and beat colon and breast cancer. The ad goes on to argue that everyone should have healthcare (Biden, 2020).

Voting was also a prominent theme with celebrities like Ludacris, Jermaine Dupri, and Magic Johnson encouraging people to get out and vote. Other ads emphasized the importance of voting and the attacks on voting rights. Many of these ads also featured Black speakers and often appealed directly to Black voters. For example, in "Life or Death," a series of Black women speak directly into the camera. They argue, "For Black women our vote has now become a life-or-death decision" and go on to list COVID-19, police violence, systemic racism, gender bias, maternal mortality of Black women, and pay inequality as problems Biden–Harris will address (Biden, 2020i). "Whatever It Takes-Angel" features a Black woman who addresses voter suppression laws saying, "They're doing it to make it harder for Black folks to vote," and encourages Black voters by saying, "If our vote wasn't so important why would they want to take it away" and "I'm gonna do whatever it takes to make sure that I can vote at my polling place" (Biden, 2020j). These ads were strategic because Biden needed more Black voters to show up for him than did for Clinton, and laws regulating voting, the closing of polling stations, and other actions of state and local governments could have served as a deterrent for Black voters. These ads not only encouraged them to vote; they used laws meant to discourage voting as motivation. This sort of strategy may have been particularly important in areas like Georgia, where Black voters pushed Biden to a narrow victory.

The sheer number of ads Biden ran provided the opportunity to tackle many issues and target a variety of audiences. This analysis looks at the videostyle as a whole, but each piece of the strategy may have been more or less prevalent in a given media market. In comparing Biden's 2020 strategy with Clinton's in 2016, it seems Biden learned from mistakes. Clinton's ads often tried to use Trump's own words against him by playing back his comments about women or persons with disabilities (Dunn & Tedesco, 2017). Both Trump and Clinton in 2016 seemed to center their strategy on persuading people to vote against the other one. Biden's 2020 strategy was different in that the underlying themes of change and optimism gave people something and someone for whom vote.

The Issues of 2020

There is no doubt the coronavirus pandemic was an important variable in the 2020 election. It was an issue that connected to many other issues such as the economy and healthcare. The pandemic also affected the campaigns. In-person events were fewer, particularly on the Democratic side. There was a greater need to communicate with voters through advertising and social media, especially since one of the debates was cancelled when Trump contracted COVID. Given this unique context, it's important to understand how the candidates approached the issue. One measure is how often the issue was mentioned in advertising. Biden's ads mentioned the pandemic in 36% of ads, significantly more than Trump's 10.2%. In this study's sample, that constituted 48 ads from Biden and 6 from Trump. The content of their ads was also very different. The act of wearing a mask in the ads communicated each candidate's position on masks and the threat of COVID-19. Biden was shown wearing a mask in nearly 89% of the ads where he appeared, while Trump appeared wearing a mask in about 8%.

Trump's strategy was largely to claim victory for overcoming COVID and getting things back to normal while also attacking Biden for his position on masks, travel bans, and immigration. The Trump strategy was largely to downplay the issue, claim it was over, and present Biden as overreacting and overreaching. Biden's ads identified COVID as an important issue, placed blame on Trump, humanized the issue, and presented policy preferences. Most of Biden's ads made a direct or indirect attack on Trump's handling of the pandemic, essentially placing blame for its effects on Trump's shoulders. Many ads linked COVID to specific issues and humanized them with a citizen speaker telling how the pandemic affected them. For example, in "Building Back Small Businesses," a woman explains the effect the pandemic and Trump's response to it have had on her business (Biden, 2020k). Numerous ads focused on the pandemic's effect on specific people, including small business owners and people of color. The second part of Biden's strategy was to provide an alternative. Ads like "Real Plans" featured Biden speaking at a podium intermixed with images illustrating the points as he lays out a plan for handling the pandemic, including a promise to increase testing, require masks, and provide necessary equipment to healthcare personnel. The ad argues that "we need real plans, real guidelines with uniform, nationwide standards" (Biden, 2020b).

The video-recorded murder of George Floyd in May 2020 in Minneapolis pushed racial justice and police violence into mainstream conversation. Protests around the country gained America's attention, and the violence that occurred at some of the protests fueled cries from both sides. The way the issue was handled in presidential advertising in 2020 reflects two distinct narratives—one centered on fear and one on hope. As has already been discussed, Trump's ads used fear appeals to characterize the protests as violent and a threat to the safety of good, law-abiding Americans. These ads framed Biden as anti-police and pro–violent crime. These ads did not mention racial inequality or Floyd. Some of Trump's other ads did mention race, but usually in reference to job creation.

The Biden campaign made Floyd's death and protests for racial justice a rallying cry for voters, particularly Black voters. One ad, "Change," even featured Floyd's sister sharing that Biden had reached out to the Floyd family. She goes on to say, "Biden is the change we need" and tells viewers that their vote matters (Biden, 2020f). The fact that more than one-fifth of Biden's ads dealt with racial justice in some way shows how important this issue was to his campaign. The strategy, however, was not based on fear, but on hope for the future. Many of his ads incorporated historical footage from the Civil Rights Movement alongside images of protests in 2020. The ads both highlighted a problem and provided hope for the future. The message was that a Biden–Harris administration could move the country forward and make it a better, safer place for Black Americans. "Rise Up" creates an emotional and optimistic mood (Biden, 2020m). It begins with a Black man saying "your vote is your voice" then moves into the song "Rise Up" by Andra Day as images are shown of contemporary Black Americans doing everyday things intermixed with current and historic protests for civil rights. The ad creates a feeling of hope and optimism.

The selection of Harris as the vice presidential candidate was itself historic, and she became an important part of both Biden's and Trump's messaging. Harris appeared in about 17% of Biden's campaign spots, which at first glance is not significantly more often than the 11.9% of Trump's ads with Pence. However, of the sample in this study, that constituted 2 of Trump's ads compared to 22 of Biden's. Harris was presented in more ways and in more contexts than Pence. Harris was the dominant speaker and made eye contact with the viewer in 13.6% of the ads in which she appeared. She was shown touching others and smiling in 50%, and she used some gestures in 22.7%. Pence, on the other hand, was never the dominant speaker and was never shown smiling, making eye contact, touching others, or using gestures.

Harris's role was active; her presence in ads had a purpose. The fact she is a woman, Black, and of South Asian descent made her a good messenger and symbol given the context of the election. For example, in the ad "Committed," Harris addresses the murder of Floyd, Breonna Taylor, and others to police violence and goes on to point out that people of different races and geographic locations "were willing to stand together, joining arms to say Black lives matter" (Biden, 2020m). Harris goes on to say, "Joe and I are committed to progress and to making sure our communities of color are safe" and "We can't do it alone. We all together can fix this." The Biden–Harris ticket was presented as a team in many ads. In "We're Listening" Harris and Biden both speak about racial justice and police reform. Harris speaks in more detail about the policy of police reform, capitalizing on her experience in the justice system, and Biden focuses more on the emotional appeal, saying, "It's about who we are, what we believe and, maybe most importantly, who we want to be" (Biden, 2020d). Further demonstrating the idea that the two were a team, many of the ads ended with the candidate approval statement and an image of both Biden and Harris.

Harris was also a point of attack for Trump. Minutes after she was announced as Biden's vice presidential candidate, the Trump campaign released an ad titled "Meet Phony Kamala Harris" that claimed she was part of the radical left, was rejected by primary voters because "they smartly spotted a phony," and that Biden was "handing over the reins to Kamala" (Trump, 2020b). Another ad titled "President Kamala" features Nancy Pelosi explaining that the 25th Amendment allows the vice president to take over "if the president suffers a crippling physical or mental problem"; then shows an image of Biden looking confused followed by text that says, "Pelosi's Plan: Remove Biden if Elected and Install Kamala"; and ends with text reading "Don't Vote for President Kamala" (Trump, 2020g). By characterizing Harris as a radical who would take over because Biden was unhealthy, Trump was able to appeal to moderates who may have been willing to vote for Biden but feared someone more radical.

Conclusion

A pandemic made the 2020 election inherently unique and elevated the importance of advertising as a means of persuading voters. Many elements—including appeals, focus, and strategies—of presidential advertising were consistent with previous elections. There were more positive than negative candidate-sponsored ads. More ads addressed issues, but many addressed both issues and image qualities. What was unique about 2020 is how the elements came together to tell the story of each candidate. The Trump campaign used several strategies that were successful in 2016—such as attacking issue stances and personal qualities of his opponent, emphasizing honesty and corruption, and focusing more on the opponent. However, Biden was a different candidate with a different strategy than Clinton. Biden's ads appealed more to the context of 2020 that included deep political divisions in the country, people suffering as a result of the pandemic, and people in the streets protesting police violence and racial inequality. Biden spoke to those issues, demonstrated he was the candidate to move the country through these challenges, and gave people hope. It is fitting that Barack Obama's vice president won the presidency with a message of hope.

References

Airne, D. & Benoit, W. L. (2005). Political television advertising in campaign 2000. *Communication Quarterly, 53*(4), 473–492. doi:10.1080/01463370500168765

Atkin, C. & Heald, G. (1976). Effects of political advertising. *The Public Opinion Quarterly, 40*(2), 216–228. doi:10.1086/268289

Benoit, W. L. (2016). American political TV spots. In W. L. Benoit (Ed.), *Praeger handbook of political campaigning in the United States: Foundations and campaign media (Vol. 1)* (pp. 123–138). Westport, CT: Praeger.

Biden, J. (2020a, August 6). *Better America* [Video]. YouTube. https://youtu.be/VyJk3H2MtzI

Biden, J. (2020b, August 14). *Real plans* [Video]. YouTube. https://youtu.be/GY5w_p5dc7k

Biden, J. (2020c, August 27). *Keep up* [Video]. YouTube. https://youtu.be/C3UsWMbUpF4

Biden, J. (2020d, September 3). *We're listening* [Video]. YouTube. https://youtu.be/MHVU3x9iKBs

Biden, J. (2020e, September 24). *What it means to serve* [Video]. YouTube. https://youtu.be/FSOGT5QvKUI

Biden, J. (2020f, October 14). *Change* [Video]. YouTube. https://youtu.be/ad8C5w4eRgM

Biden, J. (2020g, October 21) *Powerful voices* [Video]. YouTube. https://youtu.be/6JPOBePbf14

Biden, J. (2020h, October 24). *Make life better* [Video]. YouTube. https://www.youtube.com/watch?v=L_MKKBf4syI

Biden, J. (2020i, October 25). *Life or death* [Video]. YouTube. https://youtu.be/SGXHAwi4rtA

Biden, J. (2020j, October 28). *Whatever it takes-Angel* [Video]. YouTube. https://youtu.be/vCZ17QM-6jU

Biden, J. (2020k, October 29). *Building back small businesses* [Video]. YouTube. https://youtu.be/6Uf-QGDhUnI

Biden, J. (2020l, October 29) *Healthcare is a right* [Video]. YouTube. https://youtu.be/MSl0wG8Lyq0

Biden, J. (2020m, November 3). *Committed* [Video]. YouTube. https://youtu.be/lOfaaepZJ74

Bystrom, D. G., Banwart, M. C., Kaid, L. L., & Robertson, T. A. (2004). *Gender and candidate communication: Videostyle, webstyle, newsstyle*. New York, NY: Routledge.

Campbell, K. K. (1989). *Man cannot speak for her: A critical study of early feminist rhetoric (Vol. 1)*. New York, NY: Greenwood Press.

Dolan, K. (2005). How the public views women candidates. In S. Thomas & C. Wilcox (Eds.), *Women and elective office: Past, present, and future* (pp. 41–59). New York, NY: Oxford University Press.

Dunn, S. & Tedesco, J. C. (2017). Political advertising in the 2016 presidential election. In R. E. Denton (Ed.), *The 2016 US presidential campaign: Political communication and practice* (pp. 99–120). New York, NY: Palgrave McMillan.

Franklin Fowler, E., Ridout, T. N., & Franz, M. M. (2017). Political advertising in 2016: The presidential election as outlier. *The Forum, 14*(4), 445–469. https://doi.org/10.1515/for-2016-0040

Franklin Fowler, E. & Ridout, T. N. (2013). Negative, angry, and ubiquitous: Political advertising in 2012. *The Forum, 10*(4), 51–61. doi:10.1086/268289

Franz, M. & T. Ridout. 2010. Political advertising and persuasion in the 2004 and 2008 presidential elections." *American Politics Research, 38*(2), 303–329. doi:10.1177/1532673X09353507

Freedman, P. & Goldstein, K. (1999). Measuring media exposure and the effects of negative campaign ads. *American Journal of Political Science, 43*(4), 1189–1208. doi:10.2307/2991823

Gerber, A. S., Gimpel, J. G., Green, D. P., & Shaw, D. R. (2011). How large and long-lasting are the persuasive effects of televised campaign ads? Results from a randomized field experiment. *American Political Science Review, 105*(1), 135–150. doi:10.1017/S000305541000047X

Godbole, M. A., Malvar, N. A., & Valian, V. V. (2019). Gender, modern sexism, and the 2016 election. *Politics, Groups, and Identities, 7*(3), 700–712. doi: https://doi.org/10.1080/21565503.2019.1633934

Gordon, B. R. & Hartmann, W. R. (2012). Advertising effects in presidential elections. *Marketing Science, 32*(1), 19–35. doi:10.1287/mksc.1120.0745

Huber, G. A. & Arceneaus, K. (2007). Identifying the persuasive effects of presidential advertising. *American Journal of Political Science, 51*(4), 957–977. doi:10.1111/j.1540-5907.2007.00291.x

Huddy, L. & Terkildsen, N. (1993). The consequences of gender stereotypes for women candidates at different levels and types of office. *Political Research Quarterly, 46*(3), 503–525. doi:10.1177/106591299304600304

Johnston, A. & Kaid, L. L. (2002). Image ads and issue ads in U.S. presidential advertising: Using videostyle to explore stylistic differences in televised political ads from 1952 to 2000. *Journal of Communication, 52*, 281–300. doi:10.1111/j.1460-2466.2002.tb02545.x

Kahn, K. F. & Geer, J. G. (1994). Creating impressions: An experimental investigation of political advertising on television. *Political Behavior, 16*(1), 93–116. doi:10.1007/BF01541644

Kaid, L. L. (1997). Effects of television spots on images of Dole and Clinton. *American Behavioral Scientist, 40*(8), 1085–1094. doi:10.1177/0002764297040008009

Kaid, L. L. (2004). Political advertising. In L. L. Kaid (Ed.), *Handbook of political communication research* (pp. 155–202). Mahwah, NJ: Lawrence Erlbaum Associates, Inc.

Kaid, L. L. (2009). Videostyle in the 2008 presidential advertising. In R. E. Denton (Ed.), *The 2008 Presidential campaign: A communication perspective* (pp. 209–227). Lanham, MD: Rowman & Littlefield Publishers Inc.

Kaid, L. L. & Davidson, J. (1986). Elements of videostyle: Candidate presentation through television advertising. In L. L. Kaid, D. Nimmo, & K. R. Sanders (Eds.), *New perspectives on political advertising* (pp. 184–209). Carbondale, IL: Southern Illinois Press.

Kaid, L. L. & Dimitrova, D. V. (2005). The television advertising battleground in the 2004 presidential election. *Journalism Studies, 6*(2), 165–175. https://doi.org/10.1080/14616700500057205

Kaid, L. L., Fernandes, J., & Painter, D. (2011). Effects of political advertising in the 2008 presidential campaign. *American Behavioral Scientist, 55*(4), 437–436. doi:10.1177/0002764211398071

Kaid, L. L., & Johnston, A. (2001). *Videostyle in presidential campaigns.* Westport, CT: Praeger/Greenwood.

Kaid, L. L., Leland, C. M., & Whitney, S. (1992). The impact of televised political ads: Evoking viewer responses in the 1988 presidential campaign. *The Southern Communication Journal, 57*(4), 285–295. doi:10.1080/10417949209372875

Kaid, L. L., Postelnicu, M., Landerville, K., Yun, H. J., & LeGrange, A. G. (2007). The effects of political advertising on young voters. *American Behavioral Scientist, 50*(9), 1137–1151. doi:10.1177/0002764207300039

North, R. C., Holsti, O., Zaninovich, M. G., & Zinnes, D. A. (1963). *Content analysis: A handbook with applications for the study of international crisis.* Evanston, IL: Northwestern University Press.

Norton, R. & Brenders, D. A. (1996). *Communication and consequences: Laws of interaction.* Mahwah, NJ: Lawrence Erlbaum Associates.

Pinkleton, B. (1997). The effects of negative comparative political advertising on candidate evaluations and advertising evaluations: An exploration. *Journal of Advertising, 26*(1), 19–29. doi:10.1080/00913367.1997.10673515

Ridout, T., Franklin Fowler, E. & Franz, M. M. (2021). Spending fast and furious: Political advertising in 2020. *The Forum, 18*(1), 465–492. doi:10.1515/for-2020-2109

Ridout, T. N., Franz, M., Goldstein, K. M., & Feltus, W. J. (2012). Separation by television program: Understanding the targeting of political advertising in presidential elections. *Political Communication, 29*, 1–23. doi:10.1080/10584609.2011.619509

Spenkuch, J. L. & Toniatti, D. (2018). Political advertising and election results. *The Quarterly Journal of Economics, 133*(4), 1981–2036. doi:10.1093/qje/qjy010

Tedesco, J. C. (2002). Televised political advertising effects: Evaluating responses during the 2000 Robb-Allen Senatorial election. *Journal of Advertising, 31*(1), 37–48. doi:10.1080/00913367.2002.10673659

Tedesco, J. C. & Kaid, L. L. (2003). Style and effects of the Bush and Gore spots. In L. L. Kaid, J. C. Tedesco, D. G. Bystrom, & M. S. McKinney (Eds.), *The millennium election: Communication in the 2000 campaign* (pp. 5–16). Lanham, MD: Rowman & Littlefield Publishers, Inc.

Trent, J. S. & Friedenberg, R. V. (1995). *Political campaign communication: Principles and practices.* Westport, CT: Praeger.

Trent, J. S., Short-Thompson, C., Mongeau, P. A., Metzler, M. S., Erickson, A. K., & Trent, J. D. (2010). Cracked and shattered ceilings: Gender, race, religion, age, and the ideal candidate. *American Behavioral Scientist, 54*(3), 163–183. doi:10.1177/0002764210381705

Trump, D. J. (2020a, May 11) *Dangerous* [Video]. YouTube. https://youtu.be/Oz-hVIZ64xI

Trump, D. J. (2020b, August 11). *Meet phony Kamala Harris* [Video]. YouTube. https://youtu.be/fOlQj32MP_4

Trump, D. J. (2020c, September 2). *Lawless-Kenosha* [Video]. YouTube. https://youtu.be/JTfDgCCpXTE

Trump, D. J. (2020d, September 16). *For you* [Video]. YouTube. https://youtu.be/SPoO2xdfHVc

Trump, D. J. (2020e, October 6). *Joe Biden does not have the backs of police officers* [Video]. YouTube. https://youtu.be/A7F3NwCGa2U

Trump, D. J. (2020f, October 7). *Joe Biden is a Trojan horse for the radical left* [Video]. YouTube. https://www.youtube.com/watch?v=ez0TBpf2r4s

Trump, D. J. (2020g, October 14). *President Kamala* [Video]. YouTube. https://youtu.be/V_5T11wSmXI

Trump, D. J. (2020h, October 17). *Biden lied* [Video]. YouTube. https://youtu.be/aD9KfmrDrsY

Trump, D. J. (2020i, October 17). *The real Biden plan* [Video]. YouTube. https://youtu.be/9WPiSLJX0So

Trump, D. J. (2020j, October 26). *President Trump by the numbers* [Video]. YouTube. https://youtu.be/e72DT0R8_1s

Trump, D. J. (2020k, October 29). *America is stronger, safer, and more prosperous than ever before!* [Video]. YouTube. https://youtu.be/MJds60ik694

Trump, D. J. (2020l, October 29). *Joe Biden is lost* [Video]. YouTube. https://youtu.be/Y_STwJLPN_s

Valentino, N. A., Hutchings, V. L., & Williams, D. (2004). The impact of political advertising on knowledge, internet information seeking, and candidate preference. *Journal of Communication, 54*(2), 337–354. doi:10.1111/j.1460-2466.2004.tb02632.x

Winfrey, K. L. (2018). *Understanding how women vote: Gender identity and political choices.* Westport, CT: Praeger.

PART 3

Disrupting Democratic Norms

CHAPTER ELEVEN

Donald Trump, Emotional Activation, and Authoritarianism

Robert C. Rowland

There is no mystery about why former Vice President Joseph R. Biden defeated Donald Trump to win the presidency in 2020 by more than 7 million votes. Trump won the presidency in 2016 by promising to create a massive revival of American manufacturing and a job boom for the working class. In fact, despite an enormous tax cut tilted toward aiding corporations and the rich, in the first three years of his administration, Trump presided over economic growth and job creation that were a straight-line continuation of the last three years of the Obama administration, a time that Trump had decried as a near depression (Lee, 2020). In defending this record, President Trump simply lied about his accomplishments. The lies escalated over time from 6 a day in the first year of his term to 39 in his fourth and an astronomical "503 false or misleading claims [on November 2, 2020] as he barnstormed across the country in a desperate effort to win reelection" (Kessler et al., 2021, para. 1).

Moreover, his presidency was defined by gaffe after gaffe and scandal after scandal, not to mention one impeachment before the election and another after it (Lyon, 2020). Trump did not stretch democratic norms; he obliterated them. Sarah Churchwell's comment that his norm violation was so radical that "the president and his supporters regularly embrace traditions of American fascism" (2020, para. 29) is exactly on target. Moreover, Trump's gaffes and norm violation clearly offended one key Republican constituency, suburban women, who shifted strongly away from Trump (Frey, 2020). On top of his many other failures and disqualifying actions, Trump's response to the pandemic was disastrous as the United States experienced more than twice the deaths per capita of Canada (Editorial board, 2020; Lopez, 2021). In addition, the strong economy that Trump had bragged about shrank substantially by 3.5% after the pandemic forced much of the nation into shutdown (Siegel et al., 2021).

In contrast to the failures and outrages of the Trump administration, Democratic nominee Joe Biden portrayed himself as a "moderate—a practical politician, not an ideologue, eschewing left-wing favorites such as the Green New Deal, Medicare-for-all and defunding the police" (Milbank, 2020, para. 5). Biden's strategy was to offer the nation boring competence to heal the wounds of the Trump era and lower the nation's collective blood pressure. In the words of Democratic strategist Maria Cardona, the election was a contest between "competence, clarity and calm versus chaos, chaos and still more chaos" (2020, para. 13). Biden's campaign and then his new administration were defined by a "plan to be boring" (Stein, 2021). It was a winning strategy. The promise of boring competence defeated the chaos of the Trump presidency.

The real question is not why Biden won, but why the election was so close that a slight shift would have handed Trump a second term. Biden's victory "was stitched together with narrow margins in a handful of states" (Swasey & Jin, 2020, para. 1), and a shift of 44,000 votes in Arizona, Wisconsin, and Georgia would have led to an electoral vote tie, which with Republicans controlling more state delegations in Congress likely would have re-elected Trump (Kondik, 2021). Moreover, Biden's 7 million vote margin nationally should not obscure the fact that Trump received more votes than any Republican nominee in history and 7 million more votes than any previous sitting president (Colarossi, 2020; McCarthy, 2021). Biden's win was quite solid, but election fundamentals suggest he should have won in a landslide. The key to explaining the 2020 presidential election is not to explain why Biden won, but to explain how Trump used rhetoric to expand his own base of support in a situation that normally might have produced a collapse.

One clue that can illuminate the power (and weakness) of Trump's rhetoric is to recognize that his hold over core supporters did not relate to ideology, but to emotion. Unlike transformational presidents, such as Ronald Reagan and Barack Obama, whose political brands were tied to pragmatic small-government conservatism for Reagan and pragmatic more-government liberalism for Obama, Trump lacked a coherent ideological perspective. His promise to build a great wall was about as detailed as any of his policy proposals. In fact, Trump represents what has been called the "post-policy phase of Republicanism" (Plott & Goldmacher, 2021, p. A14). Moreover, much of the nationalist message calling for a tough border policy and trade sanctions was antithetical to the conservative policy vision that had governed Republican politics since Reagan.

Nor did Trump possess a strong identity as a Republican in the way that both presidents Bush and Senator John McCain did. Trump was an outsider who created a strong emotional bond with his supporters. As Jonathan Martin noted, his appeal was premised on "harnessing the grievance of the party rank and file" because "the core of his appeal is more affect than agenda" (2021, p. A19). Similarly, Timothy Pytell (2020) noted that Trump created an "emotional connection with 40% of the American people" (para. 7), a connection that has "the capacity to eclipse any rational debate" (para. 5). Conservative commentator and former speechwriter for President George W. Bush, Michael Gerson, reinforced this point, explaining that rather than ideology or an empowering narrative vision of the American Dream, "the whole Trump movement and now most of the Republican Party, is premised on the social sanctification of pre-cognitive fears and disgust," and one must add also hatred and grievance (2021, para. 3). The centrality of emotional activation to Trump's campaign and presidency has been emphasized by social scientists, ethnographic researchers, and rhetorical scholars (Rowland, 2021).

The power of this emotional bond was obvious in the period after Biden was inaugurated. Trump had presided over a political collapse of Republican power in Washington, with the loss of the House of Representatives in 2018 and the loss of both the Senate and the presidency in 2020. Normally, in such a circumstance. the party that had lost power turns sharply against the former president who presided over that loss of power, as Democrats did after Jimmy Carter's defeat and Republicans after the defeat of George H. W. Bush. Yet Trump's emotional hold on the Republican base was so strong that a presidential straw poll at the Conservative Political Action Conference in late February 2021 found that he was the leading contender for the 2024 Republican nomination by more than 30 points (McCarthy, 2021). Another sign of the emotional connection between Trump and his supporters was polling that found that more than 70% of Republicans believed Trump's outrageous and utterly false claim that he had in fact won the election (Cillizza, 2021; Zilinsky et al., 2021). They believed these claims, despite the fact that "there is not now nor has there *ever* been any evidence to back up Trump's wild claims" (Cillizza, 2021, para. 6), a conclusion attested to even by Trump's own attorney general, arch-conservative William Barr (Gurman & Gershman, 2020).

Trump's Rhetorical Activation of Negative Emotions

There are four closely related elements in Trump's rhetoric that explain how he activated the emotions of his supporters. The first element was a nationalist appeal largely to racial identity. He activated fear and anger with nationalist appeals depicting undocumented immigrants, Islamic terrorists, Black National Football League players kneeling during the national anthem, Antifa protesters, or some other group as threatening the nation. In all cases, his nationalist message was untrue but skillfully crafted to tap into a strong feeling shared by many in the White working class and among White evangelicals that they were losing a position of privilege in the nation. In so doing, he drew on the "dramatic rise of a new kind of white populism," motivated by "fear of social change; fear of terrorist attacks and other physical threats and the crisis to identity that many Whites are experiencing as they struggle to maintain their position" in a nation "in which Whites . . . will no longer be a majority within a few decades" (Taub, 2016, paras. 3, 5).

The appeal of the nationalist message was not tied to genuine dangers facing the nation. None of the groups that he cast as threatening "Others" in fact posed a serious danger to the nation. For example, undocumented immigrants commit fewer crimes on average than native-born Americans, and over the last 20 years, Antifa and all other left-wing groups have committed a total of one murder, as opposed to hundreds by right-wing and white supremacist groups (Center on Extremism, 2020; Goldman, 2021; Ingraham, 2018). Trump's activation of fear and anger was tied to threatened identity rather than to a genuine threat. The nationalist theme in Trump's rhetoric created strong emotions most powerfully among voters with an authoritarian personality structure, who fear that they are losing their country (Cox et al., 2017). This rhetoric was self-reinforcing. Researcher Karen Stenner observed that "perceptions of society being filled with groups that pose a threat to the country markedly increase intolerance of specified 'noxious' groups" (2005, p. 29). Trump's rhetoric created perceived "normative threats" that activated "the predisposition [toward authoritarianism] and increase[d] the manifestation of these characteristic attitudes and behaviors" producing strong emotional reaction and "causing those scoring high in authoritarianism to become less tolerant and more aggressive than usual" (Stenner, 2005, p. 17; Hetherington & Weiler, 2009, p. 7).

The second element in Trump's message that produced a strong emotional response was his ability to tap into grievance against elites and the media. He was, as Gerson observed, "a virtuoso at the politics of resentment" (2017, para. 1). In this way, Trump created anger and loyal support through "juxtaposition of a (corrupt) political class . . . and the people, as whose sole authentic voice the populist . . . bills itself" (Greven, 2016, Introduction, para. 1). Trump's appeal to grievance was entirely consistent with his nationalist appeals, which defined real Americans "as culturally homogenous," an approach that allowed him to stoke fear of dangerous Others and also activate a sense of grievance by blaming elites for not taking action against those Others (Greven, 2016, Introduction, para. 2).

Effective political leaders always attempt to create an emotional connection with their supporters. Transformational liberals like Obama and FDR inspired their supporters and created a strong sense of hope for better days to come. Reagan did something similar in support of his pragmatic small-government agenda. Progressive populists like Senators Bernie Sanders and Elizabeth Warren also produce strong emotional responses with their focus on how policies can address the growing rich–poor gap. Trump's emotional activation of core supporters was different from these leaders in two important ways. First, Trump's emotional activation was focused almost entirely on negative emotions such as grievance, fear, and hatred. In contrast, the transformational figures tapped into positive emotions, such as hope. Second, FDR, Reagan, Obama, Sanders, and Warren all supported policy reform. In contrast, Trump's focus was not on policy, but on selling himself as the savior of those who believed their way of life was under siege.

With the nationalist and populist elements in his rhetoric, Trump activated fear, hatred, and grievance, strongly negative emotions, that he then drew upon in presenting himself as the political outsider who could bring back a lost golden age of plentiful jobs for all and unquestioned white dominance. After winning the presidency, his persona gradually evolved from celebrity outsider to presidential strongman. The source of Trump's appeal was not his policy agenda, which was quite unspecific apart from the promise to build a Great Wall and deport undocumented immigrants. Rather, his appeal was tied to his status as a charismatic outsider who promised dramatic action, but provided few details about and almost no supporting argument for that action. In this way, he came across as a typical nationalist populist leader. Cas Mudde and Cristóbal Kaltwasser (2017) noted that "populism is generally associated with a strong (male) leader, whose charismatic personal appeal, rather than ideological program, is the basis of *his* support" and added that such leaders "connect directly to the supporters" and act as "the personification of *the* people" (pp. 42–43). In playing the role of charismatic outsider, leaders such as Trump "claim that they, and they alone represent the people" and "treat their political opponents as 'enemies of the people' and seek to exclude them altogether" (Müller, 2016, pp. 3–4).

The final element in Trump's rhetoric of emotional activation was use of a colloquial style to reinforce the other three elements in his rhetorical practice. If Trump had talked like other political leaders, he would not have seemed authentic. Instead, he adopted a style defined by expressions of grievance, bragging about accomplishments real and imagined, and a rejection of norms of decorum. This colloquial style was similar to that of other nationalist populists. The observation of Mudde and Kaltwasser that nationalist populist leaders, who are almost always male, often assume the role of "a man of action, rather than words, who is not afraid to make difficult and quick decisions, even against 'expert' advice," who uses "simple and even vulgar language" is a perfect description of Trump's colloquial style (2017, p. 64). Trump's constant attacks, his belittling of opponents, swearing in public, and so forth reinforced the other elements in his message, especially his depiction of himself as a charismatic outsider who could produce magical results.

Transformational political leaders such as both Roosevelts, Reagan, and Obama supported a policy agenda as a way of moving the nation closer to achieving the American Dream. Trump's approach was entirely different. He developed no coherent agenda and never presented an important policy speech. Even his State of the Union addresses as president were defined by expressions of grievance and demonization of Others he saw as a threat to the nation (see Rowland, 2021, Chapter 4). Instead of ideological argument, Trump used a rhetoric of emotional activation to energize his followers. While Trump's approach was ideologically incoherent and produced disastrous results, especially when the COVID-19 pandemic struck the nation, it was an extremely potent message for generating strong emotional reactions.

Nationalist Populism in the 2020 Campaign

Close analysis of the 2020 campaign demonstrates not only the dominance of the pattern I have identified in Trump's rhetoric but also that it was the only message he had, regardless of the context. Normally, presidents running for re-election extend the themes of their first campaign; lay out an agenda for a second term; respond to issues of the moment, often relating to the economy; and attack their opponent. Thus, Reagan ran for re-election in 1984, celebrating the economic revival that was labeled as "Morning Again in America" (Beschloss, 2016) and defending his Soviet policy as superior to that of Democrats. Given these norms, one might have expected that Trump would lay out an agenda for confronting the pandemic and rebuilding the economy, as well as defending the superiority of policies based in low taxes and deregulation for producing long-term economic growth. He did nothing of the kind. Rather, he doubled down on his core message with slight adaptation to focus on new dangerous Others, notably Antifa, and perceived slights that he could highlight in activating grievance and hatred against elites. While space does not allow a full discussion of all Trump's campaign rhetoric, the pattern is evident in the most important single speech of the campaign, his Republican National Convention acceptance speech; his debate performance; and his use of social media on Twitter (Thrush, 2020; Trump Twitter Archive v.2, 2020; *USA Today*, 2020).

In the convention address, Trump failed to lay out a clear agenda for a second term and made almost no attempt to defend his record on the pandemic or a host of other issues. Rather, he stuck to the four elements that produced emotional activation among supporters. Early in the address, he emphasized the nationalist theme using apocalyptic language to describe imaginary threats to the nation:

> This election will decide if we save the American dream or whether we allow a socialist agenda to demolish our cherished destiny. It will decide whether we rapidly create millions of high-paying jobs or whether we crush our industries and send millions of these jobs overseas, as has been foolishly done for many decades. Your vote will decide whether we protect law-abiding Americans or whether we give free rein to violent anarchists and agitators and criminals who threaten our citizens. And this election will decide whether we will defend the American way of life or allow a radical movement to completely dismantle and destroy it. (Thrush, 2020, para. 27)

Of course, Trump's allegation that Biden was a socialist, who supported violent anarchists, was absurd. It is a sign of Trump's commitment to the nationalist populist message that he presented such ridiculous charges in the most important speech of the campaign. Many similar passages could be cited. Notably, in discussing the pandemic, he attempted to displace blame on a dangerous Other by referring to COVID-19 as the "China virus."

Trump's airing of grievance against elites was similarly extreme. He described the Democratic Party as composed of out-of-touch career politicians and extremists:

> Our opponents say that redemption for you can only come from giving power to them. This is a tired anthem spoken by every repressive movement throughout history, but in this country, we don't look to career politicians for salvation. In America, we do not turn to government to restore ourselves. We put our faith in almighty God. Joe Biden is not a savior of America's soul. He is the destroyer of America's jobs, and if given the chance, he will be the destroyer of America's greatness. (Thrush, 2020, para. 29)

Trump was quite direct in attacking Biden as an uncaring, out-of-touch elite. He also linked the populist and nationalist themes when he claimed, "Joe Biden spent his entire career outsourcing their dreams and the dreams of American workers, offshoring their jobs, opening their borders and sending their sons and daughters to fight in endless foreign wars, wars that never ended" (Thrush, 2020, para. 30).

Along with his activation of fear, anger, and a sense of grievance, Trump presented himself as the heroic defender of real (White) America. Hitting a theme common to leaders of nationalist populist movements, he claimed that he was the personification of the real people of the nation and had fought tirelessly for them:

> From the moment I left my former life behind—and it was a good life—I have done nothing but fight for you. I did what our political establishment never expected and could never forgive, breaking the cardinal rule of Washington politics. I kept my promise. Together we have ended the rule of the failed political class, and they are desperate to get their power back by any means necessary. You have seen that. They are angry at me because instead of putting them first, I very simply said, "America first." (Thrush, 2020, para. 33)

Trump followed by claiming to have produced a string of grand successes on trade, the economy, immigration, and foreign policy. He supported these claims not with evidence, but with shameless bragging, asserting, for example, "And I say very modestly that I have done more for the African-American community than any president since Abraham Lincoln" (Thrush, 2020, para. 48). Later, he even bragged about his administration's response to the pandemic and the economic downturn that it produced, claiming success at every level. In Trump's alternative reality, his administration had done everything right by "focusing on the science, the facts and the data." In the real world, as Jeff Tollefson noted in *Nature*, "The US president's actions have exacerbated the pandemic . . ., rolled back environmental and public-health regulations and undermined science and scientific institutions. Some of the harm could be permanent" (Thrush, 2020, para. 1).

In the convention speech, Trump used the primary elements in his message to create fear and anger, amplify a sense of grievance against elites, and present himself as the strongman hero who would protect the real (White) ordinary people of the nation from largely imaginary threats, while doing little to protect them from the very real threats posed by the COVID-19 virus. He did so by using a colloquial style to demonstrate his authenticity. Trump's message was largely false, but emotionally resonant for his base of support. Gerson's characterization of the address in an opinion piece headlined as "nasty, brutish and interminable" was precisely on target (2020).

A similar pattern was evident in the second debate in 2020. I focus on the second debate because of the consensus that the first debate was an unwatchable disaster, primarily because of Trump's boorish behavior, interrupting Biden again and again (Izadi, 2020, September 29). In contrast, a number of commentators viewed the second debate as "a more substantive debate, one that offered clear contrasts in philosophy, agendas and character" (Balz, 2020, para. 6).

In fact, Trump's performance in the second debate relied on the same nationalist populist message as in other contexts. He enacted the nationalist and strongman themes by denying all responsibility for the nation's cata-strophic response to the pandemic, blaming China instead, "It's not my fault that it came here. It's China's fault" (*USA Today*, 2020, "Trump and Biden on COVID-19," para. 24). He also reinforced the nationalist message by attacking China for unfair trade policy, claiming to have solved the problem by forcing China to pay "$28 billion" to American farmers. Later, he attacked a pan-demic relief bill supported by Democrats in Congress because it was "a way of getting a lot of money from our people's pockets to people that come into our country illegally" ("On the Economy," para. 46). Even in the midst of the greatest public health crisis in a century, his focus was on non-White Others getting benefits. He also accused Biden of supporting a "catch and release" policy, which he labeled a "disaster" under which, "a murderer would come in, a rapist would come in, a very bad person would come in—we would take their names, we have to release them into the country" ("On Immigration," para. 26). He also attempted to activate fear of Black crime by attacking Black Lives Matter protesters, who he accused of "chanting 'Pigs in a blanket,' talk-ing about the police" (*USA Today*, 2020, "On Race and America," para. 31).

Trump enacted the populist theme by claiming that Biden was an out-of-touch elite. In reference to the pandemic, he said, "We can't lock ourselves up in a basement like Joe has" (*USA Today*, 2020, "Trump and Biden on COVID-19," para. 17). He also restated the populist theme by going after Biden's son, Hunter, for alleged corruption involving Ukraine and China, going so far as to claim: "His son walked out with a billion and a half dollars from China" ("On National Security," para. 36). Later he referred to allegations that Rus-sia had aided his campaign as "another . . . Russia hoax" ("On Race and America," para. 25), ignoring the fact that there had been multiple contacts between the Trump campaign and Russian operatives. Trump also presented the populist theme by claiming that Biden "is going to terminate" "great pri-vate health care" plans covering "180 million people," although Biden in fact supported expanding healthcare access, not curtailing it ("On the Economy," para. 2). Trump boiled down his attack to the claim that Biden "wants social-ized medicine," although in fact Biden had rejected proposals to enact Medi-care for all ("On the Economy," para. 8). He went even further later in the debate claiming that Biden favored "destroying your Medicare—he's destroy-ing your Social Security. And this whole country will come down" (*USA Today*, 2020, "On the Economy," para. 17).

In the second debate, Trump enacted the outsider/strongman theme most strongly at the end when he bragged shamelessly about accomplishments that were wildly exaggerated. For example, he claimed that "I got criminal justice reform done, and prison reform, and opportunity zones. I took care of Black colleges and universities," before concluding, "I'm the least racist person in this room" (*USA Today*, 2020, "On Race in America," para. 33). In actuality, Trump's record on issues related to race had been widely attacked

(Ray & Gilbert, 2020). On the economy, he claimed simply that under his leadership the nation would have "the greatest economy in the world" (*USA Today*, 2020, "On Climate Change," para. 16). As these examples indicate, rather than supporting a policy agenda with strong arguments, Trump simply bragged about accomplishments, many of which had not happened.

In the second debate, Trump spent little time laying out a second-term agenda or presenting actual policy arguments critiquing the proposals of Biden. Instead, he restated the same nationalist and populist themes that drove his campaigns and presidency, relying on a vernacular style that he had honed in dozens of campaign rallies. Although the outsider/strongman persona was more subdued than in other contexts, it came through at the end in bragging about accomplishments that were largely imaginary. Even in a debate that created pressures for substantive argument, he presented himself as what conservative commentator Jennifer Rubin (2020) labeled an "unhinged, know-nothing, narcissistic president" (para. 3).

A similar pattern is evident in Trump's Twitter postings from November 1 through the day following the election, November 4, 2020. He enacted the nationalist theme by claiming that "Biden has vowed to ABOLISH the American oil and natural gas industries", asserting that "Biden would increase refugees from terrorist nations by 700%" turning "the entire Midwest into a refugee camp," and bragging that he was "protecting your families and keeping Radical Islamic Terrorists OUT of our Country!" (Trump, 2020, November 2). Trump also labeled left-wing protesters as a major threat to the nation with several tweets attacking Antifa and other groups. In contrast, he promised to protect "our noble history, heritage & heroes," a reference to protecting Confederate monuments and those of other slaveholders, against "Antifa, the rioters, looters, Marxists, & left-wing extremists. THEY ALL SUPPORT JOE BIDEN!" (Trump, 2020, November 2). In reality, studies found that Antifa and other left-wing groups had committed almost no political violence over the previous quarter-century (Beckett, 2020).

The populist theme was present in many tweets. On November 2, Trump (2020) labeled his opponent as "Sleepy Joe Biden" and said that voting for him was "a vote to give control of government over to Globalists." On the same day, he claimed that "Biden is the living embodiment of the decrepit and depraved political class that got rich bleeding America Dry." Also on November 2, he claimed that "Biden is promising to delay the vaccine and turn America into a prison state." On the same day, he also claimed both that "Joe Biden is bought and paid for by Big Tech, Big Media, Big Donors and powerful special interests" and that "The Depraved Swamp have been trying to stop me—because they know I don't answer to THEM—I answer only to YOU. Together, we will defeat the corrupt establishment, we will DETHRONE the failed political class. . . [and] SAVE THE AMERICAN DREAM!" (Trump, 2020).

On occasion, he combined the nationalist and populist messages into a single tweet, as he did on November 2 when he said, "Every corrupt force in American life that betrayed you and hurt your [sic] are supporting Joe Biden: The failed establishment that started the disastrous foreign wars; The career politicians that offshored your industries & decimated your factories; The open borders lobbyists" (Trump, 2020). On November 1 he linked together all of the elements in his message when he said, "Joe Biden is the candidate of rioters, looters, arsonists, gun-grabbers, flag-burners, Marxists, lobbyists, and special interests. I am the candidate of farmers, factory workers, police officers, and hard-working, law-abiding patriots of every race, religion and creed!" (Trump, 2020).

In a number of tweets, he enacted the outsider/strongman theme, claiming, for example, "Our ECONOMY is now surging back faster, better, bigger and stronger than any nation on earth. We just had the best quarter of ECONOMIC GROWTH EVER recorded—a 33.1% increase, and next year will be the GREATEST ECONOMIC YEAR in the history of our Country" (Trump, 2020, October 31). The outsider theme and colloquial style came through when he claimed, "If I don't sound like a typical Washington politician, it's because I'm NOT a politician. If I don't always play by the rules of the Washington Establishment, it's because I was elected to fight for YOU, harder than anyone ever has before!" (Trump, 2020, November 2).

In his tweets on the two days before the election, Election Day, and the day after the election, Trump did not support a second-term agenda or build a case for his pandemic response or economic record. Instead, his focus was on creating fear and hatred through the nationalist message, activating grievances against political elites as a way of shifting blame away from his own failures, and bragging shamelessly about accomplishments that were always exaggerated and oftentimes imaginary. The odd punctuation, capitalization, and syntax in the tweets I have cited illustrate how Trump used a colloquial style to create a sense of authenticity.

Conclusion

Ultimately, Biden's message of boring competence reassured enough voters to win election. With a very small shift in votes, Trump could have been reelected. An ill-timed gaffe by Biden, even one that had little to do with his policies or actual capacity for governance, might have produced a very different result. That did not happen in 2020, but it very easily could have happened.

Three important conclusions follow from the analysis of the potency of Trump's message for activating strong negative emotions. First, ideological argument has quite limited power in contemporary American politics. Trump never laid out a coherent argument for his agenda as either a candidate or a president. He made hardly any effort to make a case for programs he supported in any context. Unlike previous presidents, especially Reagan and Obama who worked hard to persuade the people that their proposals would work, Trump incited hatred against Others, blamed elites for their failure to confront the Others, not to mention any attacks on him, and claimed that his programs were the best ever. Fact checkers savaged him for telling tens of thousands of outright lies. None of these failings had any discernible effect on his approval rating, which varied in a narrow range, usually in the high 30% to low 40% range (Dunn, 2020).

Cultural critics often bemoan what they see as hegemonic reason. Close study of Trump's rhetoric demonstrates that public reason is anything but hegemonic and often is powerless to confront emotionally powerful falsehoods. The decline in power of public reason is immensely disquieting. Without clear standards for distinguishing strong from weak arguments and facts from lies, there is no way to protect the nation from the charlatan, the demagogue, the bigot, or the warmonger. Reagan and Obama both thought they could win the argument and, as a consequence, their policies were grounded in the world of reason. Absent such a grounding, there are few constraints on extremism.

Second, the analysis of Trump's rhetoric of emotional activation demonstrates the power and danger of such activation. No one voted for Trump because he presented a strong case for ideologically coherent policy positions. Rather, they voted for him either because of personal or party loyalty or because of his ability to activate fear and hate, displace blame on elites, and depict himself as a heroic defender of ordinary people. It was an absurd message, but also a message that produced several million more votes for a sitting president than previously in American history. Negative emotions like hatred, fear, or a sense of grievance are dangerous because they deny the identity of entire groups of people. In other contexts, messages creating these emotions have led to genocide. Similarly, adulation for the leader is immensely dangerous because it may encourage support for dictatorial, evil, or simply incompetent policies—dangers that were obvious during Trump's term in office.

Finally, the analysis of Trump's rhetoric of emotional activation indicates that American democratic institutions are considerably more fragile than had been recognized. After the election, culminating on January 6, 2021, Trump relentlessly pushed the lie that Biden had somehow stolen the election. No evidence supported that lie, and even staunch political allies such as *Fox News, The Wall Street Journal,* and Attorney General William Barr stated publicly that Biden had won the election. Yet Trump convinced tens of millions of his supporters to support the lie, and some of the most extreme supporters attempted to overturn a democratic election through an attack on Congress. The safeguards in American democracy ultimately were sufficient and a democratic transition of power occurred, but it easily could have ended otherwise had only a few important figures in the system been less principled. The success of Trump's rhetoric in activating negative emotions along with adulation for their leader should be seen as a giant blinking warning sign about the fragility of American democracy.

References

Balz, D. (2020, October 22). Trump did what he came to do in Nashville, but Biden was ready for what came at him. *The Washington Post.* https://www.washingtonpost.com/politics/trump-did-what-he-came-to-do-in-nashville-but-biden-was-ready-for-what-came-at-him/2020/10/23/3016a3ea-14c5-11eb-bc10-40b25382f1be_story.html

Beckett, L. (2020, July 27). Anti-fascists linked to zero murders in the US in 25 years. *The Guardian.* https://www.theguardian.com/world/2020/jul/27/us-rightwing-extremists-attacks-deaths-database-leftwing-antifa

Beschloss, M. (2016, May 7). The ad that helped Reagan sell good times to an uncertain nation. *The New York Times.* https://www.nytimes.com/2016/05/08/business/the-ad-that-helped-reagan-sell-good-times-to-an-uncertain-nation.html

Cardona, M. (2020, October 16). The choice: It's competence vs. chaos. *The Hill.* https://thehill.com/opinion/campaign/521450-the-choice-its-competence-vs-chaos

Center on Extremism. (2020, February). Murder and extremism in the United States in 2019. *ADL.* https://www.adl.org/media/14107/download.

Churchwell, S. (2020, June 22). American fascism: It has happened here. *New York Review.* https://www.nybooks.com/daily/2020/06/22/american-fascism-it-has-happened-here/

Cillizza, C. (2021, February 4). Three-quarters of Republicans believe a lie about the 2020 election. *CNN* https://www.cnn.com/2021/02/04/politics/2020-election-donald-trump-voter-fraud/index.html

Colarossi, N. (2020, November 19). Donald Trump's 73.6 million popular votes is over 7 million more than any sitting president in history. *Newsweek.* https://www.newsweek.com/meric-trumps-736-million-popular-votes-over-7-million-more-any-sitting-president-history-154874

Cox, D., Lenesch, R., & Jones, R. P. (2017, May 9). Beyond economics: Fears of cultural displacement pushed the white working class to Trump. *PRRI/The Atlantic Report.* https://www.prri.org/research/white-working-class-attitudes-economy-

Dunn, A. (2020, August 24). Trump's approval ratings so far are unusually stable—and deeply partisan. *Pew Research Center.* https://www.pewresearch.org/fact-tank/2020/08/24/trumps-approval-ratings-so-far-are-unusually-stable-and-deeply-partisan

Editorial board. (2020, September 1). Opinion: Trump's disastrous virus response is veering toward another terrible turn. *The Washington Post.* https://www.washingtonpost.com/opinions/getting-to-herd-immunity -is-a-mirage-it-would-be-disastrous-for-trump-to-pursue/2020/09/01 /a72c92b8-ec76-11ea-ab4e-581edb849379_story.html

Frey, W. H. (2020, November 13). Biden's victory came from the suburbs. *Brookings.* https://www.brookings.edu/research/bidens-victory-came-from-the-suburbs/

Gerson, M. (2017, August 31). 'Trump forces' and the smashing of GOP orthodoxy. *The Washington Post.* https://www.washingtonpost.com/opinions /trump-forces-and-the-smashing-of-gop-orthodoxy/2017/08/31 /de5f440e-8e89-11e7-91d5-ab4e4bb76a3a_story.html

Gerson, M. (2020, August 28). Trump's speech was nasty, brutish and interminable. *The Washington Post.* https://www.washingtonpost.com/opinions /trumps-speech-was-nasty-brutish-and-interminable/2020/08/28 /d3a0ff96-e947-11ea-97e0-94d2e46e759b_story.html

Gerson, M. (2021, March 1). The GOP is now just the party of white grievance. *The Washington Post.* https://www.washingtonpost.com/opinions/the-gop -is-now-just-the-party-of-white-grievance/2021/03/01/67679480-7ab9 -11eb-85cd-9b7fa90c8873_story.html

Goldman, A. (2021, March 3). F.B.I. head warns senators of 'metastasizing' domestic terrorism as threat grows. *The New York Times,* A18.

Greven, T. (2016, May). The rise of right-wing populism in Europe and the United States: A comparative perspective. http://www.fesdc.org/fileadmin /user_upload/publications/RightwingPopulism.pdf

Gurman, S. & Gershman, J. (2020, December 1). Barr says no evidence of widespread voter fraud in election. *The Wall Street Journal.* https://www.wsj .com/articles/trump-campaign-files-more-election-challenges-in -wisconsin-michigan-11606849219

Hetherington, M. & Weiler, J. D. (2009). *Authoritarianism and polarization in American politics.* New York, NY: Cambridge University Press.

Ingraham, C. (2018, June 19). Two charts demolish the notion that immigrants here illegally commit more crime. *The Washington Post.* https://www .washingtonpost.com/news/wonk/wp/2018/06/19/two-charts-demolish -the-notion-that-immigrants-here-illegally-commit-more-crime

Izadi, E. (2020, September 29). 'Dumpster fire.' 'Train wreck.' A disgrace': Horrified pundits react to the presidential debate. *The Washington Post.* https://www.washingtonpost.com/media/2020/09/29/dumpster-fire -cable-news-debate-reactions/

Kessler, G., Rizzo, S., & Kelly, M. (2021, January 24). Trump's false or misleading claims total 30,573 over 4 years. *The Washington Post.* https://www.washingtonpost.com/politics/2021/01/24/trumps-false -or-misleading-claims-total-30573-over-four-years/

Kondik, K. (2021, January 9). Republican edge in Electoral College tie endures. *Sabato's Crystal Ball.* https://centerforpolitics.org/crystalball/articles /republican-edge-in-electoral-college-tie-endures/

Lee, D. (2020, October 27). Trump vs. Obama: Who has the better record on the U.S. economy? *Los Angeles Times.* https://www.latimes.com /politics/story/2020-10-27/trump-vs-obama-who-really-did-better-on -the-economy

Lopez, G. (2021, January 11). How the US's COVID-19 death toll compares to that of other wealthy countries. *Vox.* https://www.vox.com/future -perfect/2021/1/11/22220827/covid-19-pandemic-coronavirus-usa -europe-canada-trump

Lyon, G. (2020, August 13). Trump, not Biden, corners the market on gaffes. *Chicago Sun-Times.* https://chicago.suntimes.com/columnists/2020/8/13/21367815 /trump-not-biden-corners-the-market-on-gaffes-gene-lyons

Martin, J. (2021, March 2). Post-policy G.O.P: Animated by emotions, not issues. *The New York Times*, A19.

McCarthy, D. (2021, March 2). Trump's iron grip on the G.O.P. *The New York Times*, A23.

Milbank, D. (2020, October 27). 'Moderate' Joe Biden has become the most progressive nominee in history. *The Washington Post.* https://www.washingtonpost .com/opinions/2020/10/27/bidens-temperament-is-moderate-his-agenda -is-transformative/

Mudde, C. & Kaltwasser, C. R. (2017). *Populism: A very short introduction.* New York, NY: Oxford University Press.

Müller, J. W. (2016). *What is populism?* Philadelphia, PA: University of Pennsylvania Press.

Plott, E. & Goldmacher, S. (2021, February 28). "Only 68% at CPAC want to see Trump run again." *The New York Times*, A14.

Pytell, T. (2020, September 12). What is the appeal of Trumpism? *Psychology Today.* https://www.psychologytoday.com/us/blog/authoritarian-therapy /202009/what-is-the-appeal-trumpism

Ray, R. & Gilbert, K. L. (2020, October 15). Has Trump failed Black Americans? *Brookings Institution.* https://www.brookings.edu/blog/how-we-rise /2020/10/15/has-trump-failed-black-americans/

Rowland, R. C. (2021). *The rhetoric of Donald Trump: Nationalist populism and American democracy.* Lawrence, KS: University of Kansas Press.

Rubin, J. (2020, October 22). The last debate is the final straw. *The Washington Post.* https://www.washingtonpost.com/opinions/2020/10/22/last-debate -is-final-straw/

Siegel, R., Van Dam, A., & Werner, E. (2021, January 28). 2020 was the worst year for economic growth since World War II. *The Washington Post.* https://www.washingtonpost.com/business/2021/01/28/gdp-2020 -economy-recession/

Stein, S. (2021, January 26). Inside the Biden plan to be boring, *Politico.* https://www.politico.com/newsletters/politico-nightly/2021/01/26 /inside-the-biden-plan-to-be-boring-491530

Stenner, K. (2005). *The authoritarian dynamic.* New York, NY: Cambridge University Press.

Swasey, B. & Jin, C. H. (2020, December 2). Narrow wins in these key states powered Biden to the presidency. *NPR*. https://www.npr.org/2020/12/02/940689086/narrow-wins-in-these-key-states-powered-biden-to-the-presidency

Taub, A. (2016, November 9). Trump's victory and the rise of white populism. *The New York Times*. https://www.nytimes.com/2016/11/10/world/americas/trump-white-populism-europe-united-states.html

Thrush, G. (2020, August 28). Full transcript: President Trump's Republican National Convention speech. *The New York Times*. https://www.nytimes.com/2020/08/28/us/politics/trump-rnc-speech-transcript.html

Tollefson, J. (2020, October 5). How Trump damaged science—and why it could take decades to recover. *Nature*. https://www.nature.com/articles/d41586-020-02800-9

Trump Twitter Archive v.2. (2020, October 31-November 3). https://www.thetrumparchive.com/?dates=%5B%222020-11-01%22%2C%222020-11-04%22%5D

USA Today. (2020, October 23). *Debate transcript: Trump, Biden final presidential debate moderated by Kristen Welker* [Debate transcript]. *USA Today*. https://www.usatoday.com/story/news/politics/elections/2020/10/23/debate-transcript-trump-biden-final-presidential-debate-nashville/3740152001/

Zilinsky, J., Nagler, J., & Tucker, J. (2021, January 19). Which Republicans are most likely to think the election was stolen? Those who dislike Democrats and don't mind white nationalists. *The Washington Post*. https://www.washingtonpost.com/politics/2021/01/19/which-republicans-think-election-was-stolen-those-who-hate-democrats-dont-mind-white-nationalists

Reclaiming the Center: Constitutive Rhetoric and the "Moderate Ethos" in Crossover Endorsements for Joe Biden

Ryan Neville-Shepard

In the midst of the coronavirus pandemic, the Democratic National Convention in 2020 was condensed and adapted to a digital format. An event once planned to be staged for a live crowd of more than 50,000 spectators in Milwaukee was scaled back, meaning fewer "spontaneous moments that make conventions compelling political events," fewer "opportunities for up-and-coming politicians to get a breakout moment," and riskier calculations about which traditional messages to keep and which to cut (Epstein & Lerer, 2020, paras. 17–19). When former Republican Ohio governor John Kasich appeared on the first night of the convention, it was clear that the Biden campaign decided to prioritize what critics have called the "crossover speech" (Neville-Shepard, 2014). The genre, which Tom Curry (2008) of *NBC News* described as one of the most "memorable television [moments]" of a convention (para. 14), brings to mind Democrat Zell Miller's scathing attacks on John Kerry during the 2004 Republican National Convention, as well as former Democrat Joe Lieberman's surprising support of John McCain during the same convention in 2008.

It was not entirely surprising that Kasich appeared at the Democratic convention, especially since Joe Biden had been crafting his appeal to moderate voters since jumping into the 2020 presidential contest. Kicking off his campaign in Philadelphia in May 2019, the former vice president complained about politics becoming "so mean, so petty, so personal, so negative, so partisan, so angry, and so unproductive" (Biden, 2019, paras. 22–23). Alternatively, Biden promised to collaborate with Republicans to "make government work" and to find strength through compromise (para. 40). Despite falling short in early primary contests, Biden's appeal to moderates proved to be a winning message. As Sarah Longwell (2020) of *The New York Times* explained, by Super Tuesday the de facto "Never Trumpers"—or suburban White voters with college degrees who previously supported Donald Trump or sat out 2016—were showing up in record numbers for the Democrats, especially in the suburbs of Virginia, Texas, and South Carolina. According to exit polls, Longwell wrote, these voters were seeking "a Democrat they could trust to govern responsibly and end the chaos of Mr. Trump's presidency" (para. 7).

This particular path to victory relied heavily on what *New York Times* reporter Katie Glueck (2019) called the "reasonable Republican dad" (para. 13). Motivating these voters to turn out in the general election would be no small task, though. Above all, this group of voters was small, likely just 10% of those who identified themselves as Republicans. Moreover, because they were "reluctant to support a Democratic ticket," they were "waiting for allies to tell them it's OK to choose Biden over Trump" (Benen, 2020, para. 14). It was this bloc of voters that Democrats had in mind for the convention. It was why Kasich was joined by many other one-time Republican superstars, including Colin Powell, Cindy McCain, Meg Whitman, and Michael Bloomberg.

Although crossover speeches are fairly normal in a presidential campaign, the 2020 presidential election was hardly ordinary. *MSNBC* political correspondent Tom Curry (2008) noted that crossovers "matter most—and are least likely—when the endorser has been a stalwart loyalist for one party, but suddenly aligns [themselves] with the candidate of the opposing party" (para. 23). Yet 2020 saw big names from the Republican Party—including former senators, members of the House of Representatives, governors, military leaders, former Trump rivals in the 2016 Republican primary, and even former members of the Trump administration—regularly come out in support of the Biden campaign. As columnist Max Boot (2020) of *The Washington Post* summarized, "The real news [in] this election is not how many top Republicans are sticking with Trump . . . [but] how many are repudiating him" (para. 3).

While some political analysts point to Democrats for Nixon in 1972 and Reagan Democrats in 1980 as a precedent for so many elites from one party endorsing the nominee of the opposing party, *MSNBC* political constributor

Steve Benen (2020) argued "to see any kind of equivalency here is ludicrous" (para. 10). Clarifying that the crossover endorsements of previous campaigns were largely "isolated voices . . . often exaggerated to make it appear as if the White House hopefuls enjoy broad, bipartisan support" (para. 10), Benen suggested 2020 was "qualitatively and quantitatively different" (para. 11). Melissa Quinn (2020) of *CBS News* similarly wrote that the election saw "an unprecedented uprising, ranging from senior leaders to rank-and-file officials who have decided to speak out and put country over party" by advocating for Biden (para. 3). Moreover, Frank Bruni (2020) of *The New York Times* described the "anti-Trump rebellion" as "distinguished by the pedigree of the rebels," noting that even the provocateurs of the Lincoln Project were simply "strategists who worked for Bush, John McCain or Mitt Romney" (para. 17).

This chapter examines the broader category of crossover endorsements in the 2020 presidential election. While crossover endorsements have received little attention from communication scholars, existing research has described the content of those electrifying addresses at the party conventions, concluding that they work best as a form of reluctant testimony (Neville-Shepard, 2014). However, I suggest that the historic number of crossover endorsements in 2020—as seen not just during the convention, but also in op-eds, news interviews, and social media—went beyond merely persuading former Trump backers and fence sitters to help elect Biden. Instead, I argue that these crossover statements performed an important function of constituting an audience around the idea of a "moderate ethos." Rather than simply endorsing Biden, the superfluous crossover discourse in 2020 marked a critical redefinition of what it means to be politically moderate. Ultimately, I suggest that these endorsements called for a particular kind of moderate politics—what I will term "procedural centrism"—that serves as a direct backlash to Trumpism, but simultaneously undermines party-driven reforms that might help reverse the trends it allegedly condemns.

This chapter evolves over three sections. First, I contextualize the competition for the "middle" in American politics and explain how centrism is a rhetorical construct that constitutes both audiences and candidates. Additionally, I define the construct of procedural centrism and argue that especially when it is constituted by crossover endorsements, its "apolitical" politics can create significant challenges for the endorsed candidate. Second, I perform a close reading of the many crossover endorsements of 2020 to show how they constitute a specific kind of moderate politics that is perceived as a last resort, focused on character and procedure over policy, while defining extremism in a way that might build winning coalitions, but ultimately impair a party. Finally, the chapter concludes with a discussion of the implications of this study.

Constituting the Moderate

Generally speaking, to be moderate is to act outside of dominant party ideologies. Edward Carmines and colleagues (2012) summarized that while partisanship has increased in recent decades in the United States, moderate voters "whose issue preferences do not match those of either major party" lack partisan attitudes and tend to be ambivalent about candidates' parties, thus shifting their allegiances from one election to the next (p. 1633). From a candidate's perspective, the center tends to be "supra-ideological," as Matthew Lakin and Marius Ostrowski (2014) argued, meaning that it "represents the point of 'maximum' social consensus on the full gamut of domestic and international social, political and economic issues that holds any given node of party competition which sets the constraints of acceptability for political discourse" (p. 18). Reflecting the ancient Greek notion of the golden mean, to act as a moderate in politics is to avoid excess—to anchor oneself in positions between extremes especially to maximize one's chances of winning.

Political analysts' obsession with the moderate voter, at least in recent years, stems from the rise of the "Reagan Democrats." *Politico*'s Zack Stanton (2021) recounts that Yale pollster Stanley Greenberg coined the term in the mid-1980s when he noticed that many White middle-class voters in what used to be Michigan's reliable Democrat country suddenly voted for the Republican presidential candidate. According to Greenberg, these voters believed their leaders "seemed to care more about the blacks in Detroit and the protesters on campus; they seemed to care more about equal rights and abortion than about mortgage payments and crime" (para. 5). Since that transformation, Stanton argued, "the quest for the support of Reagan Democrats has defined American politics, from the rise of Bill Clinton's 'New Democrats' . . . to George W. Bush's 'compassionate conservatism,' . . . to Donald Trump's white-grievance mongering" (para. 6).

The effort to target a middle ground that once captivated the Reagan Democrats is based ultimately on the construction of an imagined audience or class of voters. As Maurice Charland (1987) wrote about the "peuple Québécois," certain narratives "'make real' coherent subjects" (p. 138), and they constitute those subjects "with a history, motives, and a *telos*" (p. 140). Constitutive rhetoric calls on a constructed people to "be true to the motives through which the narrative constitutes them" while presenting "characters as freely acting towards a predetermined and fixed ending" (p. 141). Rhetorical scholar Antonio de Velasco's (2010) work on centrist rhetoric explains how Clinton constructed an image of a political middle ground where citizens demanded that "political leaders remain close to the center in order to transcend their differences" (p. 2). By claiming to capture the center, Clinton moved beyond fashioning new policies and personalities and instead advanced "the project of reconstituting party identity to become a more effective resource for argument" (p. 18). In this way, de Velasco writes, centrist rhetoric is "an inventional metaphor to give meaning and persuasive force" to political advocacy by defining one's "fellow citizens in terms of a democratic ethos of consensus-seeking deliberation" (p. 2).

Although centrist rhetoric aims to be beyond politics, it is anything but apolitical. Those who pivot to the center, de Velasco (2010) argues, tend to "construct a vision of potential unity that remains apparent and unfinished in spite of its claim to be real and complete." However, he concludes, "Such a vision seemingly includes all," but cannot live up to that promise (p. 3). Describing the inherently political nature of such discourse, de Velasco contends, "This kind of rhetoric needs to take a side, while at the same time it needs us to believe that, on some level, it has gone beyond the ordinary and conventional taking of sides" (p. 3). Centrist rhetoric bashes division, but works by restructuring division. Its effectiveness "can only be possible because of a special connection between the conditions of assent and the contrastive act" (p. 8).

In other words, positioning a candidate and their policies in the center requires the definition of what might be considered "mainstream," and in the process portrays anything outside the mainstream as extreme. For this reason, many critics are skeptical of moderate politics. For instance, Mike Ellwanger and Adam Duncan (2014) elaborate that a "moderate choice is always moderate in *comparison* to some alternative, and only when one concedes the existence of alternative courses of action does one take on some duty to prove the superiority of the moderate choice" (p. 82). Clarifying this point, de Velasco (2010) summarizes, "To be itself, the center must become itself rhetorically; it must constantly align with a transcendence of the contingent field of political division it seeks to address" (p. 11). Thus, holding the middle is about reconstituting a candidate, party, and platform as different from some extreme, with the "middle" shifting from one moment to the next depending on which political actors or policies need to be cast as fringe.

While constituting a moderate politics is partially about finding the middle between extremes, I suggest that what is lurking in moderate rhetoric is a more specific—and consistent—critique. I call this the idea of "procedural centrism." According to de Velasco (2010), crafting a moderate ethos includes establishing a "transcendent public space" where political work can be accomplished despite ideological differences (p. 2). Defending this space requires eliminating the force of coercion so that "a free people can . . . transcend their divisions to arrive at general agreements on matters of mutual concern" (p. 2). Although such unity and consensus are fictional, what is at the core of a moderate movement is structuring democracy around a dialogue that develops when certain rules are followed. Experts on centrist rhetoric have hinted at this idea before. For instance, de Velasco's study of Clinton's centrist movement suggested the "center' was a kind of "topos from which to construct a politics based less on its identification with a singular voice of the people than on its emphasis on contingency and ideological diversity as civic goods" (p. 46). Illustrating centrism as ethotic proof, Clinton and those like him move to the center by appearing willing to listen and embrace change, all to avoid the gridlock of partisanship.

The idea of procedural centrism might always be an aspect of moderate political rhetoric, but American politics leading up to the 2020 election clearly made this critique more striking. After all, many political scholars described the hallmark of Trump's rhetorical style— both as a candidate in 2016 and as president—as a purposeful violation of democratic norms (Jamieson & Taussig, 2017; Neville-Shepard, 2019a; Rowland, 2018). Many other critics described the kind of populist rhetoric that Trump introduced to American politics as built on an outsider persona that tapped into misogynistic, sexist, and racist anger that alienated huge swaths of the electorate but also brought many new voters to the Republican Party (Kelly, 2020; Neville-Shepard & Neville-Shepard, 2020; Rowland, 2019).

On top of his divisive identity politics, critics have contended that Trump's assault on truth undermined democratic communication by destroying faith in essential institutions and rejecting deliberation as a communal goal (Kristaansen & Kaussler, 2018; McComiskey, 2017; Neville-Shepard, 2019b). If the number of crossover endorsements in the 2020 presidential election meant anything, they clearly marked a nostalgia for civility and democratic communication that was just productive enough to lead to functional government, mutual respect among opponents, and trust in public institutions. In other words, the kind of procedural centrism that I will suggest emerges from these endorsements articulated not as a moderate politics per se, but as a need to rally behind rules of conduct that would make democracy possible.

Despite the calls for civility, however, the rest of this chapter will also suggest that crossover endorsements from the 2020 campaign were not as bipartisan as they might have first appeared. By reconstituting the middle, the crossover endorsement as a genre relies on members of the oppositional party to fashion a kind of political transcendence or ethos that can then be utilized by the endorsed candidate, but they do so on the terms of the endorser. The cumulative impact of crossover endorsements is that they simultaneously enact the ethotic proof of moderate politics while constituting the moderate voter, and ultimately calling on the moderate candidate they endorse to exist within the kind of centrism they collectively imagine.

However, this rhetoric of moderation, as Ellwanger and Duncan (2014) argued, "demands that speakers signify the mood, demeanor, and language of the middle, whether or not their policy is, subjectively speaking, moderate" (p. 87). This stand against "chaos" is not without its own problems. As political theorist Chantal Mouffe (1998) argued about the "radical centre" proposed in British politics in the 1990s, the attempt to erase the divide between conservatives and liberals to create productive dialogue ignores the "relations of power and their constitutive role in society" while imagining "democracy as a struggle among elites, taking places in a neutral terrain, thereby making adversary forces invisible and reducing politics to an exchange of arguments and the negotiation of compromises" (p. 13). By casting opponents as extremists, centrist rhetoric undermines the radical change that can only come from "a vibrant clash of democratic political positions" (Mouffe, 1998, p. 14).

Constituting the Moderate Ethos in Crossover Endorsements for Joe Biden

As one crossover endorsement led to another in the 2020 presidential campaign, the genre created a moderate ethos that was illustrated by Republicans endorsing Biden, calling on Biden to perform as a moderate leader, and collectively asking voters to perform the ethos themselves. However, as moderate rhetoric is imagined against the extremes of the moment, the centrist discourse in 2020 stood out from the kinds of appeals that might have created Reagan Democrats, Clinton's New Democrats, or even Barack Obama's coalition. In this section I explain that the crossover endorsements for Biden contained a pattern of themes that portrayed centrism as a last resort, moderate ethos as based in character rather than transcendent policies, and as a protection against extremists on the right and the left.

Moderation as a Last Resort

Those making crossover endorsements for Biden in 2020 refrained from joining a moderate coalition built on policy interests. Republicans for Biden mostly articulated their move to the middle as a once-in-a-generation stand against the extremism of Trump. Offering one of the most significant endorsements after the Democratic primary, the founders of the Lincoln Project called the election the "most consequential . . . since Abraham Lincoln's reelection in 1864," adding that a stand needed to be taken against the doom spiral that had led to "a public health emergency not seen in a century, an economic collapse set to rival the Great Depression, and a world where American leadership is absent and dangers rise in the vacuum" (Conway et al., 2020, para. 1). Emphasizing that the country was facing a "transcendent and transformative period," those behind the Lincoln Project tended to foreground their opposition to Trumpism more than offering support of Biden's agenda, emphasizing that the "nation cannot afford another four years of chaos, duplicity and Trump's reality distortion" (para 14).

Cindy McCain similarly stressed the urgency of crossing over, stating, "I decided to take a stand, and hopefully other people will see the same thing," adding that it would require voters to "step out of your comfort zone a little bit" (Webb & Cooper, 2020, para. 7). In this sense, the move to Biden's camp was described as a short-term plan. McCain, for instance, explained that she had not voted for a Democrat since she was 18 and planned to remain a Republican. Kasich spoke in a similar fashion at the Democratic National Convention, describing himself as a "lifelong Republican" who in "normal times" would never think about endorsing the Democratic nominee (Yglesias, 2020, para. 5). Although he once cast himself as willing to work across the aisle, Kasich's remarks reflected that a moderate coalition in support of a Democratic president was really a last resort.

The moderate coalition for Biden Republicans, according to these cross-over endorsements, functioned primarily as anti-Trump backlash. Adopting the role of the election spoiler, the Lincoln Project summarized their mission as trying to "defeat President Trump" by "supporting a Democrat nominee for president . . . in extraordinary times" (Conway et al., 2020, para. 3). Most Republicans identified this as their sole purpose, too. Arguing that elections are "binary choices," former GOP presidential primary candidate Carly Fiorina justified her endorsement by saying, "I've been very clear that I can't support Donald Trump" (Dovere, 2020, para. 3). A Trump loss, according to this logic, was the best way to win back the Republican Party. For instance, former Pennsylvania congressman Charlie Dent argued, "If electing Joe Biden is what's needed to return the GOP to a better place where it becomes more socially tolerant, constructively engaged on the international stage and supportive of reasonably regulated free markets, all the better" (Wurzburger, 2020, "Charlie Dent," para. 4). Other Republicans saw a Trump loss as a path to long-term survival for the party. Former Illinois Governor Jim Edgar argued that Trump's politics were so extreme that Illinois was out of reach for Republicans. He summarized, "For the Party to be able to win in Illinois statewide, we need to divorce ourselves from the Trump thing" ("Former Illinois Republican," 2020, para. 5).

For many Republicans crossing over for Biden, there was less interest in a sustainable political partnership and more of a focus on winning a single election. While those like George Conway gave up on ever winning back their party, they also did not expect to find a "welcome mat in the Democratic Party" (Bruni, 2020, para. 7). Instead, as Bruni summarized in *The New York Times*, "They're not fighting to come in from the wilderness. The wilderness is a given. They're just fighting to get rid of this one sun-hogging, diseased redwood—or orangewood, as the case may be" (2020, para. 8). Some endorsing Biden were even hostile to moderate politics. Explaining that his endorsement of the former vice president was an effort to "boot Trump and Trumpism," Lincoln Project co-founder Mike Madrid added he had no interest in a moderate coalition beyond the election, stating, "There are no moderates and cowards. There are only cowards" (Wiley, 2020, paras. 5–7). In sum, if the traditional moderate message were to find a middle ground between polarizing ideologies and parties, the crossover endorsements of 2020 rejected the prospects of a sustained coalition.

Procedure Over Politics

Crossover endorsements for Biden repeatedly emphasized decency and character above policy, highlighting the kinds of traits and practices that strengthen democratic communication. Susan Del Percio, a Republican adviser for the Lincoln Project, told *CBS News* that Republicans backing Biden were largely "endorsing for the sake of decency in the country, and that's the fundamental difference between this time and every other time" (Quinn, 2020, para. 7). Biden Republicans frequently clarified that they did not necessarily support his policies, but that they thought there was something more important in the election. As Fiorina explained, "I do think character counts. I think leadership matters" (Stankiewicz, 2020, para. 2). Connecting character to the essential qualities of democratic leadership, Fiorina noted, "I think collaboration is now critical, not just collaboration across the aisle . . . collaboration between city governments wrestling with a whole host of issues, including social injustice and the federal government" (para. 4).

Others crossing over for Biden emphasized similar traits. Former Republican National Committee chair Michael Steele (2020) wrote that he disagreed with Biden's positions on many issues, but stressed that the 2020 election was "about the course of a nation and the character of her people" (para. 16). As former Pennsylvania governor and Homeland Security secretary Tom Ridge (2020) added, it was only through good character that someone could practice "intelligent leadership" to navigate "complex problems" (para. 3). Implied in all of these endorsements was the idea that democracy requires the procedures of good faith, open-mindedness, listening, honesty, and a willingness to work with opponents for the good of the country.

If the moderate ethos was defined as practicing the basic skills of democratic communication, crossover addresses in 2020 made it clear that Trump was not credible. Conway et al. (2020) described Trump as holding onto the presidency as "just one more opportunity to perfect his narcissism and self-aggrandizement," shocking and dividing audiences to feed his own ego (para. 4). Former congressman Dent noted that Trump was "an illiberal populist and nativist whose chaotic approach and managerial malfeasance have undermined the functioning of government" (Wurzburger, 2020, "Charlie Dent," para. 3). Describing the president as lacking goodwill and empathy, former White House communications director Anthony Scaramucci declared Trump was "crazy" and that "sane people have to work together to beat him" (Bowden, 2020, para. 5).

Similarly bashing Trump for his inability to be self-reflective and considerate, Ridge (2020) argued that the president "belittles, demeans, and ridicules people who disagree with him, and . . . I've never thought that loud, obnoxious, and simpleminded solutions to complex problems are the kind of qualities we want in a president" (para. 2). Steele (2020) stressed that many of Trump's ideas were legitimate, but that his communication was fundamentally undemocratic, regarding him as a demagogue and that conservatives had to "stand up against the arrogance of power and the erosion of our principles" (para. 15). Ridge (2020) also lamented that Trump's problems were not just personal failures, but problems with leadership, saying, "He sows division along political, racial, and religious lines. And he routinely dismisses the opinions of experts who know far more about the subject at hand than he does—intelligence, military, and public health" (para. 6). Character matters in democracy, these crossover endorsements conclude, because listening and relating to others is impossible if someone is thin-skinned and self-obsessed. It is this kind of ignorance, they conclude, that led the pandemic to spread unchecked, the economy to crash, and America's leadership in the world to be vacated.

Even if his policy positions were not popular with conservatives, Biden's respect for democratic practice meant he could be trusted. His good character, in other words, provided a middle ground for those who saw the country teetering toward disaster due to the inaction of a madman. Conway et al. (2020) saw Biden as a public servant who wanted "to do right by the American people" (para. 4). They added that Biden has a "long record of bipartisan friendship and cross-partisan legislative efforts" (para. 8). Others like former Arizona U.S. Senator Jeff Flake regarded Biden as someone who "unifies rather than divides," someone who "prefers teamwork to tribalism," and as someone who "summons our better angels" (Nagle & Verhovek, 2020, para. 4). Ridge (2020) claimed Biden could disagree with others while practicing "civility and respect" (para. 8). Former Secretary of Defense Bill Cohen also praised Biden's ability to see the good in a situation, claiming the country needed such a "leader with optimism and competence who gives us hope" (Russell, 2020, para. 2). Joining these voices was a team of former McCain staffers who also praised the vice president for his "history of bipartisanship," but went further in claiming he could be trusted to "remember our common interests and responsibilities" (McCain Alums, 2020, para. 2).

Praising Biden's ethos while eviscerating the incumbent president, the many crossover endorsements of 2020 were directed at moderate voters and constructed a moderate ethos they might trust. Rather than building transcendence through specific policies, these Biden Republicans focused on the democratic processes that might be restored. However, as I illustrate in the next point, this kind of procedural centrism was also self-serving for moderate Republicans as it defined extremism in a way that would limit the new moderate Democratic president from pursuing progressive action which might actually reverse the legacies of Trumpism. If he were to live up to the moderate ethos, he would need to spurn anything not considered bipartisan.

Centrism as Anti-Party Politics

Constituting the middle ground, centrist rhetoric defines mainstream politics against that which is considered too extreme. As crossover addresses tend to use members of the oppositional party to construct this middle ground, the endorsed candidate's own party may be compromised. It was not surprising that the crossover endorsements of 2020 could have affected Biden's ability to carry out liberal policy reform. After all, these endorsements reminded the moderate audience that one could disagree with Biden's politics but still trust his leadership. However, in defining centrism in relation to forms of extremism, those endorsing Biden created an equivalence between Trumpian extremism and the far left, calling on the centrist Democrat to protect his moderate base against both.

Although Trump was portrayed as an unstable conman by Republicans bucking the party's nominee, the crossover endorsements of 2020 also cast him as more extreme than a traditional conservative. Flake, for instance, insisted, "Indifference to the truth, or to the careful stewardship of the institutions of American liberty is not conservative." He added, "Disregard for the separation of powers—the centerpiece of our constitutional system—is not conservative" (Nagle & Verhovek, 2020, para. 8). Rather than representing conservativism, Flake concluded, Trump represented "rank tribalism and further division," requiring of voters a "willful amnesia in the face of more outlandish presidential behavior" (para. 9). Republican Mike Fasano, the Pasco County tax collector and former member of the Florida House of Representatives and Senate, warned voters in his state that Trump was "far removed from the Reagan Revolution," representing a new kind of conservative politics lacking "decency, compassion, integrity, and patriotism" (Taylor, 2020, para. 9). Similarly characterizing himself as a Reagan Republican, Steele (2020) endorsed Biden and warned right-leaning centrists that Trump failed to "build on the legacy of the Republican Party's founders, of which [he] is surely ignorant" as the incumbent "posited a single purpose for the GOP—the celebration of him" (para. 11).

By relying on crossover endorsements to build his moderate appeal, Biden also allowed his friendly opposition to define huge swaths of his own party as outside the mainstream. For those crossing over, Biden was constructed as a safeguard against liberalism too. Addressing a primetime audience during the Democratic National Convention, Kasich acknowledged "there are

Republicans and independents who couldn't imagine crossing over to support a Democrat" out of fear that "he may turn sharp left and leave them behind" (Yglesias, 2020, para. 10). Assuring his audience of Biden's moderate credentials, Kasich continued, "I don't believe that. I know the measure of the man. Reasonable. Faithful, respectful and no one pushed Joe around" (para. 10). Explaining the purpose of such promises, GOP strategist and Lincoln Project adviser Del Percio argued it was to make Republicans "feel secure that everything won't become Democratic rule and that Republican policies don't matter anymore" (Quinn, 2020, para. 10).

The strategy appeared effective enough that conservative stalwarts like William Kristol endorsed the Biden campaign too. Addressing readers of *The Bulwark*, Kristol (2020) called on "normal [Americans]" who "don't like demagogues of the right or the left" to pursue "responsible governance somewhere in the vicinity of the broad center" and vote for Biden in the primary (para. 1). "If you're inclined toward American constitutional democracy, the rule of law, and a free economic order," Kristol contended, then a voter would have to back Biden. "If you're not," he added, "then it's Bernie Sanders" (paras. 4–5). Despite the progressive wing reenergizing the Democratic Party, the moderate ethos created for Biden seemed to sacrifice those elements of the liberal bloc. And since Republicans were making such promises during the Democratic convention, it is safe to assume a kind of tacit approval of the message by the Biden camp. At best, such a message can win a close election. At worst, though, it risks replacing a polarized government frozen by gridlock with another.

Conclusion

This chapter examines the historic nature of the crossover endorsement in the 2020 presidential campaign. The genre, which occasionally stole the show at party conventions in the past, became the driving force for a moderate movement that could sink the disruptive Trump presidency. Yet such centrist rhetoric is constitutive by its very nature, and the overwhelming number of Republicans constituting a moderate ethos for crossover voters and the presidential candidate relying on that discourse to expand his appeal requires political communication scholars to examine the practice more closely.

As I have suggested in this chapter, the moderate movement in 2020— at least as it was given meaning in crossover rhetoric—was less about policy and more about resetting the Republican Party, reestablishing certain norms of democratic communication, and preemptively defining a moderate ethos that would also undermine liberal reforms once Biden was elected. The moderate ethos lives on. Constituting such a movement has consequences. Although the disruptive Trump presidency was brought down by a historic number of voters, many of them Never Trumpers driven from their own party, the moderate ethos has empowered those like Democrats Joe Manchin of West Virginia and Kyrsten Sinema of Arizona in the U.S. Senate to hold President Biden accountable to the moderates who got him elected. As such, when relied upon to give a moderate movement life, crossover endorsements pose a serious dilemma in that they provide perhaps the best ethotic proof of centrism, but they tend to demand the kind of compromise in return that should make most presidents and their parties wary.

References

Benen, S. (2020, August 27). Republican support for Biden's candidacy reaches new heights. *MSNBC*. https://www.msnbc.com/rachel-maddow-show/republican-support-biden-s-candidacy-reaches-new-heights-n1238411

Biden, J. (2019, May 18). Remarks as prepared for delivery by Joe Biden in Philadelphia, Pennsylvania. https://blog.4president.org/2020/2019/05/remarks-as-prepared-for-delivery-by-joe-biden-in-philadelphia-pennsylvania-on-saturday-may-18-2019.html

Boot, M. (2020, September 29). More Republicans are abandoning Trump. *The Washington Post*. https://www.washingtonpost.com/opinions/2020/09/29/biden-republicans-may-transform-american-politics/

Bowden, J. (2020, March 4). Scaramucci: 'Of course I'll campaign' for Biden. *The Hill*. https://thehill.com/homenews/campaign/486017-scaramucci-of-course-ill-campaign-for-biden

Bruni, F. (2020, July 11). The Republicans who want to destroy Trump. *The New York Times*. https://www.nytimes.com/2020/07/11/opinion/sunday/republican-party-trump-2020.html

Carmines, E. G., Ensley, M. J., & Wagner, M. W. (2012). Who fits the left-right divide? Partisan polarization in the American electorate. *American Behavioral Scientist*, *56*(12), 1631–1653. https://doi.org/10.1177/0002764212463353

Charland, M. (1987). Constitutive rhetoric: the case of the *people Québécois*. *Quarterly Journal of Speech*, *73*(2), 133–150. https://doi.org/10.1080/00335638709383799

Conway, G. T., Galen, R., Schmidt, S., Weaver, J., & Wilson, R. (2020, April 15). Opinion: We've never backed a Democrat for president. But Trump must be defeated. *The Washington Post*. https://www.washingtonpost.com/opinions/2020/04/15/weve-never-backed-democrat-president-trump-must-be-defeated/

Curry, T. (2008, July 10). The politics of cross-over endorsements. *NBC News*. https://www.nbcnews.com/id/wbna25593888

de Velasco, A. (2010). *Centrist rhetoric: The production of political transcendence in the Clinton presidency*. Lanham, MD: Lexington Books.

Dovere, E. (2020, June 25). She wanted to be a Republican president. She's voting for Biden. *The Atlantic*. https://www.theatlantic.com/politics /archive/2020/06/carly-fiorina-vote-biden/613474/

Ellwanger, A. & Duncan, M. (2014). The rhetoric of moderation in deliberative discourse: Barack Obama's December 1, 2009 speech at West Point. *Cogency*, 6(1), 63–90. https://www.academia.edu/8773642/The_Rhetoric _of_Moderation_in_Deliberative_Discourse_Barack_Obama_s_December _1_2009_Speech_at_West_Point

Epstein, R. J. & Lerer, L. (2020, August 17). The democrats are downsizing their convention to almost nothing. *The New York Times*. https://www.nytimes .com/2020/07/17/us/politics/democratic-convention-milwaukee.html

Former Illinois Republican Governor Jim Edgar says he'll vote for Biden. (2020, August 26). *WTVO*. https://www.mystateline.com/news/local-news/former -illinois-republican-governor-jim-edgar-says-hell-vote-for-biden/

Glueck, K. (2019, December 25). The 'But I would vote for Joe Biden' Republicans. *The New York Times*. https://www.nytimes.com/2019/12/25/us /politics/joe-biden-2020-republicans.html

Jamieson, K. H. & Taussig, D. (2017). Disruption, demonization, deliverance, and norm destruction: The rhetorical signature of Donald J. Trump. *Political Science Quarterly*, 132(4), 619–650. https://doi.org/10.1002 /polq.12699

Kelly, C. R. (2020). Donald J. Trump and the rhetoric of ressentiment. *Quarterly Journal of Speech*, 106(1), 2–24. https://doi.org/10.1080/00335630.2019 .1698756

Kristaansen, L. J. & Kaussler, B. (2018). The bullshit doctrine: Fabrications, lies, and nonsense in the age of Trump. *Informal Logic*, 38(1), 13–52. https://doi .org/10.22329/il.v38il.5067

Kristol, W. (2020, March 2). The simple answer: Don't overthink your Super Tuesday vote. *The Bulwark*. https://thebulwark.com/the-simple-answer/

Lakin, M. & Ostrowski, M. S. (2014). Ideology in the age of the coalition: The strange rebirth of British centrism. *Journal of Political Ideologies*, 19(1), 15–40. https://doi.org/10.1080/13569317.2013.869455

Longwell, S. (2020, March 9). 'Never Trump' Republicans will support Biden, not Sanders. *The New York Times*. https://www.nytimes.com/2020/03/09 /opinion/joe-biden-never-trump.html

McCain Alums for Joe Biden. (2020, August 26). McCain alums endorse Joe Biden for president. *Medium*. https://medium.com/@mccain4biden /mccain-alums-for-biden-73ac3682d89e

McComiskey, B. (2017). *Post-truth rhetoric and composition*. Logan, UT: Utah State University Press.

Mouffe, C. (1998). The radical centre: A politics without adversary. *Soundings*, 9, 11–23. http://banmarchive.org.uk/collections/soundings/09_11.pdf

Nagle, M. & Verhovek, J. (2020, August 24). Democratic campaign launches 'Republicans for Biden' as Flake, former GOP lawmakers endorse him. *ABC News*. https://abcnews.go.com/Politics/campaign -launches-republicans-biden-flake-gop-lawmakers-endorse/story?id =72566867

Neville-Shepard, M. (2014). Disturbing the conventions of national political conventions: Crossover addresses and reluctant testimony. In C. Palczewski (Ed.), *Disturbing Argument* (pp. 207–212). New York, NY: Routledge.

Neville-Shepard, R. (2019a). Genre-busting: Campaign speech genres and the rhetoric of outsider candidates. In S. Heidt & M. Stuckey (Eds.), *Reading the Presidency: Advances in Presidential Rhetoric* (pp 86–105). New York, NY: Peter Lang.

Neville-Shepard, R. (2019b). Post-presumption argumentation and the post-truth world: On the conspiracy rhetoric of Donald Trump. *Argumentation and Advocacy*, 55(3), 175–193. https://doi.org/10.1080/10511431.2019 .1603027

Neville-Shepard, R. & Neville-Shepard, M. (2020). The pornified presidency: Hyper-masculinity and the pornographic style in U.S. political rhetoric. *Feminist Media Studies*. Advance online publication. https://doi.org/10 .1080/14680777.2020.1786429

Quinn, M. (2020, September 24). 'This time is different': Biden attracts slew of endorsements from retired military, GOP officials. *CBS News*. https://www.cbsnews .com/news/2020-endorsements-biden-retired-military-republicans/

Ridge, T. (2020, September 27). I was a Republican governor of Pa. I'm voting for Joe Biden. *The Philadelphia Inquirer*. https://www.inquirer.com/opinion /commentary/tom-ridge-trump-biden-election-2020-vote-20200927 .html

Rowland, R. C. (2018). Donald Trump and the rejection of the norms of American politics and rhetoric. In B. R. Warner, D. G. Bystrom, M. S. McKinney, & M. C. Banwart (Eds.), *An unprecedented election: Media, communication, and the electorate in the 2016 campaign* (pp. 189–205). Westport, CT: Praeger.

Rowland, R. C. (2019). The populist and nationalist roots of Trump's rhetoric. *Rhetoric and Public Affairs*, 22(3), 343–388. https://www.jstor.org/stable /10.14321/rhetpublaffa.22.3.0343

Russell, E. (2020, August 26). Former Republican senator from Maine endorses Biden. *Portland Press Herald*. https://www.pressherald.com/2020/08/26 /former-republican-senator-from-maine-bill-cohen-endorses-biden/

Stankiewicz, K. (2020, September 20). 'Character counts'—Carly Fiorina, GOP presidential candidate in 2016, explains why she'll vote for Biden. *CNBC*. https://www.cnbc.com/2020/09/24/ex-gop-presidential-candidate-carly -fiorina-on-her-vote-for-joe-biden.html

Stanton, Z. (2021, March 4). The rise of the Biden Republican. *Politico*. https:// www.politico.com/news/magazine/2021/03/04/reagan-democrats -biden-republicans-politics-stan-greenberg-473330

Steele, M. (2020, October 20). I'm a Republican voting for Joe Biden over Trump. Because I'm an American first. *NBC News*. https://www.nbcnews.com

/think/opinion/i-m-republican-voting-joe-biden-over-trump-because-i
-ncna1243952

Taylor, J. I. (2020, October 29). 'Donald Trump is an embarrassment': 'Reagan Republican' Mike Fasano backs Joe Biden. *Florida Politics*. https://floridapolitics
.com/archives/378543-donald-trump-is-an-embarrassment-reagan
-republican-mike-fasano-backs-joe-biden/

Webb, B. & Cooper, J. J. (2020, September 22). Cindy McCain rebukes fellow
Republican Trump to back Biden for president. *Fox 10 Phoenix*. https://
www.fox10phoenix.com/news/cindy-mccain-rebukes-fellow-republican
-trump-to-back-biden-for-president

Wiley, H. (2020, July 2). These California Republicans will raise money and
campaign against Trump's reelection. *The Sacramento Bee*. https://www
.sacbee.com/news/politics-government/capitol-alert/article243952557
.html

Wurzburger, A. (2020, September 23). Cindy McCain, John Kasich & other
notable Republicans who have supported Joe Biden. *People*. https://people
.com/politics/republicans-who-endorse-joe-biden/?slide=25cfe2eb-3e77
-4c94-bd7a-c2425002bb74#25cfe2eb-3e77-4c94-bd7a-c2425002bb74

Yglesias, M. (2020, August 17). John Kasich makes the Republican's case for
Joe Biden. *Vox*. https://www.vox.com/2020/8/17/21373196/john-kasich
-dnc-speech-transcript

CHAPTER THIRTEEN

Trump's Disruptive Debate: Analyzing the Candidate Branding Costs

*Josh C. Bramlett, Benjamin R. Warner,
and Mitchell S. McKinney*

On September 29, 2020, President Donald Trump and former Vice President Joe Biden participated in the first of two general election presidential debates in the 2020 election cycle. For 90 minutes, the pair went back and forth in a debate moderated by Fox News's longtime anchor Chris Wallace. Reactions both during and after the debate were universally negative. Media pundits criticized the debate for the constant interruptions and lack of structure (Martin & Burns, 2020). Post-debate punditry labeled the debate "a dumpster fire" (Poniewozik, 2020, para. 6), "vicious" (Breuninger & Wilkie, 2020, headline), "chaotic" (Segers et al., 2020, para. 1), and "a national humiliation" (Smith, 2020, para. 1). Much of this criticism focused on President Trump, whose disruptive behavior is detailed in this chapter. Most polls found that viewers thought Biden had performed better in the first debate (Bump, 2020), and analysis of the debate dialogue found that Trump interrupted Biden or Wallace a total of 128 times for a rate of approximately one and a half interruptions per minute (Stahl, 2020).

In the intervening period between the first and final debate, the Commission on Presidential Debates (CPD) was forced to adopt new debate rules, stating, "Last night's debate made clear that additional structure should be added to the format to ensure a more orderly discussion of the issues [and] the CPD intends to ensure that additional tools to maintain order are in place for the remaining debates" (2020b). These changes prompted criticism from Trump, who tweeted, "Why would I allow the Debate Commission to change the rules for the second and third Debates when I easily won last time?" (Gregorian, 2020, para. 2). Trump was later diagnosed with COVID-19, and the CPD announced the planned second debate would be virtual (Ross, 2020). Trump refused to participate in a virtual town hall debate, and the two candidates each had separate televised town halls (Bradner & Liptak, 2020).

Both campaigns agreed to participate in a final debate even after the CPD announced that interruptions would lead to microphones being muted (Sganga & Watson, 2020). People within the Trump campaign understood that the president needed a better performance, viewing his first debate performance as "an avoidable tragedy in the president's quest for reelection" (Orr, 2020, para. 2). From a strategic communication perspective, candidates who perform well in debates can activate more favorability from supporters (Bramlett, 2021a; Warner et al., 2020). Candidates who do not perform well can be judged harshly for their poor performance, although this can be tempered by partisanship (Schrott & Lanoue, 2013; Warner et al., 2020). Trump needed to perform well in the second and final debate to overcome his disruptive first debate performance.

Candidate brand favorability is a concept centered on memory-based processing of political information (Bramlett, 2021a; Nielsen, 2016, 2017). A political candidate's brand is the composition of the brand associations retrievable from a voter's memory. The associations that are most readily retrieved from memory after viewing a debate are the most accessible brand elements of a candidate. These associations can be about the candidate's image and persona, political party affiliation, and policy positions (Bramlett, 2021a; Speed et al., 2015). Memory-based associations can be positive or negative (Bramlett, 2021a). In 2020, both candidates, and most notably Trump, were criticized after the first debate, while both candidates received more positive reviews after their second debate performances. This chapter will compare the first with the final presidential debate to understand the brand costs of Trump's disruption to normal democratic processes related to campaigning.

Our study examines voter evaluations of the candidates after each of the two general election presidential debates in 2020. We do so with a post-debate survey that examines candidate brand favorability immediately after viewing a debate. We test the candidate brand association effects of each debate performance, as well as the constraints of partisan-motivated reasoning (Mullinix, 2015; Warner et al., 2020). This design allows us to overcome a limitation of recent voter preference polling, as viewers from both parties, as well as independents, participated in our study. Polling has been found to suffer from nonresponse bias from Trump supporters (Isakov & Kuriwaki, 2020). Debate media coverage can also influence public polling taken in the hours and days following debates, as post-debate coverage can influence viewer perceptions of candidates (Fridkin et al., 2008).

Our study addresses these limitations through the recruitment of participants who viewed the debates as part of our research activity—thus debate performance will not influence one's willingness to respond to a post-debate survey, and media coverage will not influence responses because the post-debate survey is completed immediately following the debate. Thus, our results are not confounded by partisan nonresponse or media framing effects. We therefore assess immediate reactions to the first and second debate and how partisans and independents judged the political brands of both candidates.

Presidential Debate Effects

Presidential debates are viewed as a ritual of the electoral system (Greenberg, 2009), and every four years, presidential debates serve as "focal points" for campaign arguments (Carlin, 1992). Debates receive the highest television ratings of any political event and are comparable to the most viewed events on television (McKinney, 2018; Schroeder, 2008). The first debate generally receives higher ratings than other debates in a given series (Kenski & Stroud, 2005). In fact, in the 2020 cycle, 73 million viewers watched the first presidential debate and 63 million watched the second (Landrum, 2020). The prominence of the first debate in the political ritual makes the first debate in 2020 especially troubling, especially as this exchange was a disruption of democratic norms and a departure from presidential debate customs.

Voters tune into presidential debates to be informed about where candidates stand on policy issues (Benoit & Hansen, 2004; Holbrook, 1996; Jamieson & Birdsell, 1988; Jennings et al., 2020b; Jennings et al., 2021; Jennings et al., 2022). Presidential debates also serve as an opportunity for undecided voters to evaluate their vote choice (Carlin & McKinney, 1994). While primary debates produce shifts in candidate preference more than general election debates (McKinney & Warner, 2013; Warner et al., 2018a), general election debates can persuade voters through attitude change, formation, and reinforcement (Holbert, 2005; Keum & Cho, 2021; Warner & McKinney, 2013). Voters who view general election debates often come away supporting their preferred candidate more while liking the opposing candidate less (Blais & Perrella, 2008; Mullinix, 2015; Warner et al., 2020). In addition to informing and persuading voters, presidential debates typically produce positive normative outcomes such as reducing political cynicism, increasing political interest, and increasing political efficacy (Bramlett, 2021b; Drew & Weaver, 2006; Jamieson, 2015; McKinney & Warner, 2013; Pfau, 1987). The widely criticized first debate of 2020, however, may not have served as a positive democratic ritual.

The First Presidential Debate in 2020

The departure from norms was evident during the first presidential debate in 2020, even to the moderator. For instance, moderator Wallace appealed to Trump that "I think that the country would be better served if we allowed both people to speak with fewer interruptions. I'm appealing to you, please sir, please do that" (Commission on Presidential Debates, 2020a, para. 482). Unfortunately, Trump ignored this plea, along with 25 others from Wallace to follow the rules of the debate (Stahl, 2020). While much of the media criticism focused on Trump's performance, at one point Biden pleaded, "Will you just shut up man?" (Commission on Presidential Debates, 2020a, para. 146), which received criticism for how an incumbent president was addressed (Beauchamp, 2020; Grabowski, 2020). Overall, the normatively negative outcome of the first debate was best summarized by *CNN*'s Jake Tapper, who stated, "We can talk about who won the debate and who lost the debate, but I can tell you one thing for sure, the American people lost tonight because that was just horrific" (Lopez, 2020, para. 6).

The chaos and spectacle that was the first 2020 presidential debate illustrate a favored communication strategy often utilized by Trump. Before the candidates took the stage, one of our authors predicted to James McCarten of Canada's *National Observer* that "Trump's strategy will be to keep the debate from taking up the primary proposition that usually these debates are focused on when an incumbent is seeking re-election . . . Trump's antics, the taunting, the tirades, the conspiracies will all be for Joe Biden to have to clean up, to have to respond, to have to defend, all of that will keep the discussion off of the last four years and Trump's record" (McCarten, 2020, paras. 7–8). Furthermore, *The Washington Post* reported ahead of the debate that Trump planned to attack Biden on such topics as his age and his son Hunter Biden and that the Biden campaign expected "a venomous barrage" (Sullivan & Dawsey, 2020, para. 3).

Criticisms of the first debate were not only about interruptions and lack of decorum. Several of the responses from President Trump stood out for their troubling content. For example, when asked by Wallace, "What are you prepared to do to reassure the American people that the next president will be the legitimate winner of this election," Trump responded with a string of unsubstantiated claims and conspiracy theories to call into question the legitimacy of the upcoming election. He said:

> This is going to be a fraud like you've never seen. But you know what? We won't know. We might not know for months because these ballots are going to be all over. Take a look at what happened in Manhattan. Take a look at what happened in New Jersey. Take a look at what happened in Virginia and other places. . . . They're not losing 2%, 1%, which by the way is too much. An election could be won or lost with that. They're losing 30 and 40%. It's a fraud, and it's a shame. . . . It's a rigged election. . . . They have mailmen with lots of it. Did you see what's going on? Take a look at West Virginia, mailman selling the ballots. They're being sold. They're being dumped in rivers. This is a horrible thing for our country. . . . This is not going to end well. . . . This is not going to end well. (Commission on Presidential Debates, 2020a, paras. 801–826)

When Wallace directly asked Trump, "Are you willing, tonight, to condemn white supremacists and militia groups," Trump first demurred, suggesting he wasn't aware of any such groups, but finally arguing the real problem was "from the left-wing, not right-wing" and, in the end, the president told the white supremacist group the Proud Boys to "stand back and stand by" to deal with Trump's so-called "left-wing problem." Trump stated, "Proud Boys, stand back and stand by. But I'll tell you what, I'll tell you what. Somebody's got to do something about Antifa and the left because this is not a right-wing problem, this is a left-wing, this is a left-wing problem" (Commission on Presidential Debates, 2020a, paras. 614–634). Trump's exchange with Wallace (and Biden) went this way (Commission on Presidential Debates, 2020a, paras. 614–634):

> *Wallace*: Are you prepared specifically to do it [condemn White supremacists and White militia groups]. Well, go ahead, sir.
>
> *Trump*: I would say almost everything I see is from the left-wing not from the right wing.
>
> *Wallace*: So, what are you, what are you saying?
>
> *Trump*: I'm willing to do anything. I want to see peace.
>
> *Wallace*: Well, do it, sir.
>
> *Biden*: Say it. Do it. Say it.
>
> *Trump*: You want to call them? What do you want to call them? Give me a name, give me a name, go ahead who would you like me to condemn.
>
> *Wallace*: White supremacists and racists.
>
> *Biden*: Proud Boys.
>
> *Wallace*: White supremacists and White militias.

Biden: Proud Boys.

Trump: Proud Boys, stand back and stand by. But I'll tell you what, I'll tell you what. Somebody's got to do something about Antifa and the left because this is not a right wing problem, this is a left-wing, this is a left-wing problem . . .

Biden: His own FBI Director said unlike White supremacists . . .

Trump: This is a left-wing problem.

Biden: Antifa is an idea not an organization . . .

Trump: Oh you gotta be kidding.

Biden: . . . not a militia. That's what his FBI Director said.

Trump: Well, then you know what, he's wrong.

Wallace: Gentlemen, gentlemen. No, no, no, we're done, sir. Moving on to the next . . . [*crosstalk*]

White supremacists and far-right militia groups were buoyed by Trump's statements—reading them as clear endorsements. Social media accounts associated with the Proud Boys responded directly to the president by assuring him, "Standing down and standing by sir," along with two video clips of Trump's debate reply that was sent to all followers of these accounts with the accompanying tag "God. Family. Brotherhood." Yet another account associated with the Proud Boys rebranded their page following the president's shout-out by incorporating the phrase "Stand back. Stand by" as part of their social media logo (Collins & Zadrozny, 2020, para. 2). Trump's comments about the election and about these right-wing white nationalist groups were a presage to the most disruptive event of the 2020 election cycle when these very groups stormed the U.S. Capitol on January 6, 2021, in an attempt to overturn the election on the basis of the conspiracies of election fraud articulated by Trump in this debate (and elsewhere).

The Second Presidential Debate in 2020

The second presidential debate featured a different, more civil strategy from Trump. Commentators noted that Trump was more respectful of the moderator and "adopted a more subdued tone for much of the debate" (Barrow & Miller, 2020, para. 12). *Politico* reported that "he did what his advisers suggested he would do. He toned himself down, amplifying the substance of what he said over the bombast" (Siders, 2020, para. 13). Pundits complemented the performances of both candidates in the second debate. For instance, Anthony Zurcher of *BBC News* noted that "the candidates allowed each other to speak. They used respectful tones. Even when they went on the attack, they did so in a calm, deliberate manner" (Zurcher, 2020, para. 2).

Furthermore, the second debate was a more traditional debate. Reporters for *The Washington Post* wrote that "the constant interruptions from the first debate were replaced by a clearer contrast between their competing views for the country and more sharply defined exchanges of attacks and retorts" (Olorunnipa et al., 2020, para. 2). Praise was given for the moderator, Kristen Welker of *NBC News*, with Deirdre Walsh of *NPR* noting that Welker "skillfully kept the conversation moving. She followed up and pressed for answers and fairly gave both candidates opportunities to respond to the other's comments" (Walsh, 2020).

Viewers also noticed the different debate strategy. *Politico/Morning Consult* conducted polls after each debate, and for the first debate, 50% of voters thought Biden had the better performance, while 34% said Trump did (Elbeshbishi, 2020, para. 3). After the second debate, 54% thought Biden performed better, while 39% said Trump did (Elbeshbishi, 2020, para. 2). While Biden was viewed as performing better in both debates, Trump did close the gap in the second debate and garnered more support. Furthermore, 65% of viewers thought the candidates were respectful toward each other in the second debate, while only 10% thought that after the first debate (Elbeshbishi, 2020, para. 5). The first debate was clearly disruptive. The second debate was a more traditional debate where both candidates performed competently for their strategic communication aims.

Cognitive Debate Effects

Mitchell McKinney and Diana Carlin (2004) argue that televised presidential debates have three types of effects: latent, behavioral, and cognitive (pp. 210–214). Latent effects refer to normative outcomes such as shifts in political interest. Behavioral effects primarily concern changes in vote choice. Cognitive effects relate to how voters process information from a debate and what type of information voters retain from a debate. Cognitive research often examines voter learning from debates, as well as voters' psychological weighting of candidate image thoughts compared to candidate policy thoughts (Benoit & Hansen, 2004; Benoit et al., 2001; Benoit et al., 2003; Hacker, 2004; McKinney et al., 2003; Zhu et al., 1994). Debate viewers learn about policy issues and candidate image, although the extent of each is debated in the literature (McKinney et al., 2003; Zhu et al., 1994). Further, candidate image perceptions shift after debate viewing (Benoit et al., 2001; Benoit et al., 2003; Jennings et al., 2017; Jennings et al., 2020a; Katz & Feldman, 1962; Warner et al., 2019).

Cognitive effects are measured in a variety of ways focused on information processing, information acquisition, and information retention. Debate viewers process information through online processing, as well as memory-based processing (Kim & Garrett, 2012). Online processing consists of voters updating their "online tally" of information in real time as they consume political information (Bramlett et al., 2018; McGraw et al., 1990). Memory-based processing consists of retrieving thoughts related to policies and candidate personas from voters' working memory (Bramlett, 2021a; Kim & Garrett, 2012). Kim and Garrett (2012) argue that voters use both online and memory-based processing as they consume political debates. Both the real-time online processing and retrospective memory processing are guided by heuristic and deliberative thinking in ways that influence what voters think about candidates (Jennings et al., 2017; Warner & Banwart, 2016; Warner et al., 2018b). These thoughts, in real time or retrospectively, influence global evaluations of candidates (Houston et al., 2013; Jennings et al., 2017; Jennings et al., 2020a; McKinney et al., 2014).

One way to measure memory-based processing is through associative memory (Anderson, 1983; Bramlett, 2021a). Brand associative memory is measured through brand association tasks, which are a form of thought-listing (Cwalina & Falkowski, 2015; Petty & Cacioppo, 1986). Voters who consume political stimuli such as debates are asked to recall what they can about the candidates (Bramlett, 2021a; Nielsen, 2016). These associative thoughts can be positive, negative, or neutral and can be about candidate persona, policy positions, or party affiliation (Bramlett, 2021a; Cwalina & Falkowski, 2015; Speed et al., 2015). The sum total of associations comprises a candidate's brand. Josh Bramlett (2021a) defines a candidate brand as "the cumulative collection of retrievable associations in memory that voters have about a candidate" (p. 282). The extent to which brand associations toward a candidate are positive or negative comprises the candidate's brand favorability (Bramlett, 2021a; Nielsen, 2016). In sum, candidate brand associations measure how much candidate information is retrievable from viewer memory and how the favorability of this information compares between competing candidates.

Competent candidates who participate in debates can see higher positive brand favorability with their supporters than negative brand favorability with detractors (Bramlett, 2021a). Televised debates, as political marketing events, can help candidates' brand image with supporters (Bramlett, 2021a). However, how a candidate performs in a debate will influence how voters evaluate a candidate (Schrott & Lanoue, 2013; Warner et al. 2020). Exceptional or dreadful performances by a candidate can be so obvious that fellow partisans can reluctantly acknowledge the reality of that performance (Schrott & Lanoue, 2013; Warner et al., 2020). Notable examples of exceptional performances would be Bill Clinton in the 1992 town hall debate and Mitt Romney in the first 2012 debate (Schrott & Lanoue, 2013; Warner et al., 2020). Examples of poorer performances would be George W. Bush in the first 2004 debate and both Barack Obama and John McCain in the second 2008 debate (Warner et al., 2020). In essence, even when accounting for partisanship, the effects of debate viewing depend on what happens in the debates. Candidates can perform poorly and be judged harshly, or they can perform well and be lauded. Brand associations are a particularly useful way to assess these outcomes, as they can account for positive and negative thoughts directed toward each candidate (Bramlett, 2021a).

Therefore, based on our assessment of the content of the two 2020 presidential debates—supported by punditry and post-debate polling—we can expect Donald Trump to receive more negative brand associations in the minds of voters in the first debate compared to the second debate. After viewing his performance in debate 1, more negative thoughts would be more readily retrievable from viewers' memory. Therefore, we posit this hypothesis:

H1: Donald Trump will receive (a) fewer positive and (b) more negative brand associations in the first debate compared to the second debate.

Although media criticism after the first debate focused on Trump's abhorrent behavior, Biden also received some rebuke. For instance, his "will you shut up, man" line drew critiques (Beauchamp, 2020; Grabowski, 2020). Both candidates, however, were judged as having participated in a better overall second debate (Elbeshbishi, 2020). Therefore, in relation to Biden's candidate branding, we expect that:

H2: Joe Biden will receive (a) fewer positive and (b) more negative brand associations in the first debate compared to the second debate.

Although candidate performances are central to how viewers respond to debates (Schrott & Lanoue, 2013), partisans are not neutral arbiters of debate content (Munro et al., 2002). The theory of motivated reasoning holds that voters process information through a partisan lens (Bolsen et al., 2014; Kunda, 1990; Lodge & Taber, 2013). In debate viewing, voters favor the arguments of the candidate they supported before the debate (Jarman, 2016; Kim et al., 2021; Munro et al., 2002). Further, because partisanship functions as an important facet of many people's social identities (Greene, 1999), partisans are incentivized to defend and elevate the candidate from their group against attacks from the opposition (Mason, 2018), not unlike the way people root for a favored sports team (Vancil & Pendell, 1984). While we expect the first debate to have more overall negative brand associations compared to the second debate, when assessing candidate branding within each debate, we can expect more favorable associations toward one's preferred candidate and less favorable associations toward the opposing candidate. Therefore, we posit the following hypothesis:

H3: Across both debates, partisans will provide more positive and fewer negative brand associations of the ingroup candidate compared to the outgroup candidate such that Republicans will provide more positive associations and fewer negative associations of Trump and Democrats will provide more positive associations and fewer negative associations of Biden.

Although our general expectation is of partisan bias in brand evaluations, we expect the first debate to deviate from the norm. Even among Republicans, Trump's performance in the first debate should result in a reduction in Trump's brand associations, not an increase, as it was an unusually poor performance. However, because Republicans have incentive to minimize the disaster and because Democrats have incentive to exaggerate it, there should be partisan differences in the effects of Trump's poor debate on his candidate brand. Therefore, the final hypothesis posits that partisanship will moderate the comparative difference in Trump's brand from the first to final debate:

H4: The negative effect of the first debate will be weakest among Republicans such that the gap in positive and negative brand associations for Trump from the first to the second debate will be smaller for Republicans compared to Democrats and Independents.

Method

Data were collected in collaboration with a national research team composed of 12 participating universities: University of Arkansas, Cameron University, Eastern New Mexico University, Iowa State University, Johnson County Community College, University of Kansas, University of Louisville, Marquette University, University of Missouri, Salisbury University, Southern Utah University, and University of Wisconsin-Whitewater. Participants were undergraduate students enrolled in a communication or journalism course who completed the study for course credit. Research shows that student samples generate inferences about debate effects that are indistinguishable from those generated by adult samples (Benoit et al., 2003).

Participants were contacted by a member of the national research team at their home institution. When contacted, they were provided a link to a Qualtrics survey to be completed one hour prior to the live airing of one of the debates. After completing the pretest questionnaire, the Qualtrics survey provided participants a link to a Zoom session in which they viewed the live debate and received a link to a post-debate questionnaire. All procedures were approved by the institutional review board of the lead institution.

Participants

In total, 339 people completed the study, 171 for the first presidential debate and 168 for the second presidential debate. The sample was young (M_{age} = 22, SD_{age} = 6), majority female (65%), majority White (71%), and more Democratic (48%) compared to Republican (35%) or Independent (17%).

Measures

Brand Favorability

The post-debate questionnaire asked participants, "When thinking about the debate you just watched, what are 10 things that come to mind first?" They were then provided 10 textboxes to fill in whatever thoughts came to mind. After completing this form, they were presented with the text they had typed into each of the 10 lines above, one at a time, and asked, "You said [blank]. How would you rate that thought?" The questionnaire was programmed to pipe in whatever they typed in the textbox so that, for example, if a person wrote, "Trump was upset," the question would read, "You said Trump was upset. How would you rate that thought?" The response options were "positive about Biden, negative about Biden, positive about Trump, negative about Trump, none of the above." From these responses, we computed four variables capturing the total number of positive and negative thoughts about each candidate. Summary statistics are presented in Table 13.1.

Partisan Affiliation

Participants were asked, "To what extent do you consider yourself a Democrat or Republican?" This variable was collapsed from a 7-point scale ranging from "Strong Democrat" to "Strong Republican" into a three-category grouping variable such that strong Democrats, Democrats, and lean Democrats were categorized as Democrats; strong Republicans, Republicans, and lean Republicans were categorized as Republicans; and those who selected "no preference" were categorized as Independents.

Results

Hypotheses were tested using a 2 × 3 between-factor analysis of variance (ANOVA) in which party identification (Democrat, Republican, and Independent) and debate (first or second) were the between factors. Table 13.1 reports the means and standard deviations for positive and negative brand associations for both Trump and Biden. These brand associations are reported overall for debate 1 and pooled across debates for Democrats, Republicans, and Independents. Table 13.2 separates each brand association across time and party to illustrate how Democrats, Republicans, and Independents differed from the first to last debate. Table 13.3 reports the omnibus tests to determine if the brand associations differed across debates and partisanship.

The first hypothesis predicted that, overall, Trump would receive (H1a) fewer positive and (H1b) more negative brand associations after the first debate compared to the second. This hypothesis was supported in full. As

Table 13.1   Summary of Brand Associations by Debate and Partisanship

Main Effects		Debate 1	Debate 2	Republican	Democrat	Independent
	n	171	168	119	162	58
Trump Positive	M	1.05	1.68***	2.66	0.61	0.79
	SD	(2.05)	(2.36)	(2.72)	(1.53)	(1.45)
Trump Negative	M	5.23	4.17***	2.84	5.93	5.12
	SD	(3.33)	3.22	(2.99)	(2.92)	(3.29)
Biden Positive	M	1.38	2.27***	1.14	2.46	1.45
	SD	(1.93)	2.59	1.86	2.57	1.96
Biden Negative	M	2.94	2.23*	3.49	1.63	3.41
	SD	(2.94)	(2.38)	(2.76)	(2.09)	(3.17)

Note: Party scores are averaged across both debates. Significance tests for differences conducted across debate indicating whether the brand association scores are significantly different after the second debate compared to the first debate, $p < 0.05$*, $p < 0.01$**, $p < 0.001$***.

indicated in Table 13.1, on average Trump received one positive association and more than five negative associations per viewer after the first debate. However, his second debate resulted in one and two-thirds positive brand associations, a significant increase, and just over four negative associations, a significant reduction. Thus, overall, Trump's first debate performance resulted in significantly less positivity and significantly more negativity compared to his second debate performance.

The second hypothesis predicted Biden would also receive (H2a) fewer positive and (H2b) more negative brand associations in the first debate compared to the second. Again, this hypothesis was supported in full. Biden saw an increase in positive associations from not quite one and one-half to approximately two and one-third in the second debate. Overall, negative brand associations were quite a bit lower for Biden compared to Trump in each debate. In the first debate Biden received approximately three negative brand associations per viewer (compared to more than five for Trump), and this declined to about two and a quarter for the second debate.

The third hypothesis predicted partisan bias in brand associations such that Democrats would provide fewer positive brand associations of Trump and more positive brand associations of Biden compared to Republicans and,

Table 13.2 Summary of Brand Associations by Party and Debate

Interaction Effects		Republicans		Democrats		Independents	
		Debate 1	Debate 2	Debate 1	Debate 2	Debate 1	Debate 2
	n	67	52	75	87	29	29
Trump Positive	M	2.02	3.48**	0.44	0.759	0.38	1.21#
	SD	(2.63)	(2.63)	(1.33)	(1.68)	(0.94)	(1.74)
Trump Negative	M	3.57	1.9**	6.56	5.38*	5.66	4.59
	SD	(3.13)	(2.52)	(2.77)	(2.96)	(3.54)	(2.99)
Biden Positive	M	0.84	1.54	1.80	3.02**	1.55	1.34
	SD	(1.64)	(2.06)	(1.97)	(2.88)	(2.18)	(1.74)
Biden Negative	M	3.51	3.46	2.04	1.28*	3.97	2.86
	SD	(2.99)	(2.48)	(2.29)	(1.85)	(3.70)	(2.48)

Note: Significance tests for pairwise comparisons conducted with Bonferroni adjustment, $p < 0.1^{\#}$, $p < 0.05^{*}$, $p < 0.01^{**}$, $p < 0.001^{***}$.

conversely, Democrats would provide more negative brand associations of Trump and fewer negative brand associations of Biden compared to Republicans. As indicated by the party factor in Table 13.3 and mean differences reported in Table 13.1, the partisanship variable explained significant variance in brand associations for both candidates in each debate. The effect sizes reported in Table 13.3 illustrate that partisanship was a more substantial factor in explaining variance in brand associations compared to the differences in the actual quality of the candidate debate performances across the two debates. As illustrated in Table 13.1, the differences were such that Republicans provided (on average) two more positive brand associations of Trump compared to Democrats, and Democrats provided greater than two more positive brand associations of Biden compared to Republicans. Negative brand associations resulted in a similar finding—Democrats provided approximately three more negative brand associations for Trump compared to Republicans, and Republicans provided almost two more negative brand associations for Biden compared to Democrats.

The final hypothesis predicted that partisanship would moderate the differences in brand associations for Trump from the first to the second debate.

Table 13.3   ANOVA Tests of Brand Associations

Factor	DF	F	η2
Donald Trump Positive Brand Associations			
Party	2,333	42.53***	0.20
Debate	1,333	14.08***	0.04
Party*Debate	2,333	2.88*	0.02
Donald Trump Negative Brand Associations			
Party	2,333	41.25***	0.19
Debate	1,333	17.08***	0.05
Party*Debate	2,333	0.29	<0.01
Joe Biden Positive Brand Associations			
Party	2,333	11.73***	0.07
Debate	1,333	10.96***	0.03
Party*Debate	2,333	2.29	0.01
Joe Biden Negative Brand Associations			
Party	2,333	20.93***	0.11
Debate	1,333	4.29*	0.01
Party*Debate	2,333	1.07	0.01

Note: $p < 0.05$*, $p < 0.01$**, $p < 0.001$***.

We hypothesized that the nature of these differences would be such that the gap in brand associations between the first and second debates would be larger for Democrats and Independents compared to Republicans. The interaction of partisanship and debate reported in Table 13.3 indicates that party identification did moderate the difference in debates for positive brand associations for Trump, but not for negative brand associations. No interaction of partisanship and debate was predicted for Biden, and indeed none was observed.

The conditional difference in positive brand association for Trump was contrary to our hypothesis. There were no apparent differences in positive brand associations for Trump among Democrats—they scarcely found a thing worthy of positive comment for either of Trump's debate performances. Republicans, by contrast, were much more positive about Trump's second debate performance than the first, giving him three and one-half positive brand associations compared to only two for the first debate. Independents were as critical of Trump's first debate as Democrats but were more favorably disposed to his second debate performance. They increased their positive associations from less than one-half to almost one and a quarter. In sum, H4 was not supported. Although partisanship did moderate the effect of the uneven debate performances of Trump, this was restricted to positive brand associations and was more pronounced among Republicans, not Democrats.

Discussion

The 2020 presidential election featured a variety of norm disruptions from mail-in voting to virtual convention addresses to a tumultuous transition that culminated with the Capitol insurrection on January 6, 2021 (Sabato, 2021). Among the most viewed and commented upon norm disruptions was the uncivil, interruption-laden first presidential debate on September 29, 2020. The widespread criticism of the first debate drove both candidates to focus on better performances in the final debate on October 22, 2020. Our study analyzed the retrievable memory-based associations that viewers had about each candidate after each debate. We tested the influence of debate and partisanship on the brand favorability of Trump and Biden in the first and second debates.

Televised presidential debates are the most-watched moments of the campaign (Kenski & Stroud, 2005; McKinney, 2018). Televised debates provide candidates with the opportunity to promote their campaign agenda and present themselves as presidential to audiences of millions (Jackson-Beeck & Meadow, 1978; Schroeder, 2008). Debate participation allows candidates to influence what voters think about their image traits and issue positions (Benoit & Hansen, 2004; McKinney et al., 2003). Promoting one's image is central to marketing and branding (Keller, 1993; Newman, 1994). In other words, political debates provide candidates with a political marketing opportunity (Bramlett, 2021a; Nielsen & Larson, 2014). Participating in a debate can result in debate candidate branding, defined as a process where "competent candidates who participate in the marketing events of televised debates will strengthen their brand identity in the associative memory of supporters more than they will weaken it with detractors" (Bramlett, 2021a, p. 293).

In the first presidential debate of 2020, Trump received widespread criticism for his lack of decorum, as well as for his controversial statements. In the second debate, Trump rebounded with a more conventional approach. However, by that time millions of Americans had already voted (Dickinson, 2020). Therefore, the Trump campaign's approach to the debates served as a missed marketing opportunity to activate supporters and win over undecided voters.

Results from our study confirm public opinion polling following both debates. Debate viewers generated more negative brand associations toward Trump after the first debate compared to the second debate. Moreover, there were significantly fewer positive associations toward Trump in the first debate compared to the second debate. After viewing the first debate and processing the information presented on television, debate viewers came away with more readily retrievable negative associations about Trump's candidate brand. However, the aftermath of the first debate also led to more negative associations toward Biden compared to the second debate. Therefore, from a negative campaigning perspective, Trump did succeed in using his combative approach to lower the candidate brand favorability of Biden (Arceneaux & Nickerson, 2010). Still, the amount of negative brand favorability toward Biden was significantly lower than the amount of negative brand favorability toward Trump in both debates.

When assessing brand favorability within each debate, results from our study support prior research on debate candidate branding and candidate evaluations (Bramlett, 2021a; Mullinix, 2015; Warner et al., 2020). In both debates, Republicans retrieved more positive associations toward Trump than Democrats, and Democrats retrieved more positive associations toward Biden than Republicans. Similarly, Democrats retrieved more negative associations toward Trump than Republicans, while Republicans retrieved more negative associations toward Biden than Democrats. Debate viewers favor their preferred candidate regardless of performance (Jarman, 2016). However, the strength of this preference is based on performance (Schrott & Lanoue, 2013; Warner et al., 2020).

Our study observed that Republicans did have significantly more positive brand associations toward Trump in the second debate compared to the first. While Republicans still had more positivity toward Trump compared to Biden after the first debate, they came away from the second debate with a much more positive brand evaluation of Trump than after the first debate. The second debate served to reinforce and strengthen positive attitudes better than the first. Moreover, Independents had significantly more positive associations about Trump in the second debate compared to the first. From a strategic communication perspective, this may be one of the most pertinent findings of our study. Debates can help guide undecided voters toward their voting decision (Carlin & McKinney, 1994). Trump missed an opportunity to promote his brand image to undecided voters in the first debate. He rebounded in the second debate, but this occurred after millions had already voted.

Limitations and Future Directions

One limitation of our study design is that there were only two presidential debates in 2020. An additional debate would have provided a better baseline to assess the fallout of the first debate. Further, due to the polarized political landscape, we are unable to determine the extent to which Trump's negative associations may be historically high or par for the course. Because brand associations are a relatively new concept in televised debates research, we also lack historical baselines by which to compare in a presidential context. Bramlett (2021a) studied U.S. Senate debate candidate branding and found that candidates had higher in-party positivity than in-party negativity. Comparatively, while Republican viewers in our study had more positivity toward Trump than Biden, in the first debate even Republican viewers had more negative than positive brand associations toward Trump.

In other studies, Ben Warner and colleagues (2020) used changes in feeling thermometer scores to evaluate debate performances from 2004 to 2016, and Peter Schrott and David Lanoue (2013) used Gallup polling to assess debates from 1960 to 2008 to measure questions of "who won?"—which is different than assessing positive and negative thoughts toward each candidate. Warner et al. (2020) examined 30 presidential and vice presidential debate performances and found only two instances of a sizable decrease in in-party candidate feeling thermometers after watching a debate. Much more work is needed to build the empirical record necessary to establish norms and expectations for specific candidate brand scores as a measure of debate viewers' cognitive processing. Future research can continue to leverage brand associative memory to understand how people process information from televised political debates. Candidate brand associations can be linked to other variables such as candidate feeling thermometer evaluations and candidate image evaluations (e.g., Warner & Banwart, 2016).

Conclusion

Pundits and scholars will continue to think about the democratic implications of Trump's norm-disrupting first 2020 presidential debate performance. Political campaign professionals should also continue to think about the electoral implications. From a strategic communication perspective, Trump missed a major marketing opportunity in the first presidential debate of 2020. Future candidates should learn a valuable lesson from his communication missteps. While Trump received more positive candidate branding in the second debate, the brand costs and norms disruption from the first debate will linger. As Anthony Zurcher (2020) argued, "The raucous first debate probably will be what the history books remember" (para. 6).

References

Anderson, J. R. (1983). A spreading activation theory of memory. *Journal of Verbal Learning and Verbal Behavior, 22*(3), 261–295. https://https://doi.org/.org/10.1016/S0022-5371(83)90201-3

Arceneaux, K. & Nickerson, D. (2010). Comparing negative and positive campaign messages: Evidence from two field experiments. *American Politics Research, 38*(1), 54–83. https://doi.org/10.1177%2F1532673X09331613

Barrow, B. & Miller, Z. (2020, October 23). Debate takeaways: Round 2 highlights policy over petulance. *Associated Press.* https://apnews.com/article/second-debate-takeaways-trump-biden-f556ef4e356d3296d8de99e48bdd51a1

Beauchamp, B. (2020, September 29). Biden to Trump: "Will you shut up, man?" *Vox.* https://www.vox.com/policy-and-politics/2020/9/29/21494785/biden-trump-debate-will-you-shut-up-man

Benoit, W. L. & Hansen, G. J. (2004). Presidential debate watching, issue knowledge, character evaluation and vote choice. *Human Communication Research, 30,* 124–144. https://doi.org/10.1111/j.1468-2958.2004.tb00727.x

Benoit, W. L., Hansen, G. J., & Verser, R. M. (2003). A meta-analysis of the effects of viewing U.S. presidential debates. *Communication Monographs, 70*(4), 335–350. https://doi.org/.org/:10.1080/0363775032000179133

Benoit, W. L., McKinney, M. S., & Holbert, R. L. (2001). Beyond learning and persona: extending the scope of presidential debate effects. *Communication Monographs, 68,* 259–273. https://doi.org/10.1080/03637750128060

Blais, A. & Perrella, A. M. L. (2008). Systemic effects of televised candidates' debates. *The International Journal of Press/Politics, 13*(4), 451–464. https://doi.org/:10.1177/1940161208323548

Bolsen, T., Druckman, J. N., & Cook, F. (2013). The influence of partisan motivated reasoning on public opinion. *Political Behavior, 36,* 235–262. https://doi.org/:10.1007/s11109-013-9238-0

Bradner, E. & Liptak, K. (2020, October 16). 5 takeaways from the dueling Biden and Trump town halls. *CNN*. https://www.cnn.com/2020/10/15/politics /biden-trump-town-hall-takeaways/index.html

Bramlett, J. C. (2021a). Battles for branding: a political marketing approach to studying televised candidate debates. *Communication Quarterly, 69*(3), 280–300. https://doi.org/:10.1080/01463373.2021.1944889

Bramlett, J. C. (2021b). Exploring the normative and persuasive effects of televised U.S. Senate debates. *Argumentation and Advocacy, 57*(1), 37–56. https://doi.org/:10.1080/10511431.2021.1894393

Bramlett, J. C., McKinney, M. S., & Warner, B. R. (2018). Processing the political: Presidential primary debate 'live-tweeting' as information processing. In B. R. Warner, D. G. Bystrom, M. S. McKinney, & M. C. Banwart, (Eds.), *An Unprecedented Election: Media, Communication, and the Electorate in the 2016 Campaign* (pp. 168–188). Westport, CT: Praeger.

Breuninger, K. & Wilkie, C. (2020, September 29). Vicious first debate between Trump and Biden offered little on policy, lots on conflict. *CNBC*. https:// www.cnbc.com/2020/09/29/first-presidential-debate-highlights-trump -vs-biden-.html

Bump, P. (2020, September 30). Reliable polls show that Biden won the debate— so those aren't what Trump's allies are highlighting. *The Washington Post*. https://www.washingtonpost.com/politics/2020/09/30/reliable-polls -show-that-biden-won-debate-so-those-arent-what-trumps-allies-are -highlighting/

Carlin, D. P. (1992). Presidential debates as focal points for campaign arguments. *Political Communication, 9*, 251–265. https://doi.org/10.1080/10584609 .1992.9962949

Carlin, D. P. & McKinney, M. S. (1994). *The 1992 presidential debates in focus*. Westport, CT: Praeger.

Collins, B. & Zadrozny, B. (2020, September 29). Proud boys celebrate after Trump's debate callout. *NBC News*. https://www.nbcnews.com/tech /tech-news/proud-boys-celebrate-after-trump-s-debate-call-out-n1241512

Commission on Presidential Debates (2020a, September 29). *Presidential debate at Case Western Reserve University and Cleveland Clinic in Cleveland, Ohio* [Debate transcript]. https://www.debates.org/voter-education/debate -transcripts/september-29-2020-debate-transcript/

Commission on Presidential Debates. (2020b, September 30). *CPD Statement*. https://www.debates.org/2020/09/30/cpd-statement-4/

Cwalina, W. & Falkowski, A. (2015). Political branding: Political candidates positioning based on inter-object associative affinity index. *Journal of Political Marketing, 14*(1–2), https://doi.org/:10.1080/15377857.2014.990842

Dickinson, T. (2020, October 22). Debates can shake up an election. But does record early voting mean this one is too late? *Rolling Stone*. https://www .rollingstone.com/politics/politics-news/trump-debate-election-early -voting-biden-1079974/

Drew, D. & Weaver, D. (2006). Voter learning in the 2004 presidential election: Did the media matter? *Journalism and Mass Communication Quarterly, 83*(1), 25–42. https://doi.org/10.1177/107769900608300103

Elbeshbishi, S. (2020, October 24). Majority of voters say Biden won second debate, poll finds. *USA Today.* https://www.usatoday.com/story/news/politics/elections/2020/10/24/biden-beat-trump-second-presidential-debate-majority-says-poll/6025522002/

Fridkin, K. L., Kenney, P. J., Gershon, S. A., & Woodall, G. S. (2008). Spinning debates: The impact of the news media's coverage of the final 2004 presidential debate. *The International Journal of Press/Politics, 13*(1), 29–51. https://doi.org/10.1177/1940161207312677

Grabowski, G. (2020, September 30). Dignity and respect biggest losers in first presidential debate of 2020. *PR News Online.* https://prnewsonline.com/presidential-debate-analysis-Grabowski

Greene, S. (1999). Understanding party identification: A social identity approach. *Political Psychology, 20*(2), 393–403. https://doi.org/:10.1111/0162-895X.00150

Greenberg, D. (2009). Torchlight parades for the television age: The presidential debates as political ritual. *Daedalus, 138*(2), 6–19.

Gregorian, D. (2020, October 1). Trump suggests he's opposed to any rule changes for next Biden debates. *NBC News.* https://www.nbcnews.com/politics/2020-election/trump-indicates-he-s-not-open-rule-changes-next-debates-n1241726

Hacker, K. L. (2004). The continued importance of the candidate image construct. In K. L. Hacker (Ed.), *Presidential candidate images* (pp. 1–19). Lanham, MD: Rowman & Littlefield.

Holbert, R. L. (2005). Debate viewing as mediator and partisan reinforcement in the relationship between news use and vote choice. *Journal of Communication, 55,* 85–102. https://doi.org/:10.1111/j.1460-2466.2005.tb02660.x

Holbrook, T. M. (1996). *Do campaigns matter?* Thousand Oaks, CA: Sage Publishing.

Houston, J. B., Hawthorne, J., Spialek, M. L., Greenwood, M., & McKinney, M. S. (2013). Tweeting during presidential debates: Effect on candidate evaluations and debate attitudes. *Argumentation and Advocacy, 49,* 301–311. https://doi.org/10.1080/00028533.2013.11821804

Isakov, M. & Kuriwaki, S. (2020). Towards principled unskewing: Viewing 2020 election polls through a corrective lens from 2016. *Harvard Data Science Review, 2*(4). https://doi.org/:10.1162/99608f92.86a46f38

Jackson-Beeck, M. & Meadow, R. (1979). The triple agenda of presidential debates. *Public Opinion Quarterly, 43,* 173–180. https://doi.org/10.1086/268509

Jamieson, K. H. (2015). The discipline's debate contributions: Then, now, and next. *Quarterly Journal of Speech, 101,* 85–97. https://doi.org/10.1080/00335630.2015.994905

Jamieson, K. H. & Birdsell, D. S. (1988). *Presidential debates: The challenge of creating an informed electorate.* New York, NY: Oxford University Press.

Jarman, J. W. (2016). Motivated reasoning and viewer's reactions to the first 2012 presidential debate. *Speaker & Gavel, 53,* 83–101. http://cornerstone.lib .mnsu.edu/speaker-gavel/vol53/iss1/8

Jennings, F. J., Bramlett, J. C., Kenski, K., & Villanueva, I. I. (2021). Presidential debate learning as a gateway to opinion articulation, communication intentions, and information seeking. *Argumentation & Advocacy.* https:// doi.org/10.1080/10511431.2021.1949543

Jennings, F. J., Bramlett, J. C., McKinney, M. S., & Hardy, M. M. (2020a). Tweeting along partisan lines: Identity-motivated elaboration and presidential debates. *Social Media and Society, 6*(4). https://doi .org/:10.1177/2056305120965518

Jennings, F. J., Coker, C. R., McKinney, M. S., & Warner, B. R. (2017). Tweeting presidential primary debates: Debate processing through motivated Twitter instruction. *American Behavioral Scientist, 61*(4), 455–474. https:// doi.org/:10.1177/0002764217704867

Jennings, F. J., Warner, B. R., McKinney, M. S., Kearney, C. C., Funk, M. E., & Bramlett, J. C. (2020b). Learning from presidential debates: Who learns the most and why? *Communication Studies, 71*(5), 896–910. https://doi.org /:10.1080/10510974.2020.1807377

Jennings, F. J., Wicks, R. H., McKinney, M. S., & Kenski, K. (2022). Closing the knowledge gap: How issue priming before presidential debate viewing encourages learning and opinion articulation. *American Behavioral Scientist.* https://doi.org/10.1177%2F00027642211000398

Katz, E., & Feldman, J. J. (1962). The debates in the light of research: A survey of surveys. In S. Kraus (Ed.), *The great debates: Kennedy vs. Nixon, 1960* (pp. 173–223). Bloomington, IN: Indiana University Press.

Keller, K. L. (1993). Conceptualizing, measuring, managing customer-based brand equity. *Journal of Marketing, 57*(1), 1–22. https://doi .org/10.2307/1252054

Kenski, K. & Stroud, N. J. (2005). Who watches presidential debates? A comparative analysis of presidential debate viewing in 2000 and 2004. *American Behavioral Scientist, 49,* 213–228. https://doi.org/10 .1177%2F0002764205279423

Keum, H., & Cho, J. (2021). Presidential debates and voter decision making. *The Social Science Journal.* https://doi.org/10.1080/03623319.2021.1925053

Kim, Y. M. & Garrett, K. (2012). Online and memory based: Revisiting the relationship between candidate evaluation processing models. *Political Behavior, 34,* 345–368. https://doi.org/10.1007/s11109-011-9158-9

Kim, G., Warner, B. R., Kearney, C., Park, J., & Kearney, M. W. (2021). Social watching the 2020 presidential and vice-presidential debates: The effect of ideological homogeneity and partisan identity strength. *Argumentation and Advocacy.* https://doi.org/:10.1080/10511431.2021.1955446

Kunda, Z. (1990). The case for motivated reasoning. *Psychological Bulletin, 108,* 480–498. https://doi.org/:10.1037/0033-2909.108.3.480

Landrum, J. (2020, October 23). Viewership for 2nd Trump-Biden debate drops to 63 million. *AP News.* https://apnews.com/article/election-2020 -joe-biden-donald-trump-virus-outbreak-health-ad254c08bc2dfbcbbaf 258cace153fa9

Lodge, M. & Taber, C. S. (2013). *The rationalizing voter.* New York, NY: Cambridge University Press.

Lopez, G. (2020, September 30). The reviews are in: The first presidential debate was a disaster. *Vox.* https://www.vox.com/2020/9/30/21495046/presidential -debate-trump-biden-reviews-who-won-disaster

Martin, J. & Burns, A. (2020, September 29). With cross talk, lies and mockery, Trump tramples decorum in debate with Biden. *The New York Times.* https://www.nytimes.com/2020/09/29/us/politics/trump-biden-debate .html

Mason, L. (2018). *Uncivil Agreement.* Chicago, IL: University of Chicago Press.

McCarten, J. (September 29, 2020). Must-see TV: Trump, Biden to square off in first face-to-face debate of 2020 election. *National Observer.* https:// www.nationalobserver.com/2020/09/29/news/must-see-tv-trump -biden-square-first-face-face-debate-2020-election

McGraw, K., Lodge, M., & Stroh, P. (1990). Online processing in candidate evaluation: The effects of issue order, issue importance, and sophistication. *Political Behavior, 12*(1), 41–58. https://doi.org/10.1007/BF00992331

McKinney, M. S. (2018). Political campaign debates in the 2016 elections: Advancing campaign debate scholarship. *Argumentation & Advocacy, 54,* 72–75. https://doi.org/:10.1080/00028533.2018.1446818

McKinney, M. S. & Carlin, D. B. (2004). Political campaign debates. In L. L. Kaid (Ed.), *Handbook of political communication research* (pp. 203–234). Mahwah, NJ: Lawrence Erlbaum Publishers.

McKinney, M. S., Dudash, E. A., & Hodgkinson, G. (2003). Viewer reactions to the 2000 presidential debates: Learning issues and image information. In L. L Kaid, J. C. Tedesco, D. G. Bystrom, & M. S. McKinney (Eds.), *The millennium election: Communication in the 2000 campaign* (pp. 43–58). Lanham, MD: Rowman & Littlefield.

McKinney, M. S., Houston, J. B., & Hawthorne, J. (2014). Social watching a 2012 Republican presidential primary debate. *American Behavioral Scientist, 58,* 556–573. https://doi.org/10.1177/0002764213506211

McKinney, M. S., & Warner, B. R. (2013). Do presidential debates matter? Examining a decade of campaign debate effects. *Argumentation & Advocacy, 49*(4), 238–258. https://doi.org/10.1080/00028533.2013.11821800

Mullinix, K. J. (2015). Presidential debates, partisan motivations, and political interest. *Presidential Studies Quarterly, 45,* 270–288. https://doi.org/10.1111/psq.12187

Munro, G. D., Ditto, P. H., Lockhart, L. K., Fagerlin, A., Gready, M., & Peterson, E. (2002). Biased assimilation of sociopolitical arguments: Evaluating the 1996 U.S. presidential debate. *Basic & Applied Social Psychology, 24,* 15–26. https://doi.org/10.1207/S15324834BASP2401_2

Newman, B. I. (1994). *The marketing of the president: Political marketing as campaign strategy.* Thousand Oaks, CA: Sage Publishing.

Nielsen, S. W. (2016). Mapping political brands: An art and a science of the mind. *Journal of Political Marketing, 15*(1), 70–95. https://doi.org/:10.1080/15377857.2014.959682

Nielsen, S. W. (2017). On political brands: A systematic review of the literature. *Journal of Political Marketing, 16*(2), 118–146. https://doi.org/:10.1080/15377857.2014.959694

Nielsen, S. W., and Larsen, M. V. (2014). Party brands and voting. *Electoral Studies, 33,* 153–165. https://doi.org/10.1016/j.electstud.2013.08.001

Olorunnipa, T., Wang, A. B., & Dawsey, J. (2020, October 23). Second Trump-Biden debate has fewer interruptions but more counterpunches. *The Washington Post.* https://www.washingtonpost.com/politics/debate-trump—biden/2020/10/23/5b67a0d2-1478-11eb-bc10-40b25382f1be_story.html

Orr, G. (2020, September 30). "A huge misstep": Trump allies see a lost opportunity in first debate. *Politico.* https://www.politico.com/news/2020/09/30/trump-allies-debate-biden-424082

Petty, R. E. & Cacioppo, J. T. (1986). *Communication and persuasion: Central and peripheral routes to attitude change.* New York, NY: Springer-Verlag.

Pfau, M. (1987). The influence of intraparty political debates on candidate preference. *Communication Research, 14*(6), 687–697. https://doi.org/10.1177/009365087014006004

Poniewozik, J. (2020, October 23). Donald Trump burns the first debate down. *The New York Times.* https://www.nytimes.com/2020/09/30/arts/television/donald-trump-debate.html

Ross, J. (2020, October 8). CPD moves second Trump vs. Biden debate to virtual after president's COVID infection. *The Daily Beast.* https://www.thedailybeast.com/second-trump-v-biden-debate-will-be-virtual-after-presidents-covid-infection

Sabato, L. (2021). A return to normalcy? Taking stock at the end of the Trump presidency. In L. J. Sabato, K. Kondik, & J. M. Coleman (Eds.), *A return to normalcy? The 2020 election that (almost) broke America,* (pp. 1–25). Lanham, MD: Rowman & Littlefield.

Schroeder, A. (2008). *Presidential debates: Forty years of high risk TV.* (2nd ed.). New York, NY: Columbia University Press.

Schrott, P. R. & Lanoue, D. J. (2013). The power and limitations of televised presidential debates: Assessing the real impact of candidate performance on public opinion and vote choice. *Electoral Studies, 32,* 684–692. https://doi.org/:10.1016/j.electstud.2013.03.006

Segers, G., Watson, K., & Becket, S. (2020, September 30). First debate descends into chaos as Trump and Biden exchange attacks. *CBS News.* https://www.cbsnews.com/live-updates/first-presidential-debate-trump-biden-wrap-up-moments/

Sganga, N. & Watson, K. (2020, October 20). Commission on Presidential Debates says it will mute mics during parts of final debate. *CBS News.* https://www.cbsnews.com/news/debate-commission-adopts-new -rules-mute-microphones-candidates/

Siders, D. (2020, October 22). Trump came out strong. But is it too late? *Politico.* https://www.politico.com/news/2020/10/22/presidential-debate-what -to-watch-431301

Smith, D. (2020, September 30). Donald Trump ensures first presidential debate is national humiliation. *The Guardian.* https://www.theguardian.com/us -news/2020/sep/30/trump-debate-national-humiliation-analysis

Speed, R., Butler, P., & Collins. N. (2015). Human branding in political market-ing: Applying contemporary branding thought to political parties and their leaders. *Journal of Political Marketing, 14*(1–2), 129–151. https://doi .org/:10.1080/15377857.2014.990833

Stahl, J. (2020, September 30). We counted every single time Trump interrupted during the first presidential debate. *Slate.* https://slate.com/news-and -politics/2020/09/trump-interruptions-first-presidential-debate-biden .html

Sullivan, S. & Dawsey, J. (2020, September 25). Trump readies a debate onslaught—and Biden allies worry. *The Washington Post.* https://www .washingtonpost.com/politics/biden-trump-debate-attacks/2020/09/25 /f2565f36-fd91-11ea-9ceb-061d646d9c67_story.html

Vancil, D. L. & Pendell, S. D. (1984). Winning presidential debates: An analysis of criteria influencing audience response. *Western Journal of Speech Com-munication, 48,* 62–74. https://doi.org/:10.1080/10570318409374142

Walsh, D. (2020, October 23). Trump and Biden had a real debate. *NPR News.* https://www.npr.org/2020/10/23/926844747/trump-and-biden-had-a -real-debate-and-4-other-takeaways

Warner, B. R. & Banwart, M. C. (2016). A multifactor approach to candidate image. *Communication Studies, 67*(3), 258–279. https://doi.org/:10.1080 /10510974.2016.1156005

Warner, B. R., Bramlett, J. C., Hoeun, S., Manik, D. I., & Bolton, J. P. (2018a). Presidential primary debates compared: Timing of debate and size of candidate field as moderators of debate effects. *Argu-mentation and Advocacy, 54*(1–2), 122–138, https://doi.org/:10.1080 /00028533.2018.1446868

Warner, B. R., Hoeun, S., Bramlett, J. C., Galarza, R., Manik, D. I., Hase, G. E., & Engen, R. (2019). The effects of debate viewing on candidate image per-ceptions in the 2016 televised presidential general election debates. In E. A. Hinck (Ed.), *Presidential debates in a changing media environment, Vol. 1* (pp. 292–318). Westport, CT: Praeger.

Warner, B. R., Jennings, F. J., Bramlett, J. C., Coker, C. R., Reed, J. L., & Bolton, J. P. (2018b). A multi-media analysis of persuasion in the 2016 presi-dential election: Comparing the unique and complementary effects of political comedy and political advertising. *Mass Communication and Society, 21*(6), 720–741. https://doi.org/10.1080/15205436.2018.1472283

Warner, B. R. & McKinney, M. S. (2013). To unite and divide: The polarizing effect of presidential debates. *Communication Studies, 64,* 508–527. https://doi.org/: 10.1080/10510974.2013.832341

Warner, B. R., McKinney, M. S., Bramlett, J. C., Jennings, F. J., & Funk, M. E. (2020). Reconsidering partisanship as a constraint on the persuasive effects of debates. *Communication Monographs, 87*(2), 137–157. https://doi.org/:10.1080/03637751.2019.1641731

Zhu, J., Milavsky, J. R., & Biswas, R. (1994). Do televised debates affect image perception more than issue knowledge? A study of the first 1992 presidential debate. *Human Communication Research, 20,* 302–333. https://psycnet.apa.org/doi/10.1111/j.1468-2958.1994.tb00325.x

Zurcher, A. (2020, October 23). Presidential debate: Key takeaways from the Trump-Biden showdown. *BBC.* https://www.bbc.com/news/election-us-2020-54650681

Social Dominance, Sexism, and the Lasting Effects on Political Communication from the 2020 Election

Mary C. Banwart and Michael W. Kearney

Sexism in politics has long been a point of concern—and a reality—that has shaped our civic conversations and engagement, has influenced who is willing or not willing to run for office, and how we vote. One unexpected aspect of the 2016 election is very likely the way in which the juxtaposition of Hillary Clinton's and Donald Trump's candidacies—and the country's reaction to them—elevated our national dialogue around sexism. The conversation has long existed, certainly. But as Keith (2016) stated,

> Perhaps it was inevitable that with the first female nominee of a major political party on the ballot, the race for president would have undercurrents of sexism. But what wasn't inevitable is just how out in the open it has been. (para. 7)

Even with alarm bells sounding during the 2016 primaries (Bauer, 2016; Lozano-Reich, 2016) and the general election (e.g., Beinart, 2016; Cole, 2016; Keith, 2016), sexist comments and language became the norm for the election cycle. And for many, it became an acceptable one. Prior to the election, numerous studies found evidence of a relationship between sexism and support for Trump. A June 2016 study found significant correlations between scores on sexism and a likelihood to support Trump and not support Clinton, even when taking into account party affiliation and ideology (Wayne et al., 2016). A survey conducted by YouGov (Schaffner et al., 2017) found that as participants moved from low to high sexism, the likelihood to vote for Trump shifted in his favor by 30 points. In their analyses of pre-election and post-election data, academic scholars have further substantiated the indisputable role sexism played in support for Trump and against Clinton. While sexism was found to have a significant effect on vote choice that favored Trump (Banwart & Kearney, 2018; Valentino et al., 2018), it was particularly true for White women (Cassese & Barnes, 2019; Frasure-Yokley, 2018) and White men (Bracic et al., 2019).

As the country endured consistent, rhetorical threads from Trump's first term in office that perpetuated a male-centric social hierarchy in concert with themes that reinforced women as weak, as lacking strength and ability, and as dishonest (Scotto di Carlo, 2020), it is not surprising that national polls found concerns about sexism on the rise. Just prior to the 2018 midterm elections, the Pew Research Center (Hartig & Doherty, 2018) released a poll reporting that the percentage of respondents who said sexism was a "very big problem" in the country had increased by 11 points (from 23% to 34%), with 50% of Democrats and 17% of Republicans likely to view it as such. With a clear indication of sexism's role in perpetuating the tone for and influencing the outcome of the 2016 election and Trump's continued, vocal embrace of a sexist ideology, many wondered how sexism would influence the 2018 midterms.

Building on the 2016 studies, Banwart and Kearney (2018) found mixed results when analyzing the relationship between sexism and candidate image in mixed-gender U.S. Senate and gubernatorial races during the 2018 midterm cycle. While hostile sexism showed a nonsignificant relationship with how voters viewed both female and male candidates across a five-factor image scale, benevolent sexism performed quite differently. Indeed, benevolent sexism demonstrated a positive relationship with nearly every dimension of candidate image—character, leadership, charm, and competence—for male candidates running for the U.S. Senate and governor; the relationship was nonsignificant on the image dimension of intelligence. However, no significant relationship was found between benevolent sexism and the ratings of female candidates on the same candidate image dimensions.

In a study of data collected as part of the Cooperative Congressional Election Study's competitive districts survey, Schaffner (2022) found that within the most competitive U.S. House races, hostile sexism was a stronger predictor of vote choice in 2018 than in 2016. Although in 2018 the relationship between holding hostile sexist attitudes and voting Republican became stronger, the impact of hostile sexism crossed party lines; in other words, the more sexist Republicans *and* Democrats became, the more they were likely to vote Republican in 2018. However, how much of sexism's midterm relationship with vote choice could be attributed to Trump? A significant amount. Schaffner found that "one-third of the total effect of both hostile sexism and a denial of racism on the House vote in 2018 operated indirectly through voters' opinions of Donald Trump" (p. 499).

As the 2020 Democratic primary got underway, an increasing number of women stepped onto the stage. Six women ultimately sought their party's nomination for president in 2020, with then Senator Kamala Harris being tapped to run as Joe Biden's vice presidential candidate. Despite any gains, the role of sexism was still undeniable. As Senator Elizabeth Warren famously said after officially ending her campaign for the Democratic nomination, "If you say, 'Yeah, there was sexism in this race,' everyone says, 'Whiner!' If you say, 'No, there was no sexism,' about a bazillion women think, 'What planet do you live on?'" (Kurtzleben, 2020, para. 8). Granted, polling during the primary found a strong majority (84%) saying they would be "comfortable with a woman president" (para. 10). However, only one in three reported their neighbors or family would be, and a full 50% said a woman would have more difficulty running against Trump (Kurtzleben, 2020).

Ultimately, the primaries concluded with two men at the top of ticket. Did that return to an all-male set of candidates for the presidency diffuse the influence of at least gender-related dominance-oriented ideologies when voting in 2020? Or, with Trump's continued proliferation of attacks and insults on women through the 2020 cycle (Zoellner, 2020), did sexism still influence voter evaluations of the two male candidates? Through this study we extend our work from 2016 to examine the relationship between social dominance orientation, sexism, and candidate image in 2020.

Review of the Literature

Sexism as Dominance

Dahl et al. (2015) note that sexism as a construct is fundamentally situated in dominance, with an ingroup/outgroup dynamic. Through this lens, women as the outgroup are believed to be subordinate to men as the ingroup. Further, the ideology justifies the dominant status of men by submitting legitimate power to them, which in turn serves to grant a superior form of agency and justify the control they wield as the ingroup. In their seminal study developing ambivalent sexism theory, Glick and Fiske (1996) identified two facets of sexism: hostile and benevolent sexism. The theory of ambivalent sexism argues that hostile sexism (HS) and benevolent sexism (BS) both subordinate women, albeit through different attitudinal perspectives. HS is built on a specifically negative attitude toward those women who are perceived to challenge male power. BS, on the other hand, performs as a patronizing attitude, anchored in a belief that women are fragile and in need of a form of protection that is idealized—by men and women—as coming from men (Glick et al., 2004). Importantly, both facets subordinate women and connect with values of power and security (Feather & McKee, 2012).

Of specific relevance to our study, scholars have also found HS and BS associated with political ideology and issue positions (Hodson & MacInnis, 2016). For instance, when studying the relationship between political ideology, sexism, and views on abortion, conservativism positively predicted sexism, while greater sexism predicted decreased support for abortion. The study ultimately argued that the ideological divide on the issue has less to do with the issue itself and more to do with "pushback against women" (Hodson & MacInnis, 2016, p. 120).

One of the ways in which women challenge male power is by holding leadership roles, inclusive of running for office. As evidence of the incongruity, voters struggle to perceive female candidates as qualified when compared to male candidates even when they hold the same qualifications (Paul & Smith, 2008). Okimoto and Brescoll (2010) suggest this punishment is particularly harsh when women candidates are perceived as doing so for the purpose of seeking power and influence, and more so if that power is perceived to be "a personal desire for power" (p. 932). They find that male candidates do not suffer this same disadvantage. In fact, power-seeking male candidates are viewed as competent, assertive, strong, and tough, with respondents more likely to positively express a vote preference in their favor. In contrast, a power-seeking female candidate is considered less competent; is rated lower on assertiveness, strength, and toughness; and faces a moral backlash associated with anger, contempt, and disgust. It is not surprising, then, that HS has been found to predict negative responses to men *and* women who challenge traditional, stereotypical gender roles, while BS predicts positive responses to women who embody traditional, stereotypical gender roles that suggest dependence on men and allow them to remain in a more dominant role (Glick et al., 2015).

Social Dominance Orientation (SDO)

Like sexism, SDO operates from an attitudinal position of dominance, where one displays a preference for the group-based hierarchy, resulting in dominance and superiority of their own ingroup over other outgroups

(Pratto et al., 1994). In addition to a wide group of prejudices, the relationship between SDO and sexism is well documented (e.g., Christopher & Mull, 2006; Dahl et al., 2015; Feather & McKee, 2012; Fraser et al., 2015; Sibley et al., 2007). Considering that SDO is highly correlated with a competitive worldview (Perry et al., 2013), it is therefore not surprising that SDO and sexism both also share relationships with anger and perceptions of threats to masculinity (Dahl et al., 2015). The research on SDO among men is notable in that perceived threats to masculinity increase when in a situation that places them as subordinate to a woman, and even more so if the context for comparison is considered a masculine domain (Dahl et al., 2015). Dahl and colleagues (2015) also found that a threat repair response is more likely to be an ideological anger-based reaction alongside an endorsement of both SDO combined with benevolent sexism. In other words, when men in their study responded to a masculinity threat in a masculine-defined context, they did so with anger and then a process of justifying the anger in a way that restored their sense of dominance—in the form of increased endorsement of BS—and allowed them to regain their sense of power and dominance over the offending threat, which in this case was a woman.

When considering the masculine domain of politics, and based on what we know from studies on sexism, do women candidates running for office naturally create masculine threats by simply running? And is that influence found to be not only for their male opponents but also male voters in general? While SDO captures generalized prejudice, social ideologies at the group level, and sociopolitical policy preferences (for a review, see Pratto et al., 2006), it has certainly been linked to vote preference (Crowson & Brandes, 2017), political attitudes, and political orientation. For instance, SDO has been shown to predict political attitudes of conservatism and more aggressive intergroup attitudes (Ho et al., 2012), left–right political orientation (Grina et al., 2016), and a decrease in support for policies that favor racial equality and women's rights (Pratto et al., 1994). Those with a high SDO are also more likely to respond with prejudice to any outgroups who present a challenge to their dominance, influence, and superiority (Duckitt & Bizumic, 2013).

Certainly, SDO is, at its core, about dominance over outgroups. It also carries with it an added element of self-enhancing that drives reactions such as threat repair, which in turn offers additional insights as to Trump followers' enthusiastic embrace of his male-centric rhetoric that emphasized a social hierarchy, complete with an ingroup—Trump followers—who disparaged the outgroup—women—energetically, openly, and with vulgar terms. In 2016, Crowson and Brandes (2017) confirmed that SDO did in fact predict vote intentions for Trump over Clinton.

And Banwart and Kearney (2018) found that SDO was a significant, positive predictor of candidate image for Trump and a significant, negative predictor of candidate image for Clinton. Specifically for Trump, SDO predicted positive ratings on credibility, charm, and homophily. For Clinton, SDO negatively predicted ratings on her intellect and her benevolence, and as such subordinated her on image traits that could in turn justify their subordination of her credibility. As the authors conclude, "What these data do seem to clearly suggest, however, is that those with high SDO—those desiring ingroup dominance and superiority—certainly found Trump a like-minded and attractive leader, and one with whom they could identify and find similarity" (p. 434).

Candidate Image

As we did in 2016, to assess the influence of two dominance-related ideologies—sexism and SDO—on voter perceptions of Clinton and Trump, we relied on a six-factor candidate image scale for insight into how voters perceived the candidates. Examining candidate image provides more nuance to understand how voters develop a construct of the candidate and the lens through which they interpret and process candidate messages. The study of how voters use and process candidate image finds that it is not a superficial exercise. Candidate image can be linked to electoral outcomes, is found to be more important than issues in determining for whom to vote, and is developed by exposure to election-related communication in various forms (for an overview, see Warner & Banwart, 2016). Warner and Banwart (2016) also argued that past research lacked both a consistent measure for studying candidate image and one that represented the complexity necessary for a comprehensive image construct.

Based on the argument that candidate image is multidimensional and complex, we employ the six-factor scale developed by Warner and Banwart (2016). The scale is composed of character, intelligence, leadership, benevolence, homophily, and charm. In a cross-election study, the authors found that "image scores are associated with voting intention above and beyond demographic factors, party identification, and partisan affect" (p. 269). While the measure offers predictive capacity, not all traits are used with equal levels of strength in predicting vote intention. However, they all offer a unique contribution, providing "heuristics to simplify cognitive decision making about representation" (p. 278).

But very little helps us understand how voters are using dominance-oriented ideologies to inform their decision making about political candidates. And as we consider how voters make decisions in the masculine and competitive context of a political campaign, this study seeks to offer clarity in understanding the process, as well as its implications for comprehending voter sense-making. While this study focuses specifically on the presidential race featuring Biden and Trump, we argue that it also has implications for women in politics.

Hypothesis and Research Question

The purpose of this study is to extend our 2016 research to determine if the two dominance-related ideologies of sexism and SDO influenced voter perceptions of the two male presidential candidates in 2020. As in our 2016 study, we pose the following hypothesis and research question:

H1: SDO will be positively related to ambivalent (e.g., hostile and benevolent) sexism.

RQ1: Can variations in the perceptions of candidate image be explained by the SDO and/or ambivalent sexism?

Method

Respondents and Procedures

An online questionnaire was distributed via Amazon Mechanical Turk (MTurk), with workers being compensated 75 cents upon completion of the survey. Respondents ($N = 552$) were an average of 40.88 (SD = 13.24; range = 21–84) years old and consisted of 230 (41.7%) females and 260 (47.1%) males (11.2% chose not to identify as male or female). The majority of respondents were White (66.1%). The sample was about as educated as the general population, with respondents reported having completed college (42.0%), some college (16.3%), undergraduate degree (15.9%), high school (6.3%), some graduate school (5.4%), and graduate degree (1.1%), while 13% of respondents chose not to identify their education level.

Measures

Candidate Image

The ongoing project aims to better understand voter perceptions of political candidates—especially in relation to dimensions of character, intelligence, leadership, charm, benevolence, and homophily—and how those perceptions vary depending on the major party of each candidate. Building on our work on the 2016 election (Banwart & Kearney, 2018), the current study examines similar dimensions in the context of the 2020 U.S. presidential election. For consistency and interpretability, independent models

Table 14.1   Descriptive Statistics of Variables

Variable	M.	S.D.	Alpha
Sexism – benevolent	3.10	0.71	0.86
Sexism – hostile	2.84	0.90	0.91
Social domination	2.28	1.03	0.88
Character – Biden	3.33	1.09	0.79
Character – Trump	2.85	1.29	0.88
Intelligence – Biden	3.47	1.01	0.78
Intelligence – Trump	3.08	1.25	0.86
Leadership – Biden	3.56	1.05	0.86
Leadership – Trump	3.21	1.31	0.91
Benevolence – Biden	3.41	1.05	0.77
Benevolence – Trump	2.93	1.26	0.84
Homophily – Biden	3.43	1.23	0.93
Homophily – Trump	3.10	1.43	0.97

were estimated for each of the two major-party candidates. Reliability estimates for each candidate and other descriptive statistics can be found in Table 14.1.

Character. The perceived character of candidates was measured by asking respondents to indicate their level of agreement with the terms "trustworthy," "dishonest" (reverse coded), and "credible."

Intelligence. The perceived intelligence of candidates was measured by asking respondents to indicate their level of agreement with the terms "unintelligent" (reverse coded), "knowledgeable," and "smart."

Leadership. The perceived leadership of candidates was measured by asking respondents to indicate their level of agreement with the terms "strong," "poised," and "a good leader."

Charm. Perceived charm was measured by asking respondents to what extent they agreed each candidate was "charismatic," "likable," and "unpleasant" (reverse coded).

Homophily. The perceived homophily of candidates was measured by asking respondents to indicate their level of agreement with the phrases "understands people like me" (reverse coded), "understands the problems faced by people like me," and "shares my values."

Benevolence. The perceived benevolence of candidates was measured by asking respondents to indicate their level of agreement with statements such as, "I worry that <candidate> is deliberately trying to hurt America," "<candidate> doesn't care about America."

Sexism

The Ambivalent Sexism Inventory (ASI) (Glick & Fiske, 1996) was used to measure sexism in this study. The ASI consists of 22 items, with participants indicating their agreement on a 5-point scale (1 = strongly disagree; 5 = strongly agree). The measure is composed of two factors: HS and BS. The HS factor includes items such as "Most women interpret innocent remarks or acts as being sexist"; "Women are too easily offended"; and "Most women fail to appreciate fully all that men do for them." The BS factor includes such items as "Many women have a quality of purity that few men possess"; "Every man ought to have a woman whom he adores"; and "Women should be cherished and protected by men." Higher scores indicate a higher degree of sexism. Descriptive statistics and alpha reliability estimates for all variables can be found in Table 14.1.

Social Dominance Orientation

The SDO scale consists of eight items (Ho et al., 2015). Participants responded to questions on a 5-point scale (1 = strongly agree; 5 = strongly disagree). Examples of items from this scale include "An ideal society requires some groups to be on top and others to be on the bottom"; "Some groups of people are simply inferior to other groups"; and "Group equality should not be our primary goal." See Table 14.1 for summary statistics and reliability estimates.

Partisanship

To account for the link between political party preference and perceptions of party-nominated candidates, political partisanship was included as a covariate in all models. Partisanship was measured by asking respondents to locate their political views on an 8-point scale (1 = strong Democrat; 8 = strong Republican) with midpoints used to indicate whether respondents leaned Democrat (4) or Republican (5). To allow for comparisons with the 5-point scales used earlier, partisanship scores were transformed onto a 5-point scale.

Results

Hypothesis 1

We hypothesized that SDO would be positively related to ambivalent sexism. Correlation analysis supported this hypothesis, as both dimensions of ambivalent sexism were found to be positively related to the SDO: BS, $r = 0.34$, $t (534) = 8.49$, $p < 0.001$, and HS, $r = 0.59$, $t (532) = 17.04$, $p = 0.001$. Thus, hypothesis 1 was fully supported.

Research Question 1

The research question asked whether voter perceptions of candidate image could be explained by the SDO and/or ambivalent sexism (HS and BS). To answer this, ordinary least squares (OLS) models were estimated for six dimensions of candidate image for each major party candidate. To control for other important factors, models also included the covariates of age, whether male, whether White, education level, and strength of partisanship. Regression coefficients and model fit statistics for the models predicting perceptions of the Democratic candidate can be found in Table 14.2 and for the Republican candidate in Table 14.3.

Social Domination Orientation

SDO was a significant positive predictor for the Republican candidate (Trump) in every dimension and a significant negative predictor for the Democratic candidate (Biden) in every dimension except leadership. This suggests that social domination was much more likely to explain positive perceptions of the Republican candidate and negative perceptions of the Democratic candidate.

Ambivalent Sexism

Both dimensions of ambivalent sexism were included in each model as a predictor of candidate image. For both the Democratic candidate (Table 14.2) and the Republican candidate (Table 14.3), BS was positively related to candidate evaluations for nearly every dimension; the relationship was significant in every model but for perceived intellect of the Republican candidate. In the other dimension of ambivalent sexism, however, the direction of the relationship differed by political party, with HS having positively predicted evaluations of the Republican candidate across every image dimension (Table 14.3) and negatively predicted evaluations of the Democratic candidate across every image dimension (Table 14.2). As shown in Table 14.2 and Table 14.3, HS was a significant positive predictor in all evaluative dimensions for the Republican candidate and only predicted image evaluations of the Democratic candidate—and in a negative direction—on the intellect and charm dimensions.

Overall, as Figure 14.1 makes clear, the results presented here suggest that both benevolent and hostile forms of sexism were relevant in explaining voter perceptions of candidate image during the 2020 U.S. presidential election. Further, in many cases, both the size and direction of the relationships between sexism and candidate image rivaled that of the relationship between partisanship and candidate image.

Table 14.2 OLS Models Predicting Image Perceptions of Democratic Candidate

	Dependent Variable					
	Credible	Intellect	Leadership	Benevolent	Charm	Homophily
	(1)	(2)	(3)	(4)	(5)	(6)
Intercept	2.49***	3.28***	2.22***	2.49***	3.24***	1.94***
	(0.31)	(0.29)	(0.33)	(0.31)	(0.29)	(0.37)
Age	0.00	0.00	0.00	0.00	0.00	0.01
	(0.00)	(0.00)	(0.00)	(0.00)	(0.00)	(0.00)
Sex[male]	0.09	0.10	0.18*	0.09	0.12	0.14
	(0.09)	(0.09)	(0.10)	(0.09)	(0.08)	(0.11)
Race[white]	-0.11	-0.03	-0.01	-0.11	0.04	-0.05
	(0.10)	(0.10)	(0.11)	(0.10)	(0.10)	(0.12)
Education	0.14***	0.06*	0.17***	0.14***	0.08**	0.20***
	(0.04)	(0.04)	(0.04)	(0.04)	(0.04)	(0.05)
Partisanship	-0.18***	-0.13***	-0.12***	-0.18***	-0.13***	-0.18***
	(0.02)	(0.02)	(0.02)	(0.02)	(0.02)	(0.02)
Social dominance	-0.09*	-0.12**	-0.08	-0.09*	-0.19***	-0.13**
	(0.05)	(0.05)	(0.06)	(0.05)	(0.05)	(0.07)
Benevolent sexism	0.22***	0.21***	0.33***	0.22***	0.20***	0.22**
	(0.08)	(0.07)	(0.08)	(0.08)	(0.07)	(0.09)
Hostile sexism	-0.10	-0.22***	-0.11	-0.10	-0.19***	0.02
	(0.07)	(0.07)	(0.08)	(0.07)	(0.07)	(0.09)

(Continued)

Table 14.2 *(Continued)*

	Credible	Intellect	Leadership	Benevolent	Charm	Homophily
			Dependent Variable			
	(1)	(2)	(3)	(4)	(5)	(6)
Observations	456	456	445	456	455	435
R^2	0.29	0.27	0.18	0.29	0.29	0.22
Adjusted R^2	0.27	0.25	0.16	0.27	0.28	0.21
F Statistic	22.29***	20.39***	11.75***	22.29***	23.25***	15.34***

Note: $^*p < 0.05.$ $^{**}p < 0.01.$ $^{***}p < 0.001.$

Table 14.3 OLS Models Predicting Image Perceptions of Republican Candidate

			Dependent Variable			
	Credible	Intellect	Leadership	Benevolent	Charm	Homophily
	(1)	(2)	(3)	(4)	(5)	(6)
Intercept	0.90***	1.63***	0.68**	0.90***	1.17***	0.29
	(0.28)	(0.32)	(0.27)	(0.28)	(0.28)	(0.28)
Age	−0.01***	−0.00	−0.00	−0.01***	−0.01*	−0.01**
	(0.00)	(0.00)	(0.00)	(0.00)	(0.00)	(0.00)
Sex[male]	−0.09	−0.20**	−0.18**	−0.09	−0.17**	−0.03
	(0.08)	(0.09)	(0.08)	(0.08)	(0.08)	(0.08)
Race[white]	0.20**	0.16	0.21**	0.20**	0.22*	0.30***
	(0.09)	(0.10)	(0.09)	(0.09)	(0.09)	(0.09)
Education	−0.02	−0.04	0.05	−0.02	−0.04	0.05
	(0.03)	(0.04)	(0.03)	(0.03)	(0.03)	(0.04)
Partisanship	0.17***	0.18***	0.18***	0.17***	0.19***	0.19***
	(0.02)	(0.02)	(0.02)	(0.02)	(0.02)	(0.02)
Social dominance	0.24***	0.19***	0.23***	0.24***	0.22***	0.29***
	(0.05)	(0.06)	(0.05)	(0.05)	(0.05)	(0.05)
Benevolent sexism	0.19***	0.11	0.15**	0.19***	0.17**	0.14*
	(0.07)	(0.08)	(0.07)	(0.07)	(0.07)	(0.07)
Hostile sexism	0.40***	0.29***	0.49***	0.40***	0.35***	0.52***
	(0.07)	(0.07)	(0.07)	(0.07)	(0.07)	(0.07)

(Continued)

277

Table 14.3 (Continued)

			Dependent Variable			
	Credible	Intellect	Leadership	Benevolent	Charm	Homophily
	(1)	(2)	(3)	(4)	(5)	(6)
Observations	458	459	452	458	453	437
R^2	0.58	0.44	0.62	0.58	0.58	0.66
Adjusted R^2	0.58	0.43	0.61	0.58	0.57	0.65
Residual Std. Error	0.84	0.95	0.82	0.84	0.83	0.84
F Statistic	78.74***	44.35***	89.98***	78.74***	76.44***	104.47***

Note: $*p < 0.05$. $**p < 0.01$. $***p < 0.001$.

Scatter plots depict associations between perceptions of candidate image [across six dimensions] and hostile and benevolent sexism with respect to the two major-party candidates for president.

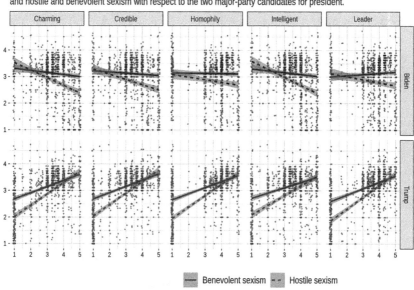

Points represent mean responses (N = 552) to related items on five-point scales.
Lines of best fit were estimated using parsimonious (no covariates) linear models.

Figure 14.1 Perceptions of Candidate Image with Hostile and Benevolent Sexism

Discussion

While in 2016 we found evidence of the two dominance-related ideologies of sexism and SDO influencing voter perceptions of Hillary Clinton and Donald Trump, the purpose of this study was to determine if sexism and SDO would also influence voter perceptions of Joe Biden and Donald Trump in 2020. Without Clinton to activate any threat to masculinity, would a correlation exist between sexism and SDO? Further, would the dominance orientation of sexism and SDO influence how voters perceived the candidates across the key image factors of an ideal candidate?

To answer these questions, we first tested whether a relationship existed between SDO and sexism. Prior research suggests a lack of consistency in the relationship between these constructs (Christopher & Mull, 2006; Sibley et al., 2007), a trend our 2016 study followed as we found a positive correlation between SDO and HS but not BS (Banwart & Kearney, 2018). Alternatively, in 2020, SDO related to *both* BS and HS. On one hand, the relationship between SDO and HS is well documented and theoretically clear. SDO is built on a perception that hierarchy and inequality are natural, and even desirable, and that the world is competitive, dangerous, and even threatening (Perry et al., 2013). HS, too, values hierarchy—specifically a gendered hierarchy—and women who challenge the gender hierarchy are subject to a threat repair response to restore masculine dominance (Christopher & Mull, 2006; Dahl et al., 2015). On the other hand, the relationship between SDO and BS is less consistent, and it can be argued that it is less transparent as well (Christopher & Mull, 2006; Christopher & Wojda, 2008; Fraser et al., 2015; Mosso et al., 2013; Radke et al., 2018; Sibley et al., 2007).

What might our study then reveal about the relationship between SDO and sexism? If we look back to 2016, Trump's open hostility toward Clinton—and toward women in general—seemed to embolden his followers to embrace those attitudes and behaviors as normal and just. Further, one could argue that Clinton's challenge to Trump in a traditionally masculine situation—that of politics and a political campaign—along with voters' validation of her competitiveness through polling data released throughout the election, likely increased the threat value to Trump and by proxy to his supporters. In other words, 2016 activated response attitudes to maintain dominance, and in so doing made it acceptable to hold and express HS views and attitudes. Further, Clinton was not a type of woman to attract the BS self-enhancing protection, as BS tends to foster dependence-oriented protection (Shnabel et al., 2016). In that scenario, Clinton's presence overall might have served as the activator of a dominance-oriented masculine threat response through HS but not of the chivalrous desire of BS to help and protect.

In 2020, HS sexist views continued to be on display from both Trump and his followers. His comments at rallies and on Twitter continued to insult and degrade agentic women in particular, which without question could serve to fuel masculine threats and dominance-orientated attitudes for those with ideals of maintaining dominance. Yet in 2020, HS was joined by BS in the relationship to SDO. As context has been shown to influence endorsement of sexist attitudes (Dahl et al., 2015), perhaps the presence of two men at the top of the ticket removed any threat and restored some stasis for those gender-dominant-oriented voters. And with the gender gap in 2020 favoring Biden, women in particular may have played a role in this shift. Based on BS research, women who are socially dominant and prefer existing hierarchical social structures—even if that structure results in their lowered status—often endorse BS attitudes as a way of resolving the dissonance (Radke et al., 2018). In particular for those women who felt at risk or uncertain about the stability and volatility of Trump—be that an economic, health, immigration, or racial insecurity—found a sense of stability in Biden, as he represented the honest, trustworthy, and responsible candidate (Rosenberg et al., 2020). Certainly, the data on SDO and sexism in both the 2016 and 2020 elections encourage us to consider a closer intersectional analysis. Doing so is likely to not only yield important answers about voting habits and expectations of political candidates but also provide an increased understanding of the complicated relationship between dominance and gender.

In this study we also sought to explore whether voter perceptions of candidate image in the 2020 election could be explained by SDO and/or ambivalent sexism. In analyzing our results, we see three main points to consider from our findings: first, the convergence of SDO, HS, and BS in predicting voter image evaluations of Trump; how HS performed uniquely differently for Trump and Biden; and the predictive value of SDO and BS in voter image evaluations of Biden.

First, although we know from 2016 that dominant-oriented ideologies played a role in predicting image evaluations of Trump and Clinton, we were interested in how they performed with a male as the opposing candidate to Trump. While our 2016 data found that HS positively predicted image ratings of Trump on all six factors and negatively predicted image ratings of Clinton (Banwart & Kearney, 2016), BS, and to a lesser degree SDO, did not consistently predict image evaluations of Trump or Clinton. However, in 2020, for Trump HS, BS, and SDO all served as positive predictors of Trump's image. In other words, it is clear that those with dominance-oriented ideologies—be that a belief in the superiority and dominance of their own group (SDO), a hostility toward women and perceived superiority over them (HS), or a belief that women are fragile and in need of protection (BS)—found Trump credible and honest, knowledgeable and smart, a good leader, likeable, and someone who shares their values and wants what is best for America. True BS attitudes were positive predictors of voter views of Trump on all image factors except intellect. While benevolence and credibility are often the most influential factors, it is worth noting that how voters view a candidate's intellect does not influence vote choice with the same strength (Warner & Banwart, 2016). Thus, although BS attitudes did not predict evaluations of Trump's intelligence, this likely was not a "deal breaker" when it came to voting at the ballot box, particularly when considering the predictive value of BS attitudes on all other factors.

Second, it is notable how HS performed differently for Trump and Biden in predicting candidate image. As we have already explained, HS positively predicted voter evaluations of Trump across all six image factors. For Biden, HS attitudes negatively predicted voter evaluations only on the image factors of intellect and charm. We surmise these ratings could be the result of a backlash against choosing Senator Harris as a running mate, although we find it of interest that a similar relationship did not emerge for the more relevant factors of leadership, benevolence, or homophily. While this lack of predictive value for Biden's image indicates other variables held more value for those voters endorsing HS attitudes, further research will be needed to fully explore this point.

In contrast, with HS positively predicting evaluations of Trump across all six image factors, our results confirm that Trump still activated an attitude of aggression toward women without a woman challenger on the ticket. On the campaign trail Trump was known to frequently insult agentic women who had risen to positions of authority, activating his followers in response. For instance, Trump called Michigan Governor Gretchen Whitmer "dishonest" (Mason & Martina, 2020, para. 4) and "a half-wit" (Zoellner, 2020, para. 49) and chastised her for not saying "thank you" with his rally crowds crying "lock her up" in response (Mason & Martina, 2020, para. 1). He called then Senator Harris "very, very nasty" (Zoellner, 2020, para. 23), insinuated she was not born in the United States, would mispronounce her name, and said if she were president it would be "an insult to the country" (Cathey, 2020, para. 1). Trump was known to ask if U.S. Representative Alexandria Ocasio-Cortez had gone to college and sexualized her; he called NBC journalist Savannah Guthrie "crazy" (Zoellner, 2020, para. 46).

What is notable, though, is that each of these women except Harris were not running against Trump for the presidency. In other words, they were not on the ballot. These results suggest that, at least in the context of politics, HS attitudes and masculine threat can be effectively activated on direct targets—such as one's political opponent—or indirect targets, such as women who are public figures but not in direct competition. Future research exploring the activating effects of women as direct or indirect threats will have important implications for women in politics and leadership roles.

Finally, we point to the strong and positive predictive value of SDO and BS in Biden's candidate image evaluations. While SDO positively predicted image evaluations of Biden across all factors, BS performed much the same with the exception of the intellect factor, which was nonsignificant. On one hand, the results are perhaps not surprising. The masculine threat that Clinton activated was no longer present with Biden, and he likely represented a traditional form of presidential candidate: male, a senior statesman with experience, a traditional family, and a wife who performs a publicly supportive role. Although those with BS attitudes embrace a broader notion that men occupy a space of dominance, it still may be challenging to fully support the aggressive, negative hostility that Trump exhibits. Therefore, Biden becomes the ideal alternative, both traditional and, of course, male. Thus, in supporting Biden voters are able to still embrace—and perhaps celebrate—a sense of homophily, wherein it is clear they remain dominant but share values with the "good one." Certainly with BS associating men with leadership positions, including a favorability toward men in prominent political offices (Cassidy & Krendl, 2019), it is not out of the question that Biden gave a desirable alternative that connected with BS beliefs, which in turn elevated the role of BS in predicting image evaluations. The prominent, predictive power of SDO for candidate evaluations also provides support for this position. And we propose further evidence for the idea that Biden appealed to a strongly BS attitude. With BS shown to be idealized by women as well (Connelly & Heesacker, 2012), combined, Biden ultimately benefitted from prejudice as he served as an alternative to Trump and Clinton, but in a way that felt far more accepted and acceptable.

Several limitations of this project should be noted. Although the questionnaire included items about real candidates shortly before the actual election day, it's possible that the timing and interface of the survey could have primed respondents to exaggerate and/or misrepresent their own views. However, given the size of the sample, we would not expect this to significantly alter the findings presented here. Nevertheless, these findings are ultimately based on only the responses from MTurk workers at a single point in time. Using only these data, it is therefore impossible to test for causality and/or exclude the possibility of unmeasured confounding variables.

In 2020, even with two men at the top of the ticket, ambivalent sexism was a clear factor in candidate evaluations. And, as our findings suggest, an overall dominance-oriented attitude played an even more influential role in 2020 than 2016. In particular, SDO, HS, and BS all served as positive predictors in voter image evaluations of Trump, even over and above partisanship. However, SDO and BS positively predicted voter image evaluations of Biden as well. Our study provides some answers about the 2020 election, but also raises more questions about how dominant attitudes develop around the role of agentic women in politics, the men who disparage them, and the men who promise to provide them with protection.

References

Banwart, M. C. & Kearney, M. W. (2018). Social dominance, sexism, and the lasting effects on political communication from the 2016 election. In B. R. Warner, D. G. Bystrom, M. S. McKinney & M. C. Banwart (Eds.), *An unprecedented election: Media, communication, and the electorate in the 2016 campaign*, (pp. 419–440). Santa Barbara, CA: ABC-CLIO.

Bauer, N. (2016). Here's what the research tells us about whether sexism is hurting Hillary Clinton's prospects. *The Washington Post*. https://www .washingtonpost.com/news/monkey-cage/wp/2016/02/05/heres-what -the-research-tells-us-about-whether-sexism-is-hurting-hillary-clintons -prospects/?utm_term=.08e83a0f0d52

Beinart, P. (2016, October). Fear of a female president: Hillary Clinton's candidacy has provoked a wave of misogyny—one that may roil American life for years to come. *The Atlantic*. https://www.theatlantic.com/magazine /archive/2016/10/fear-of-a-female-president/497564/

Bracic, A., Israel-Trummel, M., & Shortle, A. F. (2019). Is sexism for White people? Gender stereotypes, race, and the 2016 presidential election. *Political Behavior*, 41(2), 281–307. https://doi.org/10.1007/s11109-018-9446-8

Cassese, E. C. & Barnes, T. D. (2019). Reconciling sexism and women's support for Republican candidates: A look at gender, class, and whiteness in the 2012 and 2016 presidential races. *Political Behavior, 41*(3), 677–700. https://doi.org/10.1007/s11109-018-9468-2

Cassidy, B. S. & Krendl, A. C. (2019). A crisis of competence: Benevolent sexism affects evaluations of women's competence. *Sex Roles, 81*(7), 505–520. https://doi.org/10.1007/s11199-019-1011-3

Cathey, L. (2020, September 9). Trump mocks Harris' name, says having her as president would be "insult" to country. *ABC News.* https://abcnews.go.com/Politics/trump-mocks-harris-president-insult-country/story?id=72901540

Christopher, A. N. & Mull, M. S. (2006). Conservative ideology and ambivalent sexism. *Psychology of Women Quarterly, 30*(2), 223–230. https://doi.org/10.1111/j.1471-6402.2006.00284.x

Christopher, A. N. & Wojda, M. R. (2008). Social dominance orientation, right-wing authoritarianism, sexism, and prejudice toward women in the workforce. *Psychology of Women Quarterly, 32*(1), 65–73. https://doi.org/10.1111/j.1471-6402.2007.00407.x

Cole, A. (2016). Why sexism is so central to this presidential race. *Fortune.* http://fortune.com/2016/10/19/trump-clinton-sexism-presidential-debate/

Connelly, K. & Heesacker, M. (2012). Why is benevolent sexism appealing? *Psychology of Women Quarterly, 36*(4), 432–443. https://doi.org/10.1177/0361684312456369

Crowson, H. M. & Brandes, J. A. (2017). Differentiating between Donald Trump and Hillary Clinton voters using facets of right-wing authoritarianism and social-dominance orientation. *Psychological Reports, 120*(3), 364–373. https://doi.org/10.1177/0033294117697089

Dahl, J., Vescio, T., & Weaver, K. (2015). How threats to masculinity sequentially cause public discomfort, anger, and ideological dominance over women. *Social Psychology, 46*(4), 242–254. https://doi.org/10.1027/1864-9335/a000248

Duckitt, J. & Bizumic, B. (2013). Multidimensionality of right-wing authoritarian attitudes: Authoritarianism-conservatism-traditionalism. *Political Psychology, 34*(6), 841–862. https://doi.org/10.1111/pops.12022

Feather, N. T. & McKee, I. R. (2012). Values, right-wing authoritarianism, Social dominance orientation, and ambivalent attitudes toward women values and ambivalent sexism. *Journal of Applied Social Psychology, 42*(10), 2479–2504. https://doi.org/10.1111/j.1559-1816.2012.00950.x

Fraser, G., Osborne, D., & Sibley, C. G. (2015). "We want you in the workplace, but only in a skirt!" Social dominance orientation, gender-based affirmative action and the moderating role of benevolent sexism. *Sex Roles, 73*(5–6), 231–244. https://doi.org/10.1007/s11199-015-0515-8

Frasure-Yokley, L. (2018). Choosing the velvet glove: Women voters, ambivalent sexism, and vote choice in 2016. *Journal of Race, Ethnicity and Politics, 3*(1), 3–25. https://doi.org/10.1017/rep.2017.35

Glick, P. & Fiske, S. T. (1996). The ambivalent sexism inventory: Differentiating hostile and benevolent sexism. *Journal of Personality and Social Psychology*, *70*(3), 491–512. https://doi.org/10.1037/0022-3514.70.3.491

Glick, P., Lameiras, M., Fiske, S. T., Eckes, T., Masser, B., Volpato, C., Manganelli, A. M., Pek, J. C. X., Huang, L.-L., Sakalli-Uğurlu, N., Castro, Y. R., D'Avila Pereira, M. L., Willemsen, T. M., Brunner, A., Six-Materna, I., & Wells, R. (2004). Bad but bold: Ambivalent attitudes toward men predict gender inequality in 16 nations. *Journal of Personality and Social Psychology: Interpersonal Relations and Group Processes*, *86*(5), 713–728. https://doi.org/10.1037/0022-3514.86.5.713

Glick, P., Wilkerson, M., & Cuffe, M. (2015). Masculine identity, ambivalent sexism, and attitudes toward gender subtypes: Favoring masculine men and feminine women. *Social Psychology*, *46*(4), 210–217. https://doi.org/10.1027/1864-9335/a000228

Grina, J., Bergh, R., Akrami, N., & Sidanius, J. (2016). Political orientation and dominance: Are people on the political right more dominant? *Personality and Individual Differences*, *94*, 113–117. https://doi.org/10.1016/j.paid.2016.01.015

Hartig, H. & Doherty, C. (2018, October 22). More in U.S. see drug addiction, college affordability and sexism as 'very big' national problems. *Pew Research Center*. https://www.pewresearch.org/fact-tank/2018/10/22/more-in-u-s-see-drug-addiction-college-affordability-and-sexism-as-very-big-national-problems/

Hodson, G. & MacInnis, C. C. (2016). Can left-right differences in abortion support be explained by sexism? *Personality and Individual Differences*, *104*, 118–121. https://doi.org/10.1016/j.paid.2016.07.044

Ho, A. K., Sidanius, J., Pratto, F., Levin, S., Tomsen, L., Kteily, N., & Sheehy-Skeffington, J. (2012). Social dominance orientation: Revisiting the structure and function of a variable predicting social and political attitudes. *Personality and Social Psychology Bulletin*, *38*(5), 583–606. doi:10.1177/0146167211432765

Ho, A. K., Sidanius, J., Kteily, N., Sheehy-Skeffington, J., Pratto, F., Henkel, K. E., Foels, R., & Stewart, A. L. (2015). The nature of social dominance orientation: Theorizing and measuring preferences for intergroup inequality using the new SDO_7 scale. *Journal of Personality and Social Psychology*, *109*(6), 1003–1028. doi:10.1037/pspi0000033

Keith, T. (2016). Sexism is out in the open in the 2016 campaign. That may have been inevitable. *National Public Radio*. http://www.npr.org/2016/10/23/498878356/sexism-is-out-in-the-open-in-the-2016-campaign-that-may-have-been-inevitable

Kurtzleben, D. (2020, April 17). Did gender keep Democratic women from winning the presidential primary? *National Public Radio*. https://www.npr.org/2020/04/17/818952460/did-gender-keep-democratic-women-from-winning-the-primary

Lozano-Reich, N. M. (2016). The blog: Sexism, alive and well in 2016 presidential campaign. *Huffington Post.* http://www.huffingtonpost.com/nina-m-lozanoreich-phd/sexism-alive-and-well-in-2016-presidential-campaign_b_9172186.html

Mason, J. & Martina, M. (2020, October 17). Trump blasts Michigan governor Whitmer; crowd chants "lock her up." *Reuters.* https://www.reuters.com/article/us-usa-election-michigan-idUSKBN27206V

Mosso, C., Briante, G., Aiello, A., & Russo, S. (2013). The role of legitimizing ideologies as predictors of ambivalent sexism in young people: Evidence from Italy and the USA. *Social Justice Research, 26*(1), 1–17. https://doi.org/10.1007/s11211-012-0172-9

Okimoto, T. G. & Brescoll, V. L. (2010). The price of power: Power seeking and backlash against female politicians. *Personality & Social Psychology Bulletin, 36*(7), 923–936. https://doi.org/10.1177/0146167210371949

Paul, D. & Smith, J. L. (2008). Subtle sexism? Examining vote preferences when women run against men for the presidency. *Journal of Women, Politics & Policy, 29*(4), 451–476. https://doi.org/10.1080/15544770802092576

Perry, R., Sibley, C. G., & Duckitt, J. (2013). Dangerous and competitive worldviews: A meta-analysis of their associations with social dominance orientation and right-wing authoritarianism. *Journal of Research in Personality, 47*(1), 116–127. https://doi.org/10.1016/j.jrp.2012.10.004

Pratto, F., Sidanius, J., & Levin, S. (2006). Social dominance theory and the dynamics of intergroup relations: Taking stock and looking forward. *European Review of Social Psychology, 17*(1), 271–320. doi: 10.1080/10463280601055772

Pratto, F., Sidanius, J., Stallworth, L. M., & Malle, B. F. (1994). Social dominance orientation: A personality variable predicting social and political attitudes. *Journal of Personality and Social Psychology: Personality Processes and Individual Differences, 67*(4), 741–763. https://doi.org/10.1037/0022-3514.67.4.741

Radke, H. R. M., Hornsey, M. J., Sibley, C. G., & Barlow, F. K. (2018). Negotiating the hierarchy: Social dominance orientation among women is associated with the endorsement of benevolent sexism. *Australian Journal of Psychology, 70*(2), 158–166. https://doi.org/10.1111/ajpy.12176

Rosenberg, M., Borter, G., Huffstutter, P. J., Dwyer, M., & Kahn, C. (2020, November 7). "I just couldn't be silent": How American women decided the 2020 presidential race. *Reuters.* https://www.reuters.com/article/us-usa-election-women-insight-idUSKBN27N0XC

Schaffner, B. F. (2022). The heightened importance of racism and sexism in the 2018 US midterm elections. *British Journal of Political Science, 52*(1), 492–500. https://doi.org/10.1017/S0007123420000319

Schaffner, B. F., MacWilliams, M., & Nteta, T. (2017). *Explaining white polarization in the 2016 vote for president: The sobering role of racism and sexism.* [Paper presentation]. Conference on The U.S. Elections of 2016: Domestic and International Aspects, IDC Herzliya Campus, Israel.

Scotto di Carlo, G. (2020). Trumping Twitter. *Journal of Language and Politics*, *19*(1), 48–70. https://doi.org/10.1075/jlp.19034.sco

Shnabel, N., Bar-Anan, Y., Kende, A., Bareket, O., & Lazar, Y. (2016). Help to perpetuate traditional gender roles: Benevolent sexism increases engagement in dependency-oriented cross-gender helping. *Journal of Personality and Social Psychology, 110*(1), 55–75. https://doi.org/10.1037/pspi0000037

Sibley, C., Wilson, M. S., & Duckitt, J. (2007). Antecedents of men's hostile and benevolent sexism: The dual roles of social dominance orientation and right-wing authoritarianism. *Personality & Social Psychology Bulletin, 33*(2), 160–172. doi: 10.1177/0146167206294745.

Valentino, N. A., Wayne, C., & Oceno, M. (2018). Mobilizing sexism: The interaction of emotion and gender attitudes in the 2016 US presidential election. *Public Opinion Quarterly, 82*(S1), 799–821. https://doi.org/10.1093/poq/nfy003

Warner, B. R., & Banwart, M. C. (2016). A multifactor approach to candidate image. *Communication Studies, 67*(3), 259–279. https://doi.org/10.1080/10510974.2016.1156005

Wayne, C., Valentino, N., & Oceno, M. (2016). How sexism drives support for Donald Trump. *The Washington Post.* https://www.washingtonpost.com/news/monkey-cage/wp/2016/10/23/how-sexism-drives-support-for-donald-trump/?utm_term=.4890f253855d

Zoellner, D. (2020, October 30). From Greta to Gretchen: How Trump has used the office of presidency to attack dozens of women. *The Independent.* https://www.independent.co.uk/news/world/americas/us-politics/trump-attacks-women-hillary-clinton-aoc-greta-thunberg-gretchen-whitmer-b1402098.html

CHAPTER FIFTEEN

Partisan Media and Polarization in the 2020 Campaign

Benjamin R. Warner, Jihye Park, Go-Eun Kim, and Alyssa N. Coffey

Political polarization is an enduring feature of U.S. democracy. It should therefore not be a surprise that the 2020 campaign was characterized by considerable animosity across partisan lines. An astonishing 90% of Democrats and 89% of Republicans said that if their party's candidate lost, it would lead to lasting harm to the United States (Dimock & Wike, 2020). The view that political opponents are threats to the well-being of the nation is a particularly pernicious outcome of polarization because it can be used to rationalize political violence; research demonstrates that people who view the governing party as operating with malevolence will be more likely to endorse violent tactics (Warner et al., 2019). In the 2020 campaign, this link was more than hypothetical. On January 6, 2021, the U.S. Capitol was stormed by an organized mob attempting to prevent the peaceful transfer of power from the Trump administration to the newly elected Biden administration (Barry et al., 2021). This was perhaps the most significant threat to a peaceful transfer of power in the United States since the election of Abraham Lincoln in 1860.

In attempting to explain why the United States is so polarized, scholars point to a variety of factors, including the realignment of ideology and partisanship (Levendusky, 2009) and the layering of political parties with other salient social identities such as race, religion, class, and regional identification (Mason, 2018). The most common communication-related explanation for political polarization is the fragmented partisan media landscape (Garrett et al., 2014; Levendusky, 2013a; Stroud, 2010; Warner, 2010, 2018). But what role did partisan media play in the polarization that infused the 2020 campaign? Certainly, conservative partisan media contributed to the widespread and baseless accusations of election malfeasance that motivated the insurrection—partisan media are even cited in the legal defenses of people who face prosecution for their role in the attack on the Capitol (Lemon, 2021). And indeed, partisan media use has been linked to the spread of misinformation (Garrett et al., 2016) and belief in conspiracy theories (Warner & Neville-Shepard, 2014).

Given this, it is reasonable to suppose that partisan media were a central player in the polarized atmosphere that disrupted the 2020 campaign. To test this supposition, we draw on nationally representative survey data to estimate the association between partisan media use and polarization. Furthermore, we consider whether some people were more influenced by partisan media than others. Specifically, we test to see whether the association between partisan media use and polarization is stronger among those with more partisan strength, political interest, and attention to the election. We also consider the role of media from the other side—both for those who primarily consume cross-partisan media and for those who consume media from both sides. In what follows, we outline our theoretical expectations, present the results of our analysis, and consider the implications for understanding polarization in the United States.

Partisan Media and Polarization

For our purposes, political polarization will be defined consistent with research on affective (Iyengar et al., 2012) or social (Mason, 2018) polarization—the growing dislike of members of the other political party. Technically, affective/social polarization refers to the growing gap between how favorably people feel toward members of their own party compared to the negativity they feel toward the political outgroup. However, ingroup favorability has been stable over the past half-century, whereas outgroup animosity has steadily increased (Iyengar et al., 2012). Furthermore, scholarship on the negative normative outcomes of polarization focuses on this outgroup hostility (Warner et al., 2019). Thus, here we focus on the relationship between the use of partisan media and the hostility people express toward members of the other political party. This concern originates from a renewed debate about selective exposure.

The rapid onset of digital media shortly after the turn of the century coincided with a renewed debate about the effects of political media. Bennett and Iyengar (2010) suggested a new era of minimal effects because sociological and technological changes such as channel proliferation, audience fragmentation, and so forth would mute the influence of media on attitude change. They argued that audiences' ability to select congenial media, or opt out of political media altogether, would preclude substantively interesting media effects. This argument has received some empirical support (Arceneaux & Johnson, 2013; Prior, 2007)

Others leveraged the theory of selective exposure to argue that congenial media should have normatively significant effects on the electorate through either attitude change or attitude reinforcement (Holbert et al., 2010). When media consumers choose among ideological news outlets, their preference for attitude-consistent information seems to result in greater polarization (Garrett, 2009; Garrett & Stroud, 2014; Stroud, 2011). Selective exposure to like-minded information thus reinforces prior attitudes, and these stronger attitudes generate a stronger preference for ideologically congenial information, resulting in a reinforcing spiral of polarization (Slater, 2007). Most research supports the supposition that partisan media will result in greater political polarization (Dvir-Gvirsman, 2014; Garrett et al., 2014; Levendusky, 2013a; Stroud, 2010; Warner, 2010, 2018).

Two theoretical mechanisms account for the polarizing effect of partisan media: cognitive learning and intergroup competition (Sunstein, 2009). Learning new information from partisan news increases polarization because partisan media users are more familiar with arguments reinforcing their preexisting views (Dvir-Gvirsman, 2014). In addition, because users come across more perspectives that corroborate their prior beliefs, partisans become more confident that their views are correct and thus become more polarized (Knobloch-Westerwick, 2012; Sunstein, 2009).

Moreover, social identity plays a significant role in the influence of partisan media on political polarization. According to social identity theory (SIT) (Tajfel & Turner, 1979), when individuals identify themselves as a member of a group, they categorize other people as belonging to the ingroup or as members of the outgroup. These group categorizations allow people to gain positive distinctiveness with favorable intergroup comparisons by elevating the status of the ingroup and denigrating the outgroup. People also have social incentives to take stronger positions on issues that are important to their group because they receive ingroup praise by being exemplary group members. Thus, people can gain more social esteem from their group membership by expressing disdain for the outgroup. The social role of partisanship thus promotes ingroup favoritism and outgroup derogation (Greene 2004; Huddy et al., 2015; Iyengar et al., 2012; Mason 2018).

Partisan media increase the group-based incentives to polarize by providing cues that make partisan identities more salient and enhance the threat of the outgroup (Garrett et al., 2014; Levendusky, 2013a; Mason, 2018). Furthermore, because partisans feel compelled to protect and defend the favorable social status of their party, they are driven by directional goals (desire to reach to preferred conclusion that make them feel validated) rather than accuracy goals (desire to reach a correct conclusion). This results in identity-based motivated reasoning that is also linked to greater polarization (Bolsen et al., 2014; Druckman et al., 2013; Jennings, 2019).

To summarize, partisan media should increase polarization in the 2020 campaign by presenting new attitude-consistent information that affirms preexisting opinions, supplying credible ingroup exemplars who corroborate existing attitudes, providing social incentives to take stronger positions, and ensuring that attitude-consistent processing biases are dominant whenever new information about the campaign is presented. As a result, pro-partisan media users should have more incentive to denigrate the outgroup, should feel more strongly that their negative appraisals of the outgroup are correct, and should be more likely to use their partisanship as a cognitive heuristic when evaluating the political outgroup. We therefore hypothesize:

H1: Pro-partisan media use will be associated with colder evaluations of the political outgroup.

Scholarly interest in partisan media has largely focused on pro-partisan media because curiosity about selective exposure instigated this line of inquiry (Holbert et al., 2010). However, contrary to the tenets of selective exposure, people do not avoid attitude-incongruent partisan media (Garrett, 2009; Garrett & Stroud, 2014). In fact, almost one in five voters primarily consume partisan media from the other side of the political aisle (Stroud, 2011). These poorly sorted partisans were originally thought to be watching content from the other ideological perspective to counter-argue and critique (Garrett et al., 2014; Levendusky, 2013a). Thus, drawing on theories of motivated reasoning, scholars hypothesized that cross-partisan media would increase polarization. However, most empirical findings suggest the opposite, that cross-partisan media consumption reduces polarization (Feldman, 2011; Knobloch-Westerwick et al., 2015; Levendusky, 2013a; Stroud, 2010, 2011; Warner, 2018).

Feldman (2011) argues that the best expectation for cross-partisan news use is that people will be persuaded by it—a direct persuasion effect. Because message processing and attitude change follow the direction of the news content and cues, when media are clear and one-sided, people are most likely to move closer to the positions advanced by these partisan outlets. Media from the other side thus reduce polarization by increasing users' understanding

of other points of view. It is also possible that cross-partisan media acceler-
ate what Redlawsk and colleagues (2010) called the affective tipping point,
or the point at which people feel that they can no longer ignore information
that contradicts their prior beliefs. When individuals are exposed to highly
incongruent information, they are forced to face an overwhelming amount
of contrary evidence and eventually adjust their beliefs accordingly. Evidence
that people who consume media from the other side become less polarized
can be found in experimental (Levendusky, 2013a; Warner, 2010) and survey
(Garrett et al., 2014; Stroud, 2010; Warner, 2018) research. Thus, we propose:

H2: Cross-partisan media use will be associated with warmer evaluations of the
   political outgroup.

Viewers who primarily consume cross-partisan media are poorly sorted
partisans who may consume incongruent media because they lack the
political sophistication to make ideologically motivated media selections or
because they have a social motivation (Lee, 2013) that is more important to
them than ideological consistency (i.e., they are embedded in social networks
composed of largely outgroup members). However, many people consume
both pro- and cross-partisan media. In fact, Stroud (2011) estimated that
roughly the same number of media consumers supplement a pro-partisan
media diet with content from the other side (approximately 18%) as consume
exclusively cross-partisan media. There are at least two plausible motivations
to add cross-partisan media to a largely congenial media portfolio. First,
people may be motivated to watch media from the other side primarily to
critique it (Garrett et al., 2014). If this is the case, the act of counter-arguing
attitude-challenging messages should result in attitude rehearsal and greater
polarization. People may also be motivated to consume cross-partisan media
due to curiosity or because they believe the information will be useful
(Knobloch-Westerwick & Kleinman, 2012). These individuals should also
be expected to counter-argue incongruent messages to maintain cognitive
consistency. Thus, pro-partisan media should condition the effects of cross-
partisan media: for those who consume both pro- and cross-partisan media,
the effect should be to increase polarization through the attitude-rehearsal
mechanism. However, for those who consume relatively little pro-partisan
media, the direct persuasion effect described earlier is the more reasonable
expectation. We hypothesize that:

H3: Pro-partisan media will moderate the effects of cross-partisan media such
   that cross-partisan media will be associated with warmer evaluations of the
   political outgroup at low levels of pro-partisan media use, but cross-partisan
   media will be associated with colder evaluations of the political outgroup at
   high levels of pro-partisan media use.

The effects of pro-partisan media should not be uniform for all types of users. Partisan identity salience, or the extent to which people view their party membership as an important facet of their identities, is a crucial component of pro-partisan media effects. Strong partisans care more about their party affiliation and should respond more strongly to the arguments made in partisan media. When partisans select pro-partisan media, their political self-concept is activated and becomes more salient (Knobloch-Westerwick, 2012). Those for whom partisanship is more salient derive more self-worth from partisan social comparisons. Thus, it will be more important for these strong partisans to protect and defend group status (Billig & Tajfel, 1973; Huddy et al., 2015). Therefore, we propose:

H4a: The polarizing effect of pro-partisan media will be stronger for those with stronger partisan attachments.

A similar argument can be made regarding the effects of cross-partisan media. Strong partisans are more familiar with ingroup arguments and feel greater threat to their group-derived social esteem from the outgroup (Huddy et al., 2015). They thus have more motivation and ability to refute cross-partisan media. In addition, strong partisans are motivated to select cross-partisan media primarily to defend their opinions against critics (Valentino et al., 2009), thus increasing the probability that they are engaging the media with directional processing goals. Furthermore, strong partisans experience more negative emotions toward the outgroup when exposed to incongruent messages (Tesser & Leone, 1977). Conversely, weak partisans are more likely to be poorly sorted, should possess less political knowledge, and should feel less threat to their social esteem because they derive less positive distinctiveness from their partisan identity. Weak partisans are thus more susceptible to persuasion from cross-partisan media. Thus, we further hypothesize:

H4b: Partisan strength will moderate the effects of cross-partisan media such that cross-partisan media will be associated with warmer evaluations of the political outgroup for weak partisans, but cross-partisan media will be associated with colder evaluations of the political outgroup for strong partisans.

Finally, beyond partisan strength, people's general orientation toward politics should influence the effects of partisan media. Partisan media effects should be strongest for those who are less interested and attentive media users. When individuals are not interested in politics and have less political attention and knowledge, they consume partisan media passively, and they have less capacity to resist the persuasive appeals present in partisan media (Dvir-Gvirsman, 2014; Warner, 2018). Those who have little political interest will more readily accept the perspectives and incorporate the arguments advanced by partisan media. Furthermore, those with little attention to politics will likely have weaker prior attitudes and thus be more likely to fall into the attitude-formation phase of media effects (Holbert et al., 2010). Hence, we expect those with less political interest and attention to be more influenced by partisan media:

H5: Political interest and political attention will moderate the effects of partisan media such that both pro- and cross-partisan media will have stronger effects on those who are less interested and less attentive to politics. The effects will be such that pro-partisan media will reduce outgroup evaluations more among less interested and less attentive media users, whereas cross-partisan media will improve outgroup evaluations more among less interested and less attentive media users.

Method

Procedure

The study utilized the preliminary release of the 2020 American National Election Studies data (ANES, 2020). For the 2020 election, ANES partnered with Westat, Inc., to collect a probability sample of the U.S. population using a mixed-mode survey procedure. Surveys were self-administered online or completed via telephone or live-video interviews. ANES generated the probability sample from a sampling frame of 231 million U.S. citizens living in the 50 states or the District of Columbia. Eligibility requirements were such that participants needed to be 18 years of age or older, noninstitutional, and residing at the sampled address. The sample was drawn from the U.S. Postal Service digital file, which includes all residential addresses in the sampling frame. ANES also re-recruited some participants from their probability sample of the 2016 electorate. Recruitment occurred between August 18 and November 3, 2020. The American Association for Public Opinion Research response rate 3 for the survey was 40.9%.

The full ANES sample consisted of 8,280 respondents. Because our theoretical hypotheses concern only those individuals who affiliate with one of the two major political parties, unaffiliated individuals were excluded. All participants were asked, "Generally speaking, do you usually think of yourself as a Democrat, a Republican, an Independent, or what?" Those who did not identify as a Democrat or a Republican were asked the follow-up question, "Do you think of yourself as closer to the Republican Party or the Democratic Party?" Those who replied "neither" were categorized as Independents with no partisan lean and were excluded ($n = 968$, 12%).

ANES provides a "refuse" or "did not answer" option for a variety of questions. All participants who did not provide responses for variables utilized in this study were excluded from analysis. Of the 7,312 eligible participants,

1,021 (14%) had at least one incomplete response. Thus, our analyses are conducted on 6,291 (76%) of the full 8,280 ANES sample.

Participants

The 6,291 participants included in our analyses were majority White (74%; 9% Black, 9% Hispanic/Latinx, 3% Asian, 2% Native, 3% multiracial) and majority female (54%). The average age was 52 years old ($SD = 17$). A plurality (28%) described religion as being "extremely important" in their life compared to very important (19%), moderately important (19%), a little important (13%), or not important at all (21%). Most either had some post–high school education (34%), had completed a bachelor's degree (27%), or had completed a graduate degree (21%). Approximately 7% of the sample identified as gay, lesbian, or bisexual.

Variables

Polarization

Affective political polarization is the contrast between how favorably people feel toward members of their own political group and how negatively they feel toward members of the political outgroup. Although this is sometimes operationalized as the absolute value of the difference between ingroup and outgroup evaluations, such an approach combines ingroup with outgroup ratings. Much of the concern about affective polarization derives from increasing hostility toward the outgroup. Thus, for our purposes, we focus on evaluations of the political outgroup as our outcome variable.

Outgroup evaluations were measured with the feeling thermometer instrument commonly used by the ANES and often adapted for research on affective polarization (Iyengar et al., 2012; Stroud, 2010). Participants were told they would be asked to give their "feelings toward some of our political leaders" using "something we call the feeling thermometer" and that "ratings between 50 degrees and 100 degrees mean that you feel favorable and warm toward the person" whereas "ratings between 0 degrees and 50 degrees mean that you don't feel favorable toward the person and that you don't care too much for that person." Participants were asked to rate Joe Biden, Donald Trump, Kamala Harris, Mike Pence, the Democratic Party, and the Republican Party. We utilized the partisanship of the respondents to transform these ratings into outgroup ratings (i.e., Republicans respondents' ratings of Biden, Harris, and the Democratic Party; Democratic respondents' ratings of Trump, Pence, and the Republican Party). Consistent with the trend toward increasingly negative evaluations of the outgroup, the average ratings were very low ($M = 16.79$, $SD = 18.92$, $\alpha = 0.83$).

Media Use

Partisan media, in contrast with traditional media, advance persuasive arguments in favor of one political party or ideology and advocate against the alternative party/ideology. Partisan media have previously been operationalized as programing on the *Fox News* channel, conservative talk radio, conservative blogs, liberal blogs, *National Public Radio* (*NPR*), programing on *MSNBC*, and political comedy (Levendusky, 2013b; Warner, 2018; Young, 2019). The fit between the conceptual definition (advocacy media) and the actual content of some of this programing is debatable. *NPR*, for example, explicitly avoids partisan advocacy, and both *Fox* and *MSNBC* attempt to maintain divisions between their news and opinion programing. Past research has tended to justify the inclusion of these explicitly opinion-neutral media with the partisan composition of their audiences—or the "audience skew criterion" (Levendusky, 2013b, p. 569). The advantages and disadvantages of this strategy are beyond the scope of this chapter. Here, we follow previous literature.

To measure media use, ANES asks people whether they have heard or read anything about the presidential campaign on television, Internet sites, radio, and newspapers. They then ask participants whether they regularly watch, listen to, or read an extensive—although not exhaustive—list of programs or outlets within each medium. This approach to measuring media use has demonstrated predictive validity (Dilliplane et al., 2013) and is superior to alternative media use measures (Goldman et al., 2013).

Of the variety of media in the ANES survey, the following were included in our liberal media variable: the television programs *All In with Chris Hayes*, *The Rachel Maddow Show*, *The Last Word with Lawrence O'Donnell*, *The 11th Hour with Brian Williams*, *Morning Joe*, and *The Late Show with Stephen Colbert*; the NPR programs *All Things Considered*, *Fresh Air*, *Marketplace*, and *Morning Edition*; and the websites *HuffPost.com*, *NPR.com*, and *BuzzFeed.com*. The typical respondent consumed slightly more than one media source ($M = 1.28$, $SD = 1.71$, $\alpha = 0.66$), though there was substantial variance, with approximately 47% of the sample consuming zero liberal media sources, 22% consuming one, 13% consuming two, and less than 1% consuming eight or more.

The following were included in our conservative media variable: the television programs *Hannity*, *Tucker Carlson Tonight*, *The Five*, *The Ingraham Angle*, *The Story with Martha MacCallum*, *Fox and Friends*, and *Special Report with Bret Baier*; the conservative radio programs *Rush Limbaugh*, *The Sean Hannity Show*, *The Dave Ramsey Show*, *The Mark Levin Show*, *The Glenn Beck Program*, *The Mike Gallagher Show*, *The Hugh Hewitt Show*, *The Savage Nation*, *The Dana Show*, *The Thom Hartmann Program*, and *The Jim Bohannon Show*; and the websites *Breitbart.com*, *FoxNews.com*, and the *DailyCaller.com*. The typical respondent consumed slightly more than one conservative media source ($M = 1.16$,

SD = 1.59, α = 0.61), though there was substantial variance; as with liberal media, approximately 47% of the sample consumed zero conservative sources, 23% consumed one, 14% consumed two, and less than 1% consumed seven or more.

Respondents' party identification was used to transform the liberal and conservative media variables into a measure of pro-partisan media use (Democrats using liberal media and Republicans using conservative media) and cross-partisan media use (Republicans using liberal media and Democrats using conservative media). Pro-partisan media use was more common (*M* = 1.55, *SD* = 1.9) than cross-partisan media use (*M* = 0.98, *SD* = 1.27). Sixty percent of respondents reported that they used at least one pro-partisan media source, a plurality (35%) used one or two, and less than 1% used more than seven. Forty-four percent of respondents used at least one cross-partisan media source, with 36% using one or two and less than 1% using more than five.

Moderators

In addition to the direct and conditional effects of partisan media, we hypothesized that partisan media would have different effects on affective polarization depending on respondents' strength of partisanship, political interest, and attention to politics. *Strength of partisanship* was assessed with follow-up questions to the partisan identification question described earlier. Those who said they were Democrats [Republicans] were asked, "Would you call yourself a strong Democrat [Republican] or a not very strong Democrat [Republican]?" Those who said they were Independents were asked, "Do you think of yourself as closer to the Democratic Party or Republican Party?" Partisan strength was coded such that 1 = closer to Democratic/Republican Party, 2 = not very strong Democrat/Republican, and 3 = strong Democrat/Republican (*M* = 2.26, *SD* = 0.84). *Political interest* was measured by asking respondents, "Some people don't pay much attention to political campaigns. How about you? Would you say that you have been (3) very much interested, (2) somewhat interested, or (1) not much interested in the political campaign so far this year" (*M* = 2.45, *SD* = 0.68). *Political attention* was measured by asking, "How often do you pay attention to what's going on in government and politics?" with response options ranging from "always" (coded 5) to "never" (coded 1, *M* = 3.77, *SD* = 0.99).

Statistical Controls

Because the ANES preliminary release data measure all variables—be they theoretical antecedents or outcomes—at the same time prior to the election, all observed associations are merely correlational. Thus, there is no definitive way to know whether what we perceive to be the cause is not actually the effect (and vice versa). Furthermore, unobserved variable bias confounds any attempt to infer causality. In other words, the association between media use and affective polarization may be caused by some other phenomenon. For example, it is likely that people who are more interested in politics are both more likely to consume political media and more likely to express negativity toward the political outgroup (since their partisan identities are more salient). By including the most intuitive confounding variables in our model, we can control for potential unobserved variable bias. In other words, we can observe the effect of pro-partisan and cross-partisan media on affective polarization beyond what is already explained by variables such as partisan strength and political interest. Although we cannot account for all possible alternative explanations, we can include many of the most likely sources of unobserved variable bias in our models and thereby substantially increase confidence that any observed association is indicative of a true relationship between media use and polarization.

The most likely sources of unobserved variable bias are our theoretical moderators (partisan strength, political interest, and political attention). Naturally, we include these variables in all analyses. Beyond these variables, media use in general is the next most likely alternative explanation for any association between partisan media use and polarization. Information-seeking behavior should be highly correlated with the use of both mainstream and partisan media—particularly for those labeled news omnivores (Edgerly, 2015). It is possible that this information-seeking behavior will be associated with affective polarization in ways that inflate the apparent effect of partisan media. To account for this, we include a measure of mainstream media use as a statistical control. This is measured with the same procedure as our partisan media variable, but rather than including partisan media, it includes 11 television programs from network daily and weekly news, *CNN*, and *PBS* ($M = 1.1$, $SD = 1.51$, $\alpha = 0.70$).

In addition to these variables, we control for partisanship (Republican = 1, 46%); age; sex (male =1, ANES did not ask about gender, nor was there any apparent attempt to account for individuals who were not assigned a binary sex at birth); race (dummy-coded variables for Black, Asian, Hispanic/Latinx, Native American, and multiracial, with White as the excluded category); religiosity ($M = 3.18$, $SD = 1.5$); and a dummy variable indicating whether the respondent identified as gay, lesbian, bisexual, or otherwise a member of the LGBQ community. Unless reported here, summary statistics for these variables are reported earlier in the section describing participants in the ANES sample.

Results

The theoretical hypotheses about the direct and conditional effects of partisan media on polarization were tested with a series of linear regression models in which feeling thermometer toward the outgroup was the dependent variable. The results of all four models are reported in Table 15.1. The

Table 15.1 Results for Regression Models Predicting Evaluations of the Political Outgroup

	Model 1	Model 2	Model 3	Model 4
Age	−0.026	0.066***	0.057***	0.056***
Male	−0.027*	−0.008	−0.012	−0.010
Black	0.057***	0.050***	0.034**	0.033**
Hispanic/Latinx	0.067***	0.056***	0.049***	0.050***
Asian	0.055***	0.039**	0.038**	0.038**
American Native	0.027*	0.020#	0.019	0.019#
Multi-Racial	0.009	−0.003	−0.006	−0.006
GLBTQ	−0.033*	−0.027*	−0.022#	−0.020#
Religiosity	0.005	0.032*	0.024#	0.028*
Republican	0.140***	0.104***	0.099***	0.095***
Mainstream Media	—	0.027*	0.023	0.027#
Partisan Strength (ST)	—	−0.207***	−0.203***	−0.223***
Political Interest (PI)	—	−0.106***	−0.091***	−0.088***
Political Attention (PA)	—	−0.162***	−0.145***	−0.135***
Pro-Partisan Media (PM)	—	—	−0.170***	−0.284***
Cross-Partisan Media (CM)	—	—	0.134***	0.338***
PM*CM	—	—	—	−0.002
PM*ST	—	—	—	0.021***
CM*ST	—	—	—	−0.024***
PM*PI	—	—	—	−0.017
CM*PI	—	—	—	0.002
PM*PA	—	—	—	0.012
CM*PA	—	—	—	−0.004
Adjusted R^2	0.025	0.127	0.155	0.159
F	16.69	65.94	72.52	52.450
Df	10, 6219	14, 6215	16, 6213	23, 6206

Note: Standardized coefficients reported, $\#p < 0.1$; $*p < 0.05$; $**p < 0.01$; $***p < 0.001$.

first model included the sociodemographic control variables. This model only explained 2.5% of variance in outgroup feelings. The most influential variable in the model was partisanship—Republicans had warmer outgroup evaluations compared to Democrats. This is perhaps because Republicans were the governing party at the time of the election, and thus Democrats felt more outgroup threat.

The second model incorporated the variables most likely to account for any spurious relationship between partisan media and polarization: mainstream media use, partisan strength, political interest, and attention to the campaign. This model explained nearly 13% variance in feelings toward the outgroup—an increase of more than 10% from the sociodemographic model. Stronger partisans, those more interested in politics, and those who reported paying closer attention to the campaign expressed more negative feelings toward the outgroup. Those who consumed more mainstream media reported somewhat warmer evaluations of the outgroup, although this effect was too small to be substantively interesting.

The first two hypotheses predicted direct effects of partisan media. Specifically, that pro-partisan media would reduce evaluations of the outgroup and that cross-partisan media would improve evaluations of the outgroup. As reported in the column for the third model in Table 15.1, both hypotheses were supported. Pro-partisan media was associated with colder evaluations of the outgroup and was approaching partisan strength as the most influential variable in the model. Conversely, cross-partisan media was associated with warmer evaluations of the outgroup and was one of the four most influential variables in the model (along with campaign attention). This third model explained nearly 16% of variance in feelings toward the outgroup, a modest but significant improvement on the 13% explained by the previous model.

The third hypothesis predicted that the depolarizing effect of cross-partisan media would be moderated by pro-partisan media such that people who consumed both would be more polarized, whereas people who only consumed cross-partisan media would be less polarized. This hypothesis was not supported, as the interaction term for pro- and cross-partisan media reported in the fourth model of Table 15.1 was statistically indistinguishable from zero.

The fourth hypothesis predicted that the effects of partisan media would depend on partisan strength. H4a predicted that pro-partisan media would have a stronger polarizing effect on strong partisans compared to weak partisans. However, the interaction term presented in Table 15.1 shows the inverse association. To illustrate this, the interaction is represented in Figure 15.1. As the figure shows, pro-partisan media reduced outgroup evaluations the most among lean partisans (those who did not initially identify with a political party but, upon follow-up, said they were closer to one).

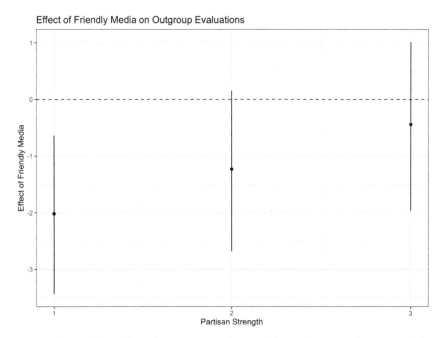

Figure 15.1   The Effect of Pro-Partisan (Friendly) Media on Evaluations of the Outgroup at Various Levels of Partisan Strength

Conversely, the effect was weaker for moderate partisans (those who initially aligned with a party but, upon follow-up, said they were not so strong partisans) and nonsignificant for strong partisans (as indicated by the error bar crossing zero).

The second prediction regarding partisan strength (H4b) was that weak partisans would be more influenced by cross-partisan media. This prediction was supported, as indicated by the interaction of partisan strength and cross-partisan media reported in Table 15.1. Figure 15.2 illustrates the nature of this interaction. The effect was strongest for weak partisans—cross-partisan media use resulted in warmer evaluations of the outgroup. Although the depolarizing effect of cross-partisan media was smaller for stronger partisans, it was persistent regardless of partisan strength. Thus, cross-partisan media use clearly results in warmer outgroup feelings regardless of partisan strength, but the effect is stronger as partisanship is weaker.

The fifth hypothesis predicted that both political interest and attention to the campaign would moderate the effects of partisan media. However, none of the four interaction terms used to test this hypothesis were significant. Partisan media exerted the same influence on outgroup feelings regardless of the level of political interest or attention to the campaign of the viewer.

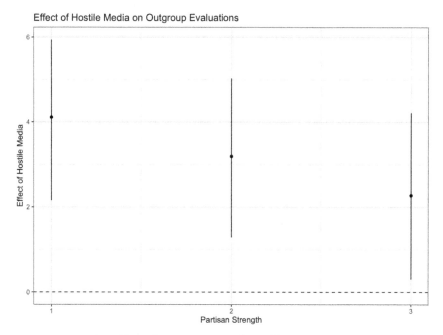

Figure 15.2 The Effect of Cross-Partisan (Hostile) Media on Evaluations of the Outgroup at Various Levels of Partisan Strength

Discussion

This chapter tested the relationship between partisan media and the highly polarized climate of the 2020 election. We found a polarizing effect of pro-partisan media consistent with past research, although we only observed this relationship among weaker partisans. Conversely, we found a depolarizing effect of cross-partisan media that was present for all partisans, although it was stronger for weak partisans compared to strong partisans. The implications of these findings, along with limitations and directions for future research, are considered next.

The effects of pro-partisan media in the 2020 campaign mirror those found in previous studies of partisan media (Garrett et al., 2014; Levendusky, 2013a; Stroud, 2010; Warner, 2018). Those who consumed more pro-partisan media also had colder feelings toward the political outgroup. During a campaign, partisan identities are especially salient because campaign communication dominates digital and legacy media in addition to interpersonal conversation. Furthermore, the prospect of winning or losing an election exacerbates the risks to the positive distinctiveness people derive from their group affiliations. The very threat of losing an election can result in more polarization

(Huddy et al., 2015). Partisan media have an incentive to emphasize both features of the campaign. First, the presidential campaign is a constant source of content that these networks can use to emotionally engage their audiences. Second, by emphasizing the stakes of the election, these media can maintain their audience's attention. Thus, if we expect polarization to generally result from the campaign, it should be no surprise that pro-partisan media contribute to this.

The more unexpected finding is that pro-partisan media primarily polarize weak partisans. We expected the reverse. Strong partisan media users have more incentive to engage in biased information processing and outgroup denigration, so in theory, they should be more influenced by the polarizing content presented in pro-partisan media. The best explanation for our unexpected finding is offered by Arceneaux and Johnson (2013), who argue that because strong partisans are already polarized, they are largely immune to partisan media effects. The antagonistic content of pro-partisan media may reflect the polarized views of their most loyal audience members rather than the cause of these views. There is some good news here. The most concerning individuals, those who are already highly polarized, do not appear to be inflamed by the uncivil content common in partisan media. However, these individuals are still remarkably polarized, so whether media are a cause or merely a symptom, the threat to democracy remains. More concerning, pro-partisan media increase polarization for weaker partisans. In other words, pro-partisan media close the polarization gap between strong and weak partisans.

We did find some good news for democracy. Those who consumed cross-partisan media were less polarized. This effect was strongest for weak partisans but was still present for strong partisans—meaning even the most polarized individuals had warmer feelings toward the outgroup if they consumed cross-partisan media. This effect held regardless of whether people also consumed pro-partisan media. In other words, even when people received all the information, argumentation, and ingroup cues that are known to increase polarization, they still benefited from the depolarizing value of media from the other side.

The depolarizing effects of cross-partisan media have been observed elsewhere (Levendusky, 2013a; Stroud, 2010; Warner, 2018) even as most existing studies hypothesize that biased processing will result in counter-arguing, attitude rehearsal, and ultimately greater polarization. Despite the antagonistic nature of the 2020 campaign, we found no evidence of this counter-arguing/rehearsal effect of media from the other side. It is becoming increasingly difficult to find any empirical support for this hypothesis despite its popularity among political theorists. Instead, we conclude with Feldman (2011) that the most likely effect of cross-partisan media is that people are influenced by the persuasive content they encounter.

Cross-partisan media thus join the small but growing list of communication strategies known to reduce affective polarization (Amsalem et al., 2022; Bond et al., 2018; Huddy & Yair, 2021; Levendusky, 2018; Warner et al., 2020; Warner & Villamil, 2017; Wojcieszak & Warner, 2020). As with most of these other depolarizing forms of communication, the effect is likely derived from an increase in understanding and perceived commonality. When people do not understand the other side, it is easy to feel divided from them and to wonder why they believe the seemingly indefensible things caricatured by political elites from their ingroup. However, when people expose themselves to outgroup media, they encounter the strongest versions of outgroup arguments. Although they are unlikely to change their vote preferences, these viewers should nevertheless have a better understanding of the nature of political disagreement and thus find it easier to empathize with those across the proverbial aisle.

Limitations

In this study, we utilized the highest-quality publicly available data to help understand the role of partisan media in exacerbating (or ameliorating) polarization during the 2020 election. ANES spares no expense to collect a probability sample that can be used to generate population inferences so that scholars of campaigns can probe the inner workings of our democracy. Nevertheless, there are important limitations to this study. First, because the data are cross-sectional, we cannot make causal inferences. Nevertheless, the associations identified here are consistent with experimental findings (Levendusky, 2013b; Warner, 2010). Second, measuring media use is notoriously difficult. Though ANES deploys a validated self-report measure of media use, behavioral measures (such as set-top television trackers and web-history capture technologies) are the only way to eliminate the bias introduced by asking people to reflect on their own media habits. Despite this limitation, our measure distinguishes between high and low partisan media users, so our theoretical inferences should be robust to self-report bias. Finally, our measure of partisan media does not distinguish between the tone of content. We grouped polemical programs such as Hannity and Carlson with programs that strive for objectivity (e.g., *NPR* and Baer). Future research should probe the nuances of partisan media to determine if the polemic content of a program dictates the nature of the effects observed.

Conclusion

The 2020 presidential election was polarized even by modern standards. In this chapter, we sought to understand the extent to which partisan media contributed to this polarization. Our findings were somewhat surprising and at least partially refreshing. It appears to be the case that consuming media from the other side reduces polarization. People who do consult sources that they disagree with have warmer feelings toward the outgroup. This finding held for weak and strong partisans alike, although the depolarizing effects were stronger for weak partisans. Despite almost a decade of hypothesizing that people's motivational biases would result in a polarizing effect of media from the other side, we circle back to the original instincts of those who renewed the debate about selective exposure: it is good to have balance in our media environment, and people should expose themselves to perspectives with which they disagree. Regarding pro-partisan media, there was evidence of a polarizing effect. People who consume ideologically congenial content have colder feelings toward the political outgroup. However, this effect was not present for strong partisans. Those who are most polarized do not appear to become more so when they consume pro-partisan media. Instead, this media serves to bring weak partisans in alignment with the more polarized members of their ingroup and, in the process, potentially shrink the number who can be counted as political moderates. In total, these findings suggest that the role of partisan media in our raucous democracy is more nuanced than we might assume. Those who chose to exclusively consume like-minded media should not be surprised by their growing ire toward citizens from across the aisle. However, those who occasionally expose themselves to the information preferred by their political rivals may discover that they understand their adversaries better and are thus less inclined to bitterness and hostility. As has always been the case, we have agency to decide what information we consume. How we utilize this agency is as influential as the media content itself.

References

Arceneaux, K. & Johnson, M. (2013). *Changing minds or changing channels?: Partisan news in an age of choice*. Chicago, IL: University of Chicago Press.

American National Election Studies. (2021, February 11). [Data set]. www.electionstudies.org

Amsalem, E., Merkley, E., & Loewen, P. J. (2022). Does talking to the other side reduce inter-party hostility? Evidence from three studies. *Political Communication*. https://doi.org/10.1080/10584609.2021.1955056

Barry, D., McIntire, M., & Rosenberg, M. (2021, May 28). 'Our president wants us here': The mob that stormed the capitol. *New York Times*. https://www.nytimes.com/2021/01/09/us/capitol-rioters.html

Bennett, W. L. & Iyengar, S. (2010). The shifting foundations of political communication: Responding to a defense of the media effects paradigm. *Journal of Communication*, 60(1), 35–39. https://doi.org/10.1111/j.1460-2466.2009.01471.x

Billig, M. & Tajfel, H. (1973). Social categorization and similarity in intergroup behaviour. *European Journal of Social Psychology, 3*(1), 27–52. https://doi .org/10.1002/ejsp.2420030103

Bolsen, T., Druckman, J. N., & Cook, F. L. (2014). The influence of partisan motivated reasoning on public opinion. *Political Behavior, 36*(2), 235–262. doi: 10.1007/s11109-013-9238-0

Bond, R. M., Shulman, H. C., & Gilbert, M. (2018). Does having a political discussion help or hurt intergroup perceptions? Drawing guidance from social identity theory and the contact hypothesis. *International Journal of Communication, 12,* 4332–4352. https://ijoc.org/index.php/ijoc/article /view/9033/2486

Dilliplane, S., Goldman, S. K., & Mutz, D. C. (2013). Televised exposure to politics: New measures for a fragmented media environment. *American Journal of Political Science, 57*(1), 236–248. doi:10.1111/j.1540-5907.2012.00600.x

Dimock, M. & Wike, R. (2020, November 13). America is exceptional in the nature of its political divide. *Pew Research Center.* https://www .pewresearch.org/fact-tank/2020/11/13/america-is-exceptional-in-the -nature-of-its-political-divide/

Druckman, J. N., Peterson, E., & Slothuus, R. (2013). How elite partisan polarization affects public opinion formation. *American Political Science Review, 107*(1), 57–79. doi:10.1017/S0003055412000500

Dvir-Gvirsman, S. (2014). It's not that we don't know, it's that we don't care: Explaining why selective exposure polarizes attitudes. *Mass Communication and Society, 17*(1), 74–97. https://doi.org/10.1080/15205436.2013 .816738

Edgerly, S. (2015). Red media, blue media, and purple media: News repertoires in the colorful media landscape. *Journal of Broadcasting & Electronic Media, 59*(1), 1–21. doi:10.1080/08838151.2014.998220

Feldman, L. (2011). The opinion factor: The effects of opinionated news on information processing and attitude change. *Political Communication, 28*(2), 163–181. https://doi.org/10.1080/10584609.2011.565014

Garrett, R. K. (2009). Politically motivated reinforcement seeking: Reframing the selective exposure debate. *Journal of Communication, 59*(4), 676–699. https://doi.org/10.1111/j.1460-2466.2009.01452.x

Garrett, R. K., Gvirsman, S. D., Johnson, B. K., Tsfati, Y., Neo, R., & Dal, A. (2014). Implications of pro- and counterattitudinal information exposure for affective polarization. *Human Communication Research, 40*(3), 309–332. https://doi.org/10.1111/hcre.12028

Garrett, R. K. & Stroud, N. J. (2014). Partisan paths to exposure diversity: Differences in pro-and counterattitudinal news consumption. *Journal of Communication, 64*(4), 680–701. https://doi.org/10.1111/jcom.12105

Garrett, R. K., Weeks, B. E., & Neo, R. L. (2016). Driving a wedge between evidence and beliefs: How online ideological news exposure promotes political misperceptions. *Journal of Computer-Mediated Communication, 21*(5), 331–348. https://doi.org/10.1111/jcc4.12164

Goldman, S. K., Mutz, D. C., & Dilliplane, S. (2013). All virtue is relative: A response to Prior. *Political Communication, 30*(4), 635–653. doi:10.1080 /10584609.2013.819540

Greene, S. (2004). Social identity theory and party identification. *Social Science Quarterly, 85*(1), 136–153. https://doi.org/10.1111/j.0038-4941 .2004.08501010.x

Holbert, R. L., Garrett, R. K., & Gleason, L. S. (2010). A new era of minimal effects? A response to Bennett and Iyengar. *Journal of Communication, 60*(1), 15–34. https://doi.org/10.1111/j.1460-2466.2009.01470.x

Huddy, L., Mason, L., & Aarøe, L. (2015). Expressive partisanship: Campaign involvement, political emotion, and partisan identity. *American Political Science Review, 109*(1), 1–17. doi:10.1017/S0003055414000604

Huddy, L. & Yair, O. (2021). Reducing affective polarization: Warm group relations or policy compromise? *Political Psychology, 42*(2), 291–309. https:// doi.org/10.1111/pops.12699

Iyengar, S., Sood, G., & Lelkes, Y. (2012). Affect, not ideology a social identity perspective on polarization. *Public Opinion Quarterly, 76*(3), 405–431. https://doi.org/10.1093/poq/nfs038

Jennings, F. J. (2019). An uninformed electorate: Identity-motivated elaboration, partisan cues, and learning. *Journal of Applied Communication Research, 47*(5), 527–547. https://doi.org/10.1080/00909882.2019.1679385

Knobloch-Westerwick, S. (2012). Selective exposure and reinforcement of attitudes and partisanship before a presidential election. *Journal of Communication, 62*(4), 628–642. doi:10.1111/j.1460-2466.2012.01651.x.

Knobloch-Westerwick, S. & Kleinman, S. B. (2012). Preelection selective exposure: Confirmation bias versus informational utility. *Communication Research, 39*(2), 170–193. https://doi.org/10.1177/0093650211400597

Knobloch-Westerwick, S., Johnson, B. K., & Westerwick, A. (2015). Confirmation bias in online searches: Impacts of selective exposure before an election on political attitude strength and shifts. *Journal of Computer-Mediated Communication, 20*(2), 171–187. https://doi.org/10.1111/jcc4.12105

Lee, A. M. (2013). News audiences revisited: Theorizing the link between audience motivations and news consumption. *Journal of Broadcasting & Electronic Media, 57*(3), 300–317. https://doi.org/10.1080/08838151.2013 .816712

Lemon, J. (2021, May 29). Capitol rioters will blame Trump, Fox News for their actions on Jan. 6. *Newsweek.* https://www.newsweek.com/capitol-rioters -will-blame-trump-fox-news-their-actions-jan-6-report-1596149

Levendusky, M. (2009). *The partisan sort.* Chicago, IL: University of Chicago Press.

Levendusky, M. (2013a). *How partisan media polarize America.* Chicago, IL: University of Chicago Press.

Levendusky, M. (2013b). Partisan media exposure and attitudes toward the opposition. *Political Communication, 30*(4), 565–581. https://doi.org/10.1080 /10584609.2012.737435

Levendusky, M. S. (2018). Americans, not partisans: Can priming American national identity reduce affective polarization? *The Journal of Politics, 80*(1), 59–70. https://doi.org/10.1086/693987

Mason, L. (2018). *Uncivil agreement: How politics became our identity.* Chicago, IL: University of Chicago Press.

Prior, M. (2007). *Post-broadcast democracy: How media choice increases inequality in political involvement and polarizes elections.* New York, NY: Cambridge University Press.

Redlawsk, D. P., Civettini, A. J., & Emmerson, K. M. (2010). The affective tipping point: Do motivated reasoners ever "get it"?. *Political Psychology, 31*(4), 563–593. https://doi.org/10.1111/j.1467-9221.2010.00772.x

Slater, M. D. (2007). Reinforcing spirals: The mutual influence of media selectivity and media effects and their impact on individual behavior and social identity. *Communication Theory, 17*(3), 281–303. doi: 10.1111/j.1468-2885.2007.00296.x

Stroud, N. J. (2010). Polarization and partisan selective exposure. *Journal of Communication, 60*(3), 556–576. https://doi.org/10.1111/j.1460-2466.2010.01497.x

Stroud, N. J. (2011). *Niche news: The politics of news choice.* New York, NY: Oxford University Press.

Sunstein, C. R. (2009). *Going to extremes: How like minds unite and divide.* New York, NY: Oxford University Press.

Tajfel, H. & Turner, J. C. (1979). An integrative theory of intergroup conflict. In W. G. Austin & S. Worchel (Eds.), *The social psychology of intergroup relations* (pp. 205–255). New York, NY: Cambridge University Press.

Tesser, A., & Leone, C. (1977). Cognitive schemas and thought as determinants of attitude change. *Journal of Experimental Social Psychology, 13*(4), 340–356. https://doi.org/10.1016/0022-1031(77)90004-X

Valentino, N. A., Banks, A. J., Hutchings, V. L., & Davis, A. K. (2009). Selective exposure in the Internet Age: The interaction between anxiety and information utility. *Political Psychology, 30*(4), 591–613. doi:10.1111/j.1467-9221.2009.00716.x.

Warner, B. R. (2010). Segmenting the electorate: The effects of exposure to political extremism online. *Communication Studies, 61*(4), 430–444. https://doi.org/10.1080/10510974.2010.497069

Warner, B. R. (2018). Modeling partisan media effects in the 2014 U.S. midterm elections. *Journalism & Mass Communication Quarterly, 11*(3), 647–669. https://doi.org/10.1177/1077699017712991

Warner, B. R., Galarza, R., Coker, C. R., Tschirhart, P., Hoeun, S., Jennings, F. J., & McKinney, M. S. (2019). Comic agonism in the 2016 campaign: A study of Iowa Caucus rallies. *American Behavioral Scientist, 63*(7), 836–855. https://doi.org/10.1177/0002764217704868

Warner, B. R., Horstman, H. K., & Kearney, C. C. (2020). Reducing political polarization through narrative writing. *Journal of Applied Communication Research, 48*(4), 459–477. https://doi.org/10.1080/00909882.2020.1789195

Warner, B. R. & Neville-Shepard, R. (2014). Echoes of a conspiracy: Birthers, truthers, and the cultivation of extremism. *Communication Quarterly, 62*(1), 1–17. https://doi.org/10.1080/01463373.2013.822407

Warner, B. R. & Villamil, A. (2017). A test of imagined contact as a means to improve cross-partisan feelings and reduce attribution of malevolence and acceptance of political violence. *Communication Monographs, 84*(4), 447–465. https://doi.org/10.1080/03637751.2017.1336779

Wojcieszak, M. & Warner, B. R. (2020). Can interparty contact reduce affective polarization? A systematic test of different forms of intergroup contact. *Political Communication, 37*(6), 789–811. https://doi.org/10.1080/10584609.2020.1760406

Young, D. G. (2019). *Irony and outrage: The polarized landscape of rage, fear, and laughter in the United States.* New York, NY: Oxford University Press.

About the Editors and Contributors

Editors

Benjamin R. Warner (PhD, University of Kansas) is an associate professor of communication and director of graduate studies at the University of Missouri. One of the nation's leading experts in political polarization and partisan media effects, he has published articles and book chapters examining the polarizing effects of partisan media, new media echo chambers, and presidential debates. He also studies the effects of viewing political comedy and discussing politics on social media.

Dianne G. Bystrom (PhD, University of Oklahoma) is director emerita of the Carrie Chapman Catt Center for Women and Politics at Iowa State University. She has contributed to 26 books—including as co-editor of *Women in the American Political System: An Encyclopedia of Women as Voters, Candidates, and Office Holders* (2019)—and has published journal articles on gender and political campaigns, the Iowa caucuses, and youth voters.

Mitchell S. McKinney (PhD, University of Kansas) is dean of the Buchtel College of Arts and Sciences at the University of Akron. One of the nation's leading scholars of presidential debates, he is the author or co-author of nine books and numerous journal articles and book chapters. He is also a frequent commentator for national and international media and has provided expert political commentary for such news media as *The New York Times*, *The Washington Post*, *USA Today*, *CNN*, *NPR*, and *BBC News*.

Mary C. Banwart (PhD, University of Oklahoma) is an associate professor of communication studies at the University of Kansas and director of the Institute for Leadership Studies. Her research focuses on political campaign communication and the role of gender in political campaigns. She has authored or co-authored book chapters and journal articles on the influence of gender in candidate presentation styles, the evaluation of female and male candidates, and how gender influences one's likelihood to feel competent to talk about politics.

Contributors

Divine Narkotey Aboagye (MS, Illinois State University) is a doctoral student in the Department of Communication at the University of Maryland, specializing in rhetoric and political culture. His research explores the intersections of presidential rhetoric, U.S. foreign policy, international law, war and chemical weapons, controversy and social movements, race and politics, the rhetoric of science, and the rhetoric of development and underdevelopment.

Josh C. Bramlett (PhD, University of Missouri) is an assistant professor of communication at Eastern New Mexico University. His research focuses on political communication in contexts such as televised political debates, political comedy, and the political uses of social media.

Jin R. Choi (BA, Gordon College) is a doctoral student in the Department of Communication at the University of Maryland specializing in rhetoric and political culture. Her overarching research interests include globalization, power, social change, belonging and citizenship, and identity.

Kevin Coe (PhD, University of Illinois) is a professor of communication at the University of Utah. His research focuses on the interaction of political discourse, news media, and public opinion, with a particular interest in the U.S. presidency and issues of identity. He is the co-author of *The God Strategy: How Religion Became a Political Weapon in America* and *The Ubiquitous Presidency: Presidential Communication and Digital Democracy in Tumultuous Times.*

Alyssa N. Coffey (MA, Saint Louis University) is a doctoral student in the Department of Communication at the University of Missouri specializing in political communication. Her research explores the effects of partisan media, especially regarding the possible harmful democratic outcomes.

Colleen Warner Colaner (PhD, University of Nebraska) is an associate professor of communication at the University of Missouri. Her research examines how communication shapes and sustains relationships in complex, diverse, and modern family structures and experiences. She focuses on children's communication experiences and abilities, with an aim to understand their unique perceptions of family relationships, and partners with mental health professionals to provide families with strategies for connecting and coping.

Andrea Figueroa-Caballero (PhD, University of California-Santa Barbara) is an assistant professor in the Department of Communication at the University of Missouri. Her research explores the link between exposure to representations of underserved groups in media content and subsequent perceptions of the self and other, as well as outcomes such as stereotyping, group esteem, and implicit bias. Her research can be found in *Communication Monographs, Journal of Cross-Cultural Psychology,* and *Journal of Broadcasting and Electronic Media.*

Ashley A. Hinck (PhD, University of Wisconsin-Madison) is an associate professor in the Department of Communication Arts at Xavier University. Her research examines how fandom and politics intersect online. She is author of *Politics for the Love of Fandom: Fan-Based Citizenship in a Digital World* (2019) and co-author of *Poaching Politics: Online Communication during the 2016 US Presidential Election.*

Taylor Hourigan (BA, Colorado State University) is a doctoral student in the Department of Communication at the University of Maryland specializing in rhetoric and political culture. Her research interests revolve around political protest and activism, specifically as carried out by young and minor-aged activists, and the ways in which power, age, gender, and race intersect in the discourses of and about these activists.

Meg Itoh (BA, The College of Wooster) is a doctoral student in the Department of Communication at the University of Maryland specializing in rhetoric and political culture. She researches in the areas in which culture, identity, and media intersect, particularly related to communication within international environments and the empowerment of minority groups.

Michael W. Kearney (PhD, University of Kansas) is a senior data scientist at Aware and holds a courtesy appointment in the Department of Communication at the University Missouri. He uses data science to analyze digital trends and human behaviors and builds tools to help others do the same.

Kate Kenski (PhD, University of Pennsylvania) is a professor in the Department of Communication at the University of Arizona. She is co-author of the award-winning book, *The Obama Victory: How Media, Money, and Message Shaped the 2008 Election* (2010). Her current research focuses on political campaign use of new media, incivility in online forums, and gender and politics.

Go-Eun Kim (MA, Korea University) is a doctoral student in the Department of Communication at the University of Missouri specializing in political communication. Her research explores political polarization and its outcomes. She also studies the effects of political debates and online political expression.

Daniel Montez (MA, Brigham Young University) is a doctoral student in communication at the University of Arizona in Tucson. His research interests include political communication, online incivility, and media effects.

Ashley Muddiman (PhD, University of Texas at Austin) is an associate professor of communication studies at the University of Kansas and a faculty research associate with the Center for Media Engagement, which is housed in the Moody College of Communication at the University of Texas at Austin. Her research examines political media effects, specifically those related to digital technologies, journalism, and political incivility.

Ryan Neville-Shepard (PhD, University of Kansas) is an associate professor of communication at the University of Arkansas. Writing in the areas of political communication, rhetorical criticism, and argumentation, his research tends to specialize in the influence of political outsiders, populist provocateurs, and conspiracy theorists.

Jihye Park (PhD, University of Missouri) is a senior research and teaching associate in the Department of Communication and Media Research at the University of Zurich, Switzerland. Her political communication research explores intergroup conflict, especially political polarization. She also studies social media effects, political debates, and elections.

Trevor Parry-Giles (PhD, Indiana University) is a professor of communication at the University of Maryland. His research and teaching focus on the historical and contemporary relationships between rhetoric, politics, law, and popular culture. He currently is exploring the role of image and character in U.S. political discourse and political judgment, the depictions of the U.S. presidency in popular culture, and Cold War rhetorics of geopolitical change and anxiety in contemporary political and popular culture.

Bryan G. Pepper (BA, University of Oklahoma) is a graduate student at the University of Oklahoma focusing on critical studies of race, class, and gender. He is currently developing several pieces of long-form fiction that trace race and the lyrical expression of posttraumatic stress disorder (PTSD).

Cameron W. Piercy (PhD, University of Oklahoma) is an assistant professor of relationships and digital media at the University of Kansas and director of the Human-Machine Communication Lab. He is interested in how humans and technologies establish and structure relationships through interaction. Specifically, he researches how new technology reshapes sociotechnical networks when organizing.

Julius Matthew Riles (PhD, University of Illinois-Urbana/Champaign) is an associate professor of communication at the University of Missouri. He researches the interplay between media use and social relationships. Specifically, he psychologically explores how exposure to social group portrayals can influence social perceptions and inclinations pertaining to those groups, the mechanisms by which social relationships influence media use, and the experience of parasocial relationships with figures in the media.

Carolyn Robbins (MA, Baylor University) is a doctoral student in the Department of Communication at the University of Maryland specializing in rhetoric and political culture. Her scholarly pursuits focus on the rhetoric surrounding mass incarceration and particularly the ways public memory, circular reasoning, and tautology come together to maintain hegemonic power structures.

Robert C. Rowland (PhD, University of Kansas) is a professor of communication studies at the University of Kansas. He has published widely on presidential rhetoric; campaign debates; the public sphere; and other topics in political communication, argumentation, and rhetorical criticism. He is the author of *The Rhetoric of Donald Trump: Nationalist Populism and American Democracy* (2021).

Matthew Salzano (MA, University of Maryland) is a doctoral student in the Department of Communication at the University of Maryland specializing in rhetoric and political culture. He studies digital media, activism, and sensation and is occasionally a Twitter bot-creator, video producer, copy editor, and journalist.

Joshua M. Scacco (PhD, University of Texas at Austin) is an associate professor of communication at the University of South Florida. He is the co-author with Kevin Coe of *The Ubiquitous Presidency: Presidential Communication and Digital Democracy in Tumultuous Times* (2021). An expert on political communication and news media, Scacco has published more than 50 academic articles, book chapters, and public research papers and provided commentary for national and local news outlets.

Kalin Schultz (BA, Villanova University) is a doctoral student in the Department of Communication at the University of Maryland specializing in rhetoric and political culture. Her research is interested in the construction of identities in the public sphere and how that has evolved and been challenged through social movements.

Xavier Scruggs (MS, Texas Christian University) is a doctoral student and instructor in the Department of Communication at the University of Missouri. His interests lie at the intersection of family and political communication, specifically how differing political beliefs/attitudes can create division and conflict within families.

Jonathon Smith (BA, Baldwin Wallace University) is a graduate student in the Department of Communication at the University of South Florida. He is studying political communication, with an interest in presidential communication. He intends to explore areas of racial identity politics and political expression and participation for his thesis.

Julia A. Spiker (PhD, University of Oklahoma) is professor of communication at the University of Akron. Her areas of research include political communication, especially the rhetoric of women leaders and the political empowerment of women and girls. Her book, *Empowering Women: Global Voices of Rhetorical Influence* (2019), presents an overarching, global picture of women's empowerment through the lens of elite women political leaders' speeches. She has more than 20 journal and book chapter publications and over 40 conference presentations.

Shelby Sturm (BA, Villanova University) is a doctoral student in the Department of Communication at the University of Maryland specializing in rhetoric and political culture. Her research interests include the construction of social identities and how these identities intersect with public understandings of democratic participation, specifically in social movements and public deliberation.

Kelly L. Winfrey (PhD, University of Kansas) is an associate professor with the Greenlee School of Journalism and Communication at Iowa State University and the coordinator of research and outreach at the Carrie Chapman Catt Center for Women and Politics. Her research focuses on political campaign communication with an emphasis on gender dynamics and has addressed such topics as gender group identification and political behavior, gender stereotypes and candidate image, political advertising, social media, and sexism in media coverage.

Index

Note: Page numbers followed by *t* indicate tables and *f* indicate figures.